3 1336 00327 6244

D1094528

OUR TROUBLED PRESS

Ten Years of the Columbia Journalism Review

OUR TROUBLED PRESS

Ten Years of the Columbia Journalism Review

EDITED BY ALFRED BALK AND JAMES BOYLAN

LITTLE, BROWN AND COMPANY — BOSTON - TORONTO

LIBRARY OF CONGRESS CATALOG CARD NO. 75–161855

FIRST EDITION

T 11/71

Published simultaneously in Canada by Little, Brown & Company (Canada) Limited

PRINTED IN THE UNITED STATES OF AMERICA

Contents

6. From Monopoly to Conglomeratism 211

7. Blights and Fixations 265

8. Folkways 303

INTRODUCTION

Elie Abel

Newspapermen are not the most inner-directed of men. As a breed they have been quick to expose the failings of others and correspondingly slow to acknowledge their own. They subscribe to no canon of ethics. Unlike plumbers or doctors, they hang no license upon their office wall. In their own circle they have been heard to argue sometimes whether journalism is a profession or at best a craft. But the argument lacks passion. Self-conscious talk about professionalism strikes many of them as pompous, the kind of thing you might expect from funeral directors or osteopaths.

Not that there is any shortage of critics among reporters. They could, if they would, tell Spiro Agnew a thing or two about the shortcomings of their business; not, however, for publication. Theirs was until recently an oral tradition like that of the Celtic bards. Newspapermen would tell other newspapermen over a glass in one snuggery or another — at Bleeck's or Costello's in New York, or at the National Press Club bar in Washington — all manner of horror stories about tyrannical city editors, fat-cat publishers, and ugly facts suppressed or glossed to please an advertiser. Formal, published criticism just happened to be outside their tradition.

True, A. J. Liebling in the *New Yorker* had written wittily and gracefully about the lapses of certain American newspapers. Don Hollenbeck had surveyed the performance of the print press on radio for CBS, followed in the age of television by Charles Collingwood. But *CBS Views the Press* was a sometime venture which had little or nothing to say about the standards of electronic journalism. As for Joe Liebling's "The Wayward Press," it died with him in 1963.

There were, of course, the trade journals: *Editor & Publisher*, *Broadcasting*, and others, which did not make a practice of questioning or criticizing their own advertisers. In short there was a void, waiting to be filled, when the *Columbia Journalism Review* was launched ten years ago in the conviction that the time had come for a bold experiment in self-appraisal. Since then the *Review* has acquired a worldwide reputation for authority, courage, and independence in media criticism.

Sir William Haley, former director general of the BBC and editor of the *Times* of London, has said of it: "I had no idea that anything of such candour, quality, and authority was being published about the press. I have never come across its equal." John Fischer, former editor of *Harper's*, has written: "Its criticism has reached a high level . . . well balanced in praise and blame." One admirer said simply: "I am exhilarated by its courage and enterprise. It is the conscience of journalism."

In a field often rightly accused of excessive reverence toward sacred cows the *Review* recognizes none. On the contrary, it delights in exposing them. One of the "dirty little secrets" that has cast a shadow on journalism, for instance, is the extraordinary amount of editorial space directly or indirectly for sale in real estate, travel, and other special sections of American newspapers. In the articles "Blighted Areas of Our Press" (page 273) and "The Fantasy World of Travel Sections" (page 281), the *Review* insists that spades be called spades.

The power of seldom-publicized regional press barons also has been examined. In "Case History: Wilmington's 'Independent' Newspapers" (page 213), Ben Bagdikian delved into the mysterious processes by which a corporate duchy, the Du Pont Company, interfered in the news operations of its two Delaware newspapers. The owners and certain staff members of both papers were heard from in loud, indignant complaint. But, as Bagdikian justly replied: "The facts remain in the article, documented and unrefuted." Similarly, in "The Indiana Primary and the Indianapolis Newspapers" (page 159) Jules Witcover exposed the blatant slanting — including misquotation of a New York *Times* editorial — indulged in by the Pulliam newspapers in their attempt to discredit Robert Kennedy. And in "Dimout in Jackson" (page 81) Edwin Williams delineated the pervasive power of the Hederman family over Mississippi's press and politics.

The *Review* has raised other storms:

The *Reader's Digest* tried to persuade the editors to halt publication of an issue, already printed, containing a less-than-flattering article about that magazine (page 291). Numerous television station managers responded with ferocity to charts in 1962 and 1966 showing local station "blackouts" of network news and public affairs programs. Supporters of freedom-of-information campaigns protested an article in 1966 that described the declining effectiveness of the congressional freedom of information committee. Nor did the Connecticut press take kindly to Robert Yoakum's detailed description of its failure of curiosity in the case of Senator Thomas J. Dodd.

But neither the rank nor station of potential targets has stayed the *Review*'s hand when criticism seemed in order. Every President in office since the *Review*'s founding has been taken to task for attempts to manipulate the news media. After Vice-President Agnew's attacks on journalists the *Review* published a special issue examining what it believed to be the media questions of highest import. The issue included a point-by-point refutation of some of Mr. Agnew's most free-wheeling statements: "The Agnew Analysis: False Premises, Wrong Conclusions" (page 179). Again, in 1970 when White House and Republican campaign officials tried to create a preelection cause célèbre over alleged violence during a presidential visit to San Jose, California, the *Review* was the first national journal to publish an analysis of the event and its coverage: "Incident at San Jose" (page 188).

On occasion the *Review* even has taken issue with its institutional godparent. In the Spring, 1966, issue, for instance, an editorial criticized the Pulitzer Prize machinery at Columbia, and editorial comment on coverage of 1968 disorders on Morningside Heights included harsh words about Columbia itself.

John B. Oakes, editor of the editorial page of the New York *Times*, and John S. Knight of Knight Newspapers are only two among a number of highly regarded media executives who have felt aggrieved enough by *Review* criticism to write demurrers. In each instance, in the conviction that publishing or broadcasting carries an accompanying obligation to provide space and time for comment and rebuttal, the magazine has published the responses. Inevitably, the *Review* makes mistakes. But it tries to set an example by acknowledging them and opening its pages to those who disagree, even when the magazine insists that it has been accurate.

How did a venerable private institution of higher learning, chartered by King George II nearly a quarter-century before the American Revolution, get into the business of tilting with the lowly and mighty of journalism and politics? In the words of Edward W. Barrett, former Dean of the Columbia Graduate School of Journalism:

> [The *Review*] sprang from the belief that American journalism, which regularly criticizes all facets of society, was itself ready to profit from fair but forthright critiques. The experiment also reflected the conviction that a national, graduate school of journalism has a duty not only to educate young professionals but also to help spur improvement in the profession.

The pilot issue was published on October 2, 1961, some nine months after John F. Kennedy became President of the United States. Like other American institutions, the news media in the sixties found themselves under challenge, forced to reexamine their methods, their standards, their goals. The issues demanding attention put American journalism to its supreme test. Certain of these ills — race and poverty and violence — were anything but new on the American scene. Some other ailments — the increasing militarization of American foreign policy, for example — were comparatively recent. All together had suddenly been thrust into high visibility after centuries or decades of neglect and forgetfulness.

Swift change — disorienting change — was the only certainty of the age, engulfing the news media no less than the rest of American society. You cannot bring the sullen heat and violence of Indochina into the living room in living color, or the black-and-white assassination of an accused assassin, or a ghostly figure clomping down on the moon's surface — both live — without affecting society in ways that have yet to be fully understood, or charted, by the social scientists. Suddenly the global village was there and we were all of us villagers, sharing the wonder or the horror, wholly unprepared.

At the start of the fifties television had reached into perhaps one American household in twenty. By the start of the sixties we had something like 100 percent saturation. The Kennedy-Nixon debates in 1960 drew tens of millions of potential voters into a single cross-country lyceum. Even in the Eisenhower era, the American people had seen filmed snippets of the presidential news conference. With Kennedy, the news conference became a live happening open to every citizen who cared to tune in. All at once television had made itself the indispensable tool of the politician and public official.

Politics itself began to change as new television-wise leaders were thrown up among the poor, the black, the alienated middle-class young. Offered no ready access to the medium, they quickly invented stratagems for capturing its attention, by *making* news. A station or network which might have said no to a polite request for air time by a militant group could hardly refuse to cover a street demonstration organized by the same group. To the purist such a demonstration may have seemed counterfeit, a species of non-event. But it had somehow become news, purists being in short supply, because it promised the producer of the evening news program what passed for action film to replace some of the "talking heads" he was otherwise stuck with.

It seems, in retrospect, unthinkable that in such a time the news media should not have been subjected to serious, continuing, and informed criticism. The idea of a critical review had been around a long time. In January, 1960, James Boylan, then assistant to Dean Barrett at the Graduate School of Journalism, summarized the idea at Barrett's request in a memorandum. Barrett, Boylan, and the rest of the school's faculty discussed the possibility of bringing out a new magazine. By June there was a formal prospectus. The magazine was titled *Columbia Journalism Review*, and quarterly publication was agreed upon.

The pilot issue published in the autumn of 1961 bore little resemblance in format to the *Review* of today. But the contents were similar. Fourteen of those first sixty pages were devoted to a careful analysis of how the American press had reported the

Kennedy-Nixon campaign of 1960. Although eleven months had elapsed since Kennedy's victory, no systematic effort had been made to examine and compare the coverage. That was reason enough, the editors felt, to go ahead. Columbia journalism students and some twenty-five correspondents across the country filed reports. Boylan had been designated the acting managing editor. Ruth K. Franklin, a Columbia journalism alumna, and Richard G. West, former managing editor of the New York *Herald Tribune*, helped design and assemble the new magazine. James S. Pope and Richard T. Baker contributed articles. There were book reviews by Liebling, Wallace Carroll, Lawrence D. Pinkham, and Louis M. Starr.

The pilot issue, mailed to some five thousand alumni and other journalists, was on the whole well received — astonishingly so, in Dean Barrett's opinion, though not all the potential subscribers were pleased. "Content — below average. Format — poor" was one reader's comment. The warmest praise came from the likes of Brooks Atkinson ("extremely interesting"); David Lawrence ("It's very good"); Mark Ethridge ("I have read almost every word of it and enjoyed it"); John Fischer ("An impressive piece of work"); and Edward P. Morgan ("A brave venture").

Volume I, number 1, carried a statement of policy that has been reprinted through all succeeding issues:

> . . . to assess the performance of journalism in all its forms, to call attention to its shortcomings and strengths, and to help define — or redefine — standards of honest, responsible service. . . . to help stimulate continuing improvement in the profession and to speak out for what is right, fair and decent.

From the beginning Dean Barrett had to make a prodigious effort to raise funds. Thus it was not until April 9, 1962, that the first regular, quarterly issue went out to subscribers. Barrett somehow persuaded the trustees of Columbia University, in effect, to advance $35,000 so that regular publication could begin with some assurance of continuing. There were private angels, too, throughout the decade; among them Louis M. Schweitzer, James P. Warburg, Frank Altschul, William Benton, George Delacorte, the Ford

Foundation, and most recently, the John and Mary R. Markle Foundation. Most important, Ambassador John Moors Cabot consented to allocating to the *Review* a portion of the income from the Maria Moors Cabot Fund, established in memory of his mother. Let the record show also that Barrett and the others were sustained by the consistent understanding and unwavering support of Dr. Grayson Kirk, Columbia's president until the time of troubles on Morningside Heights in 1968.

It has been a matter of policy from the start not to seek or accept money from newspapers, magazines, or broadcast stations—all those who might one day be subject to critical appraisal. For much the same reason, the *Review* to this day accepts no advertising.

The original tentative editorial arrangements soon gave way to a more permanent structure. Dean Barrett became editorial chairman. Boylan was confirmed as managing editor (later as editor). A faculty group of advisory editors chipped in with advice, editorial judgments, occasional articles, and book reviews. From the start the *Review* was written and edited by professionals for professionals. Contributors were paid (at a minimum rate of ten cents a word), an extraordinary practice for university-based quarterlies. On the business side Louis G. Cowan, former president of CBS–TV, became chairman of the Publishing Committee, and Sylvia Orr, circulation manager.

On the occasion of the *Review*'s fifth anniversary, Dean Barrett was able to report: "Inevitably the magazine's analyses and comments have evoked the ire of influential persons and institutions. Yet the editors have never received a complaint, an order, or a 'suggestion' from the university's trustees or administration."

On the tenth anniversary, with the *Review* now a bimonthly, his successor as dean and editorial chairman is happy to attest that the *Review* still discomfits influential persons and institutions and that its independence is still scrupulously respected by Columbia University, its trustees, and its present president, Dr. William J. McGill.

It is fair to put the question: What has the *Review* accomplished? I for one have no doubt that the news media are doing a better job today, in most cities, than they did ten years ago. But it is difficult, perhaps impossible, to measure with any precision the effect of what is, after all, only one possible agent of journalistic reform. We have reason to believe that certain crude political smears are less likely to recur in particular newspapers as a result of staff roarbacks ignited by *Review* articles. Some newspapers have been prompted by exposure in the *Review* to reconsider old, established forms of malpractice.

No less important, perhaps, is the impact upon young journalists all over the land. They read and write to us. Many of the most fascinating bits the *Review* has been able to publish about quaint journalistic customs in out-of-the-way places have been volunteered by staff members who want to see standards raised, as we do. In city after city, they have started journalism reviews of their own — a needed innovation and a form of flattery that we find particularly heartening.

We have a long way to go, no question of that. We can see that the *Review* has made a place for itself over the past ten years. It is no longer a curiosity. Busy and powerful men make a point of reading it carefully. More and more often they send us material not otherwise available. We have become a sort of clearinghouse for hard-to-get information about the media in transition, a place of assembly for the critics, a journal less scholarly than some but more readable than most.

No single periodical can hope to accomplish the reforms that seem to be called for in an industry so entrenched in the profitable old ways of doing business. Even if our effect is marginal, we are determined to carry on through the second decade, raising questions that others do not raise, discussing problems that are not elsewhere discussed at length or in depth.

We propose to do more.

To do less would be unpardonable.

ONE

The New Media Environment

ON UNDERSTANDING SOCIETY

Walter Lippmann

"For when there is panic in the air, with one crisis tripping over the heels of another, actual dangers mixed with imaginary scares, there is no chance at all for the constructive use of reason, and any order soon seems preferable to any disorder."

So wrote Walter Lippmann in *Public Opinion* in 1922.

Some weeks before his eightieth birthday, at the invitation of Professor Fred W. Friendly of the Columbia journalism faculty, Mr. Lippmann held a seminar with a small group of graduate students to discuss the contemporary applicability of this and other observations from his long and distinguished career. The text below is excerpted from the dialogue which resulted.

Public opinion has been the third force that really changed American policy on the Vietnam war. How did that come about?

Well, the war was very distant, nobody was interested in it, and the Johnson method of handling the war was to conceal it from the American people. In the first year of the fighting, this was the Johnson escalation, because before that it was not really a war in the sense that it is now. It was concealed by the fact that the army which was sent to Vietnam to do the fighting was really a professional army. It was not a drafted army. What Johnson did was to cannibalize the American forces all over the world, and build up probably the best army the United States has had in the world. But that army could last only about a year, until its term expired. During the next year or two Johnson more and more couldn't hide the fact that we were drafting men to fight that war.

Fall, 1969.

Now, drafting men to fight a war ten thousand miles away is something that no sensible great power has ever attempted. The British, in all their period of imperial rule in the nineteenth century, never conscripted Englishmen to fight in Asia. They always relied on volunteers, professional soldiers, and on mercenaries. They hired the Indians, the Gurkhas; regiments of Iranians and other people from the Middle East, and so on; but there were no Englishmen conscripted to fight around the world. Johnson, who knows no history, didn't realize what a thing he was doing when he began to conscript an army to fight a war that nobody believed in particularly anyway — nobody had ever had it explained to them, nobody could explain the reason for it — ten thousand miles away. It was that that began to arouse the American people to realize what this was. And Johnson kept getting one general after another to come forward and say we were winning it when we were not winning it. Finally the Tet Offensive came, and he tried to get generals to say we would only take 35,000 men. But finally it was leaked out from Washington that Westmoreland wanted 206,000 men. And that figure broke Johnson's back. That was when public opinion revolted. That's why Johnson had to retire.

Apparently you do believe that at least in an informal way our government is responsive to public opinion?

Well, it's responsive to the kind of thing that I was talking about, which is being for the war or against it. The fact that the country came to be against the war is very important. Whether you can get a public opinion sharpened and attuned and made accurate to more specific reforms, I'm not sure. And I think that one of the difficulties — the difficulty with television, the difficulty with this turmoil — is that you cannot refine public opinion and educate it to very detailed and complicated things. I don't expect that any large audience, for instance, could ever really understand the problem of decentralizing the schools in New York City. I think it's just too complicated and difficult. It just won't catch in the net. So I don't want to sound too optimistic about public opinion.

How many problems do you think this country can digest at one time without breaking at the seams?

Well, that's a problem I've been worried about all my life, but I have begun to realize, since I wrote *Public Opinion* and also while I was writing it, that the capacity of the general public — on which we're dependent for votes — to take on many problems is very limited. I wrote a book called *The Phantom Public* [1925], arguing that really what public opinion in the end could do was to say yes or no. It couldn't do anything very much more complicated than that. It couldn't say three-quarters or five-sixths but not two-sevenths — it isn't able to do that. That's what a scientist has to do. That's what an administrator has to do, what a public servant has to do. But public opinion as a mass can't do that. And it's one of the great unsolved problems of democracy: how are you going to make popular government — because it's always going to be popular, in the sense of involving a great many people — how are you going to make that work in the face of the problems which have become infinitely complicated even in the last twenty years?

In that regard, if in fact public opinion is not responsive to very sophisticated and very subtle problems, is the role of the media to oversimplify them in hopes of mobilizing some force?

Well, undoubtedly the mass media oversimplify. The American people are very simplistic, they want to be told that things are absolute, that they're black or white. They don't want to be bothered very long.

So what should the mass media do?

That is *the* question, I admit, but first of all, I don't know enough about the mass media. I know something about journalism, but I know very little about broadcasting. I listen to broadcast journalism, but for the news at night; I don't get the news from it. I feel utterly dissatisfied almost always. Of course, I'm very interested to see a picture of something happening. That's very interesting — a splashdown, that's wonderful. But as for the problems which are very difficult, urban problems and all, you can't find out about them. You can get a smell of them. You know a little bit about what they're like, and then you can read about them, or somebody can lecture to you about them. But broadcast journalism has not only a terribly simplifying effect, but a distorting effect, I think, because it makes everything more dramatic than it should be, more interesting, more amusing. And the world of life isn't that. It's prosaic.

The controversy over advertising of cigarettes seems to raise a central question: if the scientists and doctors who have no economic involvement in the industry are correct, and they seem to be, then there should be some public outcry about this; it's not just a problem of public opinion not getting to the legislators.

But there's a good deal of feeling. You see, this pressure has worked. Public opinion doesn't always work through big mass meetings or demonstrations.

How much do you think public opinion has become synonymous with public relations?

Well, these professionals at public relations are too much for me. There is an awful manipulation of public opinion going on all the time, no doubt about it. It's not the whole thing, though. Public relations was unable to do anything about the Vietnam war. They tried to. Johnson tried all the techniques he could to hide that war, and then to make it acceptable. And it didn't work.

How is public opinion best measured? Is the Gallup Poll, for instance, an effective measure?

The Gallup Poll is pretty good, if it's very broadly taken. But 96.3 percent, that's foolishness. The taxicab poll that most people take when they ride in a taxi and find out what the driver thinks — that has some validity. My wife comes home and tells me about the hairdressers and what they think. Very reactionary, I assure you. They're afraid to go out at night.

If you're a public man — say, a President or a candidate or a good journalist — you suddenly know what the public feeling is. Why did Johnson retire, do you think? He knew that he was beaten. And where did he get that? He got it from polls, a little bit, but mostly he just knew, as a public man very well trained in public affairs — he assumed it. I don't think you can measure everything.

Public opinion isn't instantaneous. You can't take flashlights of public opinion and get it right every time. But a man like Johnson, who is made to hear an awful lot, and the representatives in Congress who are representative in the sense that they're like the others — you talk to them and you know what people in his district are thinking or feeling, and what they're prejudiced against or for.

In 1922 you wrote that the hardest thing to report is chaos, even evolving chaos. Now, 1968 was a very chaotic year; how do you think journalism performed then?

Well, if I remember what I said in 1922, the world actually — and I think I used the phrase of William James — is a "blooming, buzzing confusion," and the mind's eye has to form a picture out of really a very chaotic thing. And that's done by the creation of stereotypes, which are ways of looking at things; and then after a while when you have these, that's all you see — what the stereotype says to you. That's all that comes through.

Now, I think that today the good reporters, both electronic and newspaper, are much more sophisticated and educated men than reporters were in 1922 when I was writing. They're much more aware of the dangers of superficiality and so on. And they strike me as extremely intelligent. I think on the whole 1968 left us rather confused. Everybody was confused, including the newspapermen, because they were dealing with a situation for which they had no preparation.

Does it seem to you that political writers of the country are swinging to the right? If so, how far to the right do you think they will go?

Well, there's no doubt that — whether that's age or personal ambition or what — men do that. It's a rule any journalist would know: it's always safer to be conservative than not. You're much less on the defensive. You have much less to explain yourself for. The Left has recently done some very vicious things, I think. But on the whole, in the lifetime of most men who are now fifty or more, the Right is the one that's done the vicious things. Fascism was very vicious. I don't think anybody can predict how far it will go, because it's action and reaction, how the Left acts and how the Right acts.

How would you compare the social rebelliousness of the generation coming of age now with the one that came of age immediately after World War I? And why, in the seven decades we have had in this century, have these two produced the greatest generation gaps?

First, of course, there was rebellion and disillusion at the end of the First World War, and that produced the twenties, in which a lot of the people who now are extremely Left just expatriated themselves. A whole colony formed in Paris of people who just couldn't stand this country. It was too awful for them. Hemingway belonged to that generation, Archibald MacLeish belonged to it. But what is new that I never knew then is the violence and disruption. They were rebellious, they made speeches, they wrote books, but they didn't come into the classroom and say, "By God, you're not teaching what we like, you're not going to teach." That didn't exist.

This man Herbert Marcuse has written a book, as you know, about the limits of toleration, and he doesn't want to tolerate people who don't agree with him. He says you mustn't tolerate people who are wrong. Those are the people he doesn't agree with. You mustn't tolerate the Right or the middle, you must only tolerate the Left, and the Left must decide whom to tolerate. Now, that philosophy, that is not new. That is a revival of a thing that started quite differently about the middle of the nineteenth century and became anarchism, with people like Bakunin, who was the great antagonist of Marx. Bakunin was a Russian nobleman who had a romantic view of the Russian serf, and if only he were in charge of things all evil would disappear from the world.

But it was an amiable and decent thing. It was impracticable, of course, and it disappeared, and now it has revived, and that is the significant and dangerous thing about the recent times. We saw it abroad. We saw it in Berkeley. We see it all around: this feeling that you must stop things from happening that you don't agree with, and that liberalism is the great enemy.

But the power of the economic system is so vast, and yet so destructive and unaware of its destructiveness, that people are frustrated, and feel they can't work within traditional lines to counter the power, and so the question really is: is the society capable of change?

It is changing all the time. It is changing much more rapidly than we know how to understand it. But can it be remade to your heart's desire? I would say no, it cannot. And that isn't because the Right is in control, it is because this is the way of life in which we are embedded. Just as primitive man was embedded in his system of tribes and so on, we're embedded in this, and we can't get out of it. It's like jumping out of your skin.

It is possible that the rebellion of the young may be a product of technology's getting out of our hands, so that we really have produced a generation that is more different from its parent generation than ever has been the case before.

I think you're absolutely right, and I think it's fundamental. The technological gap and the generation gap are the same thing. And the young people today are coming into a world for which there was no preparation in custom. There never was a world like this. Not that any revolutionist made it. It was created by technology and science. They don't know what to do about it, and the older people don't know what to do about it, either. They don't understand it themselves. That is absolutely the core of our problems. How will we be able to create a capacity to govern this enormously new and enormously complicated and very rapidly changing social environment? That is the problem. And there's no answer. We may not solve it in a generation. That's the problem today. The revolutionary — all that business — is of no importance except as a byproduct of that.

Of course, one of the most revolutionary technological inventions of our time — much more revolutionary I think than people realize generally — is contraception: The Pill. It absolutely knocked the family to pieces. The old reasons for creating and holding families together have been knocked out by this technological interference in the relationship between procreation and sexual life. And that is felt everywhere. There's no family, there's no neighborhood, there are no clans.

But how do you get around the problem of being ruled by a generation brought up in a time of slower change? Really, the problem seems to be reeducating congressmen and senators and the like, and this is the media's responsibility. But how do you get at them?

Well, this is an autobiography for me. I have lived through this. I feel it. I have felt it for years. And I have lived right in the midst of this change, never really understanding it very well and knowing I didn't understand it very well, not knowing what to do about it. I don't feel able to say what I'm going to tell a congressman to do. I myself don't know what to do. We might as well be honest about it with ourselves: we are not in a position yet to reeducate the masses because we don't know what to teach them. And that is one of the critical conditions of our time.

Is it more important for us to educate the congressmen or to educate the Middle Western farmer?

First of all, it's most important to educate ourselves. And that is really absolutely fundamental. We know what to do about a particular thing, but about the general situation we don't know. And the fact that we don't know is perhaps the beginning of wisdom. We're going to have to create the general knowledge that we don't know.

AMERICA'S TWO CULTURES

Theodore H. White

Vice-President Agnew has suggested that there is an inordinate degree of media concentration in New York City, and that therefore TV, at least, has a distorted perception of America. Do you accept this "two Americas" dichotomy?

I think what we're going through now in this country is not only a political crisis but a cultural crisis of enormous dimensions. It's a difference in cultures that divides the country and it will probably take fifty years before we can look back and see what was happening.

The frontier of the change lies in New York City. New York is moving into areas of thought and expression and emotion as strange to the country as a whole as, say, Berlin in the 1920s was to Bavaria. Berlin was the place where modern art happened, where the great experimental writing happened, where theater exploded, where the most creative and imaginative political thinking in Europe took place. Berlin in the 1920s, not Paris, was the center of the world avant-garde. But the Berlin which the world saw was completely different from the broad sweep of Germany, which eventually spat out Berlin and the Berlin culture and, to our shock, eventually chose Hitler. I don't think that the situation in the United States is anywhere nearly as dramatic as that, but the gap between the avant-garde in New York and the old Emersonian culture of the land beyond the Alleghenies has never been so great.

Winter, 1969–70. Theodore H. White, a Pulitzer Prize–winning reporter, is author of *The Making of the President* series and other books.

Is this a schism between New York and the rest of the country or between urban America, of which New York is the largest conglomerate, and the smaller towns and rural areas?

The cutting edge of the change runs through a number of urban centers, especially those deeply influenced by academia. That is, Boston, New York, Washington, Los Angeles, and San Francisco, all influenced by the great university complexes there. With this growing split in culture has come another development, which is the near-total concentration of the control of the national media in Manhattan. Basically that's a function of technology, a function of electronics, a function of the high-speed printing press and distribution mechanisms. It's a circumstance. But this concentration of thinking in the New York–Washington–Boston area puts it in the hands of villagers who, I think, have never been more remote from the broad basin beyond the Alleghenies.

This is no conspiracy. This is a circumstance. People in New York have a social life. They like to be heroes at dinner parties as well as heroes alone. To go against the dominant thinking of your friends, of most of the people you see every day, is perhaps the most difficult act of heroism you can have.

That applies to small towns also?

Of course. There was the Babbitry of the 1920s and there's the Babbitry of Greenwich Village, which is just as much a conformist group of people as is Sauk Center, Minnesota. Greenwich Village is probably more conformist than Sauk Center.

To what extent are networks news executives and reporters remote from the nation? For example, Time *notes that ten of twelve top people in TV news are from outside the East, presumably with family and other ties elsewhere? And that network bureaus and correspondents continually feed material into New York?*

First, you start with the fact that, of course, Walter Cronkite comes from Missouri, and Howard Smith from Louisiana, and Eric Sevareid from North Dakota, and so on. If you think that

Manhattan is run by New Yorkers you're mad. There are only two Rockefellers among the ten top executives of the five biggest banks in New York. The rest of the executives come from places like villages in Tennessee or Florida or Clearwater, Minnesota. New York is a place which assembles various kinds of talent. It assembles talent in a particular kind of cultural context. You have Chet Huntley, going back soon to Montana. During his sojourn in New York he has been a part of this culture and community, just as I am. Perhaps we are more sensitive. Perhaps because we came here looking for novelty, we are confusing the future with the present.

I travel more than most people, so I am really worried about this breach in American culture. I went down to the Peace March on November 15 in Washington. So did my eighteen-year-old son. He thought it was a glorious experience; he was doing his bit for peace. It did not seem incongruous to him that certain groups were marching under Viet Cong banners, and that Viet Cong banners flanked the speakers' stand, while Americans were fighting against and being killed by Viet Cong. Nor did it seem to bother the senators who spoke, or anybody else there.

This is something which does not shock or disturb here in New York. It does shock and disturb all through the Big Valley. Now why this is so, how it has come about, you would have to explore a lot more, you would probably have to explore the history of American communications, how Americans learn about their world.

For a long time American history has been taught in components and categories — American cultural history. American political history, American economic history — but no department of history teaches what I now think is most necessary: the history of American communications. All politicians operate in an environment of ideas. But, technically, this environment changes from decade to decade. Whoever shapes the ideas, whoever creates the applause or the denunciation, or whoever seizes the moral heights in the world of ideas controls the politics not of today but of ten years hence. The common phrase in New York is that the New York *Times* can't carry an election. The New York *Times* editorial page can't swing even 100,000 votes in any given contemporary

New York City election. But it affects the thinking of all executive, intellectual, and communications leadership. And ten years hence this thinking *does* shape elections; it creates the sounding board against which our politicians offer programs and leadership.

Is it significant that many of us in the media are not as affected by the New York milieu as, say, the literati who are not journalists and find it easier to turn inward and talk only to each other?

I think we are a self-selected group. We came here, or we were chosen to come here, because somehow we were ahead of the common thinking or at least were thought to be ahead of the common thinking. My point is, right now are we too far ahead? One of the paradoxes of the situation is that I have never known a group of men more fundamentally, humanly, decent or intelligent or responsible than the people who run these networks. These are absolutely authentic men. I have lived and grown up with most of these people. Charles Collingwood, Sevareid, Smith, Cronkite, Brinkley, Huntley, Edward P. Morgan are absolutely men of conscience and some of them are also men of learning. These are good people.

I don't think we would be as acutely aware of the New York concentration if we still lived in the age of radio. Radio is a voice; you have to catch the idea alone. But television is a totally different medium, which is why I would love to write a history of the media in the United States. TV is a medium where you are carrying a twelve-ton pen and you have a hundred people helping you carry the pen. It's a collective, not an individual, effort. Nobody, for example, can look at all the film that comes in. It has to be strained through staff. What the top men see is the end selection.

I did the movie version of *The Making of the President 1968*. We had two crews on the road all the time. They were young and wonderful cameramen. I was busy writing my book and reporting and I couldn't direct the film crews, so about nine months later when I finally got to Hollywood to put the film together, I found that these young people absolutely adored Eugene McCarthy and Robert Kennedy, and there was not a bad shot of either Gene McCarthy or Bobby Kennedy in the thousands and thousands of feet that we took. The images were glowing. On the other hand, these people who worked with me did not bring back one human shot of Hubert Humphrey. Everything that was taken looked sinister. He has an angular face, a pointed chin, and if you want to shoot Hubert badly, it's the easiest thing in the world. I have a personal fondness for Hubert Humphrey. I have known him for fifteen years. But I had to work with film that showed Hubert Humphrey only as a sinister character. Such problems are even more pointed when you come to the daily TV shows. You're in the hands of the hundreds of people who are feeding material to you. No single person controls television.

What was your reaction to Vice-President Agnew's interpretation of this situation?

I reacted, as many people did to Agnew that night, with a sense of rage and indignation. After about two weeks my indignation cooled off. Several paragraphs in that speech came from my 1964 book, where I described the passion of Barry Goldwater—his war against the Eastern establishment and the press he had to face. But what Agnew did, I think, was to describe a circumstance that we all recognize, and imply that it is a conspiracy. This is not a conspiracy against America or against the Midwest or against the Republican party. It is a circumstance of reality. You might just as well say that a conspiracy put the automobile industry in Detroit, or "schlock" prime-time entertainment shows in Hollywood. Things grow up and they build. National news coverage developed out of New York.

If Agnew had made that speech directly to the National Association of Broadcasters, if he had not started that speech with a defense of Nixon against the commentators and the Republican party against New York, it would have been a major speech by a public figure. He took a half truth and converted it into something else. And you have to separate the various parts of the speech. To some of those things we certainly must address ourselves. Is it good or healthy to have so much power over the American mind concentrated in a very few hands in New York City? The other part you have to separate out is, do you want the government to get into what goes over the air? And I don't want the United States Government to get into any control, any censorship, any pressure on the airwaves of the U.S.A. And there you have to say, "Mr. Agnew, if you're implying that the United States Government has got the right to censor or control what goes over the airwaves, we aren't with you and you're our enemy." And if Mr. Agnew was saying as he should have said before an association of broadcasters, "Gentlemen, there's a condition here that no one knows how to cure, you have to cure it yourselves," then I'd say he had a pretty sound proposition.

But he said something different — that the American people should rise up and let their voices be heard to make these people pliable.

That gets us right back to the culture conflict in the United States. He's saying to the Midwest it's you against them. It's you, the ordinary people of America. There has always been this suspicion of the big city on the part of rural America. And not only in rural America. It's there in Bergen County, New Jersey, there in Nassau, in every suburb.

So what should be done?

I still don't know what the people, all the people out there, can do. We may be caught in a technological dead end. Electronic reportage is different, in essence, from press reportage. Any decent-size newspaper can and should have correspondents overseas telling its community what goes on overseas. Every decent-size newspaper should have a man down in Cape Kennedy reporting on Space for his local community. But to cover technologically in pictures a thing like the Arab-Israeli war, the Vietnam war, a great assassination, a national convention requires millions and millions of dollars. You can't have a hundred TV stations in the country each giving its own point of view nationally and each reporting a national election. The coverage is so expensive it has already got beyond the budget of ABC; ABC has given up covering some major events in depth. So there are only two great corporations in the country which consistently can afford the money to do the kind of superb coverage which we get when TV is at its best — and when TV is at its best, there's nothing in the world greater.

But it takes extravagant amounts of money to do a good job on TV. Instantaneous transmission of color images costs you about ten thousand dollars for ten minutes on Telstar from Paris. So technologically we're being forced to recognize that the kind of pictorial coverage that this country requires can be afforded by only two or at most three networks. Those networks exist here in New York. How do you handle that situation?

If I were running CBS and NBC, I would stick with my present staff as the best I could possibly assemble. On the other hand, I as a citizen think there should be several more networks with other points of view. I once said on William Buckley's program, in a moment of fantasy, that if I could pass a miracle I would have three national networks, thoroughly funded, and have one on the West Coast, one in Chicago, and one in New York — all of them existing in different regional ambiences of opinion. I don't see how that will come about. I have no solutions at this point. I do say that there is a media crisis. And Vice-President Agnew approached the problem with an ax.

Local stations make money. They have evening news shows. But instead of commenting on national or international affairs, they put that responsibility on the networks. Yet Mr. Agnew directed none of his remarks to the station owners, who really have tremendous freedom and could at least build regional personalities, in the same way the Los Angeles Times *and the Chicago* Daily News *and others built their staffs in competition with the New York* Times *and the Washington* Post.

That's a good point.

Mr. Agnew seemed to be going beyond questioning philosophical differences to suggest that TV has been politicized. Do you agree?

The night before John Kennedy was elected he spoke in the Boston Arena and he concluded that the chief duty of the President of the United States is to put before the public the "unfinished business" of our time. The national media also believe that their chief duty is to put before the public the unfinished business of our time, and therefore no government will satisfy them.

Neither Eugene McCarthy nor Richard Nixon nor Lyndon Johnson nor Hubert Humphrey nor Nelson Rockefeller. Because the unfinished business of our time is enormous. There is pollution, there is racial discrimination, there is violence, there is traffic, there are all sorts of problems. No matter what any administration does, national media say why not more, why not quicker? This is where Agnew was wrong. He thinks they're just against Richard Nixon.

The national media are the national critics. Not in any partisan sense. I have known Eric Sevareid since he parachuted out of a plane in Burma during the war. I guess my closest friend at the moment is Charles Collingwood. And I don't know whether Charles, Eric, Walter Cronkite — or the ten major reporters and commentators — are Democrats or Republicans. I would bet they are ticket splitters. The national media have somehow put themselves into the role of the permanent critical opposition to any government which does not instantly clean up the unfinished business of our time. This is a strange kind of politicization.

Among newspapers, the history is that the local press is quite conservative. Has this been your observation?

This is less and less so. They are being sensitized by the influence of the national media.

There are three national newspapers in the country: the New York *Times*, Washington *Post*, and *Wall Street Journal*. Beyond that are massive and important regional publications. The Boston *Globe* has changed the politics of Massachusetts. The Chicago *Sun-Times* will be the force that destroys Dick Daley. The Los Angeles *Times* is making California better. The Portland *Oregonian*, Louisville *Courier-Journal*, Charlotte *Observer*, Atlanta *Journal* — these are all regional papers which have great and progressive influence.

What challenge, if any, do these regional media have in common with New York–based media?

I'm a working journalist. I think the great professional problem that challenges all of us is institutional reporting. Americans are not being oppressed by evil men. We are being oppressed by institutions that don't seem to work. We are all furious at the New York Telephone Company because it is falling apart. I don't know why it's falling apart, but I feel irritated, aggravated, and annoyed. People are aggravated by the railroads, by the hospital system, by the institutions of government itself. The students are aggravated by the institutions of the universities. Now, to describe and explain an institution which is going wrong is the most difficult kind of reporting to make exciting. Second only to the Vietnam war, what is bothering the U.S.A. is inflation; rising prices. Inflation is a moral disaster. But you can't describe inflation and make it interesting. If you could find one sinister backroom cabal of men who were raising prices it would be a dream story. To get into inflation you have to get into what is wrong with our institutions. They don't respond to our present needs.

That's what the young and the Eastern press are saying: that there is an institutional failure in our cities, in the quality of life. But in Dallas, Texas, or Grand Island, Nebraska, they don't see life in that perspective.

And there you get to the cultural cleavage again — for most Americans, life has gotten a lot better, in every way, than twenty years ago. Schools are better. The food is better. Architecture is better. Vacations are longer. Circumstances of daily life are more and more comfortable, except for what the draft does to their boys and inflation does to their wages. On the other hand, in New York we stress not the present progress but the problems of the near and distant future. What is happening is that this New York analysis of our environment stems from areas where the institutional crisis is most acute, yet it's heard by the people who live in the old environments and are not nearly so disturbed; that is the culture gap.

The whole structure of American party politics is breaking down, and what is breaking it is education. Education is the incubating force of change in our time. My feeling is that we are desperately in trouble in the United States. I doubt whether, since the founding of this republic, America has questioned itself and its purpose so deeply as it is doing today. Television oriented toward protest feeds our self-doubt. It may be that all of us in responsible positions in journalism have got to think of a counterbalancing reporting.

What is news today? Is it what we are achieving or that which remains to be done? You ask yourself every day, "How did we get trapped in Vietnam?" It was a blunder — an enormous blunder. But you can't toss out all of American civilization — two hundred years of it — because of one blunder in the past four or five years.

Since I object to all concentrations of power, I worry about the concentration of power in which I exist and in which I work. I have lived under systems where the government runs the news. I prefer profit makers running the news. I admit the failings of it. But I don't want anybody or any government to intrude on the gathering and dissemination of the news.

TWO

Society Under Stress

MEDIA MYTHS ON VIOLENCE

Terry Ann Knopf

Several years ago a resident of a small northern town kept insisting to a local newspaper reporter that a policeman had been shot and killed during a racial disturbance there. The reporter checked and rechecked but was unable to substantiate the story. In fact a policeman had been killed, but in another city. The man simply had heard a garbled version of the story — not an unusual occurrence in the confusion that prevails during crises.

Crisis situations increase the need for news. During most serious disturbances, news media are bombarded with calls from anxious citizens wanting information, clarification, verification of what they have heard. So important is the flow of news through established channels that its continued absence can help precipitate a crisis. In 1968 in Detroit the absence of newspapers during a protracted strike helped create a panic: there were rumors in the white community that blacks were planning to blow up freeways, kill suburban white children, and destroy public buildings; in the black community, that white vigilantes were coming into the area to attack the residents. Gun clubs sprang up in the suburbs; black leaders urged preparation of survival kits. On March 7 — nearly four months after the strike began — Mayor Cavanagh had to go on TV to plead for calm.

As racial disorders have become a familiar part of the national scene the media have demonstrated a growing awareness of their responsibilities and a healthy willingness to experiment with new policies and procedures. Technical improvements also have been made. The city of Detroit, for example, has built a press room

---

Spring, 1970. Terry Ann Knopf is a research associate at the Lemberg Center for the Study of Violence, Brandeis University.

large enough for 150 people, with independent telephone lines. Operational techniques have been modernized — the Pittsburgh police, among others, have on occasion provided a helicopter for the press. And central headquarters or "press centrals" have been established to help eliminate conflicting reports. Moreover, a number of cities have adopted or revised guidelines for reporting. These guidelines — sometimes formal, sometimes informal — urge that unnecessary interpretation be minimized, rumors be eliminated, unverified statements be avoided, and superlatives and adjectives in "scare" headlines be excluded. One set of guidelines put the matter simply: "Honest and dispassionate reporting is the best reporting."

In accordance with these guidelines, newspapers have tended to move away from the "shotgun" approach — the front-page build-up, complete with splashy pictures and boxscores of the latest "riot" news. Dramatic but meaningless predictions have also largely disappeared. In May, 1967, *U.S. News & World Report* declared that Newark was "not expecting trouble," while Cleveland was voted the city "most likely to explode — again." Cleveland failed to erupt in 1967, but Newark experienced one of the most massive outbursts in our country's history. This kind of journalism is much less common today.

There is also evidence of greater sympathy and sensitivity toward blacks. How far have we come? Consider the following comment from the New York *Times* on July 23, 1919, concerning the violent disorder in Washington, D.C.:

> The majority of the negroes [sic] in Washington before the great war were well behaved. . . . More of them admitted the superiority of the white race, and troubles between the two races were undreamed of. Now and then a negro intent on enforcing a civil rights law would force his way into a saloon or a theatre and demand to be treated the same as whites were, but if the manager objected he usually gave in without more than a protest.

These changes represent considerable improvement. But serious problems remain. Glaring instances of inaccuracy, exaggeration, distortion, misinterpretation, and bias have continued at every level — in newspapers and newsmagazines large and small, northern and southern, liberal and conservative.

The wire services are probably the most underexamined segment of the media, although as much as 90 percent of the news in some newspapers on a given day may come from the wires. One error in a wire service report from one city may be repeated in hundreds of newspapers and newscasts. In York, Pennsylvania, in mid-July, 1968, for instance, incidents of rock- and bottle-throwing were reported. Toward the end of the disturbance UPI in Harrisburg asked a stringer to get something on the situation. A photographer took a picture of a motorcyclist with an ammunition belt around his waist and a rifle strapped across his back. A small object dangled from the rifle. On July 18, the picture reached the nation's press. The Washington *Post* said: ARMED RIDER — Unidentified motorcyclist drives through heart of York, Pa., Negro district, which was quiet for the first time in six days of sporadic disorders."

The Baltimore *Sun* used the same picture and a similar caption: "QUIET, BUT . . . An unidentified motorcycle rider, armed with a rifle and carrying a belt of ammunition, was among those in the heart of York, Pa., Negro district last night. The area was quiet for the first time in six days."

The implication of this photograph was clear: The "armed rider" was a sniper. But since when do snipers travel openly in daylight completely armed? Also, isn't there something incongruous about photographing a sniper, presumably "on his way to work," when according to the caption the city "was quiet"? Actually the "armed rider" was a sixteen-year-old boy who happened to be fond of hunting groundhogs — a skill he had learned as a small boy from his father. On July 16, as was his custom, the young man had put on his ammo belt and strapped a rifle across his back, letting a hunting license dangle so that all would know he was hunting animals, not people. Off he went on his motorcyle headed for the woods, the fields, the groundhogs — and the place reserved for him in the nation's press.

More recently, an AP man in Dallas filed a story on a student takeover at Southern Methodist University. The Fort Worth *Star-Telegram* in its evening edition last May 2 put the story on the front page and gave it a banner headline:

BLACKS SEIZE OFFICE OF
S.M.U.'S PRESIDENT

Police Are Called to Stand By

DALLAS (AP) — Black students with some support from whites took over the office of the president of Southern Methodist University today and swore to remain until their demands are met. . . .

Reports from the scene said from thirty to thirty-five students were in control of [President] Tate's office.

The takeover occurred during a meeting of Tate and a campus organization, the Black League of Afro-American and African College Students.

The story had one major flaw — it wasn't true. While about thirty-five students had met with the university president, they were not "in control" of his office; nor had they "swore to remain" until their demands were met. No such "takeover" had occurred. Glen Dromgoole, a staff writer for the *Star-Telegram,* later reported what really happened. The black students had met with the president for more than five hours discussing recent demands. The talks were more friendly than hostile. (At one point hamburgers were brought in.) By the end of the meeting, agreement had been reached on most of the issues. Apparently the wire service reporter had accepted the many rumors of a student takeover.

Martin Hayden of the Detroit *News* has suggested "'an almost mathematical relationship between the level of exaggeration and the distance of news transmission." Edwin Guthman of the Los Angeles *Times* maintains that the early wire service report "is at the crux of the news media's problem." However, it is more likely that instances of misreporting remain a problem at *every* media level. The Lemberg Center for the Study of Violence, in investigating twenty-five incidents in which the news media had alleged sniping, found that, along with the wire services, local and nationally known newspapers bore a heavy responsibility for imprecise, distorted, and inaccurate reporting.

While treatment of racial disorders is generally more restrained today, the news media continue to overplay the more violent or sensational aspects of a story. The central media concern during the disorder at Cornell University last April, for example, was the emergence of the blacks from the student union. A picture of the students carrying rifles and shotguns, splashed across the nation, had a distorting effect on public opinion. The New York *Times* put the picture on page 1, and *Newsweek* used it on its cover the following week. Certain facts were largely ignored: prior to the disorder a cross had been burned in front of a black women's dormitory; the students had heard reports that carloads of armed whites were moving toward the campus; when the students emerged from the building their guns weren't loaded. What was basically a defensive response by a group of frightened students came across in the media as a terrorist act by student guerrillas.

Aspects of the disorders are dramatic and do merit extensive coverage. But the media still tend to equate bad news with big news and to confuse the obvious with the relevant. Thus when sixty-five students at Brandeis University took over a building last year it rated a story on the front page of the New York *Times* — despite the fact that there was no violence, that classes continued, and that the university suffered only minor inconvenience. I was on campus then. My only recollection of anything unusual was that on the first day or two an attendant asked to see my identification, and for the next week and a half I noticed large numbers of reporters, press cars, cameras, and other equipment. I sometimes wondered if there weren't more reporters outside than students inside the building.

The *Times*, along with most newspapers, missed the unusual climax at Brandeis. In a war of nerves with the students, President Morris Abram showed consummate skill in handling the situation, remaining flexible on the issues, mobilizing the support of the student body and faculty, and, above all, refusing to call in police. Eleven days after the crisis had begun the students quietly left the building — a dramatic victory for the Brandeis community, a dramatic example of how to handle a university crisis in contrast to fiascoes at Columbia and San Francisco State. Yet the students' departure merely merited a *Times* story about three inches long, well off the front page.

Disparities between the headlines and news stories are another problem. Often much less occurs in the story than the headline would indicate. Last year, for example, some concerned parents in Jacksonville, Florida, removed their children from Kirby Smith Junior High School after a local radio station had broadcast an exaggerated report of a fight between black and white students. The school principal later indicated that "classes continued and there was no panic." Nevertheless the Miami *Herald* headlined its story last April 25: MOMS MOB SCHOOL AFTER RIOT "NEWS." Sometimes no violence occurs in the story, dramatic headlines to the contrary. A story appearing in the Boston *Globe* last May 10 told of a peaceful rally by a small group of students at a local theological seminary. According to the *Globe*, the rally was "brief and orderly." But the headline above the story read NEWTON CAMPUS ERUPTS.

The use of the word "riot" presents another problem because it has no precise meaning in terms of current disorders. *Webster's* defines a "riot" as a "tumultuous disturbance of the public peace by three or more persons assembled together and acting with a common intent." The difficulty is that "riots" have become so frequent and come in so many sizes and shapes as to render the word meaningless. There is something ludicrous about lumping together as "riots" Detroit, with forty-three deaths, seven thousand arrests, and $45 million in property damage, and an incident in which three people break a few store windows. Yet this is precisely what the news media still do. The continued media use of the term contributes to an emotionally charged climate in which the public tends to view every event as an "incident," every incident as a "disturbance," and every disturbance as a "riot." Journalists would do well to drop the word from their vocabulary altogether.

No law says the media have to interpret and not simply report the news, but having assumed this responsibility they have an obligation to make reasonable judgments based on careful analysis. Unfortunately, journalistic attempts in the direction of social science research have been rather amateurish, particularly where new trends and patterns are concerned. The case of the Cleveland "shoot-out" is a good example. On July 23, 1968, an intense gun battle broke out between the police and a group of black nationalists led by Ahmed Evans. Before the disorder was over, 16,400 National Guardsmen had been mobilized, nine persons had been killed, and there was property damage estimated at $2.6 million. The Cleveland *Press* on July 24, 1968, compared the violence to guerrilla activity in Vietnam: ". . . it didn't seem to be a Watts, or a Detroit, or a Newark. Or even a Hough of two years ago. No, this tragic night seemed to be part of a plan."

A reporter writing in the New York *Times* of July 28, 1968, stated: "It marks perhaps the first documented case in recent history of black, armed, and organized violence against the police."

More recent reports have revealed that the "shoot-out" was something less than a planned uprising and that the situation was considerably more complicated than indicated initially. Unfortunately, following the events in Cleveland, disorders in which shots may have been fired were immediately suspected by the press of being part of a "wave." A series of errors involving a handful of cities became the basis of a myth — that the pattern of violence in 1968 had changed from spontaneous to premeditated outbreaks. Few of the nationally known newspapers and newsmagazines attempted to verify sniping reports coming out of the cities and over the wire services; few were willing to undertake independent investigations; and far too many were overly zealous in their assertions of a new "trend" based on limited and unconfirmed evidence. Unwittingly or not, the national media had constructed a scenario on armed uprisings.

Although having more time to check and verify reports than daily newspapers, the newsmagazines were even more vocal in their assertions of a "new pattern." On September 13, 1968, *Time* took note of an "ominous trend" and declared that the violence "appears to be changing from spontaneous combustion of a mob to the premeditated shoot-outs of a far-out few." The story went on to indicate that "many battles" had begun with "well planned sniping at police." Nearly a year later, on June 27, 1969 — long after investigation by a task force of the National Commission on the Causes and Prevention of Violence, by the Lemberg Center, and by the New York *Times* (which reversed itself on the Cleveland question) had cast serious doubt about premeditated outbreaks in Cleveland and elsewhere — *Time* still was talking about the possibilities of a "guerrilla summer" and reminding its readers of the time in Cleveland when "police were lured into an ambush." Once started, myths are difficult to extinguish.

The most recent myth created by the media involves an alleged "shift" in racial disturbances from large to small cities. Last July 25 a syndicated reporter for the News Enterprise Association (NEA) noted: "The socially sizzling summer has begun — but unlike recent history, it seems to be the minor, not the major, cities which are sweltering."

In an article entitled "Riots, 1969 Style," *Newsweek* declared on August 11: ". . . the traditional riot scenario is still being played out this summer — with one major difference. This season the stage has shifted from the major population centers to such small and disparate communities as Kokomo, Ind., Santa Ana, Calif., Cairo, Ill., Middletown, Conn., and Farrell, Pa."

Last September 9 the New York *Times* captioned a picture: "NEW RIOT PATTERN: Rioting in Hartford, Conn., last week . . . underscored the fact that smaller cities this summer have had more racial trouble than the big ones."

Similar stories appeared about the same time in scores of other newspapers, including the *Wall Street Journal,* the Baltimore *News American,* the Woburn (Mass.) *Times,* and the Pittsburgh *Press.*

In fact, racial disorders occurring over the past few years — not just this past summer — have been concentrated in smaller cities. About 75 percent of all outbreaks recorded in 1968 by the Lemberg Center's Civil Disorder Clearinghouse occurred outside the one hundred largest cities. For the first six months of 1969 and also for the summer no appreciable change in the percentage was noted. Furthermore, many of the cities cited as prototypes of this latest "new pattern" — Hartford and Middletown, Connecticut, Cairo, Illinois — have had disorders in previous years. The difference is that such outbreaks were completely overshadowed by a few enormous outbreaks in large cities such as Newark and Detroit.

Discovering the origin of these and other myths would be useful — a faulty wire service report, an inept reporter, an unreliable source. But aside from the fact that such a task would be almost impossible, it would miss a central point — that the system of reporting insures that errors of fact and interpretation may be repeated, compounded, and reformulated as myths. In recent years the various components of the media have become extremely interwined and dependent upon one another. The wire services, the nationally known newspapers, and the newsmagazines feed one another news and information. While the system undoubtedly speeds the flow of news to the public, it has encouraged a parrot-like character in which the various media segments tend to reproduce rather than examine one another's views.

In this respect the New York *Times* caption proclaiming a NEW PATTERN assumes greater significance. Prior to its appearance in the *Times,* I talked with Jack Rosenthal, who had been working on a story on the relatively cool summer. When the subject of a new "shift" in violence came up I indicated that such allegations were false and misleading. Rosenthal wrote a thoughtful story, dwelling on police-community relations, civic programs, and the new community spirit among blacks. His story made no mention of a "new riot pattern." Apparently the caption writer had paid more attention to what *Newsweek* and the *Wall Street Journal* were saying than to his colleague at the *Times.*

The failure of the media to tell the complete story in the case of Cornell or the right story in the case of Cleveland goes beyond a lack of initiative or an inclination to sensationalize. It also indicates a bias — one which, notwithstanding Vice-President Agnew's declarations, cuts *across* political and geographical lines. The media are no more aware of this bias than is the general public aware of its own. In part, we could call it a class bias in that those who comprise media staffs — reporters, editors, headline writers, etc. — are part of the vast American middle class and, as such, express its views, values, and standards.

Both the general public and the media share the same dislike of protestors; both are unable to understand violence as an expression of protest against oppressive conditions; both prefer the myth or orderly, peaceful change, extolling the virtues of private property and public decorum. People are expected to behave in a certain way; they just don't go around yelling and cursing or throwing rocks. Both will grant that it took a revolution to secure our independence and a civil war to end slavery (at least officially), but that was all long ago and somehow different. The bias also has elements of racism in that color is never far from the surface. It is difficult to say where the class bias begins and racist bias ends. These elements are inseparable and reenforce each other, and both manifest themselves in the thinking of the public and media alike.

A growing body of research shows that racial disorders are a part of the social process. The process includes an accumulation of grievances, a series of tension-heightening incidents such as police harassment, and a precipitating event such as an arrest which crystallizes the tensions and grievances that have mounted — the "last straw" that triggers the violence. The "typical rioter" is young, better educated than the average inner-city black, and more dissatisfied. He wants a better job but feels that prospective employers will discriminate against him. He is likely to be a long-term resident of the city. (In a survey in Detroit, 90 percent of those arrested were from Detroit, 78 percent lived in the state, and only 1 percent lived outside the state.) He is extremely proud of his race and is politically conscious. He is more interested in and informed about politics than blacks who are not involved in a disorder. He is also more inclined toward political activism. (In one survey, nearly 40 percent of the participants in the disorder — as compared to only about 25 percent of the nonparticipants — reported having been involved in civil rights activity.) Finally, he receives substantial support from the rest of his community, which does not participate but regards the violence as necessary and beneficial.

As important as the findings in these studies are, they have made virtually no impact on the vast majority of the public. Most Americans continue to believe that violence is caused by a tiny and insignificant minority, that "outside agitators" and "criminal elements" are mainly responsible for isolated outbursts that have little or no social significance. Intellectuals must share a portion of the blame for this situation. Having completed their studies, they have been notoriously reluctant to roll up their academic shirtsleeves and assume leadership in presenting their ideas to the public. There is a trace of condescension in their assumption that good ideas from above will somehow trickle down to the "masses of asses," as one academic I know calls them.

Greater responsibility for the failure to confront the public's resistance rests with the news media. They have failed to commit their power and prestige on behalf of such studies. They have failed to place the ideas before the public and push for reform in an aggressive, effective manner — settling for a splash of headlines and stories initially, and little follow-up. Instead the media have opted for the status quo, reflecting, sustaining, and perpetuating outworn beliefs of their predominantly white audience.

Historically the notion of plots and conspiracies has always had great currency in this country — and in other countries, too. Prior to the Civil War, Southerners frequently viewed abolitionists as "outside agitators" trying to stir up the happy slaves. Violent interracial clashes during World War I were said to have been instigated by the Bolsheviks, and the outbreak in Detroit in 1913 was attributed to an "Axis plot." The current wave of disorders has been blamed on individuals such as Stokely Carmichael and H. Rap Brown or, for those who like a more international flavor, "Communist infiltrators." In a survey of six northern cities by the Lemberg Center, 77 percent of all whites interviewed believed that "outside agitators" were a major contributing cause of disorders. When Los Angeles Mayor Sam Yorty recently blamed a rash of school disorders on a conspiracy of the Black Student Union, the Students for a Democratic Society, Communist sympathizers, and the National Council of Churches, he was following a long — though not very honorable — tradition.

Such allegations are usually made without a shred of evidence, except for an occasional "someone told me so." Nevertheless the media have frequently taken their cues from the public in formulating and circulating such reports. Misinterpretations of the events in Cleveland, along with assertions of a "new pattern" of premeditated violence, are blatant examples of this form of bias. But more often the bias is expressed in more subtle ways. For example, when rumors circulated that "outside agitators" were involved in a disturbance in Omaha, Nebraska, a news story appearing in the Arkansas *Gazette* last June 27 made reference to the rumors but also mentioned that the mayor had no evidence to support such reports. Yet, the headline above the story read: "OUTSIDERS" LINKED TO OMAHA RIOTING.

A look at the way in which the disorders are written up reveals, tragically, that the majority of the media and the public share essentially the same view of the violence — as meaningless, purposeless, senseless, irrational. Media treatment of the disorders following the assassination of Rev. Martin Luther King, Jr., illustrates the point. The sense of loss and injury among blacks at the time of the assassination was extremely great — far greater than among whites. The unprecedented wave of disorders — approximately two hundred — was expressive of the anger, bitterness, resentment, frustration that black people everywhere felt.

How did the media handle the disorders? Stories in just two newspapers analyzed — the Buffalo *News* of April 9, 1968 (the day of Dr. King's funeral), and the Trenton *Times-Advertiser* one day later — are fairly typical. No attempt is made to place the violence in a social context. The reference to the assassination of Dr. King is perfunctory, with only a passing mention of his funeral and a few shouts about his death. Value-laden words receive unusual emphasis. The participants are "marauders," not men; they "rove" instead of run; they move in "gangs," not groups; they engage in "vandalism," not simply violence.

We have all grown so used to viewing blacks as stereotyped criminals that it is difficult to picture them in any other role; hence such frequent press concoctions as "roving gangs," "roving vandals," "roving gangs of rampaging teen-agers," or, for variety, "a window-smashing rampage of roving gangs of Negro youths." The New York *Times* assertion last July 1 that "roving bands of ruffians" were involved in a disturbance in Middletown, Connecticut, seems somewhat feeble by comparison. The effect of such treatment by the media is to pander to the public's prejudice, reenforcing stereotypes, myths, and other outmoded beliefs. The media not only frighten the public but confuse it as well.

And let us not forget the effects on the news media. The proliferation of underground newspapers, radical publications, black journals, as well as underground radio stations on FM bands held by churches and universities, indicates that the media are failing to reach certain groups, and that they still lack sensitivity, sophistication, and skepticism commensurate with their important and strategic position.

"TRIPPING" ON THE DRUG SCENE

Marion K. Sanders

During most of last spring I was continuously at work on an article for *Harper's* magazine about drug abuse, a subject which had been one of my editorial concerns for several years. I had set myself a relatively — or so it seemed — modest task: to sort out fact from fantasy in the welter of conflicting reports about the nature of the problem and the best way to deal with it. The assignment proved difficult and arduous far beyond my expectations. In the end, I think I came reasonably close to my goal. But along the way I was repeatedly mired in a swamp of claims and counterclaims and seemingly irreconcilable differences among experts in an emotionally overcharged climate which made rational dialogue between the generations virtually impossible.

All this was vividly mirrored in the press and on TV. And several things were clear. Drug abuse among the young was reaching a crisis stage, as documented by the body count of deaths from heroin overdoses and ghastly reports of the consequences of "speed" and other hallucinogens. At the same time government officials, whose efforts to cope with the situation were manifestly unsuccessful, had set up a defensive smokescreen. Operators of various therapeutic programs were noisily touting their wares and knifing their competitors. So were the promoters of assorted schemes of "drug education," none of which seemed to be accomplishing much. Small wonder that most people were bewildered. I am afraid the majority still are. And I believe that — with some notable exceptions — the communications media have compounded public confusion.

I have now accumulated a small mountain of clippings about

Fall, 1970. Marion K. Sanders is a contributing editor of *Harper's*.

narcotics from magazines; from papers in New York, where I live; and from the contributions of friends across the country. Since spot news is ephemeral, most of this harvest belongs in the wastebasket. But leafing through it — for perhaps the hundredth time — I have compiled my private honor roll of genuinely sophisticated and distinguished reporting. (I apologize for any omissions; I do not have the resources for a comprehensive sampling of the nation's press.) To cite a few highlights:

— The *Atlantic*'s lead article in the August, 1966, issue — "White-Collar Pill Party," by Bruce Jackson — was, to the best of my knowledge, the first full account of the pervasive "drug ambiance" among adults far removed from both youth culture and the black ghettos.

— *Time*, in its issue of September 26, 1969 (at a time when hysteria about the drug problem was rising to fever pitch), put together the comprehensive, rigorously factual roundup "Pop Drugs: The High as a Way of Life," which, instead of echoing the prevailing tone of panic, soberly observed that "pop drugs hardly portend anything as drastic as a new and debauched American spirit as some alarmists believe. . . . The mounting research on drugs permits some new perspectives on their use and abuse. . . ."

— Early in 1969 Richard Severo of the New York *Times* spent months digging into the operations of the New York State Narcotics Control Commission. His report, published April 21, 1969, deflated the state's claim of a 44.2 percent success rate. "The computer has not been programmed to provide this information," he was told when he asked how long the state institution's graduates had maintained their amazing record of abstinence from drugs. He also shattered the officially fostered illusion that the facilities were primarily rehabilitation centers rather than prisons. Severo subsequently did a brilliant series on the realities of the addiction problem in New York [Sept. 23–26, 1969], in Sweden [April 10, 1970], and in Britain [March 30, 1970]. The last report was particularly valuable in dampening local enthusiasm for the "English System" under which addicts are given a free heroin supply.

One of the small gems in my collection is a terse account by Mark Tanner, which appeared in the Montgomery County (Md.), *Sentinel,* of a talk at the Prince Georges Adult Education Program by Dr. Frank C. Caprio, a Washington psychiatrist, previously on the staff of the federal narcotics facility at Lexington, Kentucky. In an effort to dispel prevailing myths about drugs, Dr. Caprio told his mostly over-forty audience that barbiturates are much more addictive than heroin and that, despite abundant research, there is no scientific evidence to indicate that marijuana is more harmful to the human body than alcohol, or is more addictive than tobacco. He went on to say that the fact that most heroin users started with marijuana is irrelevant since all heroin users have also used cola drinks, aspirin, and alcohol, and one could just as logically claim that one of these started the addict down the "road to shame." Such sensible and sober remarks are not generally regarded as "newsworthy." What does make perennial headlines is the ferocious and quite irrational antimarijuana campaign initially launched in the 1930s by Harry J. Anslinger, longtime chief of the Federal Bureau of Narcotics, and pursued with undiminished fervor (and ever diminishing effectiveness) by his successors.

Consider the complaint of John Kaplan, author of the impressive, scholarly book *Marijuana — the New Prohibition.* Kaplan, a Stanford Law School professor of criminal law who has served as a legislative consultant, was astonished last August 26 to pick up a copy of the Redwood City (Calif.) *Tribune* and read a story headlined A HORRIFYING PICTURE ON MARIJUANA DANGERS. Written by NEA Washington correspondent Ray Cromley and distributed to some five hundred papers, the report is, says Kaplan, a "perfect example" of the kind of specious reporting which "has done more to foster dangerous drug use among young people than any group of pushers yet apprehended."

Mr. Cromley — like every other journalist — has a perfect right, of course, to the opinion that marijuana is more dangerous than alcohol. But the scientific evidence, which is considerable, does not support him. (See, for instance, the *New England Journal of Medicine,* August 6, 1970.) Hence, I think one may fairly say that he breaches the boundaries of responsible journalism when he cites scientists out of context to buttress his view that marijuana invariably leads to heroin addiction and that, among other horrors, it can cause birth defects, grave psychiatric emergencies, brain damage, and cardiac failure.

Nonetheless, many "drug education" pamphlets and exhibits continue to equate the ubiquitous reefer with the heroin addict's "works" and an assortment of potentially lethal pills and capsules. What are the consequences? "You tell a kid drugs will kill him," one young ex-addict told me. "Then the kid starts smoking grass. He sees it don't kill him. So what's he going to do but say 'Shit, this didn't kill me, so I'm going to try dope next.' "

Said another: "When I was on drugs and my friends and I went visiting, we'd head for the bathroom to look for pills we could swipe. Most of the time we didn't know what they were. So we'd look at our drug education pamphlets and say, 'Oh, that's Nembutal, that's Dexedrine,' and so forth. You learn pretty quickly."

The harsh realities were expertly summed up by Terry Beresford in the Washington *Post* on August 25: "Our present drug-education programs, which is a euphemism for propaganda that adults hope will dissuade youth from drug use, are doomed to failure, as soon as children are old enough to see that the facts given them by adults are partly or wholly untrue."

William Raspberry, in his April 24 column in the *Post*, sounded a similar cautionary note.

But nowhere in the news media have I observed a serious attempt to evaluate the results of a specific drug education program, a task well within the capacity of modern social research and, it would seem, a most logical function for an enterprising journalist. Conversely, the few promising efforts at prevention undertaken by young people themselves have been given scant coverage. One of these is STASH (Student Association for the Study of Hallucinogens), which is dedicated to developing "among all 'consumers' of drug information a critical attitude toward, and an ability to come to rational conclusions about, pronouncements on drugs (including our own)." The project, which is the brainchild of Beloit College students Edmund Zerkin and James Gamage, devotes itself to distributing materials of impeccable scientific accuracy. It was mentioned in an article, "The Drug Scene in East Egg," in the New York *Times* Magazine on May 17. It seems unlikely, however, that many Sunday readers got as far as page 98, where the few paragraphs about STASH were buried. Apparently they also escaped the notice of the *Times*'s own news staff. For surely this was an item well worth following up in depth — even if it involved sending a reporter to darkest Wisconsin — by a paper that has been volubly campaigning for "effective action" against the drug menace but has been painfully short of concrete suggestions as to what form that action should take.

Front-page display, on the other hand, was accorded President Nixon's pronouncement on March 11 that "drug abuse among school-age youth is increasing at an alarming rate" — a discovery most of the nation had made at least a year earlier. Indeed, it would appear that any public official or office seeker is guaranteed respectful press attention whenever he issues a statement — however banal or preposterous — on the narcotics problem. Thus during the fall campaign readers of the Detroit *Free Press* were treated to fulsome accounts of the largely empty utterances of Michigan Governor William J. Milliken, who has a seven-part program for the instant solution of the drug problem, and of his Democratic opponent, Sander Levin, who offers a mere five-part proposal.

In New York, Governor Nelson Rockefeller similarly traded inanities with the contender, former Justice Arthur J. Goldberg. Forced to concede the failure of his own $300-million program, the governor turned his eyes to the poppyfields of Turkey. "The one way to stop heroin addiction," he announced, "is to stop heroin at the source." The Nixon Administration, he went on to say after a flying visit to Washington, knew precisely how to do this. Mr. Goldberg chose an earthier approach. Six months after his election, he promised, treatment would be available to every addict desiring it. "I will walk the streets myself to see whether open sales have stopped, and they will be stopped." Neither statement, though duly publicized, provoked a panic among the city's pushers and dealers.

The Harris Poll and others had, by this time, demonstrated that anxiety about drugs was widespread, and it was perhaps predictable that candidates would cynically exploit a tragic situation. But one might, I think, question the uncritical amiability with which the press — including one with such a knowledgeable staff as the New York *Times* — gave the politicians free rein. For instance, on August 4 Governor Rockefeller announced that he "would confer with legal and medical experts to determine whether to declare drug addiction an epidemic." The reporter for the *Times*, which had been proclaiming — and documenting — the existence of an epidemic for months, was Barbara Campbell. Apparently in search of a "new angle," she sought out Dr. Tibor Fodor, an epidemiologist expert in the control of smallpox, tuberculosis, and diphtheria, who assured her that once an epidemic was declared "the highest priority would be given to stopping the spread of the disease, finding the cause of the epidemic, and preventing future outbreaks." The question of just what form these measures would take in the case of narcotics did not come up; nor, after the *Times*'s discovery of the Fodor plan, was the governor asked to explain the nature of the evidence he would need before applying the magic label of epidemic to the drug situation.

The melancholy fact is that the drug scene is a highly marketable commodity, both in the news and entertainment media. When the President and Attorney General John N. Mitchell met in August with thirty-five TV executives to bespeak their cooperation, the response was exuberant. Drug warnings and drug "alerts" have since proliferated on the home screen. Writing from Hollywood on September 1, AP columnist Cynthia Lowry reported: "Series producers speak forcefully of 'relevance' and brag about the use of meaningful themes. Narcotics and drug abuse by the young are such popular ingredients of scripts that they threaten to become dramatic clichés. Pushers are the new villains and the terrible consequences of addiction are underlined. . . ."

Presumably the message of these scripts is "don't do it." Whether this will be the result is problematic. I recently discussed the matter with Dr. Joyce Lowinson, a psychiatrist specializing in the treatment of narcotics who has been particularly concerned with the coded drug messages in pop music. "Unfortunately," she said, "in the young, curiosity is stimulated before fear. Many of our young patients tell us that their interest in drugs was aroused by the media. Scare stories scare parents."

And it is indeed the frightened adult population that has generated the drive to "do something" about the youthful drug scene. For contrary to much wishful thinking, most young drug users are not clamoring to be rescued. As a young man who kicked heroin in his mid-twenties told me: "One thing you have to remember about drugs is that they are very functional for a kid in a rotten world which is no fun, which is ugly and dirty. Drugs take the kid out of reality and to hell with the world and all its problems."

This is why the great majority of young addicts now in therapeutic communities are not volunteers. The doors may be unlocked but their presence is required, usually by court order — a fact the programs' operators do not like to dwell on. Nor do they care to discuss results in concrete terms for the very good reason that they do not keep reliable follow-up statistics, nor has any other agency done so. The inquiring reporter or even a casual visitor is taken on a conducted tour by a courteous, cheerful young resident — usually one nearing the end of a two-year course of treatment and now preparing for "reentry" to the square world. The guide is candid and graphic about his own drug experience and eloquent in praise of his particular "house" — whether Daytop, Phoenix, Odyssey, or any of the others which use the encounter therapy pioneered by Synanon. (Odyssey has added a larger component of professional psychiatry.) One concludes that these are all worthy efforts which help some addicts, that the differences in their methods are not significant, and that there is no way of judging their accomplishments in the absence of outside evaluation.

Unable to cite objective criteria, the drug therapists in New York who are fiercely competing for public funds have waged an unremitting publicity war in which the press has lavishly cooperated. The clear winner, in lineage if not as yet in the allocation of tax dollars, is Dr. Judianne Denson-Gerber, operator of Odyssey House. Rightly applauded for sounding the alarm about the ominous spread of heroin use among the young, she has been portrayed on TV and by the newsmagazines as virtually a candidate for sainthood, with the revered New York *Times* leading the pack. The move for her canonization seems somewhat premature.

On February 26, Dr. Judy, as she is known to her charges, appeared at a televised legislative hearing with a frail twelve-year-old addict, Ralph de Jesus, seated on her lap. Millions of TV viewers and newspaper and magazine readers were shown the touching scene. In all probability, very few of them saw the minor item, a week or so later, which reported that Ralphie had stayed in Odyssey House only a few days, that he was now back in his native drug-infested habitat in the Bronx, and that there was some doubt about the veracity of the story he had told under Dr. Judy's prompting. Some months later I happened to meet an official of the school the boy attends. He told me that the heroin problem escalated markedly after Ralphie's rise to fame. The message to the young was clear: the way to get on TV is to be an addict.

Dr. Judy's publicity coup prompted her tireless rivals, the city-operated Phoenix Houses, to follow suit. On March 5 one of their fifteen-year-old residents, Maria Nevarro, told her story to an assemblage of reporters and was duly photographed with the mayor and a brace of municipal eminences registering pained concern. "Phoenix House is teaching me how to be fifteen years old," Maria said. "It's beautiful to be fifteen." The applause for Maria was deafening, according to the New York *Post* of March 6.

Much as they feud with each other, people of the therapeutic community are united on one point — their scorn for methadone maintenance as a treatment for heroin addiction. The method, pioneered by Drs. Vincent Dole and Marie Nyswander at Rockefeller University, has since been expanded and is now being used at a number of hospitals in the city. Its results have been statistically monitored by Columbia's School of Public Health Administration. As of September, 1969, the success rate was 80 percent in 2,205 cases. Eighteen percent had dropped out. Of the rest, after three years, only 2 percent had been arrested, 96 percent were in school or gainfully employed (as compared to only 29 percent on admission), and none had become readdicted to heroin.

Figures like these have not impressed the encounter-therapy zealots, nor, until very recently, the New York *Times*. In January, in response to the waiting lists — running to thousands — for admission to methadone maintenance, Governor Rockefeller allocated an extra $15 million to the programs supported by the state.

Instead of applauding this sensible step, the *Times* on January 19, in an editorial titled NO ONE ANSWER TO DRUGS (a claim never made by any methadone advocate), used the occasion to berate the governor for all the things he had not done, particularly for young addicts. (The methadone programs in New York admit only addicts over eighteen — of whom there are believed to be over 100,000 — a not negligible group.) Six months later, on June 8, the *Times* somewhat grudgingly conceded that the Columbia report on the Dole-Nyswander program showed more than two thousand patients "doing remarkably well" and called for similar evaluations of other therapies.

Methadone is a complex and controversial subject. But it is quite possible to write about it calmly and knowledgeably, as was done, for instance, by Ed Edelson of World Book Science Service in a report appearing, among other places, on October 17, 1969, in the San Bernardino (Calif.) *Sun*. Anyone who read it would have a clear understanding of its advantages and limitations.

But what was the New York *Times*'s audience to make, not only of its wavering editorial stance, but of its curious recent news coverage of methadone? My own impression is that its reporters and editors do not always read their own paper. On June 11 more than half of the first page of the second section and a large picture spread were devoted to Richard Severo's chilling account of the "rumor, intrigue, and criticism" besetting an experimental methadone program in Brooklyn which had deliberately departed from the Dole-Nyswander guidelines. On the same page was a story by Edward Ranzal about the mayor's plans to expand methadone programs, written and edited without any cross-reference to Severo's story. The next day, June 12, on page 1 was Harold M. Schmeck Jr.'s report on the federal government's plans to tighten up regulations on the use of methadone. He wrote: "The main point of the regulations appears to be to insure that methadone programs are carried out under strict medical supervision. Programs in New York that adhere to these principles would presumably not be greatly affected. . . ."

Just what this meant in relation to the Brooklyn project could not be discerned, for the question was not raised. Instead Schmeck quoted without comment the absurd assertion of Dr. Charles C.

Edwards, Commissioner of the Food and Drug Administration, that methadone had not been proved a "satisfactory" treatment — despite the fact that the *Times,* four days earlier, had given its editorial blessing to methadone. An additional note of confusion was provided on June 18 by Anthony Lewis. In one of those "let's look at the bright side of things" columns, he singled out the chaotic Brooklyn program described by Severo (but without mention of Severo's report) as an "encouraging example" of positive action.

If I have been particularly critical of the *Times* it is not because the performance of any other paper has been consistently superior. Quite the contrary; the aforementioned stories by Richard Severo would do any paper proud. But the *Times* is not only our journal of record; it is the bellwether of the whole communications flock.

I do not belittle the role of the news media generally in sounding the alarm about the drug problem and forcing public officials and school administrators to face a situation they prefer to pretend does not exist. However, careless *ad hoc* reporting of this complex subject is not useful. And I think it is clearly time to declare an embargo on nonnews about drugs, particularly the irresponsible handouts of political candidates and the contrived stunts of publicity seekers.

It would also, I believe, be helpful if more thought were given to the interpretation of real events. It is, I suppose, news when a young Kennedy or Shriver is "busted" for possession of pot. Such an occurrence could well be used to call attention to the harshness and ineffectiveness of our marijuana laws rather than the public humiliation of eminent citizens. This could be done without "editorializing." The enterprising reporter need simply include, for background, interviews with any of the thousands of middle-class parents of adolescents who have experienced or live in terror of a like calamity.

No doubt stories about the drug scene sell newspapers and magazines and boost TV ratings. But was Woodstock really, as *Time* observed on April 29, 1969, "one of the significant political and sociological events of the decade"? Was it worth the eight pages of mainly glamorous photographs which *Life* devoted to it in the same week, setting the pattern for the generous coverage accorded subsequent rock-drug orgies by the media generally? GROOVY OR GRUESOME? was the head under which the Detroit *Free Press* on August 15 published a batch of reader comments on last summer's Goose Lake fiesta in Michigan. The reporter for the *Free Press*, Bobby Mather, made her own position clear in a witty Sunday piece on September 6: "I have had enough of wild hair and beads and Indian headbands, and bare feet and bedraggled girls and drug peddlers and freaky outfits and bare bosoms and the constant obscenities and bad smells and mud and zonked-out kids sprawled on the ground."

It seems unlikely that the reporter's slant will have much impact on the reaction of readers, which seems, for the present, split straight down the generation gap. Whether it is glamorized or excoriated, there is, I think, a real danger that the drug scene is being overreported. A sad analogy is the plague of alcoholism, which was also hot news in the early days of Alcoholics Anonymous and the subject of such stirring films as *Lost Weekend* and *Days of Wine and Roses*. But who writes about alcoholism any more, even though — by the best estimates — it claims three times as many victims as narcotics? And who wants to read about it?

The reading and TV public could, in the foreseeable future, become quite as bored with the nodding addicts of Harlem, the East Village, and Haight-Ashbury as with the besotted derelicts on the Bowery. We might even see the drunken comic, once a staple of the vaudeville stage, replaced by a new figure of fun — the crazy "speed" freak. For we have a tendency in this country when we are fed up with a problem we can't cope with to treat it as a joke.

THE TROUBLE WITH SCIENCE WRITING

John Lear

The member of the United States Congress who understands science best is Emilio Q. Daddario, the Connecticut Democrat who chairs the Subcommittee on Science, Research, and Development of the House Committee on Science and Astronautics. In the preamble of a bill he recently introduced, he declared: "Emergent national problems, physical and social, are of such a nature and are developing at such an unprecedented rate as to constitute a major threat to the security and general welfare of the United States." These problems, he continued, "are largely the result of and are allied to" the rising pressure of expanding population, the rapid consumption of natural resources, and the erosion of the natural and social environment of the human species. "Widespread application of modern technology, existing and evolving," is "crucial."

This is a diplomatic but firm way of saying that technology has got out of hand and that society needs science's help to bring it back under control. Less polite echoes of Daddario's views are everywhere reverberating in choruses calling for respect for the environment. Unfortunately, the echoes diverge — as echoes will when they enter side streets from the great public squares — and some of the clamor against pollution of the environment ends as a shout against science.

Those of us who are engaged in trying to communicate truth to the mass of the people have, I think, an obligation to clarify

---

Summer, 1970. John Lear is science editor of *Saturday Review*. His work has won the Lasker Award and the Westinghouse Award of the American Association for the Advancement of Science.

the blurs in popular concepts of the antipollution issue. We might profitably begin by taking the philosophy of Daddario's bill as a model for our thinking. That measure at no point blames science alone for a predicament that scientists and nonscientists together are to blame for; on the contrary, it calls upon science to apply presently available knowledge and to acquire new knowledge to bring the use of technology into human perspective.

Science is open to misunderstanding because of serious failings in science reporting. The present situation never would have come about if science reporters had presented developments in their true perspective as the events occurred. That is my view. Admittedly, not all science writers would agree with this position. Some regard the science writer's task as essentially descriptive. Just as there is an opinion that "pure" scientists should pursue lines of experimentation without regard to consequences, so some science writers define their function as one of merely relating what scientists plan, undertake, complete, and pronounce. Interpretation of social consequences has no place in this definition.

This may at one time have been an adequate concept — though I doubt it. To understand my reservations, it is necessary only to consider the reason the press enjoys the protection of the First Amendment. That protection is given in return for maintaining eternal vigilance in all public affairs. Science and technology and their effects now are central influences on public affairs. As such they must be the subject of aggressive, informed journalistic attention.

Given this dyad of privilege and obligation, we may fairly ask why the press waited so long to focus on such developments as man's alienation from his environment. I believe my own experience with the problem is instructive. It goes back fourteen years, to the time when Norman Cousins encouraged me to establish the monthly Science and Humanity section of *Saturday Review*.

For a long time, newspapers had been undergoing mergers and chain linkages that had weakened local news interest and left publishers more concerned with providing entertainment than with obtaining information for their readers. There had been a consequent decline in old-fashioned inquiring reportage, and this reached its nadir at the very moment when science was beginning to emerge as a social force. The course of least resistance in covering science was to accept without question what the scientists said. But neither Cousins nor I were able to accept this restricted concept of science reporting. He was already known for his concern with nuclear fallout as an atmospheric pollutant. The mandate he gave me was much broader: the whole gamut of science's impact on society.

The first tenet of my philosophy was that man is an evolving creature in an evolving environment. Far from believing — as most scientific spokesmen then did — that man could conquer nature, I believed that the best he could hope for was a state of harmony between himself and all the other forms of life around him and the inanimate forces around them. In the second issue of the supplement, dated April 21, 1956, I wrote: "Incessantly [man] has tinkered, changed, invented, adapted, altered his own behavior in order to live happily among his fellowmen." Man had done all this but of late he had forgotten why, and I proclaimed our purpose: "to reestablish the common man's belief in the oneness of things."

To write about science vis-à-vis society was to me equivalent to writing about man vis-à-vis his environment. For science has always been society's agent in dealing with the environment. However, the approach evoked considerable hostile reaction. Broad-gauged scientific figures like Detlev Bronk, Caryl P. Haskins, James R. Killian, Jr., Roger Revelle, and others gave us unfailing support. But to the ordinary run of scientists what we were saying was balderdash.

When E. B. White of the *New Yorker* entered the arena in 1959, he escaped the antagonism of the scientists by coming directly to the point. In the May 16, 1959, issue of his magazine, he wrote: "Because the . . . contamination of air, sea, and soil proceeds apace, the *New Yorker* will undertake to assemble bulletins tracing man's progress in making the plant uninhabitable. This is Bulletin No. 1." For a year he wrote Bulletins No. 2, 3, 4, etc. Then he received a letter from the late marine biologist Rachel Carson urging him to write a long report on environmental pollution. Being among the readers of Miss Carson's classic book, *The Sea Around Us,* White suggested that Miss Carson do the article herself. She did, and it appeared in three issues of the *New Yorker* in 1962 under the heading, "Silent Spring." One of her paragraphs read:

> The history of life on earth is a history of the interaction of living things and their surroundings. To an overwhelming extent, the physical form and the habits of the earth's vegetation and its animal life have been molded and directed by the environment. Over the whole span of earthly time, the opposite effect, in which life modifies its surroundings, has been relatively slight. It is only within the moment of time represented by the twentieth century that one species — man — has acquired significant power to alter the nature of his world, and it is only within the past twenty-five years that this power has achieved such magnitude that it endangers the whole earth and its life. The most alarming of all man's assaults upon the environment is the contamination of the air, earth, rivers, and seas with dangerous, and even lethal, materials.

Miss Carson was attacked as an alarmist and defended as a righteous crusader. But because she was a scientist the word war generated by "Silent Spring's" appearance as a book did not take a lay vs. scientific alignment. Scientists arrayed themselves against scientists and laymen (mostly conservationists) against laymen (mostly industrialists engaged in manufacture or distribution of insecticides). Only recently did society as a whole decide Miss Carson was right.

The decision's effect on journalism has been profound. *Time* has included within its news columns a department on the environment. The New York *Times* has put a nationally reputed reporter, Gladwin Hill, on an exclusive environmental beat. The *Christian Science Monitor* gave Robert Cahn — now one of three members of the White House Council on Environmental Quality — a similar assignment after his series on the national parks that won a Pulitzer Prize in 1969. And *Saturday Review* recently expanded its Science and Humanity supplement and renamed it Environment and the Quality of Life.

Why did it take a scientist to bring the problem into focus? Why didn't a science writer do the job?

What we were suffering from was a plain case of journalistic amnesia. In dealing with science, reporters and editors alike forgot what they as journalists were supposed to be doing. Instead of treating scientists as they treat all other people — expecting them to be individual blends of good and bad (sometimes generous and sometimes greedy, sometimes right and sometimes wrong, sometimes competent and sometimes incompetent) and challenging them at every turn not clearly in the public interest — science writers generally acted as apologists for science. Editors, on their part, accepted the scientific cliché that specialization was the great desideratum, forgetting that society is a whole organism and has to be kept alive and well by general practitioners.

Take the case of the thoughtless race to the moon. It is politically expedient to hold the late President John F. Kennedy responsible for this strategic gamble. He urged it as a national goal in a message to Congress. In that same message, however, he expressed the hope that a national debate over the goal's desirability and feasibility would ensue. A few statesmen of science, including biologist Philip Abelson, editor of *Science*, the journal of the American Association for the Advancement of Science, did raise dissenting voices. But science writers generally sat on the knowledge that the vast majority of the scientific community was either lukewarm to the idea or hostile to it. The lay public, reading virtually no opposition in the news columns, presumed that the men who knew most about the subject — the scientists — were for it.

My own position is that the 1970 moon landing deadline was a mistake. But I believe that the space beyond Earth should be explored, in a consistent and reasonable manner in keeping with other more urgent goals of the American people. I believe, too, that the people should have a direct voice in the decision. To help provide them such an opportunity, *Saturday Review* in 1957 conducted the only genuine scientific study any magazine has ever made of public attitudes toward human travel in space beyond planet Earth. Our questionnaires were used as lesson texts in schools all over the globe, and huge cartons of returns were shipped to our office from as far away as Africa, India, and Australia. When we published a brief summary of our results, the Voice of America produced a special broadcast about it.

We had hoped to repeat the questionnaire periodically, thus

acquiring benchmarks of public understanding of the realities of space travel while educating the public about those realities. Had this been done the extreme dangers inherent in human voyaging in space might have sunk into popular consciousness long before the near-tragedy of Apollo 13, and the destructive effect of sudden swings in employment and unemployment of space technicians would have been pondered before being provoked. But the euphoric atmosphere generated by the science-writer apologists for the great space adventure proved too strong: computer makers, whose help was required to handle our data, declined to support our efforts, and the study died on the vine. Our original findings are stored in a national public opinion archive somewhere.

Another vividly remembered example of science writers' failure to exercise the critical faculty occurred in coverage of abuses in drug advertising. Late in 1958, a woman reader wrote to ask if I would undertake a census of antibiotics, indicating which ones were effective against what infections and which were not effective at all. I told her I thought she should obtain the answer from her physician. She replied that her physician had suggested that she write me. My curiosity aroused, I consulted academic drug research specialists, who encouraged me to expose a string of antibiotic sales promotion journals that were being edited by Henry Welch, head of the antibiotics division of the U.S. Food and Drug Administration.

I pursued Welch for months, documenting his perfidies and publishing the evidence. Other science writers showed no interest until the late Senator Estes Kefauver used my material to force Welch's resignation from the FDA. After that, the *New Yorker* related the whole story to its readers, the New York *Times* published an editorial commending *SR*'s efforts, and our magazine received Sigma Delta Chi's annual award for distinguished public service. I was gratified by the acknowledgments, but I feel that if other science writers had shown an earlier interest in Welch he would have been put in jail, where he belonged. More importantly, the drug advertisers who bought his services while the American people were paying him to protect them would have been punished.

A third instance of journalistic apathy about science involved the helpless old patients in a Brooklyn hospital who were being inoculated with live cancer cells without their knowledge or consent. Dr. Chester Southam of Sloan-Kettering Institute for Cancer Research was placed on probation for a year by New York's medical licensing authorities for his leading role in that experiment. Our magazine was the only one to print all the miserable details of the episode, although *Science* must be given credit for refusing to sit on the lid that the press as a whole imposed.

Thanks to the courage of editor Abelson and the energy and skill of muckraker Daniel Greenberg, *Science* has, in fact, become a model for candid reporting of science news. In its columns, Philip Boffey recently went so far as to suggest that even the prestigious National Academy of Sciences is not free of adulterative influence. According to Boffey's report — which has not been denied — an Academy study panel toned down its original findings to please the government agency that requested and paid for the study.

I say more power to Boffey. After all, reporters who cover the goings-on in government or in corporate boardrooms are expected to keep their eyes peeled for chicanery every day of the week. Why should scientists escape comparable scrutiny? What they do affects every facet of our lives. As taxpayers we foot the bill for their work, for it is done principally on federal government grants and contracts. The harder they resist detailed accounting of their expenditures of public funds, the more closely they should be watched. As Edmund Burke, the great British jurist, said, "Where secrecy begins, justice ends."

We have learned from books like James Watson's *Double Helix* that the white laboratory coat does not guarantee against its wearer's taking whatever advantage he considers justified by the needs of the moment. We have seen otherwise great and dedicated surgeons — Denton Cooley and Michael de Bakey, for example — squabbling like children over authority in a hospital.

I am not alone in the beliefs I am asserting. Nor do those who agree with me exist only within the ranks of journalism. Alvin M. Weinberg, director of the Atomic Energy Commission's Oak Ridge Laboratory, has publicly pleaded with his scientific colleagues to accept — no, to welcome — intrusion of Lincoln Steffens's muckraking tradition into science reporting. He has even proposed that scientists themselves become reporters of what is happening within their own bailiwicks, his grounds being that no outsider can tell the story with the verity of an insider. Perhaps Weinberg is right. I am inclined to feel that the insider has a harder time achieving a total perspective than the outsider does. In either case if both insiders and outsiders were to approach the same matters as honestly as they know how, the total effect would be more revealing than anything we have seen in print on science up to now.

A subsidiary problem must be recognized. Effective use of the English language is not a part of the American scientist's education. Before he could speak to the whole people and be understood, a scientist-reporter would have to acquire respect for the mother tongue comparable to the regard a Russian scientist has for Russian or a British scientist has for the British dialects of English. Too often, the American scientist looks upon facility with common English as a cloak for opportunism, charlatanism, or worse.

Failure to express themselves clearly does not inhibit scientists from trying to thwart readable interpretations by outsiders. I clearly remember the cries of pain and rage that rose in the scientific community after the early issues of *Saturday Review*'s Science and Humanity supplement. That any layman would dare to write about scientists and their experiments without submitting his copy to them for editing (no one would admit it was censorship) in advance of publication! When I assumed the right to say that the National Science Foundation had an obligation to assert itself in establishing priorities for research in America, a functionary of that agency tried to have the issue with my comment taken off the press.

I cannot recall how long it has been since a scientist tried to bludgeon me into submitting my copy to him. The gambit now is more wary, taking some such form as "I'll be happy to help you check your story before you print it." I gather from the persistence of such approaches that at least some other science writers are dutifully submitting copy and accepting whatever revisions are handed out. From press releases, I also get the impression that science writers generally do not check up very carefully on claims of "new" or "exclusive" discoveries. University press offices are at least as bad as, if not worse than, industrial laboratories in advancing unjustified claims.

Science writing is improving. The bulk of it now seems to be done by men and women who are both more sophisticated and more independent in their thinking than were their counterparts of twenty or even ten years ago. But most of them are still not courageous enough in facing the big public questions, such as weighing the moon voyages against other possible expenditures of public money or in exposing the danger that exists for highway accident victims if the new definitions of death sought by organ transplant specialists are commonly accepted. Again, perhaps this is because it has not become second nature to try to relate everything in science to man and his society.

It is in the area of overall evaluation that the science journalist has his greatest opportunity for public service. There is a vital need for evaluation of social processes in which science and technology are involved. Lacking the evaluative function, society will simply go on repeating the same old tired mistakes, discarding unsuccessful political programs and instituting new ones without making use of any yardsticks of performance.

How can this evaluative function be instituted and enlarged?

First, of course, the science reporter must be moved away from the "purist," restricted, merely descriptive approach. There is no better model to follow than the late J. Robert Oppenheimer. Years ago he led a movement to broaden the scientist's concept of the scientist's role. The interdisciplinary approach to research and teaching that he pressed for is now well established on many campuses. Journalists must embrace this approach to science writing, too.

The spirit of untrammeled inquiry and skepticism required of journalists in other fields must become standard in science writing. But this won't happen unless editors insist upon it. If a science reporter turns in copy replete with unanswered or half-answered questions, he must be sent back to get the rest of the facts and he must be required to say what those facts mean in terms of the ordinary reader. If science writers do not ask basic questions, editors must, both in making assignments and in handling copy. I am weary of hearing it said that all the weaknesses of science reporting will disappear when there are enough science reporters to fill the field. No larger number of reporters is going to do the job if we do not apply the critical faculty.

BEDLAM ON CAMPUS?

John Breen

Just as the news media herald the opening of the football, basketball, or baseball seasons, it has become customary for many to trumpet the onset of the "campus unrest" season. Will Harvard erupt, or Columbia or Cornell or Kent State or Wisconsin or Berkeley? The questions were asked anew this fall in editorials, features, and reports of political speeches. And fair questions they were — if based on a semblance of fact and an expectation of presenting answers in perspective.

What are the facts on campus unrest? Unfortunately, authoritative data on post-Cambodia protest last spring was not available at this writing. But the Urban Research Corporation, a Chicago organization headed by a former HEW colleague of John W. Gardner, has made a major survey of 1969. In a study covering 232 campuses from January through June of 1969, it found:

— 76 percent of the protests resulted in "no destruction or violence of any kind."

— 60 percent of all protests "did not interrupt college routine."

— "Nonnegotiable demands" were made in only 6 percent of protests; "ultimatums of various kinds" in only 13 percent.

— The "incidence of war as a major factor in protests was far less than the incidence of race or 'student power' issues."

The report added:

> Concerning the nature of black protests on campus, we found a much different pattern than the widely held impressions that they have: a) usually been violent; b) have been "led" by radical white students; and c) that black separatism has been the key issue.

Fall, 1970. John Breen, a former reporter, copy editor, and editorial writer, is assistant professor of journalism at the University of Connecticut.

The variation between the public impression and what seems to be the facts may derive from the news media's concentration on such single incidents as happened at Cornell, where protesting blacks were photographed with guns. The more violent-oriented incidents have made splashier news and may have contributed to what our findings lead us to conclude are badly mistaken public impressions. . . .

Another commonly held theory that our study seems to refute is that most college protest has been led by small radical New Left organizations. We found participation in protests to be much more broadly based. The New Left participated in only 28 per cent of all protests. . . .

Generally speaking, protests did not achieve their stated aims. At the end of the six-month period of our study, some 69 per cent of all demands presented in all protests remained unsatisfied.

In an American Council on Education study of campus disruption, "violent protest" such as the breaking or wrecking of a campus building or its furnishings was found on 3.4 percent of United States college campuses, or roughly at eighty out of 2,400 institutions of higher learning. Moreover, in a report "Campus Tensions: Analysis and Recommendations," a special American Council on Education committee headed by former Xerox executive Sol M. Linowitz stated:

Institutions have, in general, responded firmly to violence. Fifty-five per cent of the institutions that experienced violence during 1968–69 had occasion to call in off-campus police. Roughly the same percentage of institutions report that some demonstrators were arrested. Some major civil or institutional action (arrest, indictment, dismissal, or suspension) was taken against individual students at three-fourths of the institutions where there were violent protests.

What have the media been saying? In most cases, not quite what such surveys have discerned. In fact, in studying editorials, columns, and news stories about individual events one finds a pattern of generalization and misrepresentation that, cumulatively, could lead the public to almost a fantasy view of the situation.

In a May 2, 1969, editorial, for example, the Elgin (Ill.) *Courier* fumed: "At Harvard . . . terrorists bodily carried faculty members from a building." Yet, according to the Boston *Globe*, it was one dean, Burris Young, who was "picked up bodily by a young man and carried outside."

On May 19, 1969, a *U.S. News & World Report* story on "campus violence" reported that "still the campus wars went on." It added: "In the background, college buildings blazed. Arson was reported from one campus after another." Perhaps, but of seven schools mentioned, fires were reported at only three. All three were on the East Coast.

And in a *Time* magazine article, ROTC: THE PROTESTORS' NEXT TARGET, the magazine warned of the "next wave of campus protest" — but found only five schools where the "wave" might have hit. Four were in the Ivy League. The others? They are, *Time* said, at "avant-garde campuses."

The Cornell case alone resulted in a virtual five-foot shelf of errors and misinterpretation. In a James J. Kilpatrick column published in the Chicago *Daily News* on May 8, 1969, for example, the writer said: "At Cornell, everyone knew precisely which black students were involved in the seizure of Willard Straight Hall. . . . Why weren't these students expelled?"

It is doubtful, first of all, if "everyone" knew who they were. And even if someone knew each of the hundred-odd students, he would also have known that they weren't expelled because, more than two weeks before Kilpatrick asked the question, the university had promised them they wouldn't be expelled. What is not mentioned is that for several days before the column appeared, the Tompkins County Grand Jury was preparing charges of criminal trespass against eighteen black students involved in the occupation of the building — a more serious punishment, one would think, than being expelled.

Newsweek, in reporting the agreement that ended the "occupation," said that "a full faculty meeting would be called the next day to drop the judicial proceedings against the five students originally involved in the December disturbances; Cornell would give the blacks legal help to overcome any civil charges from the Straight occupation . . . provide police protection for blacks and a full investigation of the cross-burning incident."

The Cornell administrators did not agree — and in fact had no power to agree — to "drop" the judicial proceedings. What was agreed was that the dean of the faculty would recommend to the full faculty that the proceedings be dropped. The faculty, not the administration, had the power to do this. The administration also did not promise to "give the blacks legal help." In fact, the blacks were told before the agreement was signed that the university would not use its money to defend them.

As for providing police protection for blacks, what Cornell agreed to do was provide protection only for a black girls' co-op and for the Afro-American Society's center. The "full investigation" of the cross-burning incident — and the police protection for the student center — had begun even before the sit-in at Willard Straight Hall. Not mentioned in *Newsweek*'s account was what the blacks agreed to do — get out of the student union and help the university set up a campus judiciary system.

Many writers simply fail to understand how a university operates, and this failing is magnified by writing many stories like National League baseball reports, the most exciting disturbance leading the wrap-up, followed by the second most exciting, and so on until the day's disturbances have been "covered." For example, a Hartford *Courant* story combined the seizure of the Cornell student union with a hunger strike at the University of Chicago, two "arson-caused" fires at Brooklyn College, a vote at Brown University in Rhode Island to phase out ROTC, and a strike at Harvard. Another paper combined a bomb explosion at San Francisco State with the story of forty students peacefully picketing the president of the University of Minnesota.

So readers could be excused if they began to think a protest about ROTC at Harvard had something to do with protests about hiring a black fund-raiser at Mills College in Oakland, California. Indeed, based on much news media coverage and comment, readers might be excused if they failed to understand the nature and scope of campus protest at all; particularly in an election year, when uncritical reporting of and comment on self-serving statements by various candidates can only confuse the picture further.

Some reporting and comment have been excellent — accurate, thoughtful, restrained. But too many islands of inadequacy persist. American journalism must do better.

THE UNDERGROUND GI PRESS

Murray Polner

> *Remember: military targets only! Be sure you hit nothing except bases, dumps, roads, factories, bridges, trains, ships, houses, fields, forests, buildings, vehicles, or anything else that may look suspicious.*
> — *Cartoon,* Rough Draft

> *Beware! The big crack-down on mustaches, sideburns, and "long" hair is coming. . . . Bullshit! Recently, the CO of HQ & Main Support Co., 198th Maint Bn at Fort Knox gave the order that all mustaches must go. . . . Well, a couple of guys threatened to go to the IG. Within twenty-four hours that order was rescinded.*
> — Fun, Travel, Adventure

These are two examples of the personal, sometimes amateurish, always passionate journalism of the "underground" GI press — the officially frowned on, widely read and circulated new kind of servicemen's reading matter. Nearly twenty now are in existence, and their formats are simple, ranging from mimeographed sheets to photo-offset papers. Their press runs vary, some claiming as many as five thousand readers. All are irreverent; all are vigorously written.

Still, the lives of these papers remain as precarious as the traditional secret European revolutionary presses they seem to emulate. Editors are usually anonymous. Most writers will not sign their names to letters or stories. An editor of *Fatigue Press* (Fort Hood) was "busted" on a heroin charge. Roger Priest, who puts out *OM: The Liberation Newsletter* in Washington, D.C., was court-martialed by the Navy.

Copies usually are handed out free in coffeehouses, airline and bus terminals, and other off-post areas where servicemen congre-

---

Fall, 1970. Murray Polner, a Long Island resident, has written for *Commonweal, Transaction,* and other magazines.

gate, and then are quietly passed around to trusted buddies. *Rough Draft,* however, has received approval for open distribution at Fort Eustis on an issue-by-issue basis, and the Department of the Army, in a memo entitled "Guidance on Dissent," has affirmed that publication and possession of underground newspapers are protected in general by First Amendment guarantees — assuming no interference with morale or combat operations. As noted by the *Freedom of Information Digest* in a summary of the memo in September–October, 1969, the fact that a publication is critical of government policies or officials "is not in itself a ground for denial [of distribution rights]," and a commander "may not prohibit possession of an unauthorized publication," though "intent to distribute the publication" in violation of post regulations may constitute an offense.

Most papers' journalistic posture is one of defiance. Their mastheads carry prominently some variation on these statements:

This paper is your personal property. It cannot be taken away for any reason.

— The Ultimate Weapon (*Fort Dix*)

To expose those in authority who have betrayed the trust of the American people by using their power to deprive men of their constitutional rights.

— *Rough Draft*
(Tidewater Area, Virginia)

Some of their selection of subjects is predictable: demonstrations, riots in army camps, meetings, lists of friendly lawyers and organizations, instructions for contacting the Inspector General, and general news of the peace movement. What is unique is their approach. The regular press, for example, covered the Presidio "Mutiny" without favoritism. Sensationalism and shock grew out of interviews with military authorities together with guided tours of the Presidio stockade. Once the passions of the moment had died, systematic inquiry into the lives of military prisoners ended. The GI press, having nobody in the Presidio, reprinted releases originally written for civilian underground papers. Then correspondents looked into their own camp stockades from the point of view of the prisoners. "What the hell will the brass show you in a conducted tour through a stockade that a guy who's been in one can't tell you more honestly?" asked one GI editor.

Fun, Travel, Adventure (Fort Knox) ran a two-part series on "conditions at Fort Knox's stockade." The reporter, a former inmate, wrote of extreme overcrowding, insufficient food and winter clothing, medical neglect, and "extremely rough handling" and beatings. He said:

There was an IG inspection. . . . 100's [sic] of prisoners were "paroled" for the day so that the inhuman overcrowding wouldn't be noted as a gig. . . . The next day, the prisoners were stuffed back into the stockade. . . .

After a year in Nam, where the harassment . . . is at least kept to a minimum, they then return to the states and are forced to do the same candy-assed bullshit. So a guy can't take it anymore and splits.

Commented one returned GI, "Isn't there one newspaper in this country that cares enough about us to haunt the stockades and report what really goes on?"

The war, of course, is Number One topic. *Rough Draft* printed a letter from Vietnam on its first page: "I tell you in all honesty that out of the 100-plus men here at HQ, you will find not one man who would state we are right in being here. . . ."

There was this cartoon. A Pentagon general asks his aide: "When's your birthday, Rigney? November 28th? Fine, that makes it 2811 enemy casualties for the week."

Wherever there is a military unit, such items can provide an invaluable catharsis for the frustrations of military life — for which few sounding boards are available. Thus one can read such classic complaints as these:

SSG and Mrs. Richard Prim are very pleased with their new cocktail bar. SSG Prim had a couple of trainees at D Troop, 5th Recon, build it for him with army materials and tools in the supply room, on army time.

— *FTA*

"Lifer of the Month Award." Presented in February 1969 to 1 SG John Waters of A Co., Special Troops for a truly outstanding accomplishment — the Bulletin Board Orderly, continuous 8-hour shifts of staring (no reading allowed) at the bulletin board.

— *Ultimate Weapon*

We have discovered that the Special Troops S-4 is using its lawn mowing detail to cut grass for colonels in the vicinity of Post Hqs to include Colonel Weddles' own quarters.

— *Shakedown*

So it goes. Getting back at the untouchables. Embarrassing them. Calling their enemies' attention to their transgressions, real or imagined. Resorting to ridicule, the major weapon against the props of a rigid military society.

In the end, the GI papers remain amateurs, for now at least. Their content is uneven, their style sometimes turgid, their humor often simply not funny. But they also have wit and sensitivity. Their writers are angrier than any other generation of conscriptees. Their future, of course, is impossible to predict, but this much is clear: so long as the war grinds on endlessly and men are compelled to join, and so long as the mass media pretend that military life is like a television serial, the GI press will continue to thrive in circulation and influence. Given no responsive media outlet, men — young or old — will conceive and nurture their own.

PASSING COMMENT

The Ten Least Reported Stories

A favorite pastime of the season is selecting the "ten top news stories" of the year — and on this occasion the decade — just closed. Inevitably, because of the terms of the question, spot-news events are chosen. Are they any longer an accurate measure of journalism's year? We suspect they are not. As discussed elsewhere in these pages, journalism's responsibilities now extend far beyond spot-news reporting — to, among other subjects, reporting on human institutions. Accordingly, we think it appropriate that at each year-end journalists contemplate, along with presumably well-covered spot-news stories, the least reported stories of the year. For 1969 — indeed, for the sixties — we nominate these broad "institutional" stories as the ten least covered by American journalism:

Congress	Local government
Department of Defense	Medical care
The police	Education
The courts	Industry
State legislatures	The media

Comment on these selections is welcome, as are nominations in coming months for the ten least covered stories of 1970.

Winter, 1969–70.

THREE

The Racial Revolution

THEY STILL WRITE IT WHITE

Robert E. Smith

For years, the American press has referred to "regimes" in unfriendly countries, "administrations" in friendly countries; "military muscle" in Soviet May Day parades, "colorful marching units" on July 4 in this country; "puppet governments" among Communist nations (like North Korea), and "allies" among non-Communist countries (like South Korea). Daily newspapers, wire services, and television and radio stations are run by Americans and so there is an American attitude in the press.

Also, newspapers find themselves saying things like "Before you take the wife and kids out . . ." or "Joe Jones, like you and me, has to look himself in the mirror every morning when he shaves." The press is run by men and to a large extent men write and edit the news, and there is a male attitude in the press — innocuous at times, insulting at other times.

So also, whites edit and, to a large extent, write the news. There is a white attitude in the daily press and in major broadcasting — innocuous, or insulting, or perhaps even inflammatory.

There is the matter of story selection and what makes news; there is the matter of selecting "average" people, the men in the street, who always used to turn out to be white. Journalists are now aware of these problems, and seem to be compensating. But in the use of language, in the very words they use, the news media still show their whiteness. They have failed to realize how they insult a large sector of their public, in subtle and not so subtle ways.

Look, for instance, at how *Newsweek* in November described Key Biscayne: "For its people, indeed, it is paradise enow: a 6-mile island in whose habitable midsection are ensconced 4,000

Spring, 1969. Robert E. Smith is a reporter for *Newsday*.

whites, two Negroes, five motels, two hotels, four churches, a pitch-and-putt golf course, one street with sidewalks, a narrowing sliver of beach, an unending gabble of cocktail parties — and lately, to the mixed emotions of the islanders, one President-elect of the United States."

That may be *Newsweek*'s idea of paradise — that where there aren't Negroes there aren't troubles — but it's not Roy Wilkins's.

A New York *Times* article in October on the white female lead of *The Great White Hope*, said this: "Playing a part in which she has to kiss a Negro and get in bed with him on stage doesn't faze her." White readers should substitute "white" for "Negro" in the line to understand the insult. How much better it would have been to have said, "Playing a part in which she kisses a Negro . . ." or "Playing a part in which the script calls for her to kiss a Negro . . ." All the difference in the world.

The Detroit *News*, on its front page the day after the massive 1967 riots had simmered, reported: "Gov. George Romney today turned to the task of assuring 'justice under law' to the flood of human flotsam — the vicious and the merely unfortunate — swept up by police in quelling Detroit's riot. . . ."

Webster's defines "flotsam" as both "vagrant impoverished people" and "unimportant miscellaneous material." The National Advisory Commission on Civil Disorders found that half of those arrested that week in Detroit had no prior arrest record; two-thirds had no conviction records; three-fourths of the females arrested had no prior records at all. Flotsam?

Similarly, white editors, reporters, and news managers are always slightly surprised when black people behave like something other than savages. Thus, a reporter for the New York *Times*, describing President Johnson's farewell appearance before several hundred Negro government officials including a Supreme Court justice and a Cabinet member, felt compelled to report: "The President [spoke] to the well-dressed Negro officials and their wives." Of course, the real news would have been if several hundred government officials and their wives at an evening reception in Washington had *not* been well dressed!

A black attorney in Alabama chided a news reporter on this sort of thing once when asked his impressions of a White House conference of top civil rights and Negro leaders from which he had just returned. "Well," he answered, "it ended without any violence."

There are newspapermen and broadcasters who would think that was worth a headline. Just to prove the point, there is a headline that ran on the front page of the Tampa *Tribune* during the disorders there: SUNDAY NIGHT RACIAL RIOTING HAD AT LEAST ONE NEGRO HERO.

A part of the white attitude of the white press is the "articulate syndrome." At its height a few years ago but not as fashionable now, it revealed the media's surprise that black people could express themselves well. And it was a reporter's way of assuring readers he was not talking about one of your shiftless, ignorant Negroes.

Examples, chosen at random in just two weeks' checking:

From a *Newsday* sports column: "If there is going to be effective leadership among the black pros, it will come from the pro basketball players. They are the most articulate, aware and organized of the big time athletes."

From a *Newsday* article on young Negroes supporting a political candidate: "Clean-shaven and articulate . . ."

From a *Newsday* story on three black members of the "Mayor's Committee" in Cleveland: "Two of the three were lawyers, the third was the city's former chief planner. They were well-educated, articulate and middle class."

And there it is still again: In a column in the New York *Times* in January, "Charles V. Hamilton of Roosevelt University, one of the most articulate of black teachers and writers. . . ." Not inaccurate, just overused.

"Well-educated, articulate and middle class" is just one of the phrases that black newsmakers grow weary of, along with "law-abiding Negroes," "our fellow Negro citizens," "militant," "responsible Negro leaders," "reverse discrimination" (black discrimination against whites is "reverse" only from the white point of view).

The white attitude is not always an intentional thing; if it were, it would be easier to pin down and to eliminate. Often, it's hard to tell just how conscious, or how accidental, it is.

HERE COME DE TIGER said the caption under a Detroit *News*

picture last October of two Detroit Tigers ballplayers, Willie Horton and Earl Wilson, arriving in Detroit after the Tigers had won the World Series. The caption probably would have fit under any of the three or four other pictures on the page of white players arriving, but it was written for Horton and Wilson, both Negroes.

There is also a tendency, whether rooted in the old plantation fraternalism or due to many newsmen's familiarity with certain blacks as interesting characters, that results in Negroes being called by their first names in news reports while whites in a similar context are called by last names. O. J. Simpson during last fall's football season and Tommy Smith during the summer Olympics were identified on a first-name basis by sports announcers and writers more than most other athletes, for example.

The tendency was well demonstrated in a UPI dispatch from a Fort Worth track meet in February on Olympic high hurdle champion Willie Davenport, who is black. "Despite his performance," the story said, "Willie had to settle for a tie with Tom Von Ruden as the meet's outstanding athlete. Von Ruden, who managed only a ninth-place finish in the Olympic 1500 meters, set [a record] in winning the 1,000-yard run."

And then there is the "we-they syndrome." Reporters, commentators and especially editorialists find it hard to realize that their audience is made up of people of many races and colors. Too often they talk of "we" (white people) in relation to "they" (black people). What they don't realize is that one tenth or even one third (in the case of some big-city newspapers) of that "we" ain't white.

WNHC–TV in New Haven editorialized during the riots there in 1967: "The core of the crisis is that American Negroes have been deprived, denied, subjugated for decades now. And their patience is wearing thin.

"In their place, so would mine . . . so would yours.

"In fact, editorially speaking, we marvel at the patience of so many Negroes."

These were well-intentioned thoughts, but did the commentator realize that he was talking to Negroes as well as whites when he said, ". . . so would yours"?

At the same time, the New Haven *Register* was announcing in a front-page editorial: "Declaration of a state of emergency was a bitter pill for Mayor Lee — as it was, also, for a community which has made every effort to give its Negro citizens the things they have asked."

Once again, there's the implication that those "Negroes" mentioned are not really a part of "our" community, which has done so much for "them."

Similarly, an ABC–TV narrator on a well-intentioned documentary was able to intone, "We don't know what it's really like to grow up as a black." Had it occurred to him that a tenth, or a sixth, or a fourth of "we" in the audience know exactly what it's like!

It all depends on your point of view — in the language you use and the language you hear and see. Look for example at a Detroit *News* news story, not an editorial, written by a white man after the 1967 riots: "Community leaders today plunged into the hard practicalities that will take months, even years, to resolve before Detroit can be restored to normal."

Compare that with what was said one week later in a news story, not an editorial, written by a black man, in the Michigan *Chronicle,* a Negro weekly paper: "We can't go back to the status quo. In face of all the appeals from . . . city officials for a return to normalcy, it is generally agreed that this is the great danger that will undergird the fear already paralyzing much of our community. . . .

"Throughout the community there is a growing desire for change . . . change that will dig deep down into the root causes."

Here are two major newspapers in the same city talking about different "communities," one saying the community wants a restoration to "normal," the other saying that the community wants "change."

It is important to remember that one paper, the *Chronicle,* makes no claim of aiming at anything except the black community, while the other paper, the *News* (like all metropolitan papers) claims to serve all of the communities in its circulation area.

PASSING COMMENT

A New Fable (with Apologies to George Ade)

Once there was no doubt that Journalism should be all White. After all, They had Their Own churches, Their Own schools, Their Own neighborhoods, and Their Own newspapers. When the telephone rang in a White newspaper office and somebody said there had been a Shooting at Fifty-Fourth and Elm, the Editor snarled, Get me some News about White Men. Besides, you could never use One of Them as a Reporter. You couldn't send One to a DAR meeting.

The FCC thought so, too. It gave Them Their Own television stations and radio stations for Their Own preachers and gospel singers and Hair-Straightener commercials. Besides, you could never put One on Camera. What would People say in Mobile?

Journalism Schools were Different. The schools admitted Them but sometimes said, Maybe you had better go work in someplace like India, where you won't Stand Out.

That's the Way It Was until the Extremists began. Journalism had some Further Thoughts: Maybe it would be a Good Idea to hire One, just to show that Our Heart's in the Right Place. Soon there was One on camera on every television network, and lots more loitering in Commercials. And One or Two on all the Best Newspapers. When Pickets came by, Journalism could point across the newsroom and say, We have One. There He is.

But not everybody could find One. There was a Shortage of Trained Talent. Everybody called the Journalism School and said, Send us One. But the Journalism Schools said, We're Fresh Out.

And Journalism would say, How can that be? They said they wanted Jobs, didn't they?

Moral: They're Not Ready.

Winter, 1965.

INCIDENT AT ORANGEBURG: A Reporter's Notes

Jim Hoagland

In February, a chilled dry wind sweeps over the brown soil of the soybean farms thaat ring Orangeburg, South Carolina. Dust slides along the streets, past the city limits (gerrymandered to exclude Negroes) and toward Rether B. Middleton's small farmhouse. It was February 11, 1968, three days after her youngest son, seventeen-year-old Delano, had been shot and killed by state troopers. She told me about Delano's death; it was the first time she had talked to a white person about it — although there were more than fifty newsmen in this town of fifteen thousand.

Later that day, Brian Donovan of *Newsday* became the second and only other reporter to talk to the Middletons during the week following the slaying. Donovan was also the only other reporter who went to sources that should have been checked automatically — the mortician who had the youth's body, students who had been wounded and were still in the hospital, doctors who treated the youths who were killed, and students who had been on the scene. All were largely ignored by the (90 percent white) press corps.

Most of these sources were Negroes.

Delano Middleton and two other Negro teenagers were killed in the most costly racial violence in the South in this decade. The Orangeburg trouble sparked incidents across the South between Negro college student bodies and the white towns in which they are located. Orangeburg has become a national rallying cry for black militants.

Spring, 1968. Jim Hoagland, a native of South Carolina, is a reporter for the Washington *Post*.

The coverage at Orangeburg stands as a virtual case study supporting the Kerner Commission's broad indictment of the media's failure to cover both sides of race relations.

The trouble in Orangeburg began with protests over a segregated bowling alley, but the problems there lay much deeper. South Carolina State College — the only publicly supported predominantly Negro college in South Carolina — is situated in Orangeburg, and the students were convinced that they had been slighted by the state's legislature. The legislature had cut the school's budget request by $3.5 million this year. Moreover, the students chafed at the barely token integration in Orangeburg businesses and public schools.

The trail toward violence began with a student demonstration at the bowling alley on February 5, a Monday. About twenty-five of them entered the alley and refused to leave. The Orangeburg police shut it down.

There was not a word on the demonstration in Orangeburg's daily paper, the *Times and Democrat,* the next day, nor in the two other papers that cover the Orangeburg area — the *State,* Columbia's and South Carolina's largest paper, and the Columbia *Record.* The Orangeburg paper could possibly have taken off part of the pressure by looking into the situation at the bowling alley and into student grievances.

On Tuesday, February 6, the students came back. This time, the police cleared the alley by swinging clubs at the students. Some of the students fought back; at least nine were injured and treated. A dozen others were arrested. A policeman was hit with a lead pipe wielded by a student. More important, the students were convinced that they — especially the girls — had been unnecessarily beaten. One said later, "The girls were whipped for fools." The police denied this.

Next day's *Times and Democrat* reported that a "scuffle" had taken place. There was no description of the scuffle, and the main headline reported that a policeman had been hurt. The paper also had a page 1 story on the bowling alley owner's complaint about the police closing on Monday night. There were no statements from students.

On Wednesday, February 7, the students drew up a dozen

grievances recounting Tuesday's police actions, and submitted them to the City Council. The *Times and Democrat* did not report the grievances until Friday, when it printed the City Council's negative reply.

The shootings occurred Thursday night, February 8, 10:15 P.M., when a hundred state troopers confronted about an equal number of students and prevented them from leaving the campus to stage a protest march downtown.

Students had thrown bricks and wood at cars and buildings during the week, and some students who were on the scene on February 8 admit to having thrown stones at the police that night.

One of the policemen went down. His fellow troopers, perhaps thinking he had been shot, opened fire and chased the students, killing Delano Middleton and two others, and injuring at least twenty-eight. Fifteen minutes after the volley, police determined that the patrolman had not been shot but, they said, had been hit by a thrown club.

The shootings projected the conflict into the national news flow. The AP moved four night leads, beginning at 11:30 P.M., stating that two Negro students had been killed "during a heavy exchange of gunfire" in which the policeman was "struck in the head by a bullet."

Even newsmen who insist they heard sniper firing from the campus at scattered intervals during the night say there was no exchange of fire at the moment of shooting. Students and other eyewitnesses insistently deny that there was any sniping. (Yet, as late as February 15, AP moved a story saying the youths were killed "in an exchange of gunfire," without any qualification.)

The AP did file a clarification of the policeman's injury at 2:25 A.M., too late for most East Coast morning papers, including the Washington *Post* and the New York *Times,* to amend the earlier report. UPI, waiting for verification, moved the story late.

The *State,* the *Record,* the *Times and Democrat,* and the wire services were unanimous in their first accounts. There was sniper firing, they said flatly. The *Times and Democrat* did not quote any students on what happened until February 12, and then only in an AP story.

The *State* carried sixteen stories on Orangeburg February 11, but used only four paragraphs quoting students. The *State*'s entire reporting on the mood of the students and Orangeburg Negroes was one sentence: "One State College student was quoted as saying he and others were enraged by the incident."

The only early report that the students had not fired (no weapons were ever found on campus) came from Sidney Lazard on NBC's *Today* show February 9. Lazard's statement infuriated the Orangeburgers, and on the Huntley-Brinkley report that night, he dropped the reference to who fired first. Lazard said he dropped the reference not because of the criticism leveled at him by white South Carolina officials, but because it didn't fit into the later story. He still stands by his first report.

In a situation where journalistic cool was most needed, it was blown quickly. Self-serving, anonymous quotes proliferated, trigger words were splashed through news accounts. Examples:

— The *Times and Democrat*, February 9: "A source at State College . . . [said] 'there are a bunch of weird people in town.' "

— And: "Rumors flew prior to the shooting that violence was raging . . . Anxious newsmen in Columbia and Charleston queried the *Times and Democrat* . . . a person or persons with outside Orangeburg press contacts, was already heralding events that were to come."

— Publisher Dean B. Livingston's account, February 11: "I crawled over whiskey bottles and beer cans whose contents presumably helped inflame the rioters."

— And, February 12: The bowling alley "became a prime target for Negro agitation . . . and Black Power elements . . ." There are a half a dozen other references to otherwise unidentified Black Power elements.

— The *State*, February 10: "Late in the afternoon, the word went out. The core of the black militancy movement on campus had obtained arms and was preparing molotov cocktails." Again, these militants were not identified. After describing the shooting, the account ends: "The war had begun."

South Carolina papers gave extensive coverage to charges from the governor, congressmen, and city officials who blamed "black power agitators," occasionally linked with the Student Non-Violent Coordinating Committee. But there were no replies from local SNCC workers. However, there were two well-done stories concerning Cleveland Sellers, South Carolina coordinator for SNCC, who was arrested while being treated at the hospital after the shootings. The *State* resourcefully interviewed Sellers's mother and presented a well-written account of his life. Jack Bass of the Charlotte *Observer* interviewed Sellers the day before the shootings and produced an incisive story about him the day after his arrest.

After the incident of February 8, the national press moved in quickly. My paper sent me down in time to file a story on February 9.

The New York *Times* sent in Douglas Kneeland for one day, February 10. He filed one story (based on the mayor's appointment of a predictably ineffectual biracial committee, a statement from the chamber of commerce, and almost nothing from Negroes or students) and was pulled out on another assignment. After the wires moved a story saying the tension level was rising again, the *Times* sent in Douglas Robinson, who stayed with the story longer than any other out-of-state newsman.

Incredibly, *Time* magazine did not use a word on Orangeburg. *Newsweek* carried only six paragraphs, but did a good job in that space of telling what happened. The Atlanta papers did not send any staffers. Most newspapers had to depend on the wire services, which did a lackluster job.

There was little digging into what became a major point of dispute — how the students were killed. Edward T. Jones, the funeral director who had Middleton's body and who had embalmed that of one of the other students, told me that Middleton and Sam Hammond both had been shot in the back. He produced Middleton's blood-soaked clothes, with a hole in the upper back but no exit hole in the front, and a death certificate signed by the doctor who treated Hammond saying Hammond had been killed by a bullet in the back.

Newsday and my paper carried stories reporting this finding. The *Newsday* story provoked a query from UPI New York to its Columbia, South Carolina, bureau. Donovan of *Newsday* told the UPI reporter about Middleton's clothes and the death certificate. The UPI man talked to the funeral home director but UPI mentioned neither the clothing nor the death certificate.

The Associated Press also checked with the undertaker for a

story of February 12. It used one sentence on Hammond's death in the twenty-fifth paragraph, and nothing on Middleton. This story appeared in the Orangeburg paper and in the *State,* much as written. The Charleston *News and Courier* dropped the reference to Hammond.

Even more damaging to the police version of events was the story told by two students who had been wounded during the clash, and who were still at the Orangeburg hospital nearly a week later. They had wounds in the bottom of their feet and back of their legs. They said they had been deliberately shot while lying on the ground.

They were interviewed by the Washington *Post, Newsday* and *Jet* magazine. Otherwise, they were ignored. (Jack Nelson of the Los Angeles *Times* later produced an excellent roundup on how students had been wounded.)

These incidents tended to discredit the police version of why they had to kill three Negro teen-agers. That version was accepted, however, by most local newspapers, the wire services, and with one exception — later dropped — television. But that police version was heartily disbelieved by many in the Negro community, and the media's unquestioning acceptance of it gave writers like John Lewis, in the *Afro-American,* ammunition to charge that the white press was deliberately hiding the truth. This charge was taken seriously by many in a black minority with whom the press is already greatly discredited.

I don't think the charge is true, and I don't think Lewis can substantiate it. There was no conspiracy by reporters at Orangeburg. There was, however, a failure.

Enveloped in an admittedly dangerous situation, and realizing that they, unlike outside reporters, would have to rely for other stories on men like Pete Strom, the state's top policeman, and Henry Lake, the whiskey-voiced lawyer who carried a .38 pistol beneath his jacket all the time he served as the governor's top representative in Orangeburg, the South Carolina reporters were plainly in no mood to rile the police by pressing.

They covered the story largely from the Holiday Inn, which was press and police headquarters. I experienced much hostility from in-state reporters when I began asking "the wrong questions."

Hostility was, of course, the major ingredient of the Orangeburg situation, on all sides. Police growled at me my first day in town, when I asked for Middleton's name and address, "We ain't got nothing for you outsiders." (I was born in South Carolina.) Later, when I was attacked and beaten by a Negro youth who said he didn't like white reporters, two Orangeburg policemen came to the hospital to chortle about the incident as I got twelve stitches put in my head. They stood around for half an hour to get a look at me.

This is the atmosphere in which reporters had to work, moving about through the curfew enforced by M-1 toting guardsmen, on the basis of "press identification," consisting of a flimsy piece of paper on which was scrawled, in pencil, "ID" and a guard captain's signature.

Orangeburg was not happy with the attention it was receiving. Sitting in city hall, which is the front half of the Carolina movie theater (you walk by the mayor's office into the box office), the town's city manager asked me, "How should we handle the press in a situation like this? We can't have you fellows just roaming around."

He didn't have much to worry about. Little roaming was done.

For example, William Mahoney, covering for the Columbia *Record*, gave me this response when I asked him why his paper had not followed up the leads of students being shot in the back, "We talked to the governor about it and he said the FBI was conducting an impartial investigation and we would have those facts when the report was released. So we decided to wait on the report."

Such FBI reports are not made public. Stephen Pollack, head of the Justice Department's Civil Rights Division, which will get the report, told me that this specific report would not be released. Mahoney, and the rest of the South Carolina newspapers, may have a long wait.

Livingston, the editor and publisher of the Orangeburg *Times and Democrat*, gave me a different response when I asked him about the lack of probing on the shootings: "It was one of the easiest stories I've ever covered. It was a straight shooting. We got the identifications from the hospital right away, and got the ultimate in cooperation from law enforcement officials. We know what happened."

The *Times and Democrat* and the other South Carolina papers were equally simplistic when it came to why the violence erupted. It was over a segregated, all-white bowling alley, and in the view of state officials and local newspapermen, the alley was merely a target for "black power agitators" who wanted to cause violence, and the police had to stop it.

That's the way it was at Orangeburg. Two things disturb me about the coverage there, and prompted me to write this article. One of them can possibly be best expressed by some notes I jotted down as I left Orangeburg:

"Perhaps criticizing the coverage would be expecting reporters to be more than human. It was a dangerous situation. Talking to students on the campus cost me 12 stitches in the head. Also, reporters whom I have known for years and whose judgment I trust were in Orangeburg, and they too were harassed by students when they did try to talk to them. They were also angry, because they were convinced the students had thrown bricks and fire bombs for three days. When the blow-up came Thursday, these reporters are convinced, there was small arms fire from the campus, and this was enough to justify the police action.

"This may well be. The point is these reporters had their minds made up, and their stories showed it. It shouldn't have been that way, and I hope it won't be that way again."

Secondly, there was the realization that five years ago, this would have commanded extensive coverage, and stayed on page 1 for days. Orangeburg was dropped by most newspapers immediately.

It is a reflection of not only what has happened to the civil rights movement, and the press's attitude toward the racial struggle in the wake of the mega-disturbances of Newark and Detroit, but it is also a reflection of the mood of the newspapers' readers.

DIMOUT IN JACKSON

Edwin N. Williams

Coverage by the Jackson *Clarion-Ledger* of the May 13–15 disorder at Jackson State College provides a point-by-point validation of ghetto criticism of the press in the Kerner Commission report published two years ago.

The *Ledger* is the state's largest morning daily. It is the cornerstone on which the Hederman family has built a statewide publishing empire, including the state's largest afternoon daily, two weeklies, a third large daily in Hattiesburg, part ownership in radio and TV stations, a corner on the state government printing business, and other lucrative enterprises. The *Ledger* is *the* Hederman paper. The afternoon Jackson *Daily News* was a longtime rival acquired in the 1940s. The *Ledger*, much more than the *Daily News*, speaks with the voice of the Mississippi establishment.

The Hedermans, staunch Southern Baptists and political conservatives, epitomize the white power structure in Mississippi. If an agency or institution wields official power here, chances are the brothers Bob, Henry, or Zach or cousin Tom have a hand in it or are close to someone who has.

Henry is a member of the Board of Trustees of Institutions of Higher Learning, which governs the eight state-supported colleges and universities. He also is president of the Jackson Chamber of Commerce. Zach is a member of the Mississippi Memorial Stadium Commission, which controls use of the modern stadium here. Bob is a member of the Pearl River Industrial Commission, which oversees Ross. R. Barnett Reservoir, a burgeoning water recreational complex near here. His wife is on the State Library Com-

---

Summer, 1970. Edwin Williams is the Jackson correspondent for the Delta *Democrat-Times*, Greenville, Mississippi.

mission. Tom is a member of the state Research and Development Council.

The *Ledger* and its sister publication, the Jackson *Daily News*, traditionally assay the political field to insure that at least one of them backs the winner in the governor's race. After dalliance with former Governor Ross Barnett, an also-ran in the first Democratic primary in 1967, the *Ledger* joined the *Daily News* behind Congressman John Bell Williams as he trounced political moderate William Winter in the runoff. The newspapers have become less blatantly racist since the 1950s and early 1960s. Then, their news and editorial pages reflected — and contributed to — the segregationist fanaticism which culminated in violence and bloodshed when Negro James Meredith entered the University of Mississippi in 1962.

In recent years, news of Negro activities and achievements has appeared with increasing frequency in both papers. But blacks have not gained access to society pages, and black obituaries are uncommon. The *Daily News* places a page of black news in papers carrier-delivered to black homes, but that news doesn't appear in papers sold on the streets or delivered in white neighborhoods.

The Hederman papers have shown no inclination to explore the problems of blacks in Mississippi, or to use their influence to temper the truculent white supremacist policies of state political leaders. The papers have no rapport with black activist, or even moderate, leaders in this city where almost two-fifths of the 150,000 residents are black. Neither paper has made a noticeable effort to gain credibility in the black community. Neither has integrated its news staff.

When police responded to reports of disorder near Jackson State May 13, the *Ledger* police reporter took charge of coverage. He remained on the story throughout, and the *Ledger*'s lead stories became a conduit for the police viewpoint to the virtual exclusion of all others. Of the 145 column inches the *Ledger* carried in the first three days of Jackson State coverage, 73 inches — more than half — came directly from police. Another 47 inches — about a third — came from the mayor and governor. From students, on-the-scene newsmen, NAACP officials, college faculty and officials, came 16 inches — about one-tenth of the total. Nowhere in the staff-written *Ledger* stories is there a hint that many eyewitnesses dispute the official contention that police fired only in direct response to sniper fire.

The New Orleans *Times-Picayune* and Memphis *Commercial Appeal* rival the *Ledger* in morning circulation in Mississippi. Each paper maintains a full-time reporter in Jackson. Compare the lead stories in the May 16 *Ledger, Picayune,* and *Commercial Appeal.*

Clarion-Ledger:

Jackson police and Mississippi Highway Patrol officials Friday blamed dormitory snipers for a brief gun battle at Jackson State College that brought two deaths and nine injuries, one of the latter regarded as critical. They said gunshots were heard on the campus up to an hour-and-a-half before officers actually moved in to try to quell snipers.

Det. Chief M. B. Pierce . . . said policemen and patrolmen did not actually move into the campus and return fire until after a fire truck and its crew had been fired upon. He quoted a columnist for a liberal Memphis, Tenn., newspaper as saying he "abandoned" the truck and its crew after a "volley of gunfire" was aimed at it from dormitory windows.

(A brief but intense telephone conversation between the *Commercial* reporter and the *Ledger* executive editor after this story hit the streets resulted in this version in a later edition of the *Ledger:* "He [Pierce] quoted . . . a columnist-reporter for the liberal Memphis, Tennessee, *Commercial Appeal* as having told him that 'a volley' of shots burst from behind a building when the fire truck went onto the campus. . . .")

Times-Picayune:

JACKSON, Miss. — Federal and city investigations were ordered Friday into the deaths of two young blacks and wounding of a dozen others at Jackson State College after withering gunfire by officers ripped into a girls' dormitory in the early hours. . . .

An angry Negro community later blamed the gunfire on "racist" state highway patrolmen who launched a 30-second barrage of rifle and shotgun fire after hearing what they believed were two sniper shots. . . .

Commercial Appeal:

JACKSON, Miss., May 15.—Outraged Negro leaders demanded Friday that state officers who shot two youths to death and wounded nine others during an early morning confrontation at Jackson State College be prosecuted for murder and conspiracy.

State Highway Patrol officers, reportedly backed by city police, opened fire at a women's dormitory with rifles, pistols and shotguns on the West Jackson campus shortly after midnight Friday. . . .

There was sharp disagreement over reports of "sniper fire," which police said triggered the volley of gunfire. Jackson Det. Chief M. B. Pierce said there was evidence that officers were fired upon, but he declined to elaborate.

The *Picayune* story quoted wounded students, the mayor, police, black leader Charles Evers, TV newsmen on the scene when the shooting started, and a TV sound tape of the shooting. The *Commercial* story attributed information to wounded students, other student eyewitnesses, police, the mayor, the district attorney, and black leaders. The *Ledger* story attributed information to police, hospital sources, the mayor, and prepared statements by college groups and an NAACP official. No eyewitnesses other than police were mentioned in the *Ledger*. The *Ledger* reporter did not visit the campus, about a dozen blocks from the *Ledger* office.

The *Ledger* did not close its pages to black community reaction, however. In the May 16 home edition, the *Ledger* used an eight-inch AP story quoting an NAACP official who said, "There is no evidence that anyone saw a sniper or could indicate a possible direction of sniper fire." Throughout the next week, the *Ledger* used AP coverage of black community protest. But never did a *Ledger* reporter cover any black meeting or interview a black student. Never did the *Ledger* reporter waver in his use of the police "exchange of gunfire" line in recapping the events at Jackson State. Two examples:

MAY 18: The Negroes gathered . . . for a memorial service honoring two youths killed in an exchange of gunshots. . . .

MAY 23: Ultra-liberal members of Congress . . . visited the city . . . and denounced officers who fired back at sniping students. . . . Young Green was one of two persons killed in an exchange of gunfire a week ago. . . .

Never did the *Ledger* writer mention that the alleged sniper fire drew from lawmen a thirty-second barrage which riddled the end of a women's dorm with more than two hundred individual bullet holes. Never did he mention that no policeman, highway patrolman, National Guardsman, or any of their vehicles or equipment showed evidence of being hit by sniper fire. Never did he mention that lawmen used no tear gas or attempted any crowd control measures. In short, never did he allow in his story the suggestion that police did anything other than respond in kind to gunfire from the dormitory. The *Ledger* stood alone in this narrow reporting of the story.

The Jackson *Daily News,* while relying as heavily as the *Ledger* on official sources, regularly included in accounts of the shooting a paragraph saying student witnesses deny that sniper fire provoked the police barrage. The *Daily News* reporting reflects a higher degree of professionalism, not a difference of editorial opinion. The *Daily News* cartoonist, for example, came forth with an editorial page drawing depicting a white hand labeled LAW AND ORDER vigorously restraining a black arm and hand brandishing a brick labeled ANARCHY.

Although the *Ledger* adopted the police viewpoint, its pages were open to dissent. Letters and resolutions criticizing the police version and charging that lawmen overreacted were printed regularly. But openness is no substitute for competent journalism. No number of letters to the editor can make up for failure to require fair and accurate coverage in each story. A competent AP story doesn't erase a biased staff-written story.

Readers outside Jackson received better information than those in Jackson. Both AP and UPI did competent jobs on the story, as did the *Times-Picayune* and the *Commercial Appeal.* In fact, reporters for the *Times-Picayune,* Los Angeles *Times,* and Greenville, Mississippi, *Delta Democrat-Times* unearthed the only real scoops in the days following the killings.

How can one explain the *Ledger* coverage? "From the start, they played it like cops and robbers," said one ex-*Ledger* staff member. "You quote the cops, you don't quote the robbers."

It is more complex than that, however. The *Ledger* traditionally avoids stories criticizing state and local government. The Hedermans' political power is so pervasive that they can, by concerted effort, effect most political changes they think should be made. Criticism of state and local goverment is in a real way criticism of the Hedermans and their allies, since they allow goverment to be what it is. The avoidance of critical stories applies only to the *Ledger* staff, however. If AP writes a story unfavorable to government, the *Ledger* may run it, just as it runs critical letters and resolutions. But the *Ledger* will not initiate the criticism or report it if no one else does.

The Hedermans and their allies are the Mississippi establishment. If they want change, they seek it through the application of political and economic power at the top, not through investigative reporting and newspaper editorials. The police and highway patrol are part of that establishment. If the patrol, for instance, must be death with, it will be dealt with in the councils of power, not in the pages of the newspapers.

Some blacks have shown their feelings toward the Hederman papers by calling for a boycott of both the *Ledger* and the *Daily News*. They demand certain changes. Among them: fire the editor of the *Daily News* and the police reporter of the *Ledger*; resume the Jackson *Daily News* Relays, a track meet abolished after massive school integration here; hire black reporters; desegregate society pages; allow blacks as well as white newsboys to win world tours sponsored by the papers; stop printing black news on a separate sheet not included in papers sold to whites; stop editorializing in news stories. But black economic power is so minuscule compared to that of the Hedermans that a boycott seems futile. The gulf between the Hederman papers and the blacks seems destined to grow wider, rather than narrower, and the Hedermans seem unconcerned.

THE WHITE CAPTIVITY OF BLACK RADIO

Fred Ferretti

Among the dozens of changes of ownership in broadcast franchises last year were three involving William F. Buckley, Jr., columnist, TV host, and publisher of the *National Review*. With the Starr brothers of Omaha, Nebraska, he bought control of black-oriented radio stations WBOK New Orleans, WLOK Memphis, and KYOK Houston. Except for Buckley's notoriety, however, there was little unusual about the transactions. Of some 310 stations listed by the 1969 *Broadcasting Yearbook* as programming at least in part for blacks, all but sixteen were owned by whites — and no TV franchises in this country were owned by blacks. Nor was Buckley's three-station investment likely to be as unprofitable as *National Review* (which, like most magazines of comment and opinion, never is far from financial shoals): annual advertising billings on black-oriented radio stations are estimated at $35 million, and most earn profits ranging from comfortable to spectacular.

Unfortunately, most, too, are shameful caricatures of the public service image suggested by requirements for a license to use public airwaves. A black disc jockey — paid far less than white counterparts on larger stations, and with less chance of advancement — may play an Aretha Franklin record, then in "down home" accents assert that the record undoubtedly "made your liver quiver and your knees freeze." Then he will segue into a frantic plug for a "Top Forty" rock number before playing the record — deafeningly. On the hour, news will consist of a piece of wire copy

Summer, 1970. Fred Ferretti is a reporter for the New York *Times*.

ripped from a teletype and read verbatim by the same disc jockey. Required public service time will be filled mainly by pseudo-evangelist hours. And commercial sponsors will be sought willy-nilly, without sifting the "dollar-down, dollar-a-week forever" entrepreneurs from the nondeceptive advertisers.

Not all black-oriented radio stations conform to this description, of course. Station WLIB in Harlem has won two Peabody Awards, most recently in April for a program called *Higher Horizons*, which attempts to provide students from disadvantaged backgrounds with information on how to enter colleges and how to finance their education. Other black-oriented stations also provide some noteworthy public service programs. Under pressure from citizen groups which have mounted challenges to broadcast franchises, more such programming improvements seem in the offing. But, on the whole, broadcasting stations oriented toward America's black citizenry remind one of nothing so much as Newton Minow's historic description of American commercial television — "a vast wasteland."

This is not merely because, as noted in a Race Relations Information Center study by Bernard E. Garnett earlier this year, "by and large 'soul' radio still is a black-oriented version of 'Top Forty' (also known as 'bubble gum') radio, which appeals mainly to white adolescents." (Most white-oriented radio, after all, is little more imaginative than that.) There are, as Garnett points out, these related factors: "Nearly a quarter-century after a radio station first geared its entire broadcasting format to black interests, there still is no nationwide black-oriented news network. Blacks still comprise the vast minority in key executive positions at 'soul' stations. Entertainment programming is based almost entirely on 'Rhythm-n-Blues' or 'rock' music, with little or no emphasis on black performances in jazz, 'pop,' folk, or other music modes."

Such circumstances never arose in the black press. For the black press, for all its problems, always has been owned largely by blacks. Because its main commodity was news and features, it had to provide at least minimal reporting and comment on community concerns; develop black management talent; and not only respond somewhat to the black community but at times provide critical leadership. Moreover, any black individual or organization could establish a newspaper or magazine if he could raise the money and find an audience, and publishers ranging from "establishment" commercial entrepreneurs to the Black Muslims and Black Panthers have done so (see "The Black Press in Transition," Spring, 1970).

Broadcasting, however, requires not only capital but a license. Licenses are available only from the Federal Communications Commission. The FCC always has had an all-white membership and until recently almost never seriously questioned a license transfer or renewal application. Hence licenses for stations "serving" the black community could be transferred from white seller to white buyer with few questions asked, either about the relevance of programming to the black community or about the possible availability of a black owner.

Perhaps inevitably, then, in searching the list of some 7,350 commercial stations in *Broadcasting Yearbook*, one is extremely hard-pressed to find black-owned or black-managed stations. The Nashville-based Race Relations Information Center, in Garnett's report "How Soulful Is 'Soul' Radio?" lists only nine black-owned stations:

—KPRS, Kansas City, Missouri, owned by Andrew Carter. Kansas City is 26 percent black; KPRS ranks fifth in general audience ratings.

—WCHB and WCHD-FM, Detroit, owned by the Bell Broadcasting Company; president, Dr. Haley Bell, a black dentist. His two sons-in-law, Dr. Wendell Cox and Dr. Robert Bass, also dentists, are co-owners. Detroit's population is about 45 percent black. WCHB is the first-ranked black outlet, and eighth-ranked generally.

—KWK, St. Louis. Bell Broadcasting Company and Vickway Broadcasting Company, also black-dominated, both claim control; the courts and the FCC will eventually rule.

—WEBB, Baltimore; WJBE, Knoxville, Tennessee; and WRDW, Augusta, Georgia, all owned by singer James Brown, thus making James Brown Broadcasting, Ltd., of New York, the country's only black-owned and -operated radio chain. WJBE, bankrupt when Brown took it over, now ranks fourth in Knoxville, whose population is about 21 percent black. WRDW is the top-rated black station in Augusta, which is about 50 percent black, and second-ranked generally. No ranking is available on WEBB. Baltimore is about 25 percent black.

— WHOV-FM, Hampton, Virginia, owned by the Hampton Institute Mass Media Arts Department.

— WSHA-FM, Raleigh, North Carolina, owned by the Shaw University School of Communications.

The Center report notes that Atlanta's WERD, which for many years was the nation's only black-owned station, was bought by a white group in 1968. It remains black-programmed in Atlanta, a city 38 percent black.

This roster of nine black-owned stations is augmented by seven others either entirely or partially black-owned, listed by *Advertising Age* last February 9. These are:

— WGPR, Detroit, whose chief owner is Dr. William V. Banks, a gynecologist. The outlet is ranked third in Detroit's black market and twelfth generally.

— WMPP, Chicago Heights, Illinois, owned by Charles J. Pinckard, a restaurant owner. It ranks fourth among Chicago's black-oriented stations.

— WEUP, Huntsville, Alabama, owned by Leroy Garrett. It is the only black station in a city which is 9 percent black.

— WTLC-FM, Indianapolis, Indiana, held since 1968 by Frank Lloyd. The station ranks first in the black market, third generally in a city which is 28 percent black.

— WORV, Hattiesburg, Mississippi, owned by Vernon Floyd, just began broadcasting last summer.

— WWWS-FM, Saginaw, Michigan, even newer than WORV, is owned by Earl Clark, an engineer.

— WVOE, Chadbourn, North Carolina, is owned by Ebony Enterprises, principal owner Ralph Vaught, Jr. Chadbourn's population is about 20 percent black.

The list is woefully meager. More distressing are the results of the Race Relations Information Center's survey of five white-owned-and-operated "soul" radio chains. The five are:

— ROLLINS, INC., BROADCASTING DIVISION, of Atlanta, which has four stations: WBEE, Chicago; WGEE, Indianapolis; WNJR, Newark; and WRAP, Norfolk, Virginia.

— ROUNSAVILLE RADIO STATIONS, Atlanta, with four stations: WCIN, Cincinnati; WLOU, Louisville, Kentucky; WVOL, Nashville; and WYLD, New Orleans.

— SONDERLING BROADCASTING CORPORATION, of New York City, which has four stations: KDIA, Oakland; WDIA, Memphis; WOL; Washington, D.C.; and WWRL, Woodside, New York.

— SPEIDEL BROADCASTERS, INC., Columbia, South Carolina, which has six stations: WHIH, Portsmouth, Virginia, WOIC, Columbia; WPAL, Charleston, South Carolina; WSOK, Savannah; WTMP, Tampa; and WYNN, Florence, South Carolina.

— UNITED BROADCASTING COMPANY of Washington, D.C., with four stations: WJMO, Cleveland; WFAN-TV, Washington; WOOK, Washington; and WSID, Baltimore. United began an all-black-programming TV experiment on WOOK-TV in Washington. The station, with youth dance parties, filmed gospel services, old movies, and talk shows, failed to attract viewers; its call letters then were changed to WFAN-TV, and the black-oriented programming was cut to about 60 percent.

The RRIC survey of these five combines turned up these facts: in the twenty-two stations which make up the chains, there are eighty-four executive positions in station management and twenty-two news positions. Of these, blacks hold thirty executive positions and fourteen news jobs. But, the survey reported, many of these "executive" positions exist in name only. For example, on Speidel's WSOK, Charles Anthony, who does a disc jockey show, is listed as program director, news director, and public affairs director. He told the surveyors, "I wish I had the money to go with all my titles and responsibilities." WSOK also, it appears, has a sense of humor: along with its tapes sponsored by the NAACP and the Southern Christian Leadership Conference, it lists as public affairs broadcasts for its black audience fifteen-minute talks by Governor Lester Maddox and Senator Herman Talmadge. At Speidel's WYNN, Jack Singleton is listed as program director and news director, and United's WJMO has John Slade listed as station manager and news director.

Two years ago there reportedly was only one black station manager in radio, and there were so few black executives that a *Newsweek* study was prompted to observe that "on many stations only the disc jockeys and janitors are black." Generally speaking the news staffs on these stations are inadequate. In most instances they consist of one man. Often news "staffs" are part-time employees; news directors are disc jockeys who read wire copy. Public service activities generally seem to be of the support-your-community-fund variety; much of the on-the-air public service comes in packages from civil rights organizations.

Much of the news on black-oriented stations comes from the Mutual Broadcasting System, the American Contemporary Network (a division of American Broadcasting Company), United Press International Audio, or Metromedia News. But shows are pretaped and certainly not geared to local interests. There are, however, two organizations in New York — American Black Communications, Inc., and the Black Audio Network — that provide news and black-oriented features.

Barrie Beere, who runs American Black Communications, says that he has gotten the greatest response from a *Focus on Black* series of tapes done by Jackie Robinson, Ruby Dee, Ossie Davis, James Earl Jones, and Brock Peters. He has even sold these syndications to other than black-appeal stations, but says "by and large it has been our experience that the stations do not buy our service unless they can find themselves a sponsor to carry it." Jay Levy's Black Audio Network twice daily sends from New York phone feeds of several items, each thirty to forty seconds long, designed to fit into standard news broadcast formats. The service, less than a year old, last fall absorbed the Soul News Network after its founder and sole operator, Chris Cutter, had been unable to obtain regular sponsors or long-term station contracts.

There have been several other attempts at black-oriented networking. In the early 1950s Leonard Evans, founder of the black-oriented supplement *Tuesday*, launched the National Negro Network and built its client list to fifty stations — all but two owned by whites. But NNN was discontinued when white station owners began demanding, in Evans's words, "an unreasonably large share" of profits. After the assassination of Martin Luther King, Jr., black disc jockey Rudy Runnels at WIGO, Atlanta, was so deluged with phone calls asking for spot "feeds" that he organized a temporary national pool of reporters, including staff members of rival WAOK, Atlanta. Known as the American Freedom Network, the service provided coverage for some two hundred stations. And two years ago, the American Broadcasting Company was known to have been contemplating an exclusive service for black-oriented stations, but it dropped the idea when, according to an ABC source, white-owned stations proved unwilling to yield profitable local commercial time for regular network feeds.

A few weeks ago in San Diego, Chuck Johnson, former general manager of XEGM, Tijuana, announced formation of a Black Video Syndication Network to service both radio and TV stations. TV programming is to include *Black '70* (pattern on NBC-TV's *Today*); a children's quiz program with ex-boxer Archie Moore as host; and several variety shows. At this writing radio network plans remain to be announced.

Efforts to create a news network for blacks are complicated by attitudes of many white owners of black stations. They claim that audiences want rhythm and blues and "soul," and all the rest is incidental. Alan Henry, vice-president for operations of the Sonderling chain, insists: "As broadcasters, we don't dictate taste; our listeners do. 'Soul' music is what our listeners have shown they prefer, by and large, to other types. The reformists can like what they want, but the listeners dictate the programming." But Dr. S. F. Mack, associate communications director of the United Church of Christ, thinks differently. "The stations have fostered an atmosphere in which only the 'soul' format is successful. Consequently, too many blacks have gotten used to it, the way dope addicts get used to drugs."

Other authorities agree. William Wright, director of Unity House in Washington, D.C., and a force behind the Black United Front which is challenging the license of WMAL-TV, asks: "Do we need twenty-four hours of James Brown?" He answers: "No, we don't. If we're going to talk about freedom and self-determination, we need to hear our black heroes performing in other art forms. We need to talk about drug addiction, about slum landlords, about jobs, about education. But the white man gives us twenty-four hours of 'soul' because it pads his already stuffed pockets and keeps black people ignorant."

Citizen action already has been organized against several black-oriented stations. A coalition of citizen groups, for example, has complained to the FCC that Speidel's WOIC filed inaccurate data in its 1969 license application. The complaint contends that blacks received titles without pay or commensurate duties (news director Parris Eley was alleged to be a disc jockey; program director Charles Derrick was said not to have the powers of that office). The station has denied the charges, and the FCC has scheduled a hearing. United's WOOK in Washington has been accused by a citizens' group of broadcasting religious programs that offered illegal lottery numbers in the guise of scriptural references; an FCC hearing is scheduled. Rounsaville's WVOL has had a labor dispute pending in the courts since 1968. And *Variety* reported early this year on a four-city advertising boycott of United Broadcasting's properties by the Southern Christian Leadership Conference, plus a petition to the FCC opposing renewal of WJMO in Cleveland. The SCLC claims that policymaking blacks are virtually nonexistent at the station.

The most dramatic result thus far has been in Atlanta. There twenty black organizations, led by the local NAACP, have formed a coalition which won major concessions from twenty-two of twenty-eight stations — both black-oriented and general audience. Included are agreements to hire and train more blacks, earmark executive positions for blacks, step up public service activities, and consult regularly on programming.

In the end, of course, the future of meaningful "soul" radio and of black-owned and -operated stations will be only as bright or as swift to come as the increases in the number of blacks who can buy and know how to run radio stations. A singular worry at the moment is the "Pastore Bill," S.2004, introduced by Senator John Pastore. This, if passed — and it has not only a good deal of congressional approval but also the hearty endorsement of the National Association of Broadcasters — would require the FCC to renew a currently held license without consideration of rival applications if the Commission found that the licensee had served and presumably would continue to serve the public interest. Rival applicants would be considered only if the FCC decided against renewal. The "Pastore Bill" was followed by an FCC ruling under which license challengers would not be heard if current licensees substantially met the public interest.

With some justification, William R. Hudgins, president of Harlem's Freedom National Bank (the country's largest black bank), and other "soul" radio reformers fear that the "Pastore Bill" and/or the FCC ruling in effect would grant licenses in perpetuity, shutting off challenges — particularly black challenges — and thus barring black ownership of stations. Others believe that pressure on broadcasters — soul and otherwise — nonetheless will continue to mount, forcing either improvements or license denials. Those in this camp regard strides made in the sixties as direct result of challenges, of monitoring, and of pressure.

One such believer is Del Shields, outspoken WLIB disc jockey in New York and the former executive director of the National Association of Television and Radio Announcers, whose members are primarily black disc jockeys. Says Shields: "No amount of legislation will make black people continue to accept the junk that's being offered them now. The Pastore Bill will be a severe cramp, but it will not be the end. As the pressure increases all over the country, white broadcasters either will have to improve their products, sell out to black interests, or be forced out."

FOUR

The Ordeal of Vietnam

VIETNAM REPORTING: Three Years of Crisis

Malcolm W. Browne

I remember once having seen a newspaper picture of an elephant being towed on water skis under the Brooklyn Bridge. As I recall it, an advertisement for toothpaste was painted on the side of the beast, and it clearly showed in the photograph. It struck me at the time that it is really fairly easy to manipulate even the best intentioned news media, provided you have enough imaginational and gall. After all, an elephant on water skis is news of a sort, advertisement or not, and most readers are amused looking at such a picture.

This kind of press manipulation is probably innocent enough in itself. Unfortunately for foreign correspondents, similar but infinitely more sinister manipulations are frequently directed at newsmen abroad.

On the whole, most of the correspondents I have met in various parts of the world are extremely suspicious professionals who are willingly taken in by such things only rarely.

But reporting in times of crisis can be a trying and sometimes hazardous business, particularly when elements in the story are actively hostile to the free press.

One of the major pitfalls any reporter faces is the possibility of becoming an element in one of his own stories — a cardinal breach of the rules of our game. Ideally, every reporter is a detached observer, setting down fact after fact with clear-sighted fairness to all.

A few newsmen allow themselves to become actively involved in

---

Fall, 1964. Malcolm W. Browne, as senior Associated Press correspondent in Saigon, shared the 1964 Pulitzer Prize for international reporting.

their stories from the very start. Last year in Jakarta, a foreign news organization hired an Indonesian photographer to get pictures of an Indonesian mob attacking the British Embassy. The cameraman went to the riot as directed, but after a few moments he was so caught up in the patriotic fervor of smashing things that he dropped his camera and picked up a brick. The news organization fired him, of course.

In other instances, newsmen can actually become *hors de combat* covering crises. Last year, a French news agency correspondent covering a racial incident in the American South was shot to death.

On July 7, 1963, I had been taking pictures at a Buddhist street demonstration in Saigon when a brick smashed across my chest and shattered the top of my camera. Looking around, I saw my AP friend and colleague, Peter Arnett, on the ground. Blood was coursing down his face, five plain-clothes police agents were kicking him and grinding his camera to fragments.

The police squad broke off its attack as suddenly as it had begun, dashing off into the crowd of spectators like thieves. Uniformed police broke up the remains of the demonstration rapidly, and Arnett and I dragged ourselves back to the office.

The incident itself was an ugly one, and had drawn us involuntarily into the story we were trying to cover as detached observers. But worse was to come. A few hours later, uniformed police came to our office with a summons. Charges were being prepared to the effect that Arnett and I had assaulted and injured several police agents.

Our subsequent interrogation lasted about eight hours, and we were permitted no transcript of the testimony. The Saigon prosecutor's office coldly informed the United States chargé d'affaires that eight depositions filed by newsmen who had seen the incident would not be accepted in evidence. All these depositions said, in effect, that neither Arnett nor I had lifted a finger against the plainclothesmen, whose attack appeared completely unwarranted.

At this stage, we ourselves had become a story. And it fell to Arnett and me to write our own story, including complete details of the police charges, even though we knew them to be nonsense.

Ultimately, President Kennedy intervened in our behalf and the

Vietnamese government charges were dropped, but the whole thing was touchy and unpleasant.

The point was that the Ngo Dinh Diem government considered foreign correspondents enemies. This situation is true in major parts of Southeast Asia. Indonesia's powerful foreign minister, Subandrio, has publicly declared the Western press an enemy to his nation; Cambodia's Prince Norodom Sihanouk has expelled all Western newsmen; Burma's Premier refuses to grant press visas.

To be defined as an enemy is to become involved, if only to the extent of struggling for survival.

The common attitude of most Southeast Asian leaders is that the press is an element of psychological warfare and must, therefore, be rigidly controlled. Adverse reporting about a regime tends to give aid and comfort to the enemy and must therefore be eliminated.

The enemy is broadly defined as anyone or anything that tends to weaken the power of the regime. It may be a dangerous military enemy like the Viet Cong in Vietnam, or it may be a single politician with only a handful of followers. Truly objective reporting and such official attitudes, I believe, are basically incompatible, and clashes are inevitable.

Even the reporter who has never taken sides in any of the local issues before is forced to side with himself in defense of his profession against official news repressions.

Inducements and threats both are used to move the newsman in such circumstances. A newly arrived correspondent in Vietnam used to find himself the guest at constant glittering dinner parties given by high state officials. Government guides were always at his service, and the red tape of existence was cut to the bare minimum.

Several months after I arrived here, the powerful and pepperytongued Madame Ngo Dinh Nhu sent me a warm letter of thanks for an article I had written. The article had been a question-and-answer piece, quoting her extensively verbatim.

But correspondents who suggested in their articles that the war against the Viet Cong was not going as well as described in official communiqués quickly felt the lash. At first we discovered that Vietnamese military sources who once had been highly cooperative now were under strict orders not to talk to us at all. In some cases, old news sources went on talking, and most of them were found out by the government. Many were relieved of commands or even jailed.

Normally, there was no official censorship, although copies of all dispatches in Vietnam are reproduced and circulated among top officials. The only legal communication with the outer world is through the government owned and operated tele-communications center. It was, therefore, an easy matter for communications officials merely to hold up dispatches they regarded as offensive for twenty-four hours or more. As the Diem regime encountered increasing difficulties, news dispatches from Saigon were subject to longer and longer delays.

Police methods became increasingly harsh. Correspondents were tailed constantly, and the telephones of all newsmen were monitored twenty-four hours a day. Sometimes callers received sinister threats from the government. Visitors to news offices frequently were picked up and spirited off by plainclothesmen a few yards from the doors.

Correspondents were regularly expelled from Vietnam, on the direct orders of Madame Nhu.

During the 1963 Buddhist crisis, Madame Nhu's younger brother, Tran Van Khiem, let it be known that a list of foreign correspondents slated for assassination had been prepared by the government. No attempts ever were made on any of us, and the presumption was that this rumor had been put forth to rattle us.

Unfortunately, many local American officials shared the Saigon government's view that all press reporting from this country should be positive. Frequently, sins of dishonesty by the Vietnamese were compounded by United States officials.

As a trivial case in point, the Viet Cong released two United States Army prisoners on May 1, 1962, after holding them in the jungle for several weeks. The idea that the Communists would voluntarily release prisoners ran counter to the Saigon propaganda line, and its information directors let it be known that a detachment of Vietnamese troops had overwhelmed a Viet Cong camp and liberated the Americans.

This statement, with details about the valor of the government unit's commander, was passed along to correspondents by the United States military information office. Some news stories spoke of the government troops "slashing their way into a Viet Cong camp," and made the whole thing sound like a cowboy movie, in which the good guys wipe out the bad guys.

A few of us smelled a rat. The Viet Cong had never before let themselves get surprised into a jam like that, and it seemed an odd coincidence that the Americans were freed on May 1 — a big Communist holiday.

It turned out later that the Viet Cong had not only released the two men, but had sent a squad of escorts with them to make sure they got into no further trouble on the way back to the nearest government guard post.

For a long time, United States information policy tried to avoid publishing American battle casualties. On one occasion, U.S. military authorities reported to newsmen that an army enlisted man had "slightly injured his arm" on "a training exercise with Vietnamese troops, when he accidentally tripped over a wire."

But about one week later I learned that the man involved was a sergeant friend of mine, and I looked him up at a hospital. It turned out that he'd been on patrol with Vietnamese troops, all right, and he had tripped over a wire. He had tripped because the wire was connected to an electrically detonated Viet Cong land mine, which had blown away half his elbow.

Time and again correspondents were told by American authorities that U.S. information channels were kept plugged to avoid diplomatic friction with the Vietnamese government.

"If they say one thing and we say another, where does that leave us?" a United States spokesman said. "We can't offend our allies."

These official attitudes and the evidence of our own senses led to a high degree of skepticism in the foreign press corps about all official statements.

But difficult as conditions were, they were destined to become much worse. On May 8, 1963, a crisis erupted — the Buddhist upheaval. It is quite possible that the Ngo Dinh Diem regime would have survived a lot longer than it did against the Buddhist insurrection but for the role of the foreign press. Involuntarily, foreign correspondents became potent political tools — a role the dictates of our profession strictly proscribe.

Some of the key leaders of the Buddhist revolt were educated in Japan or in the West (for example, the Venerable Thich Quang Lien, a thirty-seven-year-old monk with a degree from Yale) and had a keen insight into American public opinion.

They were aware that one of Diem's major strengths was his ability to control the press strictly, keeping the less attractive aspects of his regime out of print. They also knew of the prevailing official American view, which tacitly approved of Diem's system of press control. Key Americans felt, with considerable justification, that a well-publicized Buddhist crisis could only divert energy from winning the war against the Viet Cong.

But the Buddhists were determined to override Diem's press blackout — a blackout that had permitted him to crush nearly every anti-Communist political opposition group in the country without any particular press attention. Obviously, it was a time when only the most drastic measures could have any effect against a regime flanked with tanks, a modern army, and a huge secret police apparatus. The Buddhists desperately needed the eyes of the world in support of their cause, and sought an appropriate eye-catcher.

The eye-catcher turned out to be an affable, seventy-three-year-old monk named the Venerable Thich Quang Duc, a Buddhist schoolteacher. On June 11, 1963, Quang Duc burned himself to death in the middle of a busy Saigon intersection, surrounded by 350 chanting, wailing, banner-waving monks and nuns. The police were too stunned to do much about it.

The Buddist leaders were aware that a ghastly human sacrifice like Quang Duc's would be pointless unless the Western press — the only free press in the country — carried the word to the outside world.

Chief monks had told all correspondents in Saigon several weeks earlier that two monks had volunteered for death if Buddhist demand were not met. One monk was to burn himself, and the other was to disembowel himself.

The days dragged on, and there were many street demonstrations in which nothing significant happened. Press interest lagged.

It happened that I was the only Western newsman present during the street procession in which Quang Duc died.

I have been asked why I didn't try to do something to stop that suicide once I realized what was happening. Actually, I probably could have done nothing in any case, since the monks and nuns had clearly rehearsed their roles for the ceremony many times, and had prepared methods for blocking interference. Police fire trucks were halted by monks who threw themselves under the wheels.

But frankly it never occurred to me to interfere. I have always felt that a newsman's duty is to observe and report the news, not try to change it. This attitude may be subject to criticism, but that is how I reacted on July 11, and how I would react again.

As a matter of duty, I photographed the whole horrible sequence of Quang Duc's suicide, and relayed the pictures and story as fast as possible into the Associated Press network. It is difficult to conceive of any newsman acting otherwise.

But reaction came swiftly as, I am sure, the Buddhists had anticipated. At a single blow, they had won their battle to focus world attention on their campaign. It is significant within the scope of this article that had a Western newsman with a camera not been present at Quang Duc's suicide, history might have taken a different turn.

Millions of words had been written about the Buddhist crisis, but the pictures carried an incomparable impact. I have been told that when Henry Cabot Lodge was called in to see President Kennedy about taking over the ambassadorship to Vietnam, the President had on his desk a copy of my photograph of Quang Duc.

Buddhist leaders made huge enlargements of the photograph, most of them colored in by artists, which they carried at the heads of processions. Men and women, tears streaming from their eyes, bowed in reverent prayer before the photograph. Letters reached me that back-alley vendors of "feelthy pictures" in towns as distant as Lisbon and Dar-es-Salaam were hawking copies of the photograph.

Communist China printed up huge volumes of the photograph for distribution throughout Southeast Asia. Captions described the suicide as the work of "the United States imperialist aggressors and their Diemist lackeys." A wave of suicides in Quang Duc style was reported from Burma, Ceylon, India, France, Japan, Korea, and elsewhere.

In the United States, a group of prominent clergymen used the photograph in full-page advertisements in the New York *Times* and the Washington *Post,* over the caption WE, TOO, PROTEST.

In short, that picture meant many things to many people, but none of those things did the Diem regime much good.

Diem and his family felt strongly about the matter. Madame Ngo Dinh Nhu, his sister-in-law, again denounced the Western press, and government rumors began to spread about the credibility of foreign correspondents. Diem himself asked former United States Ambassador Frederick E. Nolting, Jr., if it were true that I had bribed the Buddhist monks to murder one of their number by fire for the purpose of getting a good picture.

Heavy-handed though Diem often had been with foreign newsmen, I was stunned by this particular tactic. The president was surely well informed about all my activities, since his men had kept me under the strictest surveillance for many weeks past, and, in any case, I had never attempted to hide anything.

At any rate, strictures on the Western press grew increasingly severe. Getting any news or photographs out of Vietnam became a major smuggling operation. On one occasion, I found myself completely without resources and appealed to an American ambassador (to another country) who happened to be passing through Saigon to carry out some film and copy for me. He willingly agreed, having seen what these items were.

I will not mention his name, but if he should happen to read this, once again, I thank him with all my heart. There were all too few people willing to help newsmen in those days.

These are some of the pitfalls of reporting in crisis — physical censorship at the source, or of actual news output, harassment by authorities, and the dangers of involvement in stories, even when such involvement is wholly involuntary.

In large measure, I am convinced they can be overcome by attention to detail, hard work, and most of all, fairness at all cost. On the whole, I believe the reporting from South Vietnam was essentially fair and complete during 1963.

But there are other difficulties besides those described above.

The flow of news from the event to the reader, listener, or

viewer is essentially a two-way street. It depends not only on the news itself but on the demands of the news consumer.

The news consumer in America is a busy man or woman. He or she is leading a life of his or her own, in which news may be consumed as entertainment, as information, or a combination of the two. There is little time for detailed study of issues and complicated situations like those that pertained, for example, in South Vietnam in 1963.

Readers and editors therefore demand their news in the simplest capsules available, sometimes limiting their consumption to mere headlines.

Having once been a newspaper deskman, I have a keen appreciation for the exacting and difficult work of the headline writer. He must pack as much information as possible into a very small space. Numbers are ideally suited to headline writing.

The number of home runs, the number of weekend traffic fatalities, and the number of delegates pledged to a given political candidate all are apt subjects for headlines. So are battle casualties in Vietnam, or the number of Buddhists, or the number of square miles controlled by the Communists.

But, unfortunately, Vietnam does not lend itself well to numerical reporting, or even to the kind of simple, narrative statement required of the average newspaper lead. There are too many uncertainties, too many shades of gray, too many dangers of applying English-language clichés to a situation that cannot be described by clichés.

Obviously, there are human elements in Vietnam that can be described adequately in simple terms, because they are universal. But there are other things so alien to American social patterns and thinking that they cannot be reported simply.

War reporting in itself, for example, is technically fairly simple. Reporting a single clash with X number of casualties is not unlike reporting a sports event. By an adroit use of verbs, the writer can create an impact that comes close to reproducing reality.

But in Vietnam, the actual clashes are probably less important than the subtle thinking of people and the social upheaval of the nation. These are difficult to capture in words, and for a reader to digest.

There is nothing very dramatic, for instance, about a water

shortage and the red tape in which a well-drilling project was bogged down. Yet this situation probably has a more far-reaching effect on both the military and political status of the area than all the battles fought there to date.

This kind of thing is called "feature material," or "the news behind the news," generally published deep inside newspapers, if at all. This is reasonable, since editors know their readers are much less concerned with water shortages than with more spectacular developments.

In short, I believe one of the deficiencies of reporting is in the news consumer himself. He gets exactly as much substantial information as he asks for — neither more, nor less.

Still, the main responsibility for news falls on the correspondent, and part of that responsibility is in keeping his readers interested enough to read on.

Foreign correspondents must work harder than other kinds of newsmen, because they have so much more to cover. Even with the largest staff of assistants of any news organization in Vietnam, I still have found a seven-day-a-week schedule necessary. This is a country where communications are primitive, and in which different conditions apply in every one of the forty-three provinces.

Many newsmen here have no assistance at all, even though South Vietnam has dominated headline play for years. Most correspondents wish all news organizations would expand their foreign staffs. But for practical, financial reasons, this usually is impossible. Correspondents are expensive.

Another problem is that newsmen sometimes lack the necessary background in covering foreign assignments, particularly when the newsmen are only given a few days or weeks in a particular country. Resident correspondents have the advantage of on-the-job training and eventually became qualified to do the basic investigation and research themselves. Visitors must rely on translators, official spokesmen, and dozens of other secondhand sources who may or may not be trying to sell them a bill of goods.

I think it is significant that the late President Diem, who so deeply disliked and distrusted the Western press, frequently received visiting newsmen and women, but never granted interviews to resident correspondents. He knew that they knew too much.

The problems that have beset correspondents reporting the crises of Vietnam are not new, and they will continue in various forms here and throughout the world. Reporting will, at times, be inaccurate, deficient, or misleading. But despite his or her shortcomings, the foreign correspondent, in my mind, is one of the most fundamentally honest and dedicated human beings in the world. He loves the challenge of a really tough story more than any other opportunity, and has given up a lot of comforts to grasp this challenge.

As long as there are men and women who fit this pattern, reporting from abroad will always drag the basic truth from the snares of crisis.

TONKIN: WHAT SHOULD HAVE BEEN ASKED

Don Stillman

On the stormy night of August 4, 1964, the United States Navy destroyers *Maddox* and *C. Turner Joy* were cruising the Gulf of Tonkin off North Vietnam when the *C. Turner Joy* reported radar detection of ships closing in fast for a possible attack. Sonarmen reported tracking torpedoes from the ships. Seaman Patrick Park, the main gun director of the *Maddox*, scanned his sensitive radar for signs of the enemy. But as the destroyers maneuvered wildly for three hours in heavy swells he detected nothing. Then suddenly he reported picking up a "damned big" target, and was ordered to fire. Park recalled later:

Just before I pushed the trigger, I suddenly realized: that's the *Turner Joy*. This came right with the order to fire. I shouted back, "Where's the *Turner Joy?*" There was a lot of yelling "Goddamn" back and forth, with the bridge telling me to "fire before we lost contact. . . ." I finally told them, "I'm not opening fire until I know where the *Turner Joy* is." The bridge got on the phone and said, "Turn on your lights, *Turner Joy*." Sure enough, there she was, right in the crosshairs. I had six five-inch guns right at the *Turner Joy*, 1,500 yards away. If I had fired, it would have blown it clean out of the water. In fact, I could have been shot for not squeezing the trigger. . . . People started asking, "What are we shooting at? What is going on?" We all began calming down. The whole thing seemed to end then.

Winter, 1970–71. Don Stillman is an assistant professor at the West Virginia University School of Journalism and editor of the Appalachian monthly *The Miner's Voice*.

But it didn't end there for Park, whose statements were reported by Joseph Goulden in his excellent book *Truth Is the First Casualty*, or for the rest of the world. Hours later, President Johnson ordered the first United States bombing raids against North Vietnam. Within the week, he had demanded and received a congressional resolution that authorized him to "take all necessary steps" to "prevent further aggression" in Vietnam.

The massive American buildup in Vietnam dates from that crucial week in the Gulf of Tonkin, and in retrospect the events there proved to be a turning point in the war. At the time of the incidents, only 163 Americans had died in action in Vietnam, and the sixteen thousand American troops there ostensibly were serving as "advisers" rather than full combat soldiers. But within a year President Johnson began to use a congressionally approved "Tonkin resolution" as a functional equivalent of a declaration of war in an escalation that ultimately brought more than half a million United States troops to Vietnam. More than forty thousand were killed.

What really happened that dark night is unclear, but persistent digging by Senator J. W. Fulbright and his Foreign Relations Committee staff, by then-Senator Wayne Morse, and by a handful of persistent reporters like Joseph Goulden has given us a view of at least part of the iceberg of deception that remained hidden for years.

Reporting of the first attack on the *Maddox* on August 2 and the second alleged attack on both the *Maddox* and the *Turner Joy* on August 4 was extremely difficult because the only real sources of information were Pentagon and Navy officials and the President himself. Slowly and painfully over four years, as the private doubts of senators and reporters became public, the American people learned that in fact the *Maddox* was not on a "routine patrol in international waters," but was on an electronic espionage mission to gather intelligence information on North Vietnamese radar frequencies. As part of that mission, the *Maddox* would repeatedly simulate attacks by moving toward the shores of North Vietnam with its gun-control radar mechanisms turned on to stimulate enemy radar activity. In addition, years after the incidents stories revealed that the territorial waters recognized by North Vietnam (twelve miles) were repeatedly violated by the *Maddox*.

Two days before the first attack on the *Maddox*, the South Vietnamese for the first time conducted naval shelling of North Vietnam. Using United States "swift" boats, they attacked the islands of Hon Me and Hon Ngu. The night following the raids, the *Maddox*, approaching from the same direction as the South Vietnamese, came within four nautical miles of Hon Me. The captain of the *Maddox* intercepted North Vietnamese messages reporting the possibility of "hostile action" because the enemy believed the *Maddox* to be connected with the South Vietnamese shelling of the islands. The *Maddox* cabled: CONTINUANCE OF PATROL PRESENTS AN UNACCEPTABLE RISK. That day it was attacked.

The *Maddox* was joined by the *Turner Joy* and, after again requesting termination of the mission because of the likelihood of attack, it reported two days later that the two ships had been ambushed by North Vietnamese PT boats. The black clouds and electrical storms during that night prevented any visual sightings of hostile craft, and contradictory sightings on radar and sonar added to the confusion. The commander in charge cabled: ENTIRE ACTION LEAVES MANY DOUBTS EXCEPT FOR APPARENT ATTEMPTED AMBUSH. SUGGEST THOROUGH RECONNAISSANCE IN DAYLIGHT BY AIRCRAFT.

After lengthy questioning of crew members on both ships, the doubts grew larger. The commander cabled: REVIEW OF ACTION MAKES MANY REPORTED CONTACTS AND TORPEDOES FIRED APPEAR DOUBTFUL. . . . FREAK WEATHER EFFECTS AND OVEREAGER SONARMEN MAY HAVE ACCOUNTED FOR MANY REPORTS. NO ACTUAL VISUAL SIGHTINGS BY *Maddox*. SUGGEST COMPLETE EVALUATION BEFORE ANY FURTHER ACTION.

That evaluation did not occur, and hours later American bombers took off for North Vietnam.

Thus the espionage mission of the *Maddox*, its violation of territorial waters, its proximity and relationship to South Vietnamese shelling, and major questions about whether the second attack occurred all combined to give a much different picture of the incidents than the Administration fed the country through the news media. How well did the media handle reporting and interpretation of the Tonkin incidents?

Perhaps the worst excesses in reporting were committed by *Time* and *Life*. Both viewed the event as if the *Maine* itself had been sunk. The week after the encounter, *Life* carried an article headlined FROM THE FILES OF NAVY INTELLIGENCE that it said was "pieced together by *Life* correspondent Bill Wise with the help of U.S. Navy Intelligence and the Department of Defense." Wise was clearly fed only a small smattering of cables that contained none of the doubts about the second attack. He stated (August 14, 1964): "Despite their losses, the [North Vietnamese] PTs continued to harass the two destroyers. A few of them amazed those aboard the *Maddox* by brazenly using searchlights to light up the destroyers — thus making ideal targets of themselves. They also peppered the ships with more 37 mm fire, keeping heads on U.S. craft low but causing no real damage."

Senator Wayne Morse, in a speech on the floor of the Senate February 28, 1968, denounced the Pentagon's "selective leaking of confidential information" and *Life*'s gullibility in accepting it. "I don't know who leaked, but I can guess why," he said. "The 'why' is that someone in the Pentagon decided that the American people should see some of the messages confirming that an unprovoked attack had occurred on innocent American vessels. . . . The *Life* magazine reporter was taken in. He was 'used.' The press should be warned."

The next issue of *Life* went even further in embellishing events. It carried a picture spread headlined HEROES OF THE GULF OF TONKIN that praised the pilots who had bombed North Vietnam. "Most of the young Navy pilots had never seen combat before, but they performed like veterans," *Life* said. The planes, with two exceptions, "got back safely and their pilots, the nation's newest battle veterans, would be remembered as the heroes of Tonkin Gulf."

This kind of irresponsible puffery was evident in *Time*, too. Despite thorough and restrained files from its Washington bureau, *Time* (August 14, 1964) constructed its typical dramatic scenario of events which, though lively, was grossly inaccurate:

> The night glowed eerily with the nightmarish glare of air-dropped flares and boats' searchlights. For three and a half hours the small boats attacked in pass after pass. Ten enemy torpedoes sizzled through the water. Each time the skippers, tracking the fish by radar, maneuvered to evade them. Gunfire and gun smells and shouts stung the air.

Two of the enemy boats went down. Then, at 1:30 A.M., the remaining PTs ended the fight, roared off through the black night to the north.

Joseph Goulden, one of the few writers to interview crew members, reports that when the *Maddox* and *Turner Joy* arrived at Subic Bay several weeks after the incidents, one crew member had occasion to read both the *Life* and *Time* accounts. He quotes the seaman as stating: "I couldn't believe it, the way they blew that story out of proportion. It was like something out of *Male* magazine, the way they described that battle. All we needed were naked women running up and down the deck. We were disgusted, because it just wasn't true. It didn't happen that way. . . ."

Newsweek, which generally waved the flag far less than *Time* in its coverage of the Vietnam War, was just as overzealous in its dramatization of the second Tonkin incident (August 17, 1964): "The U.S. ships blazed out salvo after salvo of shells. Torpedoes whipped by, some only 100 feet from the destroyers' beams. A PT boat burst into flames and sank. More U.S. jets swooped in. . . . Another PT boat exploded and sank, and then the others scurried off into the darkness nursing their wounds. The battle was won. Now it was time for American might to strike back."

Even the usually staid New York *Times* Magazine was caught up in the adventure of the moment. Its August 16 picture spread on the Seventh Fleet, which had launched the planes that bombed the North, had the look of a war comic book. Headlined POLICEMEN OF THE PACIFIC, it showed planes streaking through the sky, missiles being fired, and Marines landing on beaches. It carried captions such as, "A component of the Marines is always on sea duty, ready when the call comes."

The New York *Times* news sections handled the story with restraint and, after the August 2 attack, even mentioned claims that United States destroyers like the *Maddox* "have sometimes collaborated with South Vietnamese hit-and-run raids on North Vietnamese cities." The Washington *Post*, like the *Times*, was thorough and incisive in its reporting. Murrey Marder's superb accounts even mentioned the South Vietnamese shelling on Hon Me and Hon Ngu as a possible cause for the then seemingly irrational attack on the *Maddox*.

Because transcripts of TV news shows from this period are not available, it is difficult to evaluate broadcast media performance. But the accounts of TV coverage printed in government bulletins and elsewhere indicate that some perceptive reporting did occur. NBC carried an interview with Dean Rusk August 5 in which Rusk was pressed on the question of whether the United States ships might have been operating in support of the South Vietnamese shelling units. But for the most part the broadcast media, while perhaps more responsible than some print outlets, fed viewers the same deceptive Administration leaks.

Editorial comment almost universally supported the President's response. The New York *Daily News* speculated that "it may be our heaven-sent good fortune to liquidate not only Ho Chi Minh but Mao Tse-tung's Red Mob at Peking as well, presumably with an important assist from Generalissimo Chiang Kai-shek and his Nationalist Chinese forces on Taiwan."

The Los Angeles *Times* praised United States actions as "fitting in selectivity, proper in application, and — given the clear, long-standing statement of United States intentions — inevitable in delivery." William Randolph Hearst, Jr., praised the bombing as a "fitting reply to one of the more outrageous — and implausible — aggressions committed by communism in many years." He went on to suggest that rather than limit the bombing it might be better to continue until the North Vietnamese surrendered.

The New York *Times* said: "The attack on one of our warships that at first seemed, and was hoped to be, an isolated incident is now seen in ominous perspective to have been the beginning of a mad adventure by the North Vietnamese Communists." But the *Times* did warn that "the sword, once drawn in anger, will tend to be unsheathed more easily in the future." When the Tonkin resolution went before Congress, the *Times* perceptively cautioned that "it is virtually a blank check."

The Washington *Post*'s editorial page saw the Tonkin resolution much differently. Earlier editorials mentioned "the atmosphere of ambiguity" that surrounded the first attack on the *Maddox*, but when the resolution was considered the *Post* said: "That unity [against Communist aggression] has been demonstrated despite the reckless and querulous dissent of Senator Morse. There is no substance in Senator Morse's charge that the resolution amounts to a 'predated declaration of war.' . . . This means of reasserting the national will, far short of a declaration of war, follows sound precedent. . . ."

One of the few newspapers to attack the President's account was the Charleston, West Virginia, *Gazette*, which stated that the Tonkin attacks were probably caused by the South Vietnamese naval strikes and complained of the "air of unreality" about the incidents. But the overall failure of the press to raise questions about the incidents in the editorial columns, although in keeping with the mood of the country at the time, was part of the general breakdown of the media's responsibility to act as a check on the actions of the government.

Foreign coverage of the incidents raised some of the significant points being ignored in this country. *Demokreten*, of Denmark, stated: "To create a pretext for an attack on Poland, Hitler ordered the Germans to put on Polish uniforms and attack a German guard. What the Americans did in North Vietnam was not the same. But the story sounds doubtful. . . . Why was the vessel off North Vietnamese coasts? In any case its presence there could indeed be interpreted as provocative."

New Statesman of Britain also raised doubts: "There is so little trust in official [U.S.] accounts about Vietnam that suspicion is surely understandable. . . . Is it not possible that the destroyers could not be distinguished from South Vietnamese craft that were engaged in another raiding mission?"

One American journalist who raised continuing doubts about the veracity of the Administration's accounts was I. F. Stone. In his small, outspoken sheet, Stone reported the South Vietnamese attacks on Hon Me and Hon Ngu. He was the only one to cover in detail the charges raised by Senator Morse about the incidents and the Tonkin resolution, and he even raised questions about whether the second attack even occurred. While *Time* and *Life* were adding readable embellishments to the nineteenth-century theme of "they've sunk one of our gunboats," I. F. Stone was asking the crucial questions.

One of the major shortcomings of columnists and opinion writers was their failure to ask the broad question: does the punishment fit the crime? The total damage in both attacks was one bullet hole in the *Maddox*. No United States ships were sunk, no American boys were killed or even wounded. In turn, we not only claimed to have sunk four North Vietnamese vessels but went on to the bombing of the North, sinking the major part of the North Vietnamese navy, and wiping out more than 10 percent of its oil storage tanks.

The overwhelming response of the editorialists was that President Johnson should be commended for his restraint in limiting the bombing. Among Washington journalists only Stone opined that indeed the American response was "hardly punishment to fit the crime." His small-circulation sheet received little attention.

The record of the media improved measurably as public doubts about the Tonkin incidents began to grow. Senator Fulbright, who managed the Tonkin resolution through Congress for President Johnson, began to question the facts and, in May, 1966, wrote in *Look* that he had serious doubts about the Administration's account. But the media didn't follow this up very extensively. Despite the importance of the Tonkin incidents, they were content to pass over opportunities to interview crew members of the two ships — the only firsthand witnesses — some of whom had left the service or were otherwise accessible for interviews. The first real breakthrough came in July, 1967, when Associated Press sent a special assignment team headed by Harry Rosenthal and Tom Stewart to interview some three dozen crew members. Their superb five-thousand-word account was the first real enterprise reporting on the Tonkin affair.

AP revealed for the first time that the *Maddox* was carrying intelligence equipment, and also cited for the first time that the *Maddox* had not fired any warning shots, as claimed by Secretary McNamara, but had shot to kill instead. The crew interviews indicated that there was a great confusion on board the two ships during the incident. At this point, however, there was little client interest in the story. Urban riots broke out the day it was to run. As a result, the AP report was not used by major metropolitan newspapers such as the Washington *Post*, Washington *Star*, New York *Times*, or others which might have given it the exposure it deserved. The story did appear in the Arkansas *Gazette*, however, where it was read by Fulbright, who by this time was devoting much of his attention to uncovering the true story of Tonkin.

The AP account was followed in April, 1968, by an article in *Esquire* by David Wise, who also interviewed the crews and cast further doubt on the Administration's account. These two reports and another AP account by Donald May were the only real enterprise stories that turned up new information. But John Finney, the able New York *Times* reporter, raised further questions in *New Republic* early in 1968, as did John Galloway in *Commonweal.* (Galloway has just done a splendid source book, *The Gulf of Tonkin Resolution.*)

By this time Fulbright and Morse were generating much breaking news as they prepared for the Foreign Relations Committee hearings held in February, 1968. But even during those hearings the press failed to distinguish itself. When Morse, through the *Congressional Record,* released important segments of a top-secret study done by the Foreign Relations staff, based on cable traffic and new data from the Defense Department, it took the Washington *Post* two days to recognize the significance of his statements.

The final credit for tying together the whole thread of deception surrounding the incidents must go to Joseph Goulden, whose book appeared in early fall of 1969. While covering the 1968 Tonkin hearings for the Philadelphia *Inquirer,* Goulden had filed a story on the controversial testimony of Secretary McNamara, who appeared to contradict some aspects of his 1964 testimony. The *Inquirer* rewrote the lead to make it read: "The United States did not provoke the 1964 Gulf of Tonkin incident, previously secret naval communications indicated Saturday."

Goulden left the *Inquirer,* sought out crewmen and others involved in the incident, and wrote his detailed and insightful account.

This, then, is the record on the Tonkin affair. Given its lessons, one may hope that the media will not fail so grandly if similar incidents occur. The reporting on the *Pueblo* and the *Liberty* give reason for hope. But the Fourth Estate must establish a far more independent and critical stance on government actions if hope is to become reality.

THE STORY EVERYONE IGNORED

Seymour M. Hersh

I was asked to write this article — to tell editors how they missed one of the biggest stories of the year — by an associate editor of one of the biggest newspapers in America, one of the newspapers that was very slow to fully realize the significance of the alleged massacre at Songmy. That irony, in itself, is important to me — for it convinces me that editorship, like democracy, is not dead . . . yet.

The fact that some thirty newspapers in this country, Canada, and abroad did publish my first and subsequent Dispatch News Service stories on Songmy is further proof that the nation's press is not as gutless as all that. I honestly believe that a major problem in newspapers today is not censorship on the part of editors and publishers, but something more odious: self-censorship by the reporters.

There is no doubt that many reporters had heard of the Pinkville incident (at least many have told me so). In talking to some Pentagon officials before I wrote my first story (they talked then), I was told by one general officer, "Pinkville had been a word among GIs for a year. I'll never cease to be amazed that it hasn't been written about before." Another general officer who was attached to headquarters in Saigon in 1968 said he had first heard talk of Pinkville soon after it happened. Of course, an outsider can also be amazed that generals would hear of such incidents and not demand an investigation, but the notion that *those* men thought that the press had somehow fallen on the job is, well, significant.

Winter, 1969–70. Seymour M. Hersh, a Washington newsman, won a Pulitzer Prize for his stories on Songmy. This article was adapted from a report in the *Bulletin* of the American Society of Newspaper Editors.

As everyone knows, the first mention of the incident was provided by the public information officer at Fort Benning, Georgia, who released a brief item September 6 announcing that Lieutenant William L. Calley, Jr., had been charged with murder in the deaths "of an unspecified number of civilians in Vietnam."

The AP man in the area promptly put in a query; when the Pentagon did not gush forth with all of the details, that was that. No other questions were officially asked of the Pentagon about the Calley story until I offered some carefully hedged queries around October 23. The Washington *Post* queried the Pentagon about Calley on November 6; by that time I had arranged a number of interviews — with Calley, among others — and was well on the way. The New York *Times* also began asking some questions shortly before the first story broke early November 12 for the next morning's papers.

The initial Pentagon dispatch was put on the wire by the AP and appeared Saturday morning in many major newspapers in the country, including the Washington *Post*, the New York *Times*, and Los Angeles *Times*. It would be wonderful to say I noticed it immediately, saw its significance, and dashed out with pencil and pad in hand. Of course not. I was tipped around October 20 by a source with Pentagon connections. My source simply told me that the military was planning to court-martial an officer at Fort Benning, Georgia, for the murder of about seventy-five Vietnamese civilians.

What made me drop everything (I was then finishing *The Ultimate Corporation*, a book on the Pentagon for Random House) and begin pursuing the story? For one thing, my source was good — but certainly no better than others who must have told newsmen about the incident in the twenty months since it took place. Another, more important reason, I think, was my experiences with chemical and biological warfare (CBW). I had written a book on CBW (*Chemical and Biological Warfare: America's Hidden Arsenal*, Bobbs-Merrill) that was published in mid-1968 but somehow failed to make much of a mark at first. The public and the press seemingly did not want to believe that the United States was stockpiling nerve gas at army commands overseas, nor did they want to believe that American military men would be capable of shipping trainloads of nerve gas through the American countryside without telling anyone. My book prompted very little investigative reporting.

So, I believed the story about Pinkville. And I also knew — or thought I knew — that newspapers would probably be the last to believe it. Thus I began my searches with an eye on *Look* and *Life* magazines. I won't tell who gave me leads, but suffice to say that I managed to find out who Calley was, and where his lawyer was located. I decided that the telephone was a bad interviewing instrument on the Pinkville story, and therefore interviewed every important witness or near-witness in person. I applied for and received a limited travel grant (about two thousand dollars in toto) from the Philip Stern Fund for Investigative Journalism in Washington, and began flying around to locate witnesses. (In all, I traveled more than thirty thousand miles via air.)

By early November I had a pretty good picture of what had happened, at least solid enough so I could write. I knew Calley had been charged with 109 deaths and I had the precise wording from the charge sheets. I contacted *Life;* they said they weren't interested (little did I know that they had turned down Ronald Ridenhour, the twenty-three-year-old California college student whose letters first prompted the army to study the incident). Then I went to *Look.* A senior editor there was very interested; I wrote a sketchy, but explosive, memo on what I had. They, too, decided to pass — I think, charitably, because of their four- to six-week lead time.

I really didn't know where to turn, so I simply kept doing research. David Obst, general manager of Dispatch and a Washington neighbor and fellow touch football player, had learned from me about Pinkville and was insistent on handling it. I had written a few Sunday pieces for his news service and been moderately successful; as many as six or eight responsible newspapers (including the Baltimore *Sun*) had published one or more of my earlier works. So in the end, I turned to Dispatch and committed myself to its syndication.

Why? I was convinced that if I walked into a major newspaper and laid out my story, the editors, to verify my information, would have to repeat the painstaking interview-and-more-interview process I had gone through, and then write their own story. I could respect this, but I simply wanted my story for myself. And I wanted it to be credible, which ruled out smaller magazines. This wasn't an article for a journal of opinion, like the *New Republic*, or *National Review*, for that matter — it was hard news that should be written as such.

That left Obst and Dispatch. Amazingly, as is well known, it worked. Of about fifty newspapers contacted, thirty-two or so eventually ran my first story citing the charges against Calley. This was not done on a whim; the papers carefully checked me and as many of the facts as possible. That was to the newspaper world's credit.

What happened after the first story is not. Only the New York *Times*, which had its own story, chose to follow up independently on the story, by sending Henry Kamm from its Saigon bureau to the Pinkville area to interview survivors (ABC-TV and *Newsweek* also went along). The *Times* decided to treat Pinkville as a major story and do its own reporting from the outset. Other papers avoided any hint of investigatory research and it was left to me to seek out Ridenhour (who, after my first story, had told newspapers about his role) and to interview him in California. Although he had first revealed his part in the story Friday, November 14, and I did not see him until the following Monday afternoon, amazingly I was the first reporter to personally interview him. The New York *Times* and AP had talked briefly to him by telephone, but the Los Angeles *Times* — barely thirty miles away in downtown Los Angeles — did not send a reporter. And none of the papers realized how important Ridenhour was — he had a list of eyewitnesses, many of whom were out of the service and willing to talk.

Ridenhour gave me the names and addresses of some of the eyewitnesses he had spoken to about Pinkville (he did not actually participate in the incident), and off I went. After personal interviews in Utah, Washington, and New Jersey — conducted within twenty-four hours — my subsequent story, for newspapers of November 20, was well received by the nation's press. After that second story, newspapers generally were still reluctant to comment editorially on Pinkville (with the New York *Times* and Chicago

Sun-Times being notable exceptions), although they were playing the story big. It all had suddenly become much more credible when the army announced in late November that Calley had indeed been charged with the murder of 109 Vietnamese civilians.

The last newspapers' vestiges of resistance disappeared when Paul Meadlo of Terre Haute, Indiana, submitted to a Dispatch interview and told how he had calmly executed, under orders, dozens of Vietnamese civilians. Dispatch provided information on Meadlo to CBS-TV, which ran a long interview on the Walter Cronkite show. It was a cash deal for Dispatch, with Meadlo, who had been fully informed of the possible dangers to him and his rights in the matter, not being paid one cent; but even more important was the fact that television was needed — that somehow just relying on newspapers to sear the conscience of America hadn't been working, or had been working too slowly. It took three newspaper stories and one television interview to make Pinkville a national issue; it shouldn't have.

After Meadlo came a flurry of newspaper stories quoting former members of Calley's platoon and his company. The newspaper industry, in one of those collective changes of mind that can only be found in the business, decided each man's testimony was important enough to play all over the front pages. The indiscriminate use of eyewitness statements was amazing to me; I had carefully attempted to get some kind of "feel" from each of my interviewees before quoting them. GIs are notorious liars (that point is based on a personal recollection), particularly when talking about their combat days. I think some of those who came forward did not tell all the truth.

This, of course, leads right into the issue of pretrial publicity; a major dilemma facing newspapers today. I was impressed by how important this issue was for some newspapers when they were deciding whether or not to run my first few Dispatch stories; and then surprised at how quickly the same newspapers forgot about such rights and began splashing stories across their newspaper once Pinkville became a big issue. Dispatch handled the pretrial publicity question by retaining a prominent Washington law firm and relying on it for advice. The advice generally was that the public's right to know far outweighed any disadvantages to some involved individuals. Even if a court-martial became an impossibility and some men had to be turned free, this seemed preferable to not having as full and as responsible a debate as possible — and "responsible" to me simply meant when I quoted a source I firmly believed him to be telling the truth; it was not always a question of just quoting someone accurately.

What made some responsible and careful newspapers publish my stories and others, equally as responsible and careful, not publish them? I think part of the answer is instinct, the instinct many reporters and editors feel for a story or a source. There are many blind sources one can trust, even over a telephone, while others need careful checking.

One newspaper with which I became involved was the Washington *Post*. I met with top editors of the paper early on the morning of November 12, when Dispatch broke the story. The meeting was chaired by Ben Bradlee, the *Post*'s executive editor. My story was passed around, read by all, and I answered some direct questions on the legal aspects of the charges against Calley. No one asked what seemed to me to be the obvious question: "Is this true?" After I left, I learned later, Bradlee handled that aspect by telling his staff, "This smells right." His instinct was working, at least that morning.

Nevertheless, I knew things had changed for most of the nation's press after the Meadlo interview; at least six friends in the Washington newspaper corps called me at home over the next few evenings seeking tips on where to go next or leads on involved GIs or officers who might be living in their local areas.

When the nation's newspapers begin wanting their hometown mass murderer, things are well in hand.

THE CHALLENGE AHEAD

Robert Shaplen

The longer one stays in Vietnam and the more one travels around the country, from the northernmost provinces below the demilitarized zone to the southernmost parts of the Delta, the more apparent it becomes that the war's overall effects on the Vietnamese have been cataclysmically destructive, not only in physical terms but psychologically and socially. Yet, as in all wars, the pattern is uneven. Poverty-ridden urban slums and rural wastelands are in predominant contrast to spots of "new wealth" for a minority and of considerable prosperity for a good many middle-class entrepreneurs, contractors, restaurateurs, newspaper publishers, dance hall operators, and so on, as well as for what might be called "proletarian profiteers" of the American invasion — cyclo and taxi drivers, prostitutes, and vendors of black market goods stolen from American post exchanges.

What the long-term socioeconomic results of the war have been and will be are as important as the politico-military consequences, yet they have scarcely been written about. Confining the discussion to South Vietnam, let us consider the impact of the war to date in human and social terms. The single biggest effect of the long and tragic conflict has been the urbanization of the 17 million people in the South. Some 60 percent of the people now live and work, or are unemployed and steal or beg, in and around towns and cities. Before the war, only 20 percent were urban dwellers. While scores of thousands of city-bound refugees, driven from the countryside by bombing, are gradually returning to their old rural homes or have been resettled in new areas, it seems likely that the urban and suburban population will not go below a 40 percent

---

Winter 1970–71. Robert Shaplen, who reports from Asia for the *New Yorker*, is author of *The Road from War* and other books.

level, particularly as the slow postwar process of industrialization begins.

The principal impact of urbanization has been the destruction of family life, of the close-knit family and interfamily relationships that have marked Vietnamese life — and Asian life in general — for centuries. Even in the countryside, where the fragmentation of family life has perhaps been less drastic, the war has caused the breakdown of family life as it used to exist. The families of regular army soldiers (ARVN) accompany their men from place to place but mostly live in hovels that pass for "temporary camps," and they are separated much of the time anyway. Even in the case of the Regional and Popular Force elements that stick closer to their homes, the old peaceful village and hamlet existence has been destroyed, at least for the war's duration. Politically, there has been some effort to restore local autonomy through recent staggered hamlet and village elections. This has somewhat ameliorated the social dislocation, but the effects so far are more artificial than real, and it will be some time before reunited families can live and work together again under common roofs and in common fields.

There are relatively few areas of populated Vietnam that have not felt the brunt of the war. One of them, in the Delta, is An Giang, a wealthy province dominated by the Hoa Hao sect, which has established its own accommodation with the Viet Cong. Here peasants till their land unmolested, prosperity reigns, and one could hardly tell that a war has been taking place. But almost everywhere else, in varying degree, there is ample proof that in the American effort to "save" a nation we have done much to destroy it. From the highlands to the lowlands, whole hamlets and villages (a village in Vietnam generally consists of from four to six hamlets) have been wiped out. Not long ago I flew in a helicopter over what used to be the village of Ap Bac, in the Delta near Saigon. Years ago at the beginning of the "big war" it was totally destroyed in a major battle the Communists claimed as a great victory because it proved their ability to defeat a helicopter-borne government force. Like many other such places, it has never been rebuilt. In fact, if my friend John Paul Vann, who is in charge of the combined American–South Vietnamese pacification program in the Delta, hadn't pointed out the site of Ap Bac I wouldn't have recognized it, for it was nothing but burned-out brown fields spotted with bomb craters. Even the rubble was gone.

What happened to the people of the hundreds of Ap Bacs throughout the country? The answer is, who knows? Certainly scores of thousands of ordinary civilians — no one really knows how many — were killed, and countless other thousands were permanently maimed. Many thousands more became refugees in nearby cities, including Saigon, while others have resettled in far-flung villages, probably working as tenants or more likely as sharecroppers, or living with relatives. The sons of the surviving families are in different communities either serving with the Viet Cong, or with the ARVN or the Territorial Forces, which are what the Regional and Popular Forces together are now called.

Vietnam has indeed become a nation of migrants, but the tragedy of the Ap Bacs is not universal. I have visited many other villages in the Delta that have been reestablished and repopulated with a mixture of former inhabitants and new citizens. New hamlets and villages have been created all over the country, mostly along or close to roads and highways that are protected by South Vietnamese troops, including local People's Self-Defense Forces. But these new places usually lack the natural symmetry and charm of their now-devastated tree-fringed predecessors, and many of them look like shantytowns.

The most ubiquitous sign of "restoration" in Vietnam is the gleaming tin roof. All along the Street Without Joy, the northern strip of rich coastal farmland in Quang Tri province, one can see hamlet after hamlet where shattered mud-brick homes have been rebuilt and topped with tin roofing supplied by the Americans. Flying at sunset over the once-beautiful city of Hue, one is almost blinded by the reflection bouncing off these bright new roofs. Though it will never again be as beautiful as it was, Hue, which was largely destroyed during the 1968 Tet offensive, has made an astonishing recovery. Though at least five thousand people were killed in the city — some say many more — it is prospering again, the markets are booming, and in the surrounding rural hamlets the rice harvests are once more rich and new crops of vegetables are being grown.

One of the most common results of the war has been "depeasantrification" due to widespread American bombing and defoliation. All along the roads of the country one sees small crude shacks with wooden slabs announcing GI WASH CLOTHES or COKE, BEER, SOFT DRINK or WE FIX TYRE. These places are operated for the most part by dispossessed farmers. Only as the level of the fighting has decreased — as it has done markedly in the last year, although it may pick up again — have peasants again begun to till the land; and one now begins to see many small Japanese-mechanized plows run by one man, alongside the traditional ones hauled by water buffaloes. However, Vietnam, a prewar exporter of rice, will still have to import this staple commodity indefinitely. And though the use of miracle rice seeds from the Philippines is starting to increase the yields, it will be years before the effects of the newly introduced land reform, distributing land to the tiller, will be felt. In the meantime tremendous shifts in the peasant population are continuing. Given the movement of peasants back to their old villages or to new ones, and some continued movement into towns and cities, one can only say the population as a whole is in a state of flux that is likely to continue for several years more.

What is thus evolving is a new kind of mixed urban-rural society, though I think the basic trend remains urban. Saigon-Cholon (Cholon is the Chinese section), a city of 400,000 before the war, has now swelled to 2 million, and it is not apt to diminish in size or numbers. The great majority live in slums or in areas that are so overcrowded that they are pseudoslums, where small wooden-frame or corrugated tin houses are tightly packed together in narrow lanes like so many sardine cans. One of the most familiar sights in downtown Saigon today is that of small girls, aged nine or ten, wandering around begging with their infant sisters or brothers strapped to their backs. Their mothers and fathers, if both are still alive, are working, by day and by night; the father perhaps as a cyclo driver, and the mother as a bar-girl, where she makes herself available to American soldiers, black or white, if they occasionally wander in — no guarantee against VD. The chances are that the members of such families see each other no more than four or five hours a week. Saigon, too, like the rest of Vietnam, is full of widows and vagrants.

Nobody really knows how many orphans there are in Vietnam. Recently I rode back from Paris to Vietnam with a young Belgian nurse who runs a small orphanage in Gia Dinh, the province alongside Saigon. She told me that her home regularly has about twenty-five orphans offered for adoption, and that half are Vietnamese and the other half the products of GI fathers and Vietnamese girls. It is no easy process to adopt an orphan — the paperwork alone takes about a year — so it is safe to assume that the permanent orphan population will also run into scores or hundreds of thousands.

This is only one tragic side of the war in Vietnam. What may prove equally tragic, though in a different way, is the social dislocation that will result when the Americans finally leave and the American-privileged Vietnamese are dispersed. These include not only the 400,000 or 500,000 men and women who have worked directly for the Americans but also the million or more who are their wives and sons and daughters, and perhaps their sisters, brothers, uncles, aunts, and cousins — for the circle of Vietnamese dependents is wide. Already there have been serious strikes caused by workers who have rebelled against having to go back to work at Vietnamese wages in Saigon's inflated economy, wages that are four or five times lower than what the Americans paid. The inevitable result, aside from more labor troubles, will be an acerbation of what has already occurred — an increase in the rate of crime, delinquency, and hooliganism, with all the attendant abuses of drug addiction and other forms of vice. A familiar sight along Tu Do, the main thoroughfare in Saigon, is the empty bars where the bar-girls who used to drink "Saigon tea" — high-priced colored water — with prowling American soldiers now sit by themselves, hour after hour, waiting for the stray customer and not even talking to each other; just staring emptily. The same is true in the resort cities of Vung Tau and Nhatrang, on the coast, and in other cities.

The political effects of social upheaval and dislocation are even more difficult to analyze and predict. In 1966, when the so-called Student and Buddhist Struggle Movement was destroyed in Da Nang and Hue by the government of Prime Minister Nguyen Cao Ky, with the approval and logistical support of the Americans, the Buddhists dropped out of sight as a political force. Many were jailed, some were killed, others just went underground, while still others became traditional Vietnamese *attentistes* — the French-inherited term for "waiting to see what happens." During the September, 1970, election for the Senate, the Buddhists reemerged politically, stopped their boycott of elections, and captured ten of the sixty seats in the Senate (only thirty seats were at stake this off-year election). The student movement is also active again, and while the Communist minority is responsible for most of the demonstrations and makes the most noise, the majority of student leaders and members of the important student groups are non-Communist but pro-peace. Along with the veterans — both the disabled and healthy ones — the students are likely to become more important politically in the period of readjustment that lies ahead. It may even turn out that the growing movement for peace, mostly urban-expressed, may become and remain strong enough to avert the new civil war that so many fear will follow this one.

In the countryside as well as in the cities, millions of people who are not demonstrating are simply "waiting" — waiting for the Americans to leave so they can determine who will be stronger, the government or the Communists, and therefore with whom they should make their accommodation. The easy accommodators may yet outnumber the more ardent nationalists in the South, and the ultimate outcome of such a development would undoubtedly be its domination by the North, which is partly what Hanoi means when it speaks of "protracted warfare" and of being "patient." If there is a cease-fire as a result of negotiations, and a real political contest begins, Hanoi and the Provisional Revolutionary Government it controls will quickly concentrate on the accommodators, including most importantly the fragmented religious elements in the South. The process of influencing them may take several years, if there is no new war, but the hardheaded and dedicated men of the North will meanwhile find time to rebuild their own shattered nation.

There has been much speculation and considerable writing about terrorism and the possibility of bloodbaths once this war is over. I have read countless documents in which the Communists constantly speak of eliminating "tyrants" and even list, by individual names in specific villages, the people they want to kill — mostly government cadres, teachers, and anyone who has worked for or cooperated with the Americans. On the basis of the number of assassinations and kidnappings still taking place, let alone the proven history of repression and killing that occurred in North Vietnam in 1945–1947 and again during the abortive land reform experiments in the mid-fifties, there is reason enough to believe that the Communists mean what they say. I have had long talks with ex-Viet Minh friends of mine who have outlined whole scenarios of what they think will happen "when the Communists come," of their plans to use village and town hooligans to turn people against each other, and of other terrorist tactics that have been applied before. There is no reason to believe that terror will not beget terror and that a repressive government on the Saigon side would be any less recriminatory or would eschew violence. Both sides at the Paris peace talks, in their endless propaganda, have spoken of "guarantees" against terrorism and reprisals, and if there is any attempt at a rational peace settlement an effort will undoubtedly have to be made under some sort of international supervision at least to limit the degree of such violence. The interregnum between peace and a potential Third Indochina War, however long the interval lasts — perhaps a year or two — will be crucial, and the most crucial period of all will be the first six months.

Economic dislocation and poverty also enter the equation. Although steps have recently been taken to raise the level of wages of civil servants and soldiers, the mounting inflation in the South, particularly in Saigon and other cities (the peasants in the Delta are relatively better off), threatens to burst the seams of the urban economy. At the same time the possibilities of military rebellion are not to be discounted. So long as men in the army, from the rank of private up to captain especially, but in the higher ranks as well, are not paid enough to sustain themselves and their families, the threat of armed rebellion will remain. (A hard-working whore or cyclo driver can make two or three times more a month than a general or a cabinet minister, though of course they don't have the same opportunities to make as much through corruption.) The possibilities of civil strife within a civil war are thus not to be discounted. Right now, unless the United States is willing to give Vietnam another $200 million to $300 million on top of the more than $100 *billion* the war has already cost us, the danger of economic collapse and fresh internal violence are serious. Should such outbreaks in the government's own ranks take place, the obvious beneficiaries would be the Communists.

"Vietnamization" in this sense has an inbuilt fallacy. The Vietnamese can scarcely finance the maintenance of delicate helicopters and modern jet fighter-bombers in the manner in which *we* are accustomed, let alone support an army of a million in a nation of 17 million. In fact, three-fourths of the Vietnamese national budget of some 230 billion piasters currently is devoted to military expenditures, under already inflated conditions. The social implications herein, too, are thus dire to contemplate. Grandiose postwar plans have been drawn up by combined American and Vietnamese experts — the chief American architect of the official seven-hundred-page plan has been David Lilienthal, former chairman of the Tennessee Valley Authority — but, in the opinion of most Vietnamese economists I have talked to, these long-term planners have had their heads in the clouds. Far better are some much more modest contingency plans, being worked out privately by small groups of Vietnamese in Saigon and in Paris, for postwar recovery based on agricultural improvements and then on light-industry development on a year-by-year basis.

The dichotomy of prosperity and poverty that has already afflicted the wealthy nations, notably the United States, is already evident in wartime Vietnam, too, and one shudders to think what we have wrought in this regard. In the shabby shantytown communities of Saigon and other cities, and parts of the Delta, too, one can see thousands of television aerials poking up into the sky — they are by no means restricted to fancy new modern structures being built by the get-rich-quick war profiteers and corrupt bureaucrats. The bug of the affluent society has already bitten the Vietnamese in many other ways as well, even amid the breakdown of classes and the destitution of the war. There is a generic term for it all — "the Honda society" — and it dates back several years to the policy instituted by the Americans to soak up piasters by creating a consumer climate. There is nothing wrong in every Vietnamese having a Honda (except for the increase in pollution this causes), but as one Vietnamese economist and sometime cabinet member I have known for many years says, "You shoved all these expensive things we didn't need down our throats in order to keep your kind of war going, and then, overnight, you order us into austerity and tell us to tighten our belts while we go on fighting a war we can't possibly pay for with our resources." It is no idle prediction to state that, short of the United States's continuing to give the Vietnamese $2 billion worth of economic assistance a year for at least five years after the war ends (which seems hardly likely, given the current mood of Congress), the country may simply blow up or fall apart economically, with obviously more disastrous political and social consequences.

These and other factors have contributed to the growing anti-Americanism in Vietnam. We are not, as the Communists repeatedly accuse us, "neocolonialists" in that we are not out to "conquer" or occupy Vietnam; but what we have done, unwittingly, is to create an ambience of colonialism, in social and economic ways, and the ultimate effects are not that different from what the French did before us. Perhaps they are worse in some ways, because so much more waste has been involved. In this sense the dislocation we have caused in the South, let alone the destruction by bombing and artillery, may prove to be as disastrous as the damage caused by bombing in North Vietnam.

What do the Vietnamese think of it all, and of us? They are divided and bewildered. One reads the daily translations of the Vietnamese newspapers, and talks to friends who are reporters and editors, to authors and writers of cynical songs, and the feeling one comes away with is not that they are bitter or unforgiving but that they have begun to wonder whether it was all worth the price after all. It is not that they feel they were not worth saving, or even that they did not need and welcome outside help, but that they now realize, belatedly, they could and should primarily have done more to save themselves, from Communism or anarchy, and that what we did was simply shove them over a different kind of precipice. One constantly asks oneself the question of whether a totally controlled society such as that in North Vietnam is not bound to win, one way or another, over a *partially* controlled one, such as has existed in South Vietnam since 1945.

There has been considerable difference of opinion, both in Vietnam and in the United States, about how the foreign press — especially the American correspondents — have covered the war. I think our coverage, generally, has been fairly good, though spotty. At the same time, however, far too little has been written, in any kind of depth, about either the politics or the social and economic aspects of the long conflict — and this has been made more difficult by the fact that the longer the war has lasted, the less willing the Vietnamese themselves have been to talk to any Americans, officials as well as reporters. Among other things, the Vietnamese have become mighty tired of the constantly changing American faces — the average tour of duty for a correspondent has roughly been similar to the eighteen months for an embassy official, though there have been some notable exceptions.

I have always been astonished at the lack of interest in the politics of the war shown by most American reporters. This may be due, in part, to the fact that a great many of them have been young men in their twenties who were gung-ho and eager to get out where the action was. Action stories, and action shots, were "what the American public wanted," and I do think that much of the revulsion of the war back home was caused by the overemphasis placed by television on battle coverage. It became virtually impossible, again with some rare exceptions, for a TV man to persuade his home office that there were other aspects of the war and of Vietnamese life worth shooting in film. I remember one producer, Al Wasserman of NBC, who spent two arduous months preparing an hour-long show about the politics of Vietnam at the time of the 1967 elections. He spoke to dozens of politicians and other people, both in Saigon and in the provinces, and the show was scheduled to be telecast in New York at six o'clock in the evening of what was election day in Vietnam. At the last moment this time was preempted by a golf match, and the excellent job Wasserman did was viewed by a small audience late that night.

There have been a few other good hour-long "specials" done by the networks, notably CBS's *The Mind of the Vietcong,* and for the past three years National Educational Television has conducted panel shows — discussions among correspondents — that have been informative and lively. In my opinion, most of the

Face the Nation and *Meet the Press* interview shows that have dealt with Vietnam — and there have been many — have been cut and dried and fairly stilted, with little information coming out of them, though there have been exceptions. Some of the best TV work has been done by foreigners, notably by independent French and German producers.

Comparable to the TV specials have been the occasional "blockbusters" — stories of three or four columns — usually written by departing Saigon correspondents of major newspapers or the wire services. Among the best of these that I recall were the summaries and opinions of R. W. Apple, Jr., Peter Grose, and Gene Roberts of the New York *Times,* and Robert Kaiser of the Washington *Post.* Invariably, by the time a correspondent left Vietnam, he had become pessimistic, so most of these blockbusters have tended to be gloomy, with considerable justification. During their periods of assignment, the majority of correspondents have tended to be so busy competing for daily stories, or covering routine ones, that they seldom had time to sit back and do some quiet reflection. The result has shown in the generally gray copy that often appeared on page 1 — how many men lost in how many battles, and who did what to whom.

There have been some notable exceptions to this kind of reporting. Two outstanding daily men were Ward Just of the Washington *Post* and William Tuohy of the Los Angeles *Times,* while Peter Arnett of Associated Press stood out among the wire service men. All three constantly worked hard to present a proper mixture of reporting and interpretation, and they did better than most in mixing military and political news. Perhaps because they wrote less often, some of the correspondents from other countries often did a more reflective and interpretive job. This has particularly been true of Mark Frankland of the *Observer* of London and Jean-Claude Pomonti of *Le Monde.* On the other hand, Robert Keatley and Peter Kann, both of the *Wall Street Journal,* have done similar fine work, and some excellent feature writing has been done by Bernard Weinraub and Gloria Emerson, both of the New York *Times.* Strangely enough, it has been only fairly recently that some of the most subtle and poignant reporting of this sort has begun to appear on a more regular basis. It has been as if, belatedly, we have realized what we have done not only *in* but *to* Vietnam and have looked in the mirror at our own faces as well as at those of the Vietnamese.

I sincerely doubt that either the Vietnamese or the Americans will recover from the trauma of this long and misfought, misconstrued, and often misreported or unreported war — at least not for several generations. In having sought to distinguish between involvement and intervention, I continue to feel that, originally, we made a valid commitment politically in Southeast Asia and, specifically, in Vietnam. We should not, however, have overcommitted ourselves militarily once it became clear that our efforts to initiate reforms, as far back as the period after the Second World War when the French were still in control, were getting nowhere.

But as the years have passed what has dismayed me most, beyond the damage we have wrought, is that not only have we inhibited or even helped lose a revolution that might have been won — that is, a true nationalist revolution as against a Communist one — but that we have done and suffered more than that: we have confounded and divided ourselves, and we have done the same to the Vietnamese, perhaps more seriously because more permanently. To make it worse, we are now flagellating and *mea-culping* ourselves without really attempting to discover what actually happened, why and how things went so wrong. It may be too soon for that, but given all our other national and international problems, and our short memories, I fear that when we do find time — *if* we do — to think back to Vietnam, it may be too late to learn.

PASSING COMMENT

Behind the Lines

A few journalists and news organizations reacted surprisingly to Harrison Salisbury's venture into North Vietnam. The presence of the New York *Times* correspondent in Hanoi seemed to be greeted with relative calm by the public and by most departments of government (the Pentagon being a notable exception). A pack of journalists led the shouting and finger pointing.

The most hopeful explanation of that response is to ascribe it to distaste for Salisbury's reporting or to competitiveness. The least palatable is that journalists were conceding (as they have done in past wars) that journalism stops at the front lines and the official handout takes over.

Granted, reporting from the capital of a country under attack by the United States is likely to be hard to take. Americans scarcely like to be told by American reporters that their bombs, like other bombs, kill people and destroy things. Possibly it is a mark of a public's maturity if it can absorb such facts without condemning the reporter. It is disquieting to find a few journalists who do not themselves show this maturity.

By all means, the members of Harrison Salisbury's profession should criticize, dissect, deplore (or even praise) his stories. But they should hesitate before condemning his right to report from Hanoi. They do the public and themselves no good when they suggest that journalism turn aside when asked to view sights that may disturb the official version of war.

Winter, 1966–67.

PASSING COMMENT

What's That?

Averell Harriman has unwillingly offered a demonstration that the mass media remain deaf to what they do not expect to hear. Thrice he revealed that the halt in the bombing in North Vietnam in October, 1968, had been followed by a withdrawal of Vietnamese forces — but that American forces had maintained pressure on the battlefield. Harriman first mentioned the circumstances over CBS on May 14, 1969, in an interview following President Nixon's address on Vietnam. His interviewer swept the matter aside and pressed for comment on the Nixon address. Next Harriman covered the matter again at a speech to a dinner of the American Jewish Committee on May 15. The media — and particularly the New York *Times*, which had the prime local obligation — failed to pick up the cue. Finally, on May 25, Harriman's revelations appeared far down in an interview story in the *Times*. On May 26, Harriman was quoted in the *Times* as saying, "I've always found you have to tell things twenty times before they sink into the public mind."

Summer, 1969.

FIVE

The Politics of Transition

MUST THE MEDIA BE "USED"?

James McCartney

Not long ago columnist and associate editor Tom Wicker of the New York *Times* mused at a casual lunch that he believed the Washington press corps had flopped miserably in reporting the Vietnam war. "Our failure on Vietnam is an indictment of the entire press corps," he said. "It was our greatest failure." In his opinion, Lyndon Johnson might not have been able to escalate the Vietnam conflict into a full-scale war had the press more skillfully dramatized the Administration's misrepresentations and the shortcomings of what Wicker calls its "Munich psychology"; a Tet offensive then would not have been necessary to show the public that Mr. Johnson's version of what was happening in Vietnam was false.

"I am convinced that we did our historic job in reporting it all accurately," said Wicker, who was *Times* Washington bureau chief during the period of the escalation. "We knew what the government was up to. I suppose I was one of the few people in Washington who could get the President of the United States on the phone if I had to, to check an important point. But that wasn't enough. I'm not sure in looking back now that sometimes we didn't do more harm than good by just telling it as the Administration said it was."

In retrospect, examples of Pentagon misrepresentation now seem almost inconceivable. Take Defense Secretary Robert McNamara's misrepresentations on the troop buildup. On October 14, 1966, McNamara returned from his eighth "fact-finding" mission to South Vietnam and declared, "I see no reason to expect any significant increase in the level or tempo of operations in South

---

Winter, 1969–70. James McCartney is a national correspondent for the Knight Newspapers, based in Washington.

Vietnam, nor do I see any reason to believe that deployments of U.S. forces to that country will change significantly in the future." The number of United States troops at that time was 331,000. In the months to come the troop level steadily rose at a rate of more than ten thousand a month — a massive effort. By the following April — six months after McNamara's flat statement — more than 100,000 new troops had been sent to Vietnam. McNamara's remarks were made just three weeks before the 1966 congressional elections.

The *Times* and other papers, in the traditional manner of the press, reported the statements and the figures. They held a mirror up to Lyndon Johnson's declarations and sought to report accurately all that was said. What more could one ask of the press? Wicker, among others, today asks more. It could be that the families of more than forty thousand Americans killed in Vietnam would ask more, too. For it is apparent that the press was often used by the Johnson Administration to merchandise its Vietnam policies — policies a majority of the public now believe were a mistake.

The surface story of other aspects of Mr. Johnson's salesmanship is now well known: the highly publicized "peace offensives" while more and more troops were plunged into the war, right up to his last day in the White House; the troops that would be starting home by Christmas; the light at the end of the tunnel; the innumerable "turning points" that never came. This process went on from 1965, when the President began to escalate the war, until 1968 — when Senator Eugene McCarthy and the reality of the Tet offensive provided catalysts to begin to stop it. It took almost three years for public opinion to form and to make itself felt.

The Vietnam war is only Exhibit A, the classic, still underresearched case of the using of the press by a powerful government in the 1960s. But it illustrates what the United States Government — or any other determined and talented body of men — can do with modern media if they put their minds to it and employ proven techniques.

The press is often used. The federal government is so accustomed to using it for its own ends that Presidents become annoyed and irritable when they find, to their surprise, that on some occasions they cannot do so. This is the context in which Vice-President Spiro Agnew's remarks about the news media belong. Agnew was frustrated and angry because some analysts and commentators criticized President Nixon's November 3 speech on Vietnam. Agnew had nothing to say about the fact that day after day, week in and week out, most White House ploys designed to build a favorable image of the President and his administration, are dumped undigested on a public which often does not have sufficient time or information to evaluate them on its own.

The immense prestige of the United States Presidency today leads the media to make a giant of any man who holds the job, regardless of his personal limitations. The most innocuous statement from President Nixon is often treated as though it were a pronouncement of intrinsic worth from on high.

Nixon announces a campaign against crime in the District of Columbia. It draws huge headlines, but is not implemented. In the press, Nixon is a battler against crime. Nixon tells a meeting of governors that drug addiction is a "national problem" requiring a nationwide campaign of education. His program has no teeth and represents little change. In the press, Nixon is a battler against the evils of dope. Nixon tells a White House conference that hunger must end. He has no new program, and resists efforts of conference moderates to obtain a declaration of a national hunger emergency. Says the Washington *Star,* in an eight-column streamer: NIXON PRESSES DRIVE ON HUNGER. Nixon states in his campaign for the presidency that "the war in Vietnam must end." As it turns out, his program for Vietnam is not to end the war at all, but rather to turn it over to South Vietnam so that it can continue, perhaps indefinitely. This is explained many months later by Defense Department witnesses before a congressional committee. The distinction is essentially lost in the press.

Nixon, in a nationally televised speech on Vietnam in May, claims to have taken "new" initiatives to try to break open the Paris peace talks with an eight-point proposal. White House National Security Adviser Henry Kissinger describes the proposal as "new" and "important." Five of the eight points had been proposed, in essentially the same form, by the Johnson Administration as early as 1966. The other three were repetitions of positions stated by Peace Negotiator Henry Cabot Lodge four months earlier. But the press blithely conveys the deception.

No one knows this game better than Richard Nixon, whose talents for using the press, if he could be graded, would range somewhere between B-plus and A-minus. But he still must rank behind former President John F. Kennedy, who perfected some of the techniques Mr. Nixon is using today. Kennedy created a sense of movement and excitement in Washington that persists in the Kennedy legend — and defies all logic when judged by legislation actually passed or changes actually achieved.

But it is not just the President who uses the press. So does anyone else who has a cause to plead and has the talent and imagination to calculate how it can be done. A nation can be escalated into war, but so also can an administration be toppled. The antiwar demonstrators have learned their lessons. Their use of the press at the 1968 Democratic National Convention in Chicago belongs in an anthology of masterworks.

The role of TV in this drama has often been discussed. Hubert H. Humphrey is a convert to the theory that his campaign was mortally damaged on the nation's picture tubes by a cruel juxtaposing of violence in Chicago streets with convention hall proceedings. The net impression, he has said, was that Humphrey was the candidate of violence; he never lived it down. This bit of artful staging was intentional enough on the part of the leaders of the demonstrations, although they could hardly have predicted the active cooperation of the Chicago police department, whose members responded to the plot as though they had been rehearsed.

An equally impressive feat of stage-managing, however, was performed for the written press in the weeks and months before the convention. The objective of at least some of the demonstration leaders was to create a confrontation with police. This would dramatize the establishment's "support" of the Vietnam war. If troops could be enticed to the scene, the convention could provide televised evidence of a militaristic society. But to create this confrontation, it would be necessary to have police in large numbers and, if possible, troops. Somehow city officials would have to be convinced that terror was in the wind. They would also have to be convinced that massive numbers of demonstrators would be descending — so massive as to be unmanageable by normal forces.

The campaign began across the country early in June. Predictions, freely given, were that as many as half a million demonstrators would be moving on Chicago. Some of the most effective ploys were products of the Yippies — the Youth International party. They dreamed up bizarre plots: LSD would be put in Chicago's drinking water; carpet tacks would be scattered at major interchanges of the expressway system; power stations would be threatened; the city would be brought to its knees.

Chicago's *American*, owned by the *Tribune*, proved particularly susceptible to outrageous predictions. The more egregious they became, the more seriously the *American* took them in its news columns. For months before the convention, it reported that hundreds of thousands of "revolutionaries" were coming to Chicago. Thus a tiny minority of virtually unknown, youthful revolutionaries used the press to spark the idea that the *entire* group of demonstrators would be bent on tearing the city down. A few agitators who understood the predispositions of the press toward oversimplification and sensational predictions made a major contribution to an atmosphere of fear and tension. In particular, the demonstrators understood the passion of TV for action shots. On the eve of the convention one group obligingly staged rehearsals — for the cameras — showing how they would break police lines. No statement or prediction seemed too eccentric to get TV attention.

All of this had its effect on Mayor Richard J. Daley. The mayor panicked. The degree to which he was baited is perhaps best illustrated by his decision to reject a request from antiwar demonstrators for a permit to use Soldier Field, a lakefront amphitheater that seats 100,000. Had the mayor granted that permit he would have called the bluff of the demonstrators; the crowd they eventually assembled in Chicago numbered fewer than fifteen thousand. It would have been lost in Soldier Field.

In the city's official televised report on convention-week rioting, "daily press reports" were cited as major elements in justifying security measures. Counting police, national guardsmen, and regular army troops, Daley assembled a security force of more than twenty-five thousand men. They outnumbered the demonstrators almost two to one. Just as some of the demonstrators during convention week baited the police into violence with obscene language, or by throwing human feces, some of their leaders baited Mayor Daley before the convention through the press.

As Max Ways has written in *Fortune*, "the demonstration has become the dominant form of social action" in modern American society "rather than the petition, the political debate, or the lawsuit." A demonstration provides movement and action for the cameras that no petition can. The demonstrators showed in Chicago that they can be just as adept at using the media as can the White House.

Moreover, just as a case can be made that the media were used by Lyndon Johnson in the buildup and perpetuation of the war, and by demonstrators to play a major role in driving Johnson's party from power, still another case can be made that Richard Nixon used the press more cleverly than any presidential candidate before him to find his way to the White House. This is perhaps the third side of the triangle.

Here we have the phenomenon of a presidential candidate who, early in the 1968 political year, came to a deliberate and calculated decision to bypass the writing press and carry his cause directly to the public via the imagery of TV. Like no presidential candidate before him, he was packaged as though he were a bar of soap. The quiet genius behind all this was Harry Treleaven, onetime creative director of the J. Walter Thompson Agency, with generous help from Frank Shakespeare, onetime vice-president of the Columbia Broadcasting System. The two decided on the image they wanted as early as the New Hampshire primary in February: they wanted a friendly, homey Richard Nixon, personable, experienced, well informed. Their vehicle was the TV tube, operating from a completely controlled studio situation. They would present their candidate, live and in color, being questioned by "average Americans" — handpicked by the GOP.

This was the Studio Campaign, directed to the nation's living rooms and conducted right up to election day. Only rarely was the candidate exposed to questioning from the working press that made up most of his campaign entourage. Reporters were treated to a repetition of the same, basic campaign speech in various parts of the country. The major sop thrown to them was a few extra, contrived paragraphs, to be inserted into the basic speech — a "release" for A.M.'s on a typical day, and another few paragraphs for P.M.'s. The press, as though following Wendell Willkie on a 1940 campaign train, faithfully tried night after night to make stories out of the same, repeated basic speech. And the real campaign went on over their heads, on the packaged, electronic airwaves.

Thus the candidate's major pronouncement on the crucial issue of the election — the Vietnam war — was made in a prepared statement at the Republican Convention in July in Miami. "We must end the war in Vietnam," he said. But he never was required to explain even broadly how he would do it, and throughout the campaign he was allowed to escape questioning on the subject by any sophisticated, informed panel. Indeed, the Nixon image-makers would not even let the writing reporters sit in the studios where the packaged TV programs were made. "Press Rooms" were set up in the TV studios so that reporters could have the privilege of seeing exactly what any TV set owner could see on his set at home.

The Nixon campaign for the presidency was another classic case of using the press. He used it by ignoring it, bypassing it. He used it on his own terms, and, of course, he used it effectively, from his point of view. He raised the technique of not answering legitimate questions to an art form.

These illustrations, of course, are only a sampling. J. Edgar Hoover has been spreading his personal philosophy of life and crime through release of FBI uniform crime reports for years. The fine print candidly acknowledges that uniform crime statistics are, in fact, impossible because reporting techniques and customs vary from city to city. Still, Hoover issues press releases splashed liberally with quotations from J. Edgar Hoover, representing a view of the causes of crime straight out of the nineteenth century — and the statistics are faithfully reported month after month in the nation's finest papers. An official-looking press release from the FBI is all the platform required.

Across the ideological fence, meanwhile, black militants have found an infallible formula to gain attention: the stronger the criticism of society, the harsher the judgment, the bigger the threat, the more likely it is to be on the tube. Or in the papers. Stokely Carmichael and Rap Brown became masters of the technique. By using the media carefully to build national images and reputations, they have distorted the image of America's black community, prompting many a member of the white middle class to cower in his suburb waiting for the revolution — while in-depth studies universally indicate that the overwhelming majority of the black community is deeply committed to the preservation of the established social system.

In fact, in this age of media manipulation, reporters at times seem to beg to be used. The "background" session, in which government officials decline to be identified or quoted directly, continues to thrive, not only in Washington but now in the provinces as well. By the standard Washington rule the reporter is permitted to use information thus imparted "on his own authority." He is permitted, in other words, to report the government line as though it were Gospel without mentioning that it is the government line. There even are regular "background breakfasts," organized like social clubs, which compete for officials' favor. The most successful current group is operated by Washington reporter Godfrey Sperling, Jr., of the *Christian Science Monitor*, who had the wisdom to assemble a blue-ribbon panel of newspapermen when he initiated the enterprise in 1966. It is successful in the sense that top government officials accept invitations to the breakfasts. As a result, Sperling is having trouble restricting membership. At least two other breakfast groups have been formed since, at least partially as competitors.

The breakfasts are a useful way of allowing reporters to get to know officials and to question them at some leisure and in some depth outside the formal confrontation of a press conference. Many reporters who participate have deep-seated reservations about the "background" syndrome, but feel that they must take advantage of the only opportunities they may have to question officials. For the government, the backgrounder can be an invaluable propaganda tool. Government officials are often anxious to take advantage of the platform. Anonymity, however, rarely seems to breed either courage or candor.

Must the media be used? Are they, like a Greyhound bus, a public carrier that should accept all, equally, who wish to ride? What, if anything, can the media do to avoid being used?

Various newsmen believe that "using" of the media can be reduced, but their approach to achieving this probably would give Spiro Agnew insomnia. For they believe, in effect, that rather than having too many analysts and commentators, the media have too few. Rather than doing too much analysis, the media do too little. If so, newspapers must hire reporters and writers with the background and brains to qualify as independent analysts in major fields of government. Then if a President stands up and says that it is important to the nation that it fight a war in Asia, the reporter will have the background and training to challenge the President. Hence, the future role of newspapers would be to supply more criticism, examination, and questioning.

"We once did the hard news," says Tom Wicker. "But TV has taken that over. Our job now must be in the area of depth, questioning, and analysis."

If there was a media failure on Vietnam, what exactly was it? Was it a failure to interpret and analyze available material, or was it a failure to discover and report — and possibly dramatize — what was really happening? Joseph Goulden, former Washington bureau chief for the Philadelphia *Inquirer*, in a book called *Truth Is the First Casualty*, examines the story of the Gulf of Tonkin incident of 1964, which Lyndon Johnson seized upon to gain a congressional blank check to wage war in Vietnam. Through personal interviews with participants, Goulden makes a convincing case that the incident was a fraud. One key witness had never talked to a reporter until Goulden traced him; then his story exposed the incident as a sham. What might have happened if reporters had found that witness in 1964?

In the same way, David Kraslow and Stuart H. Loory of the Los Angeles *Times* have exposed Johnson's diplomatic strategy. The two were given eight months' reportorial time, and an unlimited budget, to try to piece together the behind-the-scenes story of Johnson's Vietnam diplomacy. Their series of articles in the *Times* and their book, *The Secret Search for Peace in Vietnam*, leave little doubt that Johnson's strategy was to talk peace and make war. His objective was a military victory, and it was not abandoned until the very end of his administration. Kraslow and Loory, both top reporters, were not able to complete their research and publish it until spring, 1968 — after the Tet offensive and Clark Clifford had changed the complexion of the war. What might have happened if some other great news organization had undertaken a mission similar to Kraslow's and Loory's a year earlier?

A "used" press is in many ways a passive and timid press whose staff members take the statements and explanations and rationalizations and handouts and background sessions and pass them along to the reader or the viewer and then go home to the suburbs to watch *Laugh-In*. If the Vietnam war could indeed have been reversed or slowed by the media, it is hard to believe it could have been done without aggressive, challenging, controversial reporting. It certainly could not have been done on the back pages. It would have to have been done at the tops of front pages, with stories for which reporters had excavated facts to show that the Administration was lying. It is hard to believe it could have been done by a press corps that could adopt a phrase like "credibility gap."

If the media are to avoid being used, they must recognize that the most common technique employed by those who would use them, in or out of government, is the staged or pseudo-event — what some have called the "media event." The speech, the announcement, the statement by the Secretary of Defense, the antiwar demonstration, the press conference called by the black militants, the press release from J. Edgar Hoover, even the appearance at breakfast by a cabinet member — all share one thing in common. All are a way in which a salesman for a point of view may present his case. The problem in this fast-moving society is to put hundreds of these pseudo-events, staged daily, into a context that bears a relationship to their importance.

Here is a prominent way in which the media fail. They continue to be victimized by the old "hard-news" formula in which not enough is said about who is doing the talking — and why. As one newsman put it, "A congressman can still get up on the floor of the House and make a cogent argument that we ought to recognize Red China and the wires still put it out with a tone of shock that suggests the man is probably a red. The world has changed, but the hard-news reporters haven't."

No rule of journalism forbids a reporter from attempting to set the scene for what he is reporting. Some newsmen in Washington will identify information as coming from a "backgrounder" in which the source declined to be identified. That helps. But it would also help if stories went deeper in suggesting a President's motivation, or even the possible motivation of the director of the FBI. It would have helped in Chicago had more effort been invested in determining who was whom among potential demonstrators, and who spoke for how many. It would have helped if reporters covering the Nixon campaign had taken time to investigate and explain his image-making techniques, which Joe McGinniss so adroitly exposed in *The Selling of the President*. With more and more pseudo-events becoming legitimate news, the necessity for providing background for an event becomes greater and greater.

It is necessary to recognize, too, that the nature of news — or what is called news — is changing. Because of the infinite complexity of modern society, many things are "news" that can't be learned in police stations: attitudes in the black community or among youth; the influence of the military; the economics of hunger; the adequacy of public education or health care; the will of the people in South Vietnam; the way images are made. All these may bear directly on the lives of readers and, having importance to them, may be "news," though not events.

The news media still must try to hold up a mirror to the world, to reflect it as accurately as possible to readers or viewers. But the picture can hardly be accurate if the media are largely occupied with reflecting the views of pleaders of causes, or dramatizing "happenings," or blandly transmitting the official government line. The press must not turn itself over to those who would use it. Editors and writers must seek out the questions that require answering and set out to find the answers for themselves.

PRESS AGENT — BUT STILL PRESIDENT

Ben H. Bagdikian

For a time during World War II this writer was an instructor in aerial navigation, an exercise that required one student navigator to direct the plane to a practice target while a second navigator, in the same plane but out of touch with the first, tracked where the plane had been and where it was headed. One night the first navigator said the plane would hit the target at 11 P.M. and the target would be El Paso. Asked where we would be at eleven, the second navigator wrote, "Albuquerque." At eleven o'clock a large city loomed out of the night. Both men looked jubilant. On the ground I had to tell the second man we were not in Albuquerque but in El Paso. He was stunned. He pulled out his log, full of statistics like compass headings and celestial fixes, waved it in front of my face and cried, "But that's impossible! I've got the figures to *prove* we're in Albuquerque!" He did have the figures to prove it. But the sign on the tower said El Paso and all the natives claimed to be Texans.

This episode came to mind when the President in his June 1 press conference described the care with which he decided to send the Marines to Santo Domingo: "I had 237 individual conversations during that period and about 35 meetings with various people. . . ."

The President is a lover of statistics and of appearances and in the fierce gamesmanship that has developed in the White House he has proved himself an indefatigible practitioner of the art of

---

Summer, 1965. Ben H. Bagdikian, a frequent contributor to the *Review*, is an assistant managing editor of the Washington *Post*.

public relations. This has presented special problems for the press corps, but not simply because a President tries to put himself in the best light, because all do that. It has dawned only recently on Washington correspondents just how deeply committed the President is to his public relations practice.

Joseph Kraft, writing in *Harper's,* believes the President's troubles with the press "stem largely from the inability of the press to see the President as just another flack."

What happens if the press has to view the President of the United States as "just another flack"?

The problem is not the existence of public relations in the White House, which has to consider its "image" if for no other reason than to know whether it is being understood. But there is flackery and flackery and the White House has pushed the technique of PR to the point of negative returns.

Some White House deceptions are forgiven as part of the job. President Eisenhower would have been wiser to refuse comment on the U-2 shot down over Russia. As a national leader the President has to keep himself open to negotiations for the national good and if he publicly associates himself with all the dirty tricks that go on behind the scenes he damages his power — not because he tells the other side anything it doesn't privately know, but because he becomes a public symbol of the dirty tricks with whom other national leaders cannot negotiate. Precisely because the President is more than a promoter of his own program and reputation, more than proprietor of government agencies, but also a symbol of national aims and values, it is important that he be listened to — and speak — as something more than a shrewd public relations man.

Some of the deceptions have been important. For weeks President Johnson told the public it was being misled by reporters who said the government was considering widening the war in Vietnam. The reporters were correct and the President wrong. The White House has implied that it consulted the Organization of American States before committing troops to the Dominican Republic, but it never told the OAS beforehand that it was considering troops.

Other illusions are of interest chiefly within the trade, such as the time the President gave a backgrounder in Texas but asked correspondents to put on a Washington dateline (which most did).

The problem is partly the astonishing portion of presidential attention given to public relations. No President has monitored his public image with more zeal. He often pulls popularity poll results out of his pocket. He adds up hours of time given to the press and it is enormous, though much of it is ritualistic or non-useful. In one extended session a French correspondent whispered to an American that he had a Paris deadline coming up and had to leave. The President was holding forth on the White House south balcony. The American whispered back that the Frenchman couldn't possibly leave. "But we've been here for an hour and a half and he is saying nothing and I have a deadline." The American hissed, "Would you leave if Charles de Gaulle were doing this?" The Frenchman stiffened and whispered, "Charles de Gaulle would not spend fifteen minutes talking about the rust on his balcony."

The President and his staff seem to ring like burglar alarms whenever and wherever the name "Johnson" appears in print or is uttered on the air. A small item in a West Texas paper mentioned Billie Sol Estes in connection with the President in a three-paragraph story on the inside; the editor claims he got a telephone call from the White House in time to kill the item in later editions. One television correspondent was awakened in the middle of the night by the White House, which had heard that he planned to make some critical remarks the next day. A newspaper correspondent wrote a critical morning story and got three telephone calls from White House aides before breakfast. The *New York Review of Books*, a medium-highbrow publication, ran a scathing review of Johnson's Vietnam policy and its editors got a phone call from a White House aide suggesting that in the future they have Vietnam books reviewed by Joseph Alsop (who approves of the Johnson policy).

The President has three television sets for simultaneous viewing of the three networks, plus an AP and UPI ticker. Apparently he watches them more closely than some of the editors. One night a startled wire service editor in Washington got a White House call later preserved in the house organ, *UPI Reporter*, as follows:

"Hello?"
"Hello, Pat, this is Lyndon Johnson."
"Yes, Mr. President."
"Say, I have here . . . (pause) . . . A1O1N from Johnson City, Texas, about the homestead, by Kyle Thompson. Let's see . . . (pause) . . . you say in there that there's going to be a fee for the tour. Well, that's not right at all. The idea is to give it to the people."
"Just a minute, Mr. President, and I'll get the story."
"You see what it says. It says 'the home was opened to the public for fee tours.' That isn't right. You see, it's for free. That's the idea. Do you see that?"
"Yes, Mr. President. It looks like they dropped the 'r' in the word 'free.' I guess they omitted it in transmission."
"Well, Pat, it sure does mean just the opposite of what we mean."
"It sure does, Mr. President. I'll fix it."
"Well, we want it to be free."
"Certainly, Mr. President. I'll straighten it out right away."
"I'd appreciate it if you would clean this up for me."
"I certainly will, Mr. President."
"We hope you will take the necessary steps to straighten this out."
"Yes, sir, Mr. President."
"Thank you, Pat."
"Thank you for letting us know, Mr. President."

But the problem is not just quantity of presidential time and intervention. Some of it is less meticulous than his editing of UPI typos and some of it has such an implausible ending that it can only harm his credibility. He likes to be the miracle worker, so takes pains to knock down stories predicting what he will do. In December he complained that the Washington *Evening Star* reported falsely that he would propose a 3 percent pay raise for federal workers. The *Star* dutifully reported the presidential complaint. Then the President proposed a 3 percent pay raise for federal workers.

At about the same time, the President complained that the Washington *Post* falsely reported that he planned to ask for a $4 billion cut in excise taxes. "The President is described as feeling that the $4 billion figure couldn't be further wrong," the news story said. The then press secretary, George Reedy, said, "That figure bears no relationship to any decision that has been made."

The President proposed an excise tax cut of $3,964,000,000, which bears a relationship to $4,000,000,000 as 99.1 to 100.0.

Nor is it unknown that a responsible White House aide will confirm a reporter's story before it is printed, and after the published story causes unexpected embarrassment another equally responsible White House aide will tell reporters that the story is wrong and was never checked with the White House.

While doing all this, the President maintains sympathetic relations with editors and publishers beyond anything known before. Lyndon Johnson is the only Democratic President in this century who seems to be on better terms with newspaper publishers than with the working press. This isn't bad; it is merely astonishing. I. F. Stone, an incorrigible heretic in a town with increasing pressures for journalistic orthodoxy, has written: "Johnson sometimes seems to think the Constitution made him not only commander-in-chief of the nation's armed forces but editor-in-chief of its newspapers."

Among the institutional casualties of this crushing program of public relations are the press briefings by the press secretary, which have decreasing content, and the presidential press conference, which becomes increasingly rhetorical. Even the semiconfidential backgrounder has often been reduced to an absurdity. On April 7, for example, such a session was held to give prior interpretation of the President's Johns Hopkins University speech offering unconditional discussions on Vietnam. The briefing was given in the White House by Secretary of Defense Robert McNamara, then-Acting Secretary of State George Ball, and special assistant McGeorge Bundy. Ordinarily it is not cricket to print names of briefing officers but in this case the White House disclosed them by staging a make-believe start of the briefing for television and radio for the 6 P.M. newscasts to help build public interest in the speech.

When it came to the nonattributable Q-and-A, the cameras were shut off but the same spirit of charade continued to pervade the session. Max Frankel of the New York *Times* asked why the government had waited so long to make public its aims and its basis for settlement in Vietnam. Secretary Ball said that there was no delay, that the government had always had the position presented in the President's speech.

"Are you saying," Frankel asked, "that this speech is not news, that we should treat it as old stuff?" Ball replied that the government had always held the same position, though the "formulations" might be new and, he added as a parting shot, "it may be a little clearer to you." To which John Scali, ABC diplomatic correspondent, rose to say, "Since this has all been said before, would the Secretary please refresh the reporters' memories on the last time anyone in the government offered unconditional discussions on Vietnam?" There was general laughter and no answer.

The White House seems so obsessed with keeping the news record favorable that it is defensive about firsthand journalism that it could find useful. The press helped dispel some of the wild confusion within government on the Dominican *coup d'etat* with reporting from the scene that was better than official diplomatic and military reporting.

The same was true in Vietnam. John Mecklin, chief information officer in Saigon during the time when David Halberstam of the *Times* and Malcolm Browne of the AP were official dirty words, writes in his book, *Mission in Torment,* that Halberstam and Browne were essentially correct in their reporting and the government essentially wrong.

The White House obsession with PR would be easier to handle if it came from another source. Most correspondents learned to cope with flackdom a long time ago: they react when special pleaders originate news; they recognize the implausibly rosy release; they instinctively check with the opposition; they treat with contempt a man who deliberately flim-flams them.

What is special here is Kraft's observation: most reporters have trouble looking at the President as just another flack. He is not just another flack. He is a PR man in his obsession with image, his unrestrained attempts to create illusion for tactical reasons, and his concern with appearances no matter how implausible. But he is also President of the United States, carrying the burdens of his office seriously.

The problem is that Lyndon Johnson appeals to reporters with all the dignity and power of his position as President and when this does not produce the results he wants, begins manipulating them and the news in ways that are not highly regarded even at the Press Club bar. He is trying to have it both ways. The weakness of many correspondents is that the President is too valuable a source in the competition for news to be ignored as a lesser PR man would be. But deeper than that is the conflict the President creates in many serious correspondents who respect the office of President and the man in it, but whose professional standards tell them that what is going on is common, ordinary press agentry.

The President and his aides often seem to ignore the demands of professionalism upon correspondents, which require exercise of independent judgment based not on personality or pressure but on honest discrimination. Too often correspondents are asked to choose between disrespect for the reader and disrespect for the President.

One simple answer may be to report the unabashed intervention of the White House into the news process. The dialogue in *UPI Reporter* was seen widely in the trade, but it was not on the UPI wire. Ordinarily this would be healthy avoidance of narcissism. But perhaps the time has come to report the President not only as originator of news but also as editor of it.

THE INDIANA PRIMARY AND THE INDIANAPOLIS NEWSPAPERS

Jules Witcover

In a presidential election year, the Washington beat spreads far beyond the capital into those states that emerge as battlegrounds for the major-party nominations. Most of these primary-election states are traditional — New Hampshire, Wisconsin, Oregon, California. But this year, Senator Robert F. Kennedy's unexpected decision to make Indiana the first test in his race for the Democratic nomination sent reporters off into unfamiliar primary territory. Their lengthy visit in turn gave Indiana's two largest newspapers — the Indianapolis *Star* and the Indianapolis *News* — an unusual opportunity to show members of their own fraternity what they could do with a major national story. The political writers, editors, and columnists who flocked to the state in April and early May made the *Star* and the *News* daily reading and as primary date approached the papers' coverage became the source of nearly as much conversation among them as the campaign itself.

Long before Kennedy publicly proclaimed in a talk to local ministers that the Indianapolis dailies were "the worst newspapers in the country" (replacing New Hampshire's *Union-Leader* on his personal list), out-of-state newspapermen had passed judgment of their own. No poll was taken, of course. But it was very clear from all the talk at breakfast tables, on the campaign planes and buses, and in the nightly bull sessions that the consensus did not treat the Indianapolis papers kindly.

When, in the closing days of the Indiana campaign, Pierre Salinger urgently requested an investigation by the American

---

Summer, 1968. Jules Witcover, a member of the Los Angeles *Times* Washington bureau, has written books about Robert Kennedy and Richard Nixon.

Society of Newspaper Editors in behalf of Kennedy, most reporters dismissed the plea for what it was — an eleventh-hour political ploy. But they did not argue with Salinger's premise — that the papers had displayed an "outrageous and callous disregard for fairness" in covering the campaign.

Salinger specifically had wanted ASNE's freedom of information committee to look into the papers' "journalistic practices and ethics" and to issue a report before the primary — which at that late date was impossible. Vincent S. Jones, the ASNE president and Gannett Newspapers executive, predictably rejected the request. "We don't have any authority like that," he said. "We don't police our members and we don't investigate our members."

Eugene C. Pulliam, publisher of both Indianapolis papers, said in a statement from Phoenix, where he owns the Arizona *Republic*:

> Bobby Kennedy is like all spoiled children. When he doesn't get what he wants, he bellyaches about it. The facts are Kennedy and his entourage received more space in the Indianapolis *Star* and the Indianapolis *News* than any other candidate, largely for the reason he brought his whole family, including his mother, to Indianapolis and they made news and we printed the news and the pictures.
>
> Of course we are opposed to his candidacy because we don't believe men who spend millions of dollars in a primary campaign should be given the nomination for the highest office in our government. Editorially, we have tried to make it clear that Indiana, at least, is not for sale. But in our news columns we have given Kennedy a far better break than he has given any of his opponents.

In the heat and the rush of the primary, there was no time to check on Pulliam's statement. But afterward, I surveyed for the *Review* the rag files of the *Star* (morning) and the *News* (evening) from the day Kennedy filed for the primary (March 28) through election day (May 7). The check, seeking to gauge only the quantitative performance of the papers, measured column inches of staff-written copy concerning each of the three Democratic candidates — Kennedy, Senator Eugene J. McCarthy, and Governor Roger D. Branigin, Indiana's favorite son and the Pulliam papers' editorial choice. All editorials and other opinion pieces including syndicated columns were excluded, as were campaign roundup stories in which more than one candidate was mentioned. To keep the task within reasonable bounds, no effort was made to compare headline sizes or photo coverage, although in both cases Branigin appeared to have an edge. Finally, to give the papers every benefit of doubt, all stories about Kennedy — unfavorable as well as favorable — were included in his total: those, for example, in which he was charged with excessive campaign spending, and with "injecting racism and religion" into the campaign.

From March 28 through May 7, the survey showed, Branigin had received 664 column inches of staff copy in the *Star*, compared with 459 for Kennedy and 382 for McCarthy. In the *News*, the breakdown was Branigin, 384 column inches; Kennedy, 253; McCarthy, 202.

Sheer volume of space, of course, does not in itself prove editorial bias. The flow of news is uneven; in a political campaign, one candidate often is more active than another, says more, or creates more public interest. Among out-of-state reporters who covered all three candidates, that candidate in the Indiana primary clearly was Kennedy. His crowds dwarfed those of the other two, and in fact the campaign rapidly began to revolve around him as a personality. Kennedy himself — the outsider, the big spender, the Bobby-come-lately — became the dominant issue. Yet in the forty days surveyed, he made page 1 in the *Star* only eleven times and in the *News* only six times in the editions kept in the papers' own rag files. Branigin stories were on page 1 of the *Star* seventeen mornings (sometimes two or three stories on the same day) and on page 1 of the *News* fourteen evenings. McCarthy, who was treated offhandedly until the late stages, made page 1 of the *Star* three days, and two days in the *News*, in the editions checked.

Almost from the beginning, Kennedy had difficulty breaking prominently into the *Star* and the *News*. Although he was mobbed when he flew into Indianapolis on the night of March 28 to file his candidacy, the fact that he "had to fight his way through a crowd of about 4,000 wildly enthusiastic supporters at the Statehouse" didn't appear until the nineteenth paragraph of the lead story. Ahead of that fact came an endorsement of Branigin by the state's attorney general, the labeling of Kennedy's candidacy as "cutthroat competition" by McCarthy's state chairman, and excerpts from a Branigin statement accompanying his own filing — performed by his two sons while the governor was returning home from Florida.

A week later, Kennedy was in Indianapolis when he learned of the assassination of Dr. Martin Luther King, Jr. He proceeded to a rally in a Negro district, where he informed the crowd of Dr. King's death and then gave a speech urging racial reconciliation that was reported across the country as a major incident in that eventful night. In the *Star*, an account of the speech appeared in a page 1 story under a pro-Branigin cartoon and a headline reading YOUNG HOOSIERS BACK "FAVORITE SON" BRANIGIN. The story led with the news that a new statewide youth group had been formed for the governor, and that the Indiana headquarters of the Branigin-for-President Committee would open the next day, and only then got into the Kennedy speech on Dr. King. The *News* ran its account, under a Kennedy headline with a staff photo, on page 5 that afternoon.

On April 24, two weeks before primary day, the *Star* began an intensive campaign in behalf of Branigin. For six straight days, stories favorable to the governor appeared on page 1, with Kennedy and McCarthy stories, when there were any, well inside. The Branigin stories dealt with state labor support he was receiving, his attacks on his two Democratic foes for criticizing Johnson, his shock at their rate of campaign spending, and a vice-presidential boomlet for Branigin detected by the *Star*'s Washington bureau but apparently by nobody else. There were three pro-Branigin cartoons on page 1 during the six days, the first of which, entitled "Guests in the House — !", depicted Branigin sitting politely at the dinner table while McCarthy and especially Kennedy, sitting on either side of "Mrs. Indiana," made advances toward her that never would have gotten past the old Hays Office in the movies. Nearly every day there was another labor endorsement from this or that local or county council. As far as I could determine, however, Indianapolis readers never were advised that the state council of the AFL-CIO had balked at pressure from George Meany in Washington and had declined to endorse Branigin.

From what one read in the Indianapolis papers during this stretch, one had reason to conclude that Branigin was conducting a whirlwind campaign around the state, voters hailing him everywhere. But reporters who went out with him found him going from county courthouse to small local gathering to county courthouse without causing much of a ripple most of the time. In the town of Marion on April 24, he entered the Grant County courthouse virtually unrecognized and was introduced to employees there by the county treasurer, Fred A. Millspaugh, who supplied them with cards on which they might get the governor's signature. The next day in the *Star*, readers learned that Branigin "was besieged for autographs." The same story devoted twelve inches to a "reception" in Marion without noting the attendance was only eighty or so loyal party workers who sat stiffly on wooden folding chairs while their boss gave them an old-time political pep talk.

On April 29, as the final week of campaigning started, the local citizenry was treated to an eight-column banner in the *Star* that proclaimed BRANIGIN VIEWED FOR V.P., under an overline: "NATURAL" HUMPHREY RUNNING MATE. The story, by Washington bureau staffer Ben Cole, said Branigin was "being considered among 'three or four' prominent Democrats as a possible running mate" for the Vice-President. The story quoted "a spokesman in the Humphrey high command" as saying that "Governor Roger D. Branigin's name is now being frequently mentioned as a possible running mate, along with three or four others." By whom it was being mentioned, the story didn't say, but it noted that "one of the party's highest figures confided recently that Branigin would be a 'natural' for the Vice Presidency, capable of giving the office the charm, identity and humor given to it by former Vice Presidents. . . ." The story went on to say Humphrey "would find in Branigin the capacity for first-rate liaison with the states" because of his experience and popularity with other governors. There was no reference to other factors that would have seemed certain to bar Branigin's selection: his advanced age (sixty-five) the fact that like Humphrey, he comes from a Midwest state; the uncertainty that even Branigin could enable the Democrats to carry his own state in November, especially against Richard Nixon. That afternoon, the *News* also proclaimed: "BRANIGIN A TOP CHOICE FOR VICE-PRESIDENT."

On April 30, Kennedy finally made page 1 of the *Star*, thus ending Branigin's six-day monopoly (although there also were two Branigin stories on the page that day). But Kennedy could have done without the breakthrough. MCHALE RAPS KENNEDY'S USE OF RACISM, RELIGION, the headline said. The story reported that Frank M. McHale, a former Democratic national committeeman, had accused Kennedy "yesterday" of "injecting racism and religion into Hoosier politics." McHale, further identified as "a former American Legion national committeeman who was named a Knight of St. Gregory by Pope John XXIII," was said to have based his racism charge on a speech in which Kennedy told Indiana University School of Medicine students that Negroes "carry the major portion of the struggle in Vietnam." What Kennedy had said was that Negroes carry a disproportionate share of the war in terms of the Negro population. McHale was quoted as saying religion was injected into the campaign when Kennedy's wife, speaking before a state meeting of the National Council of Catholic Women, thanked Archbishop Paul C. Schulte of Indianapolis for "inviting" her, when in fact he had not. McHale was quoted as saying she had made "a deliberate attempt to make Hoosier Catholics think that Bobby has official sanction." The story appeared Tuesday morning. The last paragraph read: "McHale made his remarks before a group of veterans following the spring conference of the Indiana American Legion on *Saturday* [italics mine]."

Also on April 30, the *News* ran a banner and story over the page 1 nameplate that said BRANIGIN'S MOVES AVERT STATE FINANCIAL CRISIS. The reader could have been forgiven if he had understood this to be spot news. Rather, it turned out to be a general review of the governor's economic policies since he took office in 1965. The same afternoon, Kennedy was mobbed in Indianapolis's Monument Circle, causing a traffic jam. In the edition checked, a two-column headline on page four below the fold said KENNEDY SHAKES HANDS ON CIRCLE.

Meanwhile, back at the *Star*, an effort of nearly a month to persuade Indiana voters Kennedy was "buying" the election reached its zenith. Up to that time, the paper had been running entirely legitimate stories discussing campaign expenses and quoting the state Democratic chairman, Gordon St. Angelo, who was accusing Kennedy and McCarthy of spending $2 billion in Indiana between them. Other newspapers outside Indiana were exploring the campaign costs as well, and in fact the New York *Times* had just run an editorial criticizing the system under which large sums of money were spent in primaries, to the disadvantage of poor candidates.

On May 1, at the bottom of the *Star*'s page 1, an editorial was printed under the headline: IS INDIANA FOR SALE? ASKS THE NEW YORK TIMES. A precede said simply, "This was the lead editorial in the April 30 issue of the New York Times." No mention was made of the fact that references in the *Times* to Branigin's campaign, and to Indiana's failure to have an effective law on reporting of campaign expenses, had been deleted. The editorial as reprinted had a sentence that said, "Gov. Roger D. Branigin, the 'favorite son' candidate, is the leader of a state party organization." In the original, that sentence continued: "which controls thousands of patronage jobs and which still engages in the ancient and disreputable practice of levying a two percent tax on the salaries of state employees."

In the same issue, the *Star* had Kennedy on page 1 for the second straight day (along with two pro-Branigin stories). The headline on this one said KENNEDY WON'T JOIN "POOR MARCH," an accurate summation of his response to a question from a minister about his participation in the march. Kennedy had said he wouldn't march because he was running for President. (It was at this same ministerial meeting that Kennedy called the Indianapolis papers "the worst newspapers in the country." The *Star*, reporting on that meeting, made no mention of the statement, and referred only parenthetically to "a digression which indicated his displeasure with some news coverage he encounters in Indiana.")

By this time, the Indianapolis papers were being criticized from all sides. Their coverage of the campaign was finding its way into many correspondents' stories and at least two television networks, the Columbia Broadcasting System and the Public Broadcasting Laboratory, were working on special reports. *Star* and *News* executives were approached for comment and were well aware that their papers had come under unusual and unfavorable scrutiny among visiting newsmen.

On Friday, May 3, the *Star*'s coverage abruptly changed. In the lower left-hand corner of page 1 under a four-column headline, THREE DEMOCRAT CONTENDERS "SELL" HOOSIERS THEIR BRAND OF POLITICS, stories on McCarthy, Kennedy, and Branigin appeared side by side. McCarthy and Kennedy each got only one column under the head and Branigin got two, but it was a great improvement. Above the fold, however, was a cartoon showing a folksy gent with pipe and DEBT FREE INDIANA printed across his chest, sitting on his front stoop while another gent in top hat and tails, and labeled EASTERN EXTREMISTS, asked him: "Come Now, Surely You Don't Want to Live Like a Cornball All Of Your Life!" One "Walter Crankcase" was thrusting a microphone into "Debt Free Indiana's" face as a photographer from the "Liberal Press," "Bunkley and Hinkley" and "Assorted City Slickers" looked on.

On Saturday, May 4, Kennedy and McCarthy were on page 1 again with Branigin and Republican Richard Nixon, all receiving two-column readouts under a banner across the bottom of the page: CAMPAIGNERS IN INDIANA TOUCH PEACE TALKS, POLITICAL SPENDING. And no cartoon. It seemed to augur a turned-over leaf. But came Sunday, May 5, and an eight-column banner over a lead story that said: "Bonna Printing Company failed to meet its deadline yesterday for delivering election supplies for the Tuesday primary, partly because the firm devoted much of its time to print campaign materials for Senator Robert F. Kennedy (D-N.Y.), it was learned yesterday." A three-column picture, with the overline TUESDAY'S ALMOST HERE, showed a local voting official inspecting precinct supplies on hand. WILL BONNA PRINTING COMPANY HAVE NECESSARY MATERIAL READY? the caption asked. (The next day's *Star*, under a one-column head at the bottom of page 15, provided the answer: Yes. An all-night rush job got most of the supplies out, the story reported.) Sunday's *Star* also had a front-page editorial about the earlier New York *Times* "Is Indiana For Sale?" editorial. Although stories elsewhere had pointed out that the *Star* had cut derogatory information about Branigin from the *Times* reprint, *Star* readers still were in the dark.

By Monday, the day before the election, page 1 was back to normal. A secondary banner proclaimed PRIMARY HINGES ON UNDECIDED VOTER, with a deck, DEMOCRATS CLAIM UNKNOWN FACTOR

TO HELP BRANIGIN. In the top center of the page, Branigin in a photo beamed at constituents in a Saturday appearance and the overline read THE SMILE OF VICTORY? Under the picture was a Washington bureau story headlined BRANIGIN IS COMMITTED TO UNITY OF NATION AND PARTY, JESUIT SAYS, with the following lead:

> Washington — An exclusive article in the Jesuit magazine, *America*, presents Governor Roger D. Branigin as a Democrat deeply committed to unity of nation and of party.
>
> The interview, conducted by the Rev. Harry J. Sievers, S. J., assistant editor of *America*, shows the Indiana governor to be a far different man from the chauvinistic bumpkin conjured up in anti-Hoosier newspapers at Washington and New York this election weekend.
>
> The seaboard press and some TV stations are ridiculing Indiana and its governor as so ingrown and atavistic they should be closed off from the rest of society behind a modern Hadrian's wall. . . .

Across the very bottom of page one, not marked as an advertisement, ran these words: "Vote for Indiana — Vote for Branigin."

Finally, on election day, the *Star*'s eight-column banner proclaimed BRANIGIN PREDICTS VICTORY. The page 1 cartoon was a nonpartisan appeal to citizens to vote, but under it ran two more pro-Branigin stories. The headline on one said TEAMSTERS, GARY NEGRO GROUP ENDORSE BRANIGIN. The headline on the other was MOTHER WORKING FOR BRANIGIN GETS THREATENING PHONE CALL. The story identified the woman as a Negro who said the caller had "a heavy voice like a Negro" but "did not identify himself as a supporter for any presidential candidate." Those observers of the election who were aware the Negro vote was expected to go overwhelmingly to Kennedy marveled at the coincidence of these developments on the eve of the election. Kennedy and McCarthy both made page 1 on election day — with a one-column head for each.

Through all this, the *News* and the *Star* ran paradoxically well-balanced editorial and opposite-editorial pages. The *Star*, particularly, printed various columns disagreeing with its own conservative bent and numerous letters to the editor not only supporting Kennedy but going after the *Star* vigorously for its own news coverage of the campaign. But once, when columnist Joseph Kraft on April 28 suggested that Indiana, "one of the last backwaters in the country, has finally entered the mainstream" and that it was bad news for Branigin, the *Star*'s editors couldn't control themselves. They inserted an editor's note into the column that said: "This article by Joseph Kraft, long-time columnist-friend of the Kennedy family, ridiculing Indiana, is typical of the propaganda being turned out by pro-Kennedy writers to push the candidacy of Senator Robert F. Kennedy." But the Kraft column was printed nevertheless — with a long editorial that led off: "Get rid of your horse-and-buggy, your lightning rods, chamber pots, kerosene lamps, bustles and McKinley buttons. Indiana is emerging from antiquity. The word comes from Joseph Kraft, columnist, whose perception is matched only by the fluidity of his prose. . . ." Letters on both sides flowed in, and were printed, including one on May 3 from a woman who said that the *Star*, rather than attributing the Kraft column to pro-Kennedy motives, "should bring its editorial policy into line with 20th Century American reality. There should be no more editorials about such fictional conditions as 'the sovereign state of Indiana.' The cartoons about the Democratic primary exemplify politics at the dirtiest extreme. . . ."

The staff cartoons in both the *Star* and the *News*, and the editorials themselves, showed none of the ambivalence of the op-ed page. Even after the election, on the next day the *Star*'s cartoon showed Kennedy straddled over the ropes of a boxing ring, one eye blackened, but saying with a toothy grin, "Tough Fight Ma, But I Won!" as the referee tried valiantly to lift Bobby's right glove — a huge money bag. But perhaps the best cartoon of the primary period appeared in the *News* on April 20. It showed the top of a manufacturing plant of some kind, marked "Indiana Primary Campaign," with seven big smokestacks pouring forth thick, black soot. The building was not further identified, but regular readers of the *Star* and *News* could have been forgiven if they thought it was a self-portrait.

On election day, after reviewing the Indianapolis newspapers' performance during the campaign, I called on Eugene S. Pulliam, assistant publisher of the papers and son of their owner, and asked him if he cared to comment on their coverage. "I do think that in the earlier part of the campaign, as far as positioning stories, we got overeager," he said. "But I think that was rectified." Pulliam declined to comment on how decisions were made concerning play of stories and suggested I write to his father in Phoenix. I did so, asking the senior Pulliam to comment also. He sent back two statements, one the response to Salinger's appeal to the ASNE, and the other a postmortem on the election. It said:

Senator Kennedy won in Indiana because he had the most money and the largest number of election day workers. He completely dominated the Negro vote. He brought his whole family, including his wife, sisters — and even his mother — to Indiana. As a result, they made more news than either of the other two candidates and we printed it. His statement that he was "completely blacked out of the *Star* and *News*" is ridiculously untrue. He and his entourage received more space than either Branigin or McCarthy. Evidently he thought his stories and picture should be on page one every day.

If Branigin had had one-half the money Bobby spent in Indiana, Branigin would have won hands down. The blunt truth is, this primary depended on which candidate had the most money to spend.

During the entire campaign we had no complaints from the Democrats regarding our coverage of the primary — and none from Kennedy until the day before the election when Pierre Salinger made his absurd attack on both the *Star* and *News*. [Note: Salinger's attack came two days before the election.]

We editorially opposed Kennedy largely for the reason that we do not trust his judgment in either domestic or foreign affairs; but more importantly, because we do not believe that only millionaires can run for the presidency. If this becomes a fact in American politics, our whole elective system will be destroyed.

It may well be, as the publisher of the Indianapolis *Star* and *News* said, that the Indiana primary "depended on which candidate had the most money to spend." The two newspapers, and especially the *Star*, obviously felt their role was to be a kind of equalizer — not merely reporting and analyzing what happened in the campaign, but using their news columns in numerous instances as only thinly disguised free advertising for Branigin. Reporting on excessive campaign spending is not only valid but commendatory, but even in this area, the two papers relied heavily on criticisms from Branigin's campaign chief, Gordon St. Angelo, the state Democratic chairman, and offered little in the way of staff enterprise and investigation. Out-of-state newsmen such as Roger Mudd of the Columbia Broadcasting System, Richard Harwood of the Washington *Post*, and Robert Walters of the Washington *Evening Star* produced stories on this aspect of the campaign that were more revealing, enterprising, and balanced than anything that appeared in either of the Indianapolis papers.

The use of editorials and cartoons to project a newspaper's point of view is, of course, a tradition of American journalism, and a strength when exercised straightforwardly and responsibly. Readers have become accustomed to finding such opinion matter on the editorial pages, but there is no firm rule that prevents the placing of an editorial or a cartoon on page 1 for reasons of special emphasis. But when the line between a newspaper's editorial point of view and its reportage of the news becomes so blurred that the average reader no longer can be expected reasonably to discern where fact ends and opinion and propaganda take over, the community — and the integrity of the news business — are ill-served.

CHICAGO GHOST STORY

Norman Glubok

You can be certain in Chicago that just as sure as there is an election, someone will charge "vote fraud." It happened in 1960 when Richard Nixon lost Illinois by eight thousand votes and his supporters asserted that the election was stolen from him in Chicago. It happened again in 1964 — this time, weeks before the ballots were even cast.

A few weeks after the 1960 election, three political science professors at the University of Chicago — Herman Finer, Jerome G. Kerwin, and C. Herman Pritchett — studied newspaper coverage of the Republican attempt to win a recount. The finding of the professors, all acknowledged Democrats: "We conclude that the charges that wholesale election fraud was perpetrated in Chicago were baseless and unsubstantiated . . . Chicago's title to its reputation as a city of good government and decent intention deserves protection from irresponsible defamation."

If the professors were unhappy with press coverage in 1960, they would not have been likely to find much cause for satisfaction in 1964.

Chicago's 1964 "ghost voter" battle started five weeks before the election. SHERIFF OPENS VOTE FRAUD WAR, proclaimed an eight-column, page 1 headline in the Chicago *Tribune.*

The story, by Robert Wiedrich, began: "Sheriff Richard B. Ogilvie charged yesterday that there may be as many as 150,000 ghost voters on Chicago election rolls and called for 1,000 volunteers to make an independent canvass." (A "ghost voter," as used here, was a name appearing on the rolls that did not represent an actual qualified voter.)

Winter, 1964–65. Norman Glubok, a former Chicago reporter, is a member of the CBS-TV news staff in New York.

The *Tribune* article said that Ogilvie, a Republican, had called for action "to prevent a recurrence on November 3 of wholesale ballot stealing that marked the 1960 presidential and 1962 general elections." It quoted Ogilvie as saying: "It has been estimated that there are between 50,000 and 150,000 ghost voters on the election rolls of Chicago. When an election can be decided by as few as 2,500 votes, as it has been the case in some past campaigns, then the casting of phony ballots is of prime concern."

The *Tribune* story was based on a news conference the previous afternoon, September 30. The other three major Chicago dailies also covered the conference. The *Tribune*-owned afternoon *American* gave the story a one-column headline: OGILVIE DECLARES GHOST VOTER WAR, and five inches of type. It did not mention the "150,000 ghosts." The other afternoon newspaper, Marshall Field's *Daily News*, also played down the story: OGILVIE ASKS VOTER SURVEY AID was the one-column headline. The story ran seven inches, and the second paragraph noted: "Ogilvie said this effort could easily expose from 50,000 to 150,000 phony registrations." The other Marshall Field newspaper, the morning *Sun-Times*, used a two-column headline on a thirteen-inch story. OGILVIE PROPOSES A VOTER SCREEN, it said. Unlike the three other newspapers, it quoted an official, the counsel, of the Chicago Board of Election Commissioners, target of the sheriff's criticism: "I think Ogilvie is attempting to take over the conduct of this election for his own political purposes."

On almost every day that followed, the "ghost voter" drive was in the newspapers. The *Tribune* gave the story by far the biggest play, followed by its subsidiary, the *American*.

The sheriff's campaign won editorial support from the *Tribune*. PURGE THE GHOSTS, was the *Tribune*'s head on its editorial October 2. It called on "good citizens of all political beliefs" to get behind Ogilvie. The *Daily News* had a similar editorial on October 7, headed PURGE THE POLL LISTS.

On October 12, the *American* differed with the *Tribune* with an editorial headed ARE THE FRAUDS ALL HERE? The *American* called Ogilvie's effort "laudable" but added: "Our satisfaction would now be complete if someone would undertake a really thorogoing campaign that, for a change, would not be based on the assumption that frauds take place only in Chicago, and are committed only by big city Democrats."

Once the actual canvass of the rolls began, the *Tribune* splashed the story across page 1 every day. GHOST VOTE HOMES FOUND was the banner in the October 12 *Tribune*. The story called attention to "obvious and blatant" violations of the election laws and listed such "fraudulent registrations" as thirty voters registered at a vacant lot address. Thirty-four others registered from three vacant buildings.

The *Daily News* ran a story on the same canvass, but in the third paragraph added something missing from the *Tribune* story. The *News* quoted the election board's head as saying that the canvass was not accurate because many persons had moved or died, and the canvassers were using two-year-old lists.

The next morning's *Sun-Times* had a three-column headline on page 3: 64 GHOST VOTERS ALREADY PURGED, HOLZMAN REPORTS. The story told of the claim by the board's chief that many of the alleged ghost voters had already been stricken from lists by the board's own canvassers. The same edition of the *Tribune* put the information in the eleventh paragraph and disposed of it in two sentences. The same *Tribune* story printed without attribution the "fact" of the existence of "100,000 to 150,000 ghost voters."

The high point of the effort came on October 18, when the *Tribune* headline read SUSPECT 3,000 ON VOTE LIST. The subhead noted ONE OF THE 'ELIGIBLES' IS A BOY, 8. The story told how a sheriff's canvasser had "surprised and shocked" a Mr. and Mrs. Louis Knox of 1451 S. Kostner, by informing them that their son, Robert, was registered to vote.

The next day the election board pointed out that the Robert Knox registered to vote at 1451 S. Kostner was a seventy-four-year-old man, the great-grandfather of the eight-year-old boy. Furthermore the canvassers had gone to the wrong address; the youngster lived at 1449 S. Kostner. But this explanation, in the *Tribune*, was tagged on the end of a twenty-inch story. The headline said VOTER TEAM FINDS 4,000 UNQUALIFIED.

At the end of the canvassing, the sheriff's counsel announced that his five hundred volunteers would challenge 3,456 names, according to the *Daily News*. The *News* quoted the board's response

— that 3,456 names are "fewer than have appeared in the obituaries since the last day of registration." The *News* also quoted the board's chief to the effect that the board's own canvassers had purged 141,000 persons from the lists.

The election board scheduled three days of public hearings, beginning October 22, for persons who had received notices to appear and defend their right to vote. ANGRY VOTERS CHALLENGE "GHOST" LABEL, was the *News* headline on a story that told of "a shouting match" at the hearings.

The *Tribune* story the next morning said: "*New* violence erupted last night . . ." The "violence" turned out to be a pushing match between a volunteer canvasser and a Democratic precinct captain.

Three days after the hearing ended, the election board issued its findings. On October 27, the board's lawyer reported that 2,941 persons were stricken from the rolls. Of this number, he said 1,817 were the result of Republican challenges; the remaining 1,124 were brought by Democratic workers. All four of the newspapers played the story straight. The *Sun-Times* story was on page 18. The *Tribune* story was on page 1, with a one-column headline.

The only newspaper to follow up was the *Daily News*. On October 29 the *News* story was headed GOP EVALUATES GHOST VOTER DRIVE. The subhead told the story: TOTAL OF 1,817 TAKEN OFF ROLLS FAR SHORT OF 150,000 GOAL. The story quoted the sheriff as blaming the "weak election laws" and the Chicago board of election commissioners. Five days before the election, the ghost voter story was laid to rest.

Four weeks after the election, I asked Professor Finer what he thought of the 1964 coverage. "If anything," said Finer, "the ghost voter search this time was more flagrant than it was last time, because it was an organized campaign. What strikes me is that at least one newspaper in this city, and you know which it is, tried to revive the whole thing. It is wicked in a democracy to have fraudulent voting. But it is also wicked to procure votes by fraudulent newspaper tricks." Finer suggested that the entire campaign was designed to frighten qualified voters out of voting.

The Republican sheriff saw the election coverage differently: "I thought we got more support than we could ordinarily expect from the *Tribune*," said Ogilvie. "The *Tribune*, I felt, played it as a straight news story. The *Tribune* gave it the most space, but I felt all the papers played it straight." Asked how he had arrived at the estimate of 150,000 ghost voters, Ogilvie replied: "That was an educated guess on my part. I did it by arithmetic. I figured the number of bad wards, the number of precincts in existence, the investigations we had earlier, and I multiplied a kind of average. I don't remember exactly, but I have the figures somewhere around the office."

AN EDITORIAL:

The Attack on the Press

The *Columbia Journalism Review* has sometimes been accused of being too critical of facets of American journalism. Now, however, it has the privilege of taking the offensive on behalf of America's news media. The campaign attacks on the news integrity of *all* media *as a class* have been unfair, irresponsible, and, in some cases, vicious.

Sweeping charges of print and broadcast "distortion" and "suppression" of news have long been a standard technique of the shabbiest demagogues — of Huey Long, Father Coughlin, Earl Browder, and Fritz Kuhn. Protests against editorial-page views have been a commonplace, too, as in the old Democratic "one-party press" complaint. What distinguishes the recent wave of attacks is that they have been broadside assaults on the integrity of *news* reporting and have come from what would normally be considered a "respectable" part of the political spectrum.

From large-scale sampling of press and broadcasting output, investigation of charges, and examination of other available material, five clear points emerge:

1. Barry Goldwater has been the object of editorial-page, column, and commentary criticism far more widespread and vigorous than that encountered by any Republican nominee within memory. There is nothing unfair or dishonest in this fact alone; editorials, columns, and commentaries are expected to take sides, so long as they do not descend to scurrility. Such anti-Goldwater comments, moreover, are nearly equaled in vigor by certain conservative columnists' attacks on Lyndon Johnson and on the integrity of businessmen supporting him.

Fall, 1964.

2. There have been isolated cases of news reporting reflecting unjustly on Goldwater. One example was a broadcast report from Bonn implying a deliberate juncture of Goldwater and Nazi remnants.

3. Such cases of injustice in news reporting, however, have been rare and exceptional. In general, Senator Goldwater's activities and utterances, like the President's, have been reported generously, honestly, and literally, in news columns and broadcasts.

4. Specific charges of unfairness, with documentation, have been few. The editors of the *Review* have systematically sought out those issuing generalized denunciations and requested them to supply examples. Thus far specific citations, aside from the handful of commonly cited examples, have been rare.

5. What the more agitated partisans have viewed as unfairness has generally stemmed from (1) the partisans' tendency to blur the distinction between news and clearly labeled comment and (2) the confusing output of the candidate himself. One need only study the record (as was ably and honestly done by Hedley W. Donovan, for example, in the September 18 *Life*) to recognize that no recent presidential candidate has equaled Mr. Goldwater in imprecise use of the English language, oversimplification, and seeming self-contradiction. One eminently balanced editor, Erwin Canham of the *Christian Science Monitor*, summed up the problem this way: "In 35 years of political reporting and editing, I have never met a public figure who is more difficult to cover fairly. You have to work very hard to protect the man against his own indiscretions . . ."

The whole spectacle suggests two conclusions:

First, the media have a responsibility to society and themselves to demand specific chapter and verse citations from those who charge "distortion," "misrepresentation," and "suppression." When any such citations are forthcoming, they should be reported and discussed publicly. Society can only gain from such discussion of specific charges.

Second, the media have a responsibility to resist intimidation, which is the admitted aim of some who denounce them. Today's political reporter must be more than a stenographer; he must use intelligence as well as shorthand. Modern journalism must of course report faithfully what a candidate says, but it must also put his words in the context of a campaign's issues, his previous positions, and the facts of record. There is abundant evidence every day that this can be done fairly and impartially.

It is just such reporting in context, when it is done well, that has been a major advance in the journalism of the last decade — and not a betrayal, as some critics would have it. This has been true of broadcast journalism as well as newspapers. To retreat from this progress out of fear of being slandered would be a loss for journalism and for society.

THE AGNEW ANALYSIS:

False Premises, Wrong Conclusions

[*On November 3, President Nixon's*] *words and policies were subjected to instant analysis and querulous criticism.*

MIKE WALLACE: The fact of the matter was that the speech was in the hands of the analysts . . . two hours ahead of time, and they all went over to be briefed on his speech by Henry Kissinger. Then they . . . listened to the speech and made their comments. So it was hardly any more instant analysis than the kind . . . that is done by overnight newspapers.

HERBERT KLEIN: I'd have to agree with that.

— *Sixty Minutes,* CBS-TV, November 25.

When President Kennedy rallied the nation in the Cuban missile crisis, his address to the people was not chewed over by a round-table of critics. . . .

Would the Vice-President believe Sander Vanocur, Ray Scherer, Frank McGee, David Schoenbrun, Roger Mudd, George Herman, Richard C. Hottelet, and Douglas Edwards? The date on that is October 22, 1962.

— Fred W. Friendly, speech, November 21.

We do know that to a man these commentators and producers live and work in the geographical and intellectual confines of Washington, D.C., or New York City. . . . We can deduce that these men read the same newspapers. They draw their political and social views from the same sources.

Winter, 1969–70.

It is true that we live in New York . . . but not a single one of the network newsmen . . . comes from New York or even from that Eastern establishment area: David Brinkley [is] from North Carolina; [Chet] Huntley from Montana; Howard K. Smith from New Orleans; Dan Rather from Houston, Tex.; Eric Sevareid from South Dakota; Harry Reasoner from Iowa . . . Frank McGee from Oklahoma. This is a cross-section of America in its own way.

— Walter Cronkite, *Sixty Minutes*

Is it not fair and relevant to question its [TV news'] concentration in the hands of a tiny, enclosed fraternity of privileged men elected by no one . . . ?

No, I was not elected. But I submit that I could not have arrived at my present post without two score of news executives having made individual and independent judgments about me along the way. And I might add that none of these men ever asked me about my personal opinions. . . . Had I ever violated their trust, I would not have been in their employ the following day.

— Elmer Lower, president, ABC News,
speech, December 10

Do they allow their biases to influence the selection and presentation of the news?

Well, we all have our prejudices, we all have our biases, we have a structural problem in writing a news story or presenting it on television as to time and length, position in the paper, position on the news broadcasts, and these things are all going to be affected by our own beliefs, of course they are. But we are professional journalists. This is the difference. We are trying . . . to be objective.

— Walter Cronkite, *Sixty Minutes*

As with other American institutions, perhaps it is time that the networks were made more responsive to the views of the nation and more responsible to the people they serve.

What does that mean, "made"? He could have said, "Perhaps it is time the networks became more responsive." . . . It seems to be an implicit threat to station owners.

— Mike Wallace, *Sixty Minutes*

I'm asking whether a form of censorship already exists when the news that 40 million Americans receive each night is determined by a handful of men responsible only to their corporate employers. . . .

Censorship must be official, or it isn't censorship. Newsmen editing news is not censorship, even if they do their jobs badly. As for official censorship, it is Mr. Agnew who raises that specter.

— Reuven Frank, president, NBC News,
memo to staff, November 26

If we are to believe a recent report of the House of Representatives Commerce Committee, then television's presentation of the violence in the streets [*of Chicago*] *worked an injustice on the reputation of the Chicago police.*

Police violence was a fact of convention week. Were the policemen who committed it a minority? It appears certain that they were — but . . . there has been no public condemnation of these violators of sound police procedures and common decency by either their commanding officers or city officials. . . .

— "The Walker Report," National Commission
on the Causes and Prevention of Violence, 1968

But a single company, in the nation's capital, holds control of the largest newspaper in Washington, D.C., and one of the four major television stations, and an all-news radio station, and one of the three major national news magazines — all grinding out the same editorial line. . . .

The Washington *Post*, *Newsweek*, WTOP-TV, and WTOP radio decidedly do not "grind out the same editorial line." . . . They disagree on many issues . . . Washington is one of the most competitive communications cities in America by any objective standards. It is one of only three cities left with three major newspapers under separate ownership, all of them first rate.

— Mrs. Katharine Graham, president,
Washington Post Company, November 20

. . . and this is not a subject that you've seen debated on the editorial pages of the Washington Post *or the New York* Times.

In fact, in an editorial on March 13, 1969, headed "Competition and Monopoly," the *Times* stated: "The constitutional guarantee of freedom of the press provides the press with no warrant for seeking exemption from the laws prohibiting monopoly. If anything, the sanctity attached to press freedom by the First Amendment makes it the special obligation of the press to fight for the broadest extension of that freedom." This is a sentiment that the New York *Times* has expressed repeatedly and still holds.

— Arthur Ochs Sulzberger, president
and publisher, New York *Times*, November 20

When three hundred Congressmen and fifty-nine Senators signed a letter endorsing the President's policy on Vietnam, it was news — and it was big news. . . . Yet the next morning the New York Times *. . . did not carry a word. Why? Why?*

The New York *Times* printed the story. Unfortunately, it failed to make the edition that reached Washington but was carried in a later edition of the *Times*. Moreover, the *Times* has given considerable attention to that story as it developed.

— Arthur Ochs Sulzberger, November 20

The day when the network commentators and even the gentlemen of the New York Times *enjoyed a form of diplomatic immunity from comment and criticism of what they said is over. . . . [The] time for blind acceptance of their opinions is past.*

Such a day, of course, had never dawned (at least) in the state whose punitive legislation against the *Times* some years ago produced the U.S. Supreme Court's controlling libel precedent.

— Harry S. Ashmore, Los Angeles *Times*

I'm raising these questions so that the American people will become aware of — and think of the implications of — the growing monopoly that involves the voices of public opinion. . . .

If it was suspected from his initial speech . . . it was confirmed by the second: the rap was not against journalists but against liberals, actual or assumed. . . . If Agnew . . . were really interested in responsible news judgment and unbiased reporting, as he professed to be, he would have had to include *Time* magazine, the Chicago *Tribune,* and a host of right-wing newspapers with broadcast properties . . . which apparently earn their exemption through sympathy with the Administration.

— *Variety,* November 26

Attorney General John N. Mitchell says the Nixon Administration has no intention of using the anti-trust laws to break up news media concentration. Questioned on a National Educational Television network program after Vice-President Agnew's "monopolization" charge, the Attorney General said such action is "the last thing in the world we have under consideration."

— *Publisher's Auxiliary,* December 13

PASSING COMMENT

The Subpoena Dilemma

It has not been an auspicious season for governmental relations with the press and broadcasting. The President, to insulate himself from regular direct questioning, has taken to holding only infrequent press conferences. "If *I* consider that the press and the public need more information than *I'm giving* through press conferences, *I'll* have more [emphasis added]," he said in December. The Vice-President, after suggesting that his November assaults on the news media were his last, has resumed the attacks and appears committed to continuing them. And, with at least tacit approval if not active cooperation from the Attorney General, newspaper, magazine, and TV journalists have been subjected to an unprecedented barrage of generalized "fishing-expedition" subpoenas of notes, still pictures, TV film "outtakes" — even travel vouchers and expense accounts.

It would strain credulity to suggest that all these occurrences were dictated from a single office in Washington. The conspiracy theory of human events is no more attractive or logical when used by the media than when employed against them or in connection with distasteful trends or unpleasant events they must report. But all these occurrences have political overtones, and all appear to reflect an attitude prevalent in the upper echelons of the Administration. That is, that there should be a new order of relationships between government and the news media; the media should be less critical of leaders of the party now in power; indeed, the media should mirror the leaders' philosophy more than they now do, and should even accede to becoming a de facto arm of the Attorney General's office.

Spring, 1970.

Nowhere is this governmental attitude more apparent than in the subpoena epidemic. Newsmen, like other citizens, for years have been called as witnesses in trials, but normally only to attest to the authenticity of published or broadcast material (unless, of course, the journalists were party to a lawsuit). Crime reporters, at their discretion, have informally exchanged selected information with police or the FBI in order to cultivate news sources. And newsmen covering civil rights activities in the South on occasion have provided evidence to authorities to prevent gross miscarriages of justice — some of them against journalists. But in these instances reporters' cooperation has been discretionary; involuntary release of notes, film, off-the-record confidences, or the identity of confidential sources has rarely been sought. Instead there has been informal bargaining and, usually, a compromise in which a subpoena, if employed at all, is narrowly drawn and merely ratifies the terms of the agreement. Even in the most critical national-security situations — wars, presidential assassinations — or in riots in Watts or Detroit or Newark, blanket compromising of journalistic privilege never has been attempted.

With the disorders accompanying the 1968 Democratic Convention in Chicago the situation began to change. Vast quantities of photos, film, and videotape were subpoened from the networks, newsmagazines, and Chicago media — by prosecutors, defendants, grand juries, and a presidential commission. Because physical and not merely "verbal" violence had occurred, because police were instrumental in escalating it, because newsmen were among the victims of police brutality, and because confidentiality of news sources was not threatened, the media tended to cooperate. NBC alone reportedly spent $150,000 to reproduce film and videotape to comply with subpoenas. The Chicago *Sun-Times* and *Daily News* photo libraries and darkrooms were immobilized for weeks to reproduce thousands of photos. No media organization was paid for the time and materials involved in complying with the subpoenas.

Then subpoenas were served on *Time*, *Life*, *Newsweek*, NBC, and four Chicago dailies for notes, files, unpublished photos, or untelevised film dealing with the SDS Weathermen; on CBS-TV and on San Francisco-based New York *Times* reporter Earl Caldwell for untelevised film and personal notes on dealings with the

Black Panthers; and on *Fortune* for notes, tape recordings, and other "raw" files in connection with an antitrust action involving industrialist James J. Ling. Attorney General John Mitchell, after several subordinates had consulted with media organizations, in February issued what columnist Jack Gould called a "mini-apology" and promised "steps to insure that, in the future, no subpoenas will be issued to the press without a good-faith attempt by the Department of Justice to reach a compromise acceptable to both parties prior to the issuance of a subpoena." Then a subpoena was served on CBS-TV newsman Mike Wallace and producer Paul Loewenwater for "outtakes" of an interview with Black Panther leader Eldridge Cleaver in Algiers, plus notes, correspondence, and expense accounts. A second subpoena also was served on Earl Caldwell. The Attorney General's "assurance" obviously was no insurance at all.

The question is not whether journalists should resist all subpoenas. Obviously they cannot, nor do they seek to. The question is whether government can and should enlist independent American newsgathering organizations as investigative collaborators in action against dissident political organizations (in this case, primarily the SDS and Black Panthers) — no matter how abhorrent to most Americans the doctrines and tactics of such organizations may be; whether American journalism can hope to fulfill its First Amendment mission if newsmen are suspected of being akin to Soviet citizens who are at once journalists-spies-informers; indeed, whether American law enforcement agencies, which are the appropriate employers of undercover men, have reached such a low state of efficiency that they cannot maintain their own surveillance of potentially dangerous organizations.

To be free, the press and broadcasting must be able to gather as well as disseminate information. Privilege in editorial relationships and confidentiality of sources are crucial to that function. As Max Frankel explained in the February 6 New York *Times:*

> In private dealings with persons who figure in the news, reporters obtain not only on-the-record comments but also confidential judgments and facts that they then use to appraise the accuracy and meaning of other men's words and deeds. Without that access and

without such confidential relationships, must important information would have to be gathered by remote means and much could never be subjected to cross-examination. Politicians who weigh their words, officials who fear their superiors, citizens who fear persecution or prosecution would refuse to talk with reporters or admit them to their circles if they felt that confidences would be betrayed at the behest of the Government.

Sweden, recognizing this, long has had a national law that not only guarantees journalistic confidentiality but requires it — any newsman who reveals a confidential source can be prosecuted. More than a dozen states in our country also guarantee journalistic confidentiality. If bills recently introduced are passed, the federal government and several other states will provide similar guarantees. For now, however, the news media face a dilemma: if they comply with blanket, "fishing expedition" subpoenas, they break faith with confidential sources and undermine credibility among already hostile segments of the community, groups who must have access to the media and about whom the public must have information. If they refuse to comply, in the absence of any clear statutory protection they hand the Administration another weapon that can be used to pummel at least some media organizations into docility.

In this situation the proper strategy seems to be the one the media appear to have adopted: to foster maximum publicity about government tactics, giving ground only grudgingly while trying to muster the understanding and support of the bar, civil liberties groups, and congressmen.

INCIDENT AT SAN JOSE

Mel Wax

San Jose best can be described as the Los Angeles of Northern California. It is a sprawling, fast-growing, characterless city, with a polyglot population of whites, blacks, and Chicanos. Its civic auditorium, built in 1934, is vaguely Spanish in appearance, with yellow stucco on the outside and red Spanish tiles on the roof. Part of the building is one story high; part, two stories. Behind it, to the north, is a parking lot some hundred yards square. There, Americans learned from their print and broadcast media the weekend before last November's national election, the President of the United States and his official party were violently attacked by a rock-throwing mob, following an Oct. 29 political rally for Republican Senator George Murphy.

Time said [Nov. 9]: "Nixon emerged into the darkness to confront several thousand hostile demonstrators. . . . The eggs began to fly even before the motorcade moved out to run the gauntlet between two walls of unfriendly citizens. Dozens of rocks were thrown, some the size of a potato. They bounced off the President's well armored car, and they smashed windows in the press and staff buses trailing behind. . . ."

Newsweek's report of the incident said: "A roiling, cursing crowd of them, 2,000 strong, laid siege to the San Jose, Calif., municipal auditorium while the President was inside speaking, met him coming out, nearly struck him with a stone, and forced his car and his motorcade to run a gauntlet of eggs, rocks, and chunks of glass the size of baseballs."

Larry Stammer wrote in the San Jose *News* [Oct. 30]: "A surg-

---

Winter, 1970–71. Mel Wax, a Nieman Fellow, is anchorman/editor of *Newsroom*, the Peabody Award–winning news program on public TV station KQED, San Francisco.

ing mob of rock-throwing, obscenity-chanting radicals, representing what President Nixon decried as 'the worst in America,' attacked the Presidential motorcade here Thursday in the most violent outburst against Nixon since his election."

Earl Behrens, political editor of the San Francisco *Chronicle*, wrote: "A crowd of angry demonstrators threw rocks, eggs, and bottles at President Nixon's limousine and entourage last night as he left a spirited political rally in San Jose."

This was the general tenor of the reporting that night.

The President himself, flying to San Clemente, issued a statement from Air Force One saying, in part, "the stoning at San Jose is an example of the viciousness of the lawless elements in our society." Senator Murphy said, "This was as vicious a crowd as I've ever seen in my life."

The next day in the San Jose *Mercury* Police Chief Ray Blackmore was quoted by reporter Jim Larimore as saying that the attack was "without question our most serious confrontation with militants and radicals in San Jose." Walter Cronkite reported the "stoning" of the presidential party.

And yet, despite heavy photo coverage by White House press traveling with the President, by the California press traveling with Murphy and Governor Reagan, and by the local press covering a presidential appearance, nobody came up with a picture of anybody throwing a rock. And for all the supposed violence in the presence of some 428 police, highway patrolmen, and Secret Service agents, there were only four arrests. Three were on misdemeanor counts; one was a felony charge for an attack on a police officer by a member of the Peace and Freedom Party — a charge that later was reduced to a misdemeanor. Nobody was charged with attacking the President or his motorcade.

One policeman broke his finger. Some of the crowd was maced. But there is no record of anybody being hit with a rock, bottle, or other weapon.

Steve Lighthill of CBS, among other network cameramen at the scene, was bawled out by superiors because he had no film of the "riot." He was there. He said there was no riot.

Mark Gladstone, a stringer for *Time*, couldn't believe the reports he had seen in the press. (This was before *Time*, in New

York, gave them credence.) When he left the San Jose Civic Auditorium with the President he saw two projectiles in the air; they looked to him "like wadded up pieces of paper."

By Tuesday of the following week, even Police Chief Blackmore had changed his tune. Associated Press, in a dispatch from San Jose, quoted him as saying, "A few rocks were thrown. There was a verbal attack. That was the so-called violence." Blackmore, who was in the car behind the President's, said his car was not hit and he personally did not see anything hit the President's car.

What did happen in San Jose? Tom DeVries, who covered the presidential visit for *Newsroom*, had telephoned during the program to say that demonstrators there were a peaceful, happy, cheerful crowd. There was no violence. The next morning, despite the big stories everywhere, DeVries said, "It didn't happen." Then he told his version of what he thought had happened.

DeVries, a former Chicago *Sun-Times* staff member, is an honest, able, sensitive, first-class reporter, and I trust him. I told him to go after the story; to get all the attribution he could; to find out what others who were there had to say.

The parking lot where the incidents took place is bordered on the east and west sides by chest-high cinder-block fences broken only by two traffic control posts operated by AMPCO Auto Parks; and on the north side by an open fence of metal stakes and wire, fronting on Park Avenue. Normally there is no exit to Park Avenue, but at the Secret Service's request an exit was created there. Two stakes were pulled out, the wire was cut, and asphalt was snuggled between the sidewalk curb and the roadway so cars and buses wouldn't jolt when they bumped down to the street.

Park Avenue was one of three possible exits from the rear of the auditorium. This improvised northern route was the one eventually chosen. A Marine Corps helicopter hovering overhead also was available for an airborne getaway, if the Secret Service thought the President's life would be endangered by more conventional transport. Because the parking lot is blacktopped, rocks or other missiles would have to be imported.

That there was a demonstration in San Jose should have come as no surprise to anybody. Two hours before Nixon arrived there was a rally at San Jose State College, seven blocks from the auditorium. The *Stanford Daily*, in nearby Palo Alto, quoted Jane Franklin of the Bay Area Revolutionary Union as having said the day before the rally: "A riot will begin at 5:30 at Seventh and San Carlos Streets in San Jose." Demonstrators had asked for a parade permit. (It was not granted, but they paraded, anyhow.)

On *Newsroom* the night after the San Jose incident DeVries said in part:

> It was an astoundingly mixed group. . . . Among them were Head Start parents. . . . There were some for "Free Angela Davis." There were unemployed engineers with long, very wordy signs about how funds should be increased for the Federal Department of Transportation. . . .
>
> I ran into some shipfitters and machinists — hardhats we sometimes call them — who don't have jobs, and who wanted "Paychecks, Not Welfare." And there was a "Cool It Squad," sponsored by Congressional Candidate Stuart McLean (a Democrat), whose incumbent opponent was inside basking with the President. And, of course, there were those who wanted no SST; those who wanted clean air or water; and those who think that the President isn't ending the war fast enough, or, maybe, at all.

When Nixon arrived at the auditorium, some twenty minutes early, he smiled and waved at the crowd. The people booed, or cheered, according to their politics. There was no violence, all agree. The President sat with Murphy, Reagan, and a host of local politicians in the office of Nick Lickwar, the civic auditorium manager. He was relaxed, smiling. He could hear the demonstrators outside, but they didn't seem uppermost in his mind. "He told me San Jose State used to beat Whittier College (Nixon's alma mater) all the time," Lickwar recalled. "He said it was his first time in the auditorium, and he talked about how much San Jose has grown."

The crowd inside was almost entirely pro-Nixon. Even the usual campaign hecklers seemed to be missing. Nixon reminded his audience that they were outside. "The Secret Service told me there are 900 demonstrators outside the hall, shouting hatred for the United States, and obscenities," he said. "But I've got news for them. Those violent few, those radical few, are not the majority of young America, and they're not going to be the leaders of the future."

Following the speech, the President was supposed to make an appearance in two rooms in the building where he had been seen on closed-circuit TV. But he passed that up and stepped outside to the parking lot, where the demonstrators were.

San Jose Police Captain Lewis Hallers said the Secret Service had approved letting demonstrators into the northern half of the parking lot. Leroy Aarons of the Washington *Post* quoted Captain Haller as saying: "As long as we could protect it, and the President was looking for votes, they felt people should be allowed to congregate in the lot." Haller added: "The President was advised that there were these people out here, and they were screaming and yelling." Many people in the crowd, to get a better look at the President, climbed on the roofs and hoods of cars parked in the lot. Some roofs caved in. Some tires were slashed. Some radio antennas and windshield wipers were broken.

Nixon emerged casually. He seemed to be in no hurry to get away. According to Lickwar, who was with him at the time, somebody threw an egg. It spattered on the pants leg of a Secret Service man. "I didn't see anything else thrown," Lickwar said, "but of course it was hard to see. It was dark, and the lights we had set up in the parking lot weren't very bright." Again, there were both cheers and boos. There was no violence, then.

DeVries reported:

Pete Lauffer, who's a reporter for KSAN here in San Francisco, was with the President when he came out of the hall, and he was chatting, Lauffer told me, about football in California. Glancing at the shouting crowd, Nixon — Lauffer told me — climbed on the hood of his limousine and held his arms up in the victory, or peace sign — "taunting his critics," as Syd Kossen said this afternoon in the [San Francisco] *Examiner*. Marty Schramm, White House Correspondent for *Newsday*, who was standing there, heard the President say: "That's what they hate to see."

Lauffer of KSAN told me that "the vibes were bad," and that one egg hit a Presidential bodyguard. Most reporters working outside in the crowd, including myself, saw nothing. I did see the local police run a wedge of officers, followed by two-wheeled motorcycles, through the crowd to clear a corridor for the motorcade. And I saw people who were slow, maced. It was really the only time during that period when the caravan corridor was being cleared that I felt anything like the surge you get in a crowd, the kind of excitement you get when something has happened. The only time, also, I saw it in the faces or in the actions of the police.

The President paused to chat with newsmen for a few minutes before getting into his bulletproof limousine with Reagan and Murphy. All three then flashed the V-sign from inside the car.

Police Chief Blackmore gave a prearranged signal. A double file of tactical squad police, using mace and sticks on laggards, forced open a path to the exit on Park Avenue. Two police motorcycles and four squad cars gunned through the demonstrators in the path opened by the tactical squad. The motorcade stopped once when a Secret Service man, lunging for a car, missed and fell, sprawling flat on the parking lot pavement. He narrowly escaped being run over by a police car.

Earl Behrens, the San Francisco *Chronicle*'s political editor, was four cars behind the President's. He bruised his knee when the procession jammed to a stop. With him were reporter Carol Kilpatrick and wire service men from AP and UPI. Behrens said he saw people throw rocks, and a young man swinging a heavy belt at the cars. "But our car was not hit," Behrens said.

Haller, who was in charge of "outside security" for the San Jose Police, recalled seeing a "hail of missiles." He said they consisted of "windshield wipers torn from parked cars, some broken glass, a gear shift lever, and eggs." No rocks. Reagan said so many rocks hit the presidential car "it was like being inside a drum." "They must have been at least the size of half a brick by the sound they made," Senator Murphy added.

DeVries quoted a number of other eyewitnesses. One was Walter Reynolds, an employee of the Stanford University Medical Center: "I cannot reconcile these reports — those in the press today, these reports of riot, rocks, and damage — with what I saw. The remarkable thing I saw was absolutely nothing. Nobody was talking. There was no excitement."

DeVries said of NBC reporter Roy Cullin: "I saw him this morning and asked him if he'd seen rocks or bottles or any kind of stuff thrown. He just looked at me and shook his head and said, 'Nothing.' "

Of Mike Mills, a reporter for KRON-TV, NBC outlet in San Francisco: "He, like the rest of the reporters that were there with film crews, got no film of the rocks and the bottles and the eggs. He said this afternoon: 'That's because there weren't any.' "

How, then, if nothing happened, did windows get broken on two press buses? DeVries explained: "Those who did see or rather probably feel things thrown were those apparently in the White House press bus, and the police in San Jose. The White House press bus had several (four) windows broken, and the people who were on that bus were very interested and very excited, I think, by what happened. . . ."

Reporters on the press buses said the brunt of the "attack" took place as they came off the sidewalk and made the right turn on Park Avenue heading for San Jose's municipal airport. No police were there. Blackmore told the Grand Jury: "The reason this block was not covered by police officers was that it was the alternate route for the motorcade to take, and was chosen by the Secret Service. We were not instructed to put men there, nor in any way was it indicated that this would be the exit the President was to take. Therefore the area was not policed."

DeVries continued:

I called down to San Clemente this afternoon and talked to Henry Hubbard, who's with the traveling party that's been accompanying the President on this campaign tour. Hubbard works for *Newsweek* magazine. He told me that something like a "volley of rocks" hit the bus. They couldn't see anything, but they could hear the banging as they came against the side.

That's the White House press bus, a big chartered Greyhound that came out and, incidentally, had on the side of it a huge sign with perhaps two-foot-high letters that said: WHITE HOUSE PRESS. And it was followed by a bus that said PRESIDENT'S GUESTS, also in large letters. Those are the two buses . . . in which people say something hit them. Hubbard told me that the volley of rocks hit the side of the bus just as it turned into that corridor that had been cleared moments before for the President and the motorcade by those motorcycles. He said the volley lasted a few seconds, but the crowd — in Hubbard's opinion — was a very mean one. . . .

After the cars left, I wandered around the parking lot. . . . I saw nothing on the ground — no broken eggs, no rocks, no bricks. . . . Nothing like that.

DeVries's story raised a lot of questions. Others in the press began to take a second look. The New York *Times* sent Robert E. Semple, Jr., and Steven V. Roberts, head of its Los Angeles bureau, and the Washington *Post* dispatched Leroy F. Aarons. Andy Jokelson recapitulated for the Oakland *Tribune* a week later. *Time*'s San Francisco bureau sent a reporter to reconstruct the event. He filed a report, at this writing not yet published.

Indeed, others apparently had second thoughts, even while the story was building. Associated Press had been first with reports of violence. An AP memorandum said:

When the first stone was thrown at President Nixon's motorcade, AP members had a bulletin almost immediately. Just a few minutes later came a detail-rich 300-word add. The super-quick work was by AP White House staffer Frank Cormier, who scored a beat of almost ten minutes. Cormier, in a telephone car four vehicles behind Nixon's limousine, sensed the impending trouble and opened a phone circuit to the Los Angeles bureau, talking with Night Superintendent Don Morine. . . .

A crowd shouting "two, four, six, eight [sic] we don't want your ----ing war," threw eggs and rocks the size of potatoes as Nixon's motorcade left the rally. The rocks bounced off Nixon's bulletproof limousine and smashed windows of the press cars and staff buses trailing behind. Cormier's car was hit by several missiles that sounded like cannon balls. Nothing stopped his dictation, though.

William German, executive news editor of the San Francisco *Chronicle*, was less enthusiastic about the reports he was getting off the wires. His photographer at the scene said he didn't see anything untoward. Behrens was in the motorcade. The New York *Times* Service story didn't mention anything being thrown at the motorcade until far down in the report. It didn't read like a riot report.

"The wire reports were confusing," German said. "We toned them down, and took the middle road. Who saw what was never really made clear. It was a case where attribution was needed. Frankly, I wished to hell I knew more about it. I felt a little naked. . . . It was very strange. With all the coverage a presidential appearance gets, it was strange there were no immediate eyewitnesses."

Nonetheless the general tendency was to go along with the prevailing and most sensational story. The morning after the incident, for example, the Ridder papers' San Jose *Mercury* carried the headline: NIXON BLASTS TUNNEY IN SAN JOSE SPEECH. Below the fold on page 1 there was a three-column head: YOUNG MILITANTS HURL EPITHETS AT PRESIDENT. And an overline: VIOLENCE MARS RALLY. But the emphasis was on verbal violence.

That evening, the Ridders' San Jose *News* carried a banner line: S.J. OUTBURST THE "WORST" . . . NIXON MOB VIOLENCE, and a deck: ROCKS, BOTTLES THROWN. The next morning the *Mercury* caught up. The lead story by political editor Harry Farrell began: "A shockwave jarred the nation's conscience Friday, after Thursday night's stoning of the presidential party — an act which added San Jose to the gazetteer of infamous American violence sites."

At this writing no reporter or anyone in the crowd has come forth who actually saw the President's car being hit by anything. *Newsweek*'s Hubbard said he saw evidence of a splattered egg on the car later at the airport. The next week at San Clemente the Secret Service showed some newsmen the limousine. They found, according to Oakland *Tribune* reporter Andy Jokelson, "at least a dozen fresh chips in the car's paint, at least two chips in the glass, and two small dents." Presumably the damage occurred at San Jose.

The Secret Service issued a statement saying damage to the car "could only have been done by rocks or other hard objects." Arthur Godfrey, a Secret Service agent riding in the President's car, estimated it had been hit ten times. General manager Don Wickham and operational manager Ken Lampton of AMPCO Auto Parks told reporter Jokelson that among the debris were a few dozen rocks, soft drink cans, many sticks — such as those used to support placards — ten to twenty bottles, a metal post, broken glass, and "at least two bricks." Between 60 and 70 percent of the debris was said to be in the general area where the motorcade passed.

Their statement was challenged by John P. Adams, a twenty-one-year-old AMPCO employee who helped clean up the lot that night. "There wasn't that much junk around," Adams said. Chief Blackmore said police picking up Thursday night found only "one bottle and a few rocks."

Some reporters thought the crowd in the parking lot might have been as high as two thousand. Most press accounts went along with the "nine hundred" figure the President cited when he referred to the demonstrators during his speech. Western Greyhound Lines said six windows — two on one bus, and four on another — were broken. So it went.

Our mail on the incident was significant. Many viewers sent us clippings of newspaper stories describing the "riot." (Testimony to credibility of the print medium.) Some echoed the sentiments of the viewer who complained: "The report given by Mr. Tom DeVries was a discredit to *Newsroom*. He became an apologist for the actions of a few people who were present that did not wish to protest peacefully."

Roughly half the mail was complimentary:

— Hooray for Tom DeVries. He was there, and he told it like it was. We were there, too, and we were astounded at today's press reports — on national TV — who did not tell it like it was.

— The furor and panic created by the media probably have not been matched since the Orson Welles radio account of the invasion of the man from Mars.

— It came as something of a shock to realize and have to admit that my TV screen was as black as the bottom of a skillet and that about all I could recall seeing was a man stand up above the crowd with raised arms — clearly making the V sign with both hands, a perfect target.

Ron Ziegler, the President's press secretary issued the following statement from San Clemente on election day:

Following the San Jose incident there, of course, has been a lot of discussion and conjecture about it. I think everyone agrees it was an unfortunate affair. As the President said, this violent act by a few should not reflect on San Jose, nor should it reflect on the capabilities of the San Jose Police force.

However, one thing, unfortunately, should be stated clearly, and this is the assessment of those riding in the presidential car and in the presidential motorcade. That is that the President's car and the motorcade came under a barrage of rocks as it left the San Jose Auditorium. It should be further said that reporters from various news organizations inspected the presidential limousine and noted chips in the roof glass and other parts of the car.

I give these comments, not to make specific issue with all of those who are discussing the San Jose incident, but simply to state two things — that published and broadcast reports of the incident were in no way exaggerated. It was a serious and unfortunate incident that I personally would hope never would occur again around the President of the United States and those accompanying him.

The same day, Police Chief Blackmore said, "The barrage on President Nixon was verbal. It was not physical. This so-called riot has been exaggerated."

Whatever the truth of the opposing views, it was not a proud day for the presidency, for the police, or, unhappily, for the press.

In broadcasting, the most humorous by-product long has been the spontaneous slip of the tongue; in print journalism, the typographical error, transposed line, or other inadvertency that can surprise an editor as thoroughly as it can a reader. Like the news and features of which they are a part, these minor monuments to serendipity usually perish with each calendar page's turn. The inside back cover of each *Columbia Journalism Review*, however, is devoted to preserving at least a sampling of the more worthy printed mutations brought to the editors' attention. Titled "the lower case," the department may not "always leave 'em laughing," but it unfailingly keeps us smiling.

—The editors

Segregated advertising

This ad appeared in the Michigan Education Journal for April 1, 1964:

It also appeared in the Alabama School Journal, but apparently the fourth passenger was moved to the back of the bus:

Double threat

UPI moved the following on August 3, 1964:

> WASHINGTON, AUG. 3 (UPI)--PRESIDENT JOHNSON SAID TODAY HE HAS ORDERED THE NAVY TO DOUBLE ITS DESTROYER FORCE OFF NORTH VIET NAM AND TO PROVIDE THE VESSELS WITH SUFFICIENT AIR COVER TO DESTROY ANY ATTACKING FORCE.

> HE SAID A DESTROYER WOULD BE ADDED TO THE ONE ALREADY ON PATROL, THUS DOUBLING THE FORCE.

Don't mention it

Whose face was reddest? The copy reader who failed to delete the parenthetical comment, the reporter who couldn't spell, or the managers whose policies were put in an embarrassing light? The clipping is from the next-to-last paragraph of a story printed in the Sacramento Union on June 18, 1964:

> Mrs. Brantner, whose Indian name means "The Bride of the God of Big Lagoon," will bring with her authentic Indian costumes, some weighing over 30 pounds, for display in a store window. (Rhodes but their not advertisers.) There will also be Indian paintings on display.

Short count

What's a synonym for visiting civil-rights workers? A headline writer at Mississippi's Jackson Clarion-Ledger offered this answer on July 31, 1964:

> **Invaders Tell Story To Students**
>
> UNIVERSITY — A male and a female COFO worker from

The News bites

Here is the lead of a story (which also supplied the page-one banner) in the New York Daily News for October 5:

> **In the view of hundreds of persons who stood by, a 28-year-old man was repeatedly stabbed yesterday afternoon by a burly Negro who had tried to force his attentions on the victim's attractive red-haired wife in Times Square.**

At no point was the story attributed to either the police or the victim or his wife; the News offered it as pure fact. Came the dawn of October 6, and it was a new story:

> Mrs. Sandra Zaia, 24, an attractive redhead, was charged last night with obstructing justice by telling cops that a burly Negro masher had stabbed her husband in Times Square Sunday afternoon. Before being booked, she admitted that the assailant was an ex-boy friend but refused to identify him, police reported. the hospital that she gave at the

Have you seen this man?

An early edition of The New York Times of August 24 carried this story with its surprising photo. The same picture appeared in later editions with correct story and head, "City of Edinburgh Gives Menuhin a High Honor"

Forgetful Thief Leaves Photo of Himself Behind

Bender

Yehudi Menuhin

Special to The New York Times

NORWALK, Conn., Aug. 23—Local police who are seeking a camera thief have more than routine clues to go on. They have an excellent likeness of the culprit himself.

Richard Harty, a clerk in the Hilgert & Gough photography store, was demonstrating a Polaroid camera to a prospective buyer and gave him a demonstration of its capability. The man decided on a more expensive model valued at about $200 and asked that it be wrapped.

When Mr. Harty returned from a back room with wrapping paper, the man said he had changed his mind and left. A few minutes later the clerk noticed that a camera was missing from a display rack and called the police.

Mr. Harty was not only able to give them the model, number of the stolen camera, but presented the investigating officers with a sharp picture of the thief himself.

Crystal-ball reporting

When two girls disappeared from the University of Texas in July, The Associated Press sent out a story from Austin saying that an unnamed "psychic" from Dallas had offered her visions to Austin police. The story produced the following headlines in The Houston Post and the Houston Chronicle on July 24:

Seer Says Co-Eds To Be Found Soon

Tells Vision of 3 Men in Girls' Car

Psychic Predicts Finding UT Co-eds

On the next day, The Houston Post went the AP one better by digging up a "mystic" of its own in Miami:

2 Men Abducted Co-eds, Mystic Says

The girls were found murdered, and the assortment of psychics contributed neither to the finding of the bodies nor the solution. Their only function, it turned out, had been to supply banner headlines on slow days.

Sail on

There was only a shade of difference between the report of Robert Manry's Atlantic crossing in Time (left) of August 27, and Newsweek (right) of August 30:

> Manry napped during the day and sailed at night so that he could signal away ships that might otherwise have run him down in the dark.

> Throughout all this, Manry sailed on, putting out a sea anchor each night so that he could sleep and during the day keeping a sharp eye out for big ships that might run him down.

Ghost town?

An item in Life's "Washington Report," July 23, not only carried a non-existent dateline, but misspelled the former name of Santo Domingo:

> **A STILL ELUSIVE DOMINICAN PEACE**
>
> CUIDAD TRUJILLO
>
> From recent sounds out of Washington one might conclude that a Do-

Next question?

Is no question too difficult—no answer too blunt for Parade magazine's "Personality Parade"? In the August 15 issue, it tackled this one:

> **Q.** ***What is the basis of the feud between Lyndon Johnson and Bobby Kennedy? —S.T. Hunt, Ft. Worth, Tex.***
>
> **A.** Their personalities clash.

Headlines anonymous

Houston Chronicle, June 26, 1967 (they meant Rockefeller):

Many Governors Still for Roosevelt

West Yellowstone, Mont. (UPI) — The two who talked about presidential nomination ... Gov. Nelson ... Rockefeller's Rockefeller ...

Publisher's Auxiliary, July 1 (about time):

Dailies Get Ready For 20th Century

RICHMOND, Va.—The daily ...rooms are changing along wit...

Columbus Citizen-Journal, July 6 (one letter missing from Congo):

Paratroops Seize 2 Cong Airports

St. Paul Pioneer Press, July 7, 1967.

It Happened Last Night — St. Paul Pioneer Press, Fri., July 7, '67

Sophia, Audrey Hepburn Expecting

Speaking of accuracy

As if the Columbia Journalism Review offices were not just four floors from the American Press Institute, the following appeared in the Review's spring issue. Page 41:

Bows

¶ To J. Montgomery Curtis as he leaves the executive directorship of the American Press Institute at Columbia to join the Knight Newspapers and to his former associate and able successor, Walter Everett. Their pragmatic guidance of newspapermen's ... has ... make API ... effe...

Same issue, back cover:

...day 4,648 stu...s in John...on High School pursued their studies intelligently and industriously. Meanwhile, one of their classmates killed the principal. — *Montgomery J. Curtis, former executive director of the A...*

Overlappers

Herblock's cartoon for The Washington Post (left) of July 11 and Conrad's for the Los Angeles Times of July 12:

"Some of You May Be Wondering How This Summit Was Reached"

Arab Summit Conference

Headlines (and miscellaneous captions) anonymous

The Washington Post, October 20, 1957 (corrected in final edition)

Photos by AP and UPI

Price Daniel faces newsmen on the Independence: Govs. Godwin, Virginia, and Winthrop Rockefeller, Arkansas, chat, as do Maryland's Agnew and New York's Rockefeller . . . and latter's wife enjoys the sea breeze.

Scoop from St. Louis Globe-Democrat, October 19, 1967

LANDS ON PLANET

Soviet Spacecraft Finds No Human Life on Venus

Minneapolis Star, October 3, 1967 (typo for 135):

STILL IN INSTITUTION

Deaf-Mute, Believed Retarded, Has 35 IQ

The Tampa Tribune, August 18, 1967

School Boss Says Kirk Sewed 'Crop of Shame'

The Houston Post, September 27, 1967 (woman referred to is Louise Day Hicks, opponent of Negro pupil-busing):

Negro Woman Wins Boston Primary Race

From the Seattle Post-Intelligencer, July 28, 1967:

Obituaries

Fri., July 28, 1967

Many persons died this week in and near Seattle. And that accounts for the large number of obituaries appearing in this morning's Post-Intelligencer.

Look-alikes

John Kenneth Galbraith, on page 69 of The New York Times of November 8, 1967, had a twin appear on page 70 (right).

John Kenneth Galbraith

Paine, Webber Admits New General Partner

Fabian Bachrach

Samuel A. Gay

The admission of Samuel A. Gay as a general partner

Composing-room humor?

The first babies of 1968 appeared in The Seattle Times of January 1 next to the line identifying the edition:

NIGHT SPORTS FINAL

Mrs. Robert Douglas smiled at her infant son, Robert Harry Palmer Douglas 3rd, the first baby reported born in Seattle in 1968.

Mrs. Manuel del Villar held her first child, a boy, the second infant born in the Seattle area on New Year's Day.

Typography anonymous

Minneapolis Star, October 3, 1967 (the intended word was contraceptive):

Contractive Beer Suggested

ADDITIVE CALLED POSSIBLE

San Francisco Examiner, August 24, 1967:

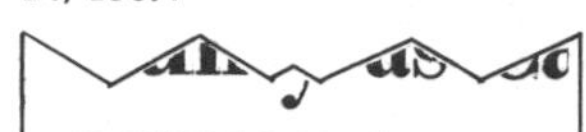
BEVERLY HILLS — (UPI) — Joey Gibson, 21, whose nude, fold-out photograph graced the June issue of Playboy magazine, has been convinced of prostitution.

The attorney for the plati-

The Cincinnati Enquirer, December 13, 1967:

Viola! UC Students 'Create' A Paris Cafe

Audience of one: Boston Globe, January 14, 1968

N.E. Newsman to Hear Sen. McCarthy Jan. 25

AP Wirephoto

WHEN COMPETING CANDIDATES GET TOGETHER, YOU CAN BET ON A HANDSHAKING SESSION

From left at California delegation caucus at Dem convention are Vice President Hubert Humphrey, Minnesota's Sen. Eugene McCarthy, South Dakota's Sen. George McGovern. The man behind McGovern wasn't identified.

Retouchers anonymous

The photo at left ran in The Denver Post on August 27, 1968. The caption refers to a man between Senators McCarthy and McGovern, but he has been wiped out by the retoucher—all but his disembodied right hand

Representative James Corman, Democratic candidate for Congress in California's 22nd District, sent the photo above to The Van Nuys News. Corman appears third from the right in a check presentation for International Orphans, Inc.

But when the News printed the photograph on September 8, 1968, Corman was missing from the line-up, despite his precaution of not standing at the end of the line. (The News was backing his opponent; Corman won the election.)

Headlines anonymous

Ambiguity in the Fall River, Massachusetts, Herald-News, March 20, 1969

Police Patrol Reading After Riots

Emphasis in the Spokane Daily Chronicle, January 11, 27, and 28, 1969

Snow Siege Due to Tighten Grip

Snow Tightening Grip on Region

Winter's Snowy Grip Tightening

Overstatement in the Hollywood, California, Citizen-News (February 10, 1969). Head refers to principals in the Clay Shaw conspiracy trial in New Orleans

PARTY BY KILLERS PROBED

Anachronism in The Arizona Republic, Phoenix, January 15, 1969, where the headline writer chose to ignore the Braves' two moves, to Milwaukee in the 1950's and to Atlanta

Glendale to seek Boston Braves training pact

Tried and true

Paragraphs from the Des Moines Register account of the state girls' basketball tournament, March 17, 1968, and March 15, 1969

ly, 113-107, in overtime.

If the madcap struggle between the state's two top-ranked teams wasn't the best title game in history, it will do until someone figures out a better one.

It was the first loss in 30

morial Auditorium.

If it wasn't the biggest surprise in the history of this tournament, it will do until someone comes up with a better one.

The Trojanettes, fired by a 56-

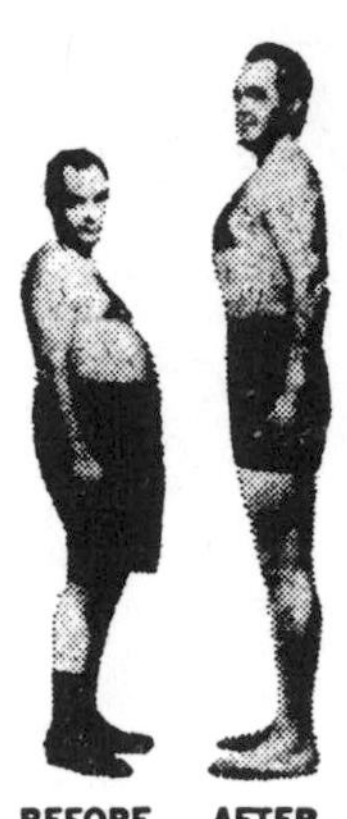

Miracle department

An ad for a health club in The Washington Post for March 18, 1969, showed these two figures. If the taller is estimated at six feet, the health-club treatment added one foot to his height

Daughter Calls on Truman; She Says He's in Good Shape

KANSAS CITY, Feb. 24 (AP) —Former President Harry S. Truman's daughter, Mrs. Clifton Daniels, visited her 84-year-old father today for the first time since he had entered a hospital here with intestinal flu.

She told newsmen later that she had spent an hour with her father after arriving by plane from Little Rock, Ark.

Her father, she said, is fretting to return home to nearby Independence. In fact, she said, when he learned she was to arrive he let it be known he would like to go to the airport to meet her. His doctors refused.

Mrs. Daniels said that her father was in good condition. She came only because she theater appearance in Little Rock.

The sure touch

Nothing is surer than errors in stories about a newspaper's own brass. Thus, The New York Times for February 25, 1969, added a terminal "s" to the name in a story on the managing editor's wife

Young Men Rise in Publisher Ranks

BILL D. MOYERS

At 36, publisher of *Newsday*, Long Island, N.Y., Mr. Moyers started his career in journalism as a reporter for the *Marshall* (Tex.) *News Messenger* in 1949 while a student in high school. He became assistant news editor of KTBC, the Austin radio, tv station owned by Mrs. Lyndon B. Johnson, while a student at the University of Texas. He served in several capacities as assistant to Lyndon Johnson when Mr. Johnson was Senator, Vice-President and President. He was named President Johnson's press secretary in 1965 and resigned from this post in 1966 to become publisher of *Newsday*.

MARSHALL FIELD

At 28, publisher of the *Chicago Sun-Times* and *Daily News*, Mr. Field is the son of the late Marshall Field IV, who was publisher of the papers at the time of his death in 1965. The publisher title was not used until Mr. Field was named to the post last Oct. 1. Mr. Field worked briefly in the editorial department of the *Boston Globe* while a student at Harvard, and after graduation worked for the old *New York Herald-Tribune*. After the death of his father he began a training program with Field Enterprises Inc. and worked in each of the company's 23 divisions and subsidiaries. He was elected senior vp in 1968.

ARTHUR OCHS SULZBERGER

At 44, president and publisher of the *New York Times*, Mr. Sulzberger was named to the post in 1963 at the age of 37 by his father, Arthur Hays Sulzberger, chairman of the *Times*. Arthur (Punch) started his journalistic career as a cub reporter for the *Times* in 1952. He worked on the foreign news desk and as a foreign correspondent until he became assistant to the publisher in 1955. In 1957, he was appointed assistant treasurer, a post he held until named to the top position.

GEORGE RANDOLPH HEARST JR.

At 43, publisher of the *Los Angeles Herald-Examiner*, Mr. Hearst is a grandson of William Randolph Hearst. He started his journalistic career in 1948 on the staff of the old *Los Angeles Examiner*. From 1954 to 1956 he served as assistant to the business manager of the *San Francisco Examiner*. He joined the old *Herald-Express* in 1956 as assistant business manager, and was named business manager in 1957. He succeeded his uncle, David W. Hearst, as publisher of the *Herald-Examiner* in 1960 at the age of 33, when David became vp and director of Hearst Corp.

OTIS CHANDLER

At 43, senior vp, Times Mirror Co., publisher of the *Los Angeles Times*, and vice-chairman of the board. Mr. Chandler joined the Times Mirror Co. in 1963 and moved from department to department as an apprentice at the *Times* and *Mirror-News*. He became assistant to the president of the *Mirror-News* in 1957 and marketing manager of the *Times* in 1959. He became publisher of the *Times* in 1960, at 33, when his father, Norman, left the post to devote himself to expanding the parent organization.

THOMAS V. H. VAIL

At 44, editor and publisher of the *Cleveland Plain Dealer*. Mr. Vail, son of Herman L. Vail, president of Forest City Publishing Co., joined the old *Cleveland News*, also published by Forest City, in 1949 as a reporter. He became political editor in 1953 and remained in that post until he joined the *Plain Dealer* in 1957. He became a vp in 1961. He has been on the board of directors of the Bureau of Advertising, American Newspaper Publishers Assn., and a member of Sigma Delta Chi.

PETER B. CLARK

At 42, chief executive officer of the Evening News Assn. and publisher of the *Detroit News*. Mr. Clark, a great grandson of James E. Scripps, founder of the *News*, joined the parent company in 1960, became a vp in 1961, and in 1963, at age 35, was named to his present post. Member: American Newspaper Publishers Assn., American Society of Newspaper Editors, and the Adcraft Club of Detroit.

JOHN COWLES JR.

At 41, president and chief executive officer of the Minneapolis Star & Tribune Co., a post he succeeded his father in at the age of 39, in 1968. Mr. Cowles joined the company in 1953, was named a vp in 1957, and became editor of the *Minneapolis Star* and *Tribune* in 1961. He is a member of the American Society of Newspaper Editors and Sigma Delta Chi.

WILLIAM P. HOBBY JR.

At 38, president of the Houston Post Co. and executive editor of the *Houston Post*. Mr. Hobby started with the paper in 1957 as assistant secretary-treasurer. He became associate editor in 1959, managing editor in 1960 and exec vp in 1963. He was elected to his present post in 1965, succeeding his mother, Oveta Culp Hobby, in the post of president at that time. He is a member of the American Society of Newspaper Editors.

So you want to be a publisher?

If so, this *Advertising Age* feature (April 20) suggests, fortune is most apt to smile on you if you are the offspring of a publisher.

Women's Liberation really is broad-based

—Chicago *Sun-Times,* May 21.

Army Tries a New Idea

—Washington *Post,* June 7.

Mayor Assails 'Criminals' Who Disrupt Pubic Affairs

—Banner headline, Baltimore *News-American,* May 14.

HUBERT H. HUMPHREY

Argentina's Junta Picks Obscure Army Man As President

BUENOS AIRES — Brig. Gen. Roberto Marcelo Levingston, a relatively obscure Army careerist, was named by the military junta last night as the new president of Argentina.

Levingston, 50, replaced Lt. Gen. Juan Carlos Ongania, who was overthrown Monday

Earlier in the week, the junta announced it was drawing up a new charter that would make the president and the armed forces chieftains "co-legislators."

The junta is made up of Lt. Gen. Alejandro Lanusse, commander of the army; Adm. Pedro Gnavi, head of

Juxtaposition triumphant

(Above) Peoria *Journal Star,* June 14.

(Below) New York *Post,* April 17.

The Addicts: Which Way Out?

Series by Jay Levin • Today: Methadone • Page 41

THE WAY IS DOWN

Mrs. Howard Hughes Gets Around, But Manages To Remain Invisible

—Sacramento *Bee,* December 12, 1969.

Press Is Banned From UCD Dead-Horse Probe

DAVIS — An inquiry into the mysterious deaths of 11 horses was closed to the press and public here because the information involved "doctor-patient" relationships.

More than 20 persons attended the 3½-hour session yesterday at the University of California campus here, seeking to find out what killed horses pastured next to a Humble Oil Co. refinery near Benicia, Solano County.

A university administration spokesman said the press was excluded because discussions covered "privileged material" and "doctor-patient" relationships.

Doctor-what?

—Sacramento *Bee,* February 12, 1970.

Good fortune department

—London *Express* dispatch, New York *Post,* March 31.

Twenty-eight-year-old tailor Yuksel Conker pointed to a row of collapsed homes. He explained his wife and father were still buried there.

Conker was more fortunate than many. Before it was over, his entire family had been wiped out.

Here in Rochester, the National Petition Committee is a conspicuous example of the right way to protest. In a half-page advertisement in this newspaper yesterday, local people and organizations who support the committee aims noted

Establishment view

—Rochester *Democrat and Chronicle,* May 18.

Brooks Hays in Racing Post

RALEIGH, N. C., Jan. 16 (UPI)—Brooks Hays, the Arkansas Representative who was defeated for re-election in 1958 during the Little Rock school integration crisis, was named today to head North Carolina's race relations agency. Mr. Hays will be chairman of the North Carolina Good Neighbor Council. The chairmanship is a pol-

Racing-ism at wor

—New York *Times,* January 17.

De Gaulle Keels Over and Dies at 79

De Gaulle Dies While Watching TV

De Gaulle Dies While Playing Solitaire

—Philadelphia *Bulletin*, Nov. 10, 1970 (top) Two-Star; (center) Two-Star Suburban North; (bottom) Two-Star Metropolitan Midday Stocks.

Firemen Go To Bathroom

Brattleboro firemen went to Stone Fence Inn on Putney Road at 10:20 last night to investigate smoke. Cause was an overheated motor in a bathroom fan. Firemen disconnected the fixture.

—Brattleboro, Vt., *Reformer*, June 22, 1970.

11-year-old son of a decreased U.S. Air Force colonel was reported in good condition today

—Kenosha, Wis., *News*, Sept. 25, 1970.

24-PART INTENSELY PERSONAL SERIES FROM

Lady Bird's Diary . . . Five Turbulent Years as White House Mistress

—Atlanta *Constitution*, Nov. 14, 1970.

'It's What I've Always Wanted'

Sex No Handicap for Vet

—Feature on woman veterinarian, Springfield, Mass., *Daily News*, Nov. 25, 1970.

of the Reds' dugout.
But the decision stood. And Anderson refused to complain after the game, explaining quietly:
'y for the U.S. balance of payments
"The umpire didn't beat us—Baltimore did it by putting three over the fence.

—Denver *Post*, Oct. 11, 1970.

Neighborhood workers were awarded a plague for winning the competition with the men in the business drive. Mrs. Pat

—Boulder, Colo., *Daily Camera*, Oct. 2, 1970.

Unplanned stop

LONDON (AP)—A British airliner made an unscheduled landing in Manchester on a flight from Dublin when a warning light indicated a passenger mistook it for the toilet.

—Eugene, Ore., *Register-Guard*, Oct. 13, 1970.

5 Pollution Documentary
10 12 Nixon Address
President Richard Nixon delivers a campaign speech at Miami Convention Hall.
ghostly and menacing presence.
9:00 2 Advocates (to 10)

—Miami *Herald*, Oct. 27, 1970.

Asked whether he believes, as many young people do, that only something drastic and revolutionary can change society, Trudeau replied:

Police guard for judge

—Toronto *Telegram*, Oct. 24, 1970.

York ... campaign.
Beaming his appeal directly at Republicans, Goodell said at a Columbia University dedate yesterday: "I tell you this man makes Richard Nixon look like a radical."
Goodell then ran down a list of Nixon proposals and pro-

NEW YORK — Republican Sen. Charles E. Goodell told Columbia University yesterday that Conservative James L. Buckley "is the kind of man that makes Richard Nixon look like a liberal."
In a 90-minute debate, moderated by Columbia University President William J. McGill, R...

—Jack W. Germond (left), Woodie Fitchette (right), in Rochester, N.Y. *Democrat and Chronicle*, Oct. 27, 1970.

WEATHER:
Always Fair

THE JOHNSON CITY GOOD NEWS

The Only News
Is Good News

THURSDAY, APRIL 20, 1967

Polls Go 99.9 Per Cent For LBJ

Senate Abolishes Foreign Relations

Fulbright Applies For Fellowship

A [illegible] County [illegible] when Circuit Judge Albert V. Bryan Jr. signed a court order yesterday bringing boundaries [illegible] the Supervisors.

The [illegible] when Virginia Attorney General Robert Y. Button ruled that the [illegible] were not affected by the [illegible] plan adopted for Supervisor elections in February.

The County was required by the voter-approved Urban County Plan to redraw its [illegible] boundaries on the basis of equal population. An eighth district was created at the time.

Yesterday's action also increased the number of elected

Peter Hurd Joins Housepainters Union

Two of the districts received new names, and it was [illegible] would become confused if they [illegible] under the old district names and supervisors under the new name.

The primary function of the Fairfax [illegible] is to issue

RFK Quits Senate to Head Family Book Co.

Seeks To Publish Lady Bird's Memoirs

The new [illegible] would run [illegible] White House [illegible] Independence Avenue sw. and east to the Capitol.

It would have stations at McPherson Square, at the Federal Triangle on 12th Street nw., at 10th and Independence Avenue sw., at 7th Street and Independence Avenue sw., at 4th and C Streets sw., and just south of the Capitol on South Capitol Street.

The new line would then [illegible] up with the subway that

[illegible] from each district.

The new [illegible] both supervisor and [illegible] this year from the [illegible] new electoral divisions. They will take office Jan. 1.

De Gaulle Asks Return of NATO

Welcomes LBJ To Paris

Several citizens' groups in the Adams-Morgan area have protested the planned [illegible] of the Columbia Heights line, which would have had stops along Columbia and Park Roads nw.

Both the elimination of that line and the addition of the Southeast [illegible] were approved by the National Capital Planning Commission on Thursday. It also urged the WMATA to give "high priority" to planning a replacement [illegible] Columbia Heights line, possibly with a subway along [illegible] Streets nw.

HoChiMinh Asks LBJ Ranch Invite

Sends Hat Size

[illegible] the Freshman Drill Team, Texas A&M University third, the [illegible] University fourth, the University of Wisconsin [illegible], fifth, the Andrew D. Turner Memorial Drill Team, Howard University sixth, [illegible] University's [illegible], and seventh, Saint Peters College.

Homemakers of America Elect Wallace

He Renounces Politics

The [illegible] High School band of [illegible], S.C. was second place.

Third place went to the Thomas A. [illegible] High School band, Alexandria, Va.

Fifteen bands, including [illegible] musicians, took part in the two-day competition.

CIA Panel Probes Missing .1%

By Lynda Bird

A small crowd gathered on the Ellipse yesterday to watch Villanova University's [illegible] Company march off with first place in the National Cherry Blossom Festival ROTC Drill Team Competition.

The meet, held outdoors for the first time in its [illegible] history, attracted [illegible] teams from all over the Nation. Both male and female teams competed for the highly coveted honor of being named the best drill team in the nation.

Trophies in the shape of the Washington Monument were presented at the conclusion of the meet. First place in the [illegible] division was presented to Ohio University's Army ROTC [illegible]. The second place trophy went to the [illegible] Drill Team from [illegible] State University. Third place was awarded to the Angel Flight from [illegible] State University.

Luci Has Boi

The band [illegible] were Ambassador and Mrs. Charles S. A. Ritchie of Canada [illegible]

State of Texas Dedicated As Johnson National Park

The [illegible] from the White House [illegible] G Street nw. through the downtown [illegible] district and Judiciary Square to Union Station.

A move was made at the

The Connecticut Avenue line is now scheduled to be built first. But Gleason is known to feel that the G Street subway, which is pivotal to the system, should be pushed ahead.

George Hamilton Enlists After Mother Joins WACS

No Washington area [illegible] was presented this year because the Turner team from Howard University received the [illegible] award.

The Falls Church High School band, directed by [illegible], won first place in the annual Cherry Blossom Festival band contest Thursday. It was

Positivism

Complaints by the Johnson administration about the lack of positive-thinking news led to the effort produced as a dinner program by the Women's National Press Club of Washington.

SIX

From Monopoly to Conglomeratism

CASE HISTORY: WILMINGTON'S "INDEPENDENT" NEWSPAPERS

Ben H. Bagdikian

The Wilmington, Delaware, newspapers, the *Morning News* and the *Evening Journal,* are according to a standing editorial masthead, "independent" newspapers. A formal resolution issued by their owners on April 13, 1936, and presumably still in force, instructs the editors that the policy of the paper is, among other things, to "avoid blind partisanship . . . never to misrepresent the facts either in their news or editorial columns; never to resort to suppression except for the public good . . . always to give all sides a fair hearing on all public questions."

In this the two papers are no different from hundreds of others across the United States that also call themselves "independent" and solemnly declare that their owners insist on editorial freedom and want no fiddling with the news. As in Wilmington, their owners don't really mean it, or else the words mean one thing to editors and something else to owners.

Creed Black is an intense Kentuckian, thirty-nine years old, with reportorial and editorial experience on *Stars and Stripes,* the Chicago *Sun,* the Chicago *Herald-American,* the Nashville *Tennessean,* and the Savannah *News-Press.* He seldom turns his back on a controversy ("I don't mind a fight") and until June 1 of this year was vice-president and executive editor of the two Wilmington papers.

Black's departure from Wilmington is not unusual in the tribulations of the trade — it was an enactment of a ritual that goes on through American newspaperdom with all the unhappy regu-

Summer, 1964.

larity of Aztec sacrifices; and if some way is not found to end this combat the free-enterprise press could go the way of the Aztecs. For what Creed Black did overtly goes on silently and secretly in editorial offices and board rooms all over the country, in election years more than ever.

The owner of the two Wilmington papers is the Du Pont Company, which is to Delaware what God is to Heaven. More precisely, the owner is the Christiana Securities Company, a holding company that is to Du Pont what the Church is to God. Christiana was formed in pre-World War I days to buy out a faction of Du Ponts during one of the bitter family feuds. It now owns 27 percent of the Du Pont Company and all the stock of the News-Journal Company, which, with the exception of a paper of 13,600 circulation in Dover, publishes the only dailies in Delaware.

The Du Pont Company is run by an executive committee of nine men, called the ExComm. The Du Pont family interest in the company and other concerns is exercised through Christiana, whose ruling group has some seats in ExComm. There is a single room on the ninth floor of the Du Pont Building in Wilmington where the secretary of Christiana can cast one ballot to constitute a "stockholders' meeting" of the News-Journal Company.

The News-Journal Company has a board of directors of ten men. Four of them are working executives of the paper, including, until recently, Creed Black. They also include the papers' president and editor, Charles L. Reese, Jr, son of the Du Pont chemist who led the company's research to international stature in World War I. There are two "outside men," that is, non-Du Pont. They are Ralph K. Gottshall, president of Atlas Chemicals, once a Du Pont firm, spun off after antitrust action but still in friendly symbiosis with its parent. The other is J. J. B. Fulenwider, vice-president of Hercules Powder, another former Du Pont firm separated by antitrust order, with 300,000 of its shares now owned by Christiana. A seventh member of the board is Robert H. Richards, Jr., counsel for the paper, a director of the Du Pont bank, the Wilmington Trust, until recently Republican National Committeeman from Delaware, and son of the legal genius who created Delaware's friendly corporation laws and guided the formation of Christiana.

The three ownership directors are Henry Silliman, son-in-law of Irénée du Pont; Robert R. M. Carpenter, Jr., known as "Bobby," nephew of the president of Christiana, himself on the board of Christiana and owner of the Philadelphia Phillies baseball team; and Henry B. du Pont, president and patriarch of Christiana and until recently vice-president of ExComm. H. B. du Pont is the ruling man in the ownership, with Carpenter increasingly influential.

The Du Ponts and the press have had a long joint history. The family first appeared in the Delaware press on January 1, 1806, when one of the papers in town (Wilmington then had a population of 3,500 and two newspapers; it now has a population of 100,000 and two newspapers) carried a grocery store ad for smoked herring, Old Peach Brandy and "Dupont & Co's. gunpowder." Since that time their printed presence has been more dramatic. Like any normal family, they have no love for adverse publicity, but their wealth and power have given them more than their share of it. It is a huge family, with about 1,600 contemporary members, 250 of them important in the empire and a handful of them potent leaders. It is a large but close-knit group.

For the last seventy-five years the news has often been intolerable for the Du Ponts, since their prominence made their most embarrassing private moments terribly public. These moments were plentiful, with family scandals and fights, suicides, bordello shootings, spectacular intrafamily marriages and divorces (HE MARRIED A BARMAID, a Chicago *Daily News* headline said of a Du Pont on November 12, 1889) and senatorial investigations of the "munitions lobby" in the 1930s. All of this gave the family good reason to fear the press.

Alfred I. du Pont saved the company for the family, and helped plunge it into the newspaper business. After most of the clan had voted to sell out to their closest competitor, Alfred formed a troika of leadership in 1902 with his cousins, T. Coleman du Pont and Pierre S. du Pont (with the help of Pierre's ingenious assistant, John Jacob Raskob). The three cousins took over the $24,000,000 enterprise with a total cash outlay of $2,100 — the incorporation fees.

The newspaper appendix to the Du Pont anatomy was acquired

after the family declared war on Alfred, not so much because of his spectacular divorce and remarriage to his divorced cousin but because when he did this he inserted a flamboyant announcement of it in the Wilmington *Morning News*. When he got back from his honeymoon, Coleman told him, "Al, now you've done it," and said he should get out of the company. Alfred refused and the fight was on, Alfred on one side with about one-fifth of the clan, and Coleman and Pierre on the other, with the bulk of the family. The feud involved politics; Coleman had ambitions to be a senator or even President. Alfred started a new bank and deliberately made his building two stories higher than the twelve-story Du Pont Building one block away.

Henry A. du Pont, on Coleman's side, bought the Wilmington *Evening Journal*. In response, Alfred bought the Wilmington *Morning News* and six downstate papers and there followed a journalistic firefight that shredded state politics, the company, and the family. When Coleman's political drive collapsed, Alfred ran a headline in his paper: BANG! T. C. DU PONT'S BOOM BLOWS UP! The explosive figure of speech was considered unforgivable bad taste in a family that lived (and sometimes died) by gunpowder.

When Alfred got his second divorce in 1906, nothing appeared in any Wilmington paper, but there was a full account in the Philadelphia papers, an enduring pattern that continues to this day on sensitive Du Pont family or Du Pont Company news.

World War I made the company what it is today, but the postwar depression caught Alfred personally $10,000,000 in debt. He sold out his share of the company and the *News* to his family enemy, Pierre. The same faction of the family then took control of the company and of every daily paper in the state.

Over the years the family shaped itself by shrewd decision and careful selection of in-laws to govern the company in a more orderly fashion, ruthlessly weeding out incompetent members from company leadership in the most discriminating nepotism in the country. The Wilmington newspapers were only afterthoughts in this process and they settled down to conventionality and drab dignity.

In 1960, the executive editor, Fendall Yerxa, left to return to the New York *Herald Tribune* and a management consultant firm combed the country for an acceptable professional to take his place. They came across Black, who was ready to leave Savannah. The *Morning News* and *Journal-Every Evening* (as it was then called) were not very different from most papers: the owners insisted that within broad principles agreed upon beforehand, the editors were free to put out the best product they could.

Two other prominent American newspaper editors took a look and decided not to take a chance. One of them asked what would happen if he decided to endorse a Democrat. When he was told that this would be a decision for the board of directors he said good-by and went to the nearest hotel and "got stiff." On the other hand, previous editors had not found the job intolerable and Reese, the president and editor, is a respected man in the trade. Black took the job.

The technical history thereafter was comforting. Their names were simplified to *News* and *Journal*. The typography was reformed; one paper had looked like the prewar *Herald Tribune* and the other like the postwar Baltimore *Sun*. Some of the old content (SANDWICHES/ON MENU and MASONIC CLUB/AIDE TO SPEAK) disappeared to make room for harder news from new bureaus. An inbred staff was leavened with younger talent selected from other papers and from universities. In four years the combined morning and evening circulation went from 106,000 to 125,000. The 1963 revenue and profit were up 25 percent to the highest level in the papers' history. What was more significant, the old picture of the Wilmington papers as Du Pont Company house organs began to fade. Younger editors even asked if the Du Ponts still owned the paper.

Despite professional appearances, inside troubles had begun in 1961. The starting point was *Operation Abolition*, the House Un-American Activities Committee film that was used as a set propaganda piece for right-wing causes. The Delaware state police were showing the film under official auspices to schoolchildren, churches, and civic clubs. The paper editorialized against the official showings as dangerous precedent for political indoctrination by the police, using a factually dubious piece of work.

This stand brought severe pressures from the owners. An Un-American Activities Committee staff member and the narrator of the film, Fulton Lewis III, was a guest at the home of H. B. du Pont, where the papers were severely criticized by a group made up largely of right wing Delawareans. The film later was shown at a program sponsored by Mrs. H. B. du Pont and Carpenter.

H. B. du Pont ordered the papers not to comment editorially on the film. Instead, for two months the news columns carried attacks against the paper by the state police chief. The letters columns carried attacks on the papers and on the patriotism of the staff. The editors themselves were ordered to remain silent. The owners' old resolutions — never to resort to suppression and always to give all sides a fair hearing — were invoked, in vain.

At about this time the papers provoked the disapproval of the president of the University of Delaware, an institution close to the Du Ponts, who served on its board of trustees. The dispute seemed to be over the reporting of campus controversies, which the university regarded as bias on the part of the dailies. H. B. du Pont ordered the papers to suppress a number of items involving the university.

It was at this point that Bobby Carpenter, nephew of H. B. du Pont, was placed on the board of the papers. It was plain that the papers were being enlisted in a passionate political crusade. From this time on there was growing acrimony between the editors and the owners.

In 1962, the editors proposed that they interview major candidates for state office from both parties to help them editorialize during the campaign. This was approved. But when the editors decided to back the Democratic candidate for Congress as "the lesser of two evils," there was a special meeting of the board of Christiana Securities. Christiana is probably the richest investment trust in the world, with assets of more than $3,000,000,000, but that day its attention was directed to the cosmic subject of an editorial that compared the demerits of two candidates for Congress and came up with a begrudging net in favor of the Democrat. Christiana had the editorial rewritten outside the newspaper office. It finally appeared, watered down from the original. The papers did endorse one Democrat openly — the candidate for state auditor.

Other clashes came quickly. When Shell Oil wanted to build a refinery in Delaware, the owners ordered the papers to stop comment on the issue. When Congress was considering legislation for relief of the Du Ponts in selling their General Motors stock under court order, the papers were told not to criticize Senator Byrd, chairman of the Senate Finance Committee. During the same period, the Du Pont Company public relations department asked the paper not to run on page 1 a statement on the matter by Harris McDowell, Democratic member of Congress from Delaware, for fear it would anger a friendly senator.

H. B. du Pont also told the paper to put the damper on stories of public charges of mismanagement at the Wilmington airport, whose chief activity is handling the business of a private aviation corporation in which H. B. du Pont has an interest.

Some idea of the clash between owner ideologies and professional practices can be seen in the complaints of board members. The significance of these conflicts is not so much in the views of the owners (who, of course, have views, as do all interested citizens) as it is a revelation of what happens when an owner fails to understand the role of the monopoly newspaper and the discipline of news.

Henry Silliman and Robert Richards, both members of the paper's board, formally requested through Richards that the paper give a prominent play to a family wedding. "I do not know if this is in accordance with your policy or would require a deviation from your rules. If the latter is true, there should be exceptions to every rule. . . ."

At a time when Richards was on the paper's board and also Republican National Committeeman from Delaware, Richards complained bitterly to the editors that the paper's reporter had written a conventional news account of a Democratic rally when he should have turned it into a pro-Republican essay. Richards even wrote his own anti-Democratic story as an example of how the paper should have carried it, though presumably Richards was not at the rally himself. "This was a matter which, if properly handled, could, in my opinion, have been very useful to the Republican Party and their success at the polls in November," he wrote.

When Wilmington began having racial troubles, H. B. du Pont told his editors: "A continual overplaying of integration in our papers certainly plays right into the hands of the radical element of our population . . . many of the writers on your staff seem to have a degree of dedication to certain causes which would make them appear to be quite far to the left."

Most revealing is the collection of complaints issued by Carpenter to the executive editor:

On an editorial praising President Kennedy's Supreme Court appointments: "Why should we devote space to one who is an enemy of private enterprise and the capitalistic system?"

When editors asked him if his complaints about their comments on a bill by Representative McDowell meant the paper should oppose everything McDowell was for, the answer was, "I would say, Yes."

When an editorial criticized some Republican choices of candidates: "Are we endorsing the Democratic Party by criticizing the Republican Conventions? . . . Could we not become a house organ for the conservative cause?"

When he objected to running a letter to the editor signed by sixty-four University of Delaware students favoring integration, the editors asked if they should close the column to all letters from students. His answer was, "Yes."

On an editorial noting that French Socialists had outmaneuvered French Communists: "Should the *News-Journal* take the position of favoring actions of any Socialist Party? I believe it is a grave error for a subsidiary of Du Pont to follow the philosophy of the ultra-liberal whose objectives are destruction of capitalistic systems."

It is apparent in retrospect that two conflicting developments had occurred. The Wilmington papers, as with most metropolitan dailies in this country, were in fact broadening their professional and social scope. This was in line with the growing sophistication of the overwhelmingly Democratic or moderate Republican urban audience. At the same time, the owners seemed increasingly rigid in their demands for ultraconservative orthodoxy and family convenience, both in the news columns and editorials.

With the 1964 election campaign approaching, and with Senatory Barry Goldwater involved, it was obvious to the editors that something had to be done to resolve these conflicts. The editors pressed the owners for a statement of what they expected of the papers, some mandate that could be followed. When the editors suggested that the papers be committed to the Republican cause with editorials to "focus on an objective appraisal of the chances of the various candidates," H. B. du Pont objected that this idea would "leave editorial writers free to snipe at candidates for the Republican nomination for President."

Black asked mostly for consistency. In a memo noting that he had received orders from four or five separate owners plus the public relations department of the Du Pont Company, he asked, "How many bosses are we expected to please and take orders from?" (He had, for example, run the names of large holders of General Motors stock, as released to the national press by the Du Pont Company public relations office and had received bitter castigation from two members of the Du Pont family.)

On May 19, 1964, the owners of the Wilmington *News* and *Journal* gave their answer. They said that Charles M. Hackett, executive assistant in the public relations department of the Du Pont Company, would be the boss of news and editorial operations of the papers, with Black serving under him. Black quit. The day before, the announcement was made that the Wilmington papers had won five of fifteen possible first prizes in a publishers' association judging of papers in Pennsylvania and Delaware.

The ending followed tradition. Black wanted to publish his letter of resignation, which said, in part: "I, for one, need no further evidence that the ownership wants the *Morning News* and the *Evening Journal* operated as house organs instead of as newspapers." H. B. du Pont vetoed the idea. After the first edition of May 19, carrying simply the news of his resignation, Black posted his letter on the newsroom bulletin board and the Philadelphia papers printed it before Wilmington did.

H. B. du Pont, at the time, denied Black's assertion and said the newspapers "have never been and never will be operated as a house organ for any organization. Christiana Securities Corporation reaffirms their determination that the News-Journal Newspapers be operated independently with the objective of being a constructive influence in the community, in the state, and in the nation."

Efforts to obtain further comment from the papers' management during the preparation of this article were unsuccessful. H. B. du Pont was unavailable for comment. Robert Carpenter, when asked about his role in requesting changes in the newspapers' content, said, "I wouldn't want to comment on the subject." Charles L. Reese, Jr., president and editor of the newspapers, also declined to discuss it.

The depressing quality of the Wilmington episode is that it is not unusual. Few families are so powerful, organized, or dominant in their state as are the Du Ponts, but newspaperdom is filled with owners whose assumptions of their responsibilities are based on their nonnewspaper businesses and whose journalistic enterprises are peripheral both to their personal experience and their daily attention. Unlike the McCormicks and the Ochses, such owners do not have to live with the day-to-day consequences of their decisions, nor face constituents whose information and opinions they oversee.

Decision making in newspapers has a fundamental difference from that of most enterprises. Success in conventional business has a simple measure: survival and profit making. Both are essential to newspapers but a paper that only survives and only shows a profit can be a failure as a newspaper. The newspaper is a community educational institution run for profit. The owner's relationship to the news he prints is something like a university trustee's relationship to reading material selected for archaeology courses.

There are hundreds of dailies in which editorials on certain subjects are as predictable as a catechism, whose news departments are designed to overreact or underreact to certain kinds of news, notably financial and political, not because of incompetence or sensationalism but because of the impulse to create a picture closer to the dreams of the ownership. Nor is it unusual for owners to believe that their paper's staff is filled with radicals dangerous to the point of doubtful patriotism. Owners, typically, are conservative Republicans, and staffs — in journalism, as in most fields — tend to be Democrats.

If there were a tradition within newspapering to contain this distrust and tension between owners and staff, as there is in universities, it could result in a pluralism with the advantage of a checks-and-balances system. But there is no such tradition. Too many owners have been alienated too long from the social realities their staffs must perceive and report (and amid which the staff lives and owners generally do not). The Boston *Transcript* was perhaps the last metropolitan daily that lived within a closed elite. The power of both the *Transcript* and its elite were changed with the Depression. Millions of words in thousands of editorials will not bring back the mid-twenties.

There are continual legislative and vigilante attacks on freedom of the press. It will be an uncomfortable time when the owners of newspapers have to depend for preservation of this freedom on the understanding of constituents with whom the owners have been out of sympathy and, worse, out of touch, for thirty years.

When Creed Black resigned he got the unexpected sympathy of some prominent citizens of Delaware, partly because not many hired hands publicly dispute the Du Ponts. Some publishers wrote him that owners will never learn. Editors sympathized with him. And one bright university student who had planned a newspaper career wrote: "I have always had a few doubts about the newspaper business . . . if this is at all typical of the behind-the-scenes actions in the fourth estate, I'll have no part of it."

THE *CHRONICLE:* SCHIZOPHRENIA BY THE BAY

David M. Rubin and William L. Rivers

To those who know the San Francisco *Chronicle* only casually through visits and hearsay, the paper is synonymous with Herb Caen. This is understandable. As the cleverest local-tidbits columnist in the three-dot school of journalism, Caen is to the *Chronicle* what Gideon is to Bibles. But to those who know well the long battle with Hearst and Scripps-Howard for dominance in San Francisco, the synonym for the *Chronicle* is executive editor Scott Newhall.

Since his appointment in 1952, Newhall has been leader of a quintet of executives who have pushed the paper from third in San Francisco (with 154,608 circulation) to first in 1969 (circulation 480,233). Newhall and associates — president and editor Charles de Young Thieriot, news editor Bill Garman, managing editor Gordon Pates, and city editor Abe Mellinkoff — contrived a splashy paper which buried Scripps-Howard in San Francisco and wounded Hearst. The executives fashioned a joint operating agreement with Hearst which has given the *Chronicle* undisputed control of the lucrative morning market. Newhall's *Chronicle* is now by far the largest and most influential newspaper in the San Francisco Bay Area, a nine-county region of nearly 5 million residents encompassing San Francisco, Oakland, San Jose, and dozens of smaller cities.

Fall, 1969. William L. Rivers, who wrote *The Opinionmakers* and is co-author of *Responsibility in Mass Communication* (revised edition), is professor of communication at Stanford. David M. Rubin is an advanced Ph.D. candidate there. This article is adapted from their book, *The San Francisco Bay Area Press*.

With thick shoulders, short, muscular arms, and knotty hands, Newhall is not the picture of the genteel newspaper editor. A wooden leg (the result of an infection contracted in 1936 in Acapulco) interrupts but does not slow his gait. His face, especially with a five o'clock shadow, is ruggedly sinister. He looks vaguely like a man who might be featured in a *Look* exposé of the Mafia. His phrases are sometimes similarly tough. In an interview with the famous Berkeley *Barb*, Newhall was forthright about the quality of the daily press and the aims of the establishment, of which Newhall's boss, Charles Thieriot, is a charter Bay Area member:

We have to play it cooler than you underground papers. We have to keep the Establishment anesthetized so they don't feel the pain as we stick the needle into their archaic veins and give them a transfusion. . . .

The press is in danger; not the kind of Hollywood danger, but the danger of dissolving into a gray mass of non-ideas. The underground press will replenish the straight press and keep it alive.

But it was a Newhall editorial of February 27, 1969, that made him the talk of San Francisco and gave readers an unforgettable glimpse of the strong personality that has distinctively stamped the *Chronicle*. The editorial was a reaction to a public Board of Education meeting on the volatile issue of bussing-integration. A number of citizens and a *Chronicle* photographer at the meeting were beaten by small groups of thugs opposed to the bussing plan. The attackers escaped unidentified. Newhall's editorial called the men "self-appointed heirs of Hitler's brownshirts," "professional thugs," and "intellectually underprivileged . . . overnourished apes." He closed the editorial with a challenge (which, at this writing, has not been answered):

The members of this band of social neanderthals are obviously too insecure and too frightened to come forward and identify themselves. But, if they should miraculously care to do so, they can either call GA 1-1111, extension 463, or come to this writer's office, which is Room 332 on the third floor.

On the other hand, if this phantom squad of bullies cares to take umbrage at these remarks and wishes to continue its typical cowardly and disgraceful activities, it can catch the executive editor of this paper almost any week night on the darkened Fifth Street sidewalk at the side entrance to the *Chronicle*. He leaves the building at approximately 8 P.M. each evening on his way home.

Or, if they prefer, they can catch him quite alone in his San Francisco residence. The address is 1050 Northpoint Street. Simply ask the doorman for Apartment 708 and you will be escorted to the elevator.

Although the *Chronicle* is not really the crusading muckraker this sketch of Newhall might indicate, it is certainly a maverick among metropolitan dailies. One editor, with some justification, has called it "the only above-ground underground paper in the United States." Once a country club haven for talented reporters, the *Chronicle* now has a staff as hip as the city. One young reporter said with pride, "If there was a wholesale pot bust in San Francisco tomorrow, 80 percent of the city-side reporters and copydesk would be in jail."

How the *Chronicle* became what one of its columnists calls "a daily satire on American journalism" is instructive. Beginning in 1935, when Paul Smith, twenty-six years old, took over as executive editor (Newhall joined the paper as a photographer that same year), the *Chronicle* tried to become either the "New York *Times* of the West" or the "Western New York *Herald Tribune*." Most observers of the period remember the *Chronicle* under Smith as *Times*-like, with an emphasis on national and international reporting, sometimes quite heavy. But there was also a strong emphasis on flavorful writing of the sort usually associated with the late *Herald Tribune*. Smith went on recruiting forays to the East—and indeed, everywhere—and lured bright young reporters and editors with promises of "a machine gun in every typewriter." This was a heady period.

Since its founding, the *Chronicle* has been operated by members of the de Young family and their relatives. The "de Young" of that time was George Cameron, uncle of current *Chronicle* publisher Charles de Young Thieriot. Smith enjoyed Cameron's confidence and was so influential in Republican politics that he accompanied former President Hoover, who was still the grand poohbah of the GOP during the 1930s, on a trip to Europe. Smith was asked by reform-minded Republicans in 1939 to run for mayor of San Francisco. Leaders brought him a stack of petitions carrying 47,000 signatures of San Franciscans who would back him. Smith turned them down, saying that he wanted to continue to direct the *Chronicle.*

How he achieved this status can be stated simply: Smith produced a sturdy, informative, interesting failure. He offered urbane, cosmopolitan San Franciscans a chance to support a quality newspaper, but most of them declined. By commercial standards, so did the *Chronicle.* A sick circulation list and lean advertising revenues combined with the impending retirement of Cameron and the accession of Charles Thieriot to suggest to Smith that his power would be reduced. So in 1952, he moved on to Crowell-Collier, eventually taking *Chronicle* reporter Pierre Salinger with him. (While Salinger was working for *Collier's* magazine, which died before he could write much for it, he met the Kennedys.)

Newhall, who under Smith had become editor of the *Chronicle*'s Sunday magazine *This World,* then became executive editor with the mission of overtaking Hearst's *Examiner.* News editor German, who, with columnist Art Hoppe, is known as a leader of the *Chronicle*'s intellectual underground, has written deftly of the paper's strategy in a widely circulated memo:

> What strength there was in the old *Chronicle* had always been with the upper level of the population, the upper level economically and intellectually. Home-delivered circulation was proportionately high. Street sales were low. Strategy and tactics called for attracting many non-readers of our eggheadish newspaper into our tent, and, once there, keeping them from drifting out again. It was also essential that our core of serious readers not be so disaffected by the raucousness of our new spiel that they pack up and go elsewhere.

The concern for serious readers was sometimes hidden as the *Chronicle* plunged rapaciously after circulation. A daily banner was added to the street edition, which was "no longer reserved for the most consequential news of the day," German continues. "The banner under its new concept was to be a piece of promotional advertising for the sale of that day's edition, much in the manner of a headline on the cover of a slick magazine." Leads were set in larger type, and white space was splashed around heads and pictures. Reporters were encouraged to reflect their own reactions to events — which German has called the *Chronicle* "cult of personality."

Newhall recognized the value of a daily surprise, and the most successful circulation builders were a scattershot collection of wild pseudostories, some of them running for weeks, which provided a sharp contrast to the straight journalism of other Bay Area dailies. Jonathan Root waged a campaign against poor coffee in San Francisco restaurants under such front-page banners as A GREAT CITY IS FORCED TO DRINK SWILL.

Reporter George Draper played up a press agent's campaign to clothe naked animals, which led to the founding of chapters of SINA (Society for Indecency to Naked Animals). This received national attention when Draper tried to start a chapter in the U.S.S.R. And in 1960, outdoors editor Bud Boyd was sent into the wilderness of the High Sierras to act as "The Last Man on Earth."

Boyd, his wife, and their three children were to portray the sole survivors of an H-bomb attack and test man's ability to survive. The *Chronicle* asked in a front-page note: "Could an average city-dweller exist in the wilderness tomorrow with little more than his bare hands?" Daily dispatches tried to answer that question. One reported a "night of terror" during which the Boyds fought for "survival against cold and exhaustion." At the height of considerable interest in the series, the rival morning paper, Hearst's *Examiner,* sent a reporter to the Sierras. His first dispatch carried reports from "unassailable sources" that the Boyds had left their camp. At the campsite, the *Examiner* reporter found (and documented with pictures) fresh eggs, empty spaghetti cans, chipped-beef containers, kitchen matches, Coke bottles, enough toilet paper to start a fire, and other amenities suggesting that the Boyds had not been exactly deprived during their wilderness sojourn. *Chronicle* and *Examiner* executives waged an editorial battle over the series, with Boyd and Newhall even appearing on the *Chronicle*'s television station, KRON-TV, to present a "report to the people."

It was left to the afternoon *News-Call-Bulletin,* then so near its end that it was barely involved in the competitive struggle, to provide a masterful closing touch. City editor Harry Press assigned one of his reporters to test man's ability to survive in lush Golden Gate Park. The reporter wrote touchingly of his ordeal and was pictured surrounded by caviar, champagne, and voluptuous blondes.

The *Chronicle* had other weapons, notably a string of highly literate columnists. Some had started with the paper before the Newhall regime. Others were taken on by Newhall; some of these were reporters whose distinctive styles had caught Newhall's eye. Before Newhall was through, he was publishing so many local columns that his *Chronicle* sometimes seemed to be a "views-paper." And although the *Chronicle*'s huge package often seemed to add up to little more than a ton of feathers, it offered the most provocative writers in the Bay Area, with Herb Caen and political satirist Art Hoppe the acknowledged stars.

Some of Newhall's ideas for columns were highly effective and original. The lead column in the sports section was given to Charles McCabe, an elegant stylist from the city side who had offered no evidence that he knew the difference between a touchdown and the left-field foul line. From the first, McCabe operated outside the routine of the sportswriter, and he seemed never to develop the rapport with athletes, coaches, general managers, and owners that subtly ties the hands of so many who write about sports. The result was a column, aptly titled "The Fearless Spectator," that was the most refreshing in the world of athletics.

Nearly all the views the *Chronicle* offered were liberal. After the death of Lucius Beebe, whose Sunday column carried some of the most outrageously reactionary judgments in the most delightful phrases, not a conservative voice could be heard. The only editorial balance came at election time in the unsigned editorials. Although the editorials often sounded the same liberal themes voiced by the columnists, the *Chronicle* endorsed many conservatives (including George Murphy in his 1964 Senate race against Pierre Salinger). In effect, the paper talked Democratic and voted Republican.

This was the scattershot lineup Scott Newhall threw into the battle for dominance in San Francisco. It worked. The pattern of merger which would reduce San Francisco from four independent dailies to two with a Siamese-twin relationship began to take shape. First the afternoon Scripps-Howard *News* and the Hearst *Call-Bulletin* combined, with Scripps-Howard taking editorial control and Hearst running business, advertising, production, and distribution. Then in 1962, Scripps-Howard sold its 50 percent interest to Hearst, which gave Hearst the afternoon *News-Call-Bulletin* as well as the morning *Examiner.*

Then the New York *Times* introduced its heralded western edition. A *Times* executive later admitted that the Los Angeles *Times,* on its way to becoming a great paper under Otis Chandler, was thought to be too strong to allow the New Yorkers really to succeed in Southern California, but that they did expect to do well in the North. They were mistaken. A poor record in the first year and strike troubles at home soon caused the western edition's demise.

The *Chronicle* and the *Examiner* continued to battle for morning superiority, with the *Chronicle* ahead 351,489 to 301,356 by 1964. The Chronicle Publishing Company was in excellent financial health because of profits from KRON-TV — a situation which, ironically, soon was to cause publisher Charles Thieriot considerable difficulty. In a Senate hearing on the "Newspaper Preservation Act" (then known as the "Failing Newspaper Act") in July, 1967, he first said that with the exception of 1956 the *Chronicle* had lost money "in modest proportions" through 1964. Only then, he testified, did the *Chronicle* "break even." The circulation war with the Examiner, he explained, was fought with KRON-TV profits. But in December of 1967, in a letter to Michigan Senator Philip Hart, Thieriot reversed his position, perhaps because he realized that using TV profits to drive a competitive newspaper to the wall might be damaging at license renewal time for KRON-TV (which has proved to be the case). Thieriot wrote: "Before depreciation, newspaper operations showed a small and manageable loss in 1955, a profit in 1956, somewhat larger but manageable losses in 1957 and 1958, and, as indicated above, a profit for each year commencing with 1959 through September, 1965, with the single exception of 1962."

Despite the contradiction, it is clear that the *Chronicle* was not a failing newspaper. Indeed, of the three San Francisco newspapers published in 1964, it may be that only Hearst's afternoon *News-*

Call-Bulletin was failing; its circulation was down to 183,176. Hearst sued for peace with a scheme that would kill the *News-Call-Bulletin*, move the *Examiner* to the afternoon, give the *Chronicle* the morning market, and insure solvency for both the *Examiner* and the *Chronicle* through profit splitting. Why did not Hearst simply kill the *News-Call-Bulletin* and move the *Examiner* to the afternoon without making a deal with the *Chronicle?* The only answer seems to be the lure of a guaranteed profit. Bruce Burgmann, who has been battling what he calls "Superchron" ever since the agreement, has charged as much in his monthly San Francisco *Bay Guardian*. *Chronicle* executives do not offer a better explanation.

On October 23, 1964, the two companies agreed to form the San Francisco Newspaper Printing Company, with stock to be owned equally by the Chronicle Publishing Company and Hearst. The new corporation would perform the mechanical, circulation, advertising, accounting, credit, and collection functions for both papers. When the agreement was submitted to the Department of Justice, August 30, 1965, the Attorney General replied that he did not *for the present* plan to institute antitrust action. On September 1, incorporation papers were filed in Carson City, Nevada, and on September 12 the merger went into effect. Neither paper has ever given its readers a full account of these actions.

Yet even with the secure place thus won as the Bay Area's largest and most influential newspaper, the *Chronicle* has not abandoned the editorial strategy that the executives thought necessary to gain dominance. Indeed, the strategy has become a full-blown philosophy. As German has written: "The formula at the *Chronicle* calls for a combination of fact, truth, and fun. Each edition each day should approach the goal of informing and entertaining most of the people most of the time." Newhall expresses the same thoughts more colorfully, likening the front page to a circus barker saying, "Hurry, hurry, hurry, the girls are just about to take off their clothes." Once inside, the reader finds a story about Vietnam — or so the theory runs.

The theory, however, undergoes considerable strain. The *Chronicle* is edited to be read so quickly that the reader who cares about social and political affairs is likely to finish the edition with the guilty feeling that he has been having more fun than reading a newspaper should give him. A fast reader can go through most *Chronicle* stories in a minute or two. The news ethic, as city editor Mellinkoff sees it, is, "Will someone read the story? If the story is not read, it's not news." German believes that a good test of a story's value is whether people will talk about it. This has led to permissive editing that shocks many San Franciscans. "We decided," German says, "not to be any more bluenosed than the society in which we lived. When a topless bathing suit was first designed and debated, we fitted out a model in the first such suit and published her picture in a prominent position in the paper."

The emphasis on snappy, readable stories is so antithetic to long-running series that the *Chronicle* publishes fewer than does any other metropolitan paper in the Bay Area. Those it does run are usually memorable, either because a reporter is deeply interested in the subject, as Bill Moore was in exposing the unhappy conditions in Chinatown, or because the reporter hit on a subject that titillates, as when a long series reported on the short movies in which women "act" as undraped love objects — movies known to San Franciscans as "beavers." These series are exceptional because, as Mellinkoff says, "a paper should be complete in itself." A *Chronicle* reporter adds that it is almost "unheard of" for a reporter to be sprung loose from his daily assignments to write a deep story. This is somewhat paradoxical, for Newhall holds and the paper has argued editorially that radio and TV have taken over the spot-news world, and it is now the task of the newspaper to explain, interpret, and clarify. Newhall complains that some of his deskmen are so old-fashioned that they do not understand interpretation.

Where Newhall has succeeded in making his influence felt is in promoting personal journalism on the part of reporters. The *Chronicle*'s coverage in May, 1969, of the "People's Park" controversy in Berkeley was notable for reporter involvement with police and demonstrators. Informative and readable stories also sprang from the arrest and incarceration of reporter Tom Findley at the Santa Rita Prison Farm after a mass bust, and from the attendance of other *Chronicle* writers at "People's Party" meetings. One *Chronicle* editor holds up as models Norman Mailer's story of the march on the Pentagon and his account of the Democratic National Convention in Chicago, explaining: "We're feeling our way toward a new method of communication in print without the stereotypes of what a paper is supposed to look like."

The *Chronicle* has also been feeling its way toward a new kind of international reporting — with wildly mixed results. Although the paper has no bureaus abroad (and none in Washington), it buys stories from stringers in foreign countries. (The costs of this operation may be gauged from a letter, which fell into the hands of a rival paper, inquiring when the letter writer would receive a twelve-dollar check for his dispatch from India.) There is little danger that these stringers will duplicate the work of the many foreign reporters for wire services and other newspapers. As one *Chronicle* editor said: "We have a general disinterest in detailed coverage of foreign economics and politics. We think our readers are more concerned with whether or not they use Saran Wrap in Kuala Lumpur than with New York *Times*-type foreign coverage."

Chronicle editors instruct their stringers to try to determine what people are talking about over lunch in cities around the world. In theory this is an exciting idea and one not very far afield from the relatively recent desire among other foreign editors to have their operatives report on the fabric of life around the world. But judging from what appears in the *Chronicle*, the stringers eavesdrop on peculiar lunchtime conversations: They find that Parisians never talk about Pompidou, de Gaulle, the Common Market, French glory, or French philosophy; the English never talk about the government's austerity program, the rise of the red-brick universities, taxes, or the problems of the pound. In fact, lunch-table conversations over the world are startlingly alike: Everyone everywhere is apparently talking about sex, voodoo, witchcraft, drinking (in India, Trivandrum is talking about "Toddy Tapping"), or some form of eccentric behavior.

This may be oversimplifying, but not much. When a young *Chronicle* reporter heard our judgment of his paper's international coverage and urged us to look again because a new, more serious line was beginning, we checked the next two issues. One reported that Tokyo was talking about "Coffee Shop Classes," and the next that Colombo, Ceylon, was talking about "Human Smuggling."

It is all fun, and it may be the only kind of foreign news most subscribers will read. But one shudders to think of the masses of copy the editors junk every night, some of it penetrating reportage. For the *Chronicle* not only receives such conventional services as AP and UPI; Newhall also has the special news services provided by the New York *Times,* the Los Angeles *Times*-Washington *Post,* the North American Newspaper Alliance, and the London *Times.* Not only does the *Chronicle* scrap an overwhelming percentage of all this; its territorial arrangements keep these special services out of nearly all the other Bay Area newspapers. Nor can the rival papers publish *Chronicle* columnists — and this may be the chief reason the *Chronicle*'s circulation is more than twice that of any other Bay Area paper. Newhall prefers homegrown columns. His eye for a distinctive style is so sharp that no rival paper comes close to providing as much cleverness and titillation.

This leadership begins with Herb Caen and Art Hoppe. It is no more rewarding to try to define Caen's qualities than it is to try to dissect a joke, but certain values are clear. Unlike many of his colleagues, Caen works. His column is usually packed with pointed information and anecdotes. He sometimes fills it with one of those "essays" so dear to the columnist who is straining for something to say, but ordinarily his prose poems to San Francisco and environs appear only on Sundays (he writes the Sunday column the preceding Tuesday) or when he is trying to catch his breath after a vacation. Most of his writing is lean; he has an unusually sensitive ear for the quip or anecdote only marginally worth printing, and he apologizes for printing it with a deprecating phrase as effective as Johnny Carson's rueful and engaging recovery line: "That was a little bit of humor there."

Caen is much more than a gossip columnist, if only because the spread and intensity of his readership give him unusual influence. He may ride a political horse for only a sentence or two, but then a few days later another sentence appears on the same or a similar theme, and a week later, an anecdote — and suddenly Herb Caen's political leanings are quite clear. They are distinctly liberal leanings.

Hoppe, who is less widely known than Art Buchwald and Russell Baker, may nonetheless be the nation's best political satirist. Although Buchwald has greater celebrity — he is a genuinely funny man whose column misses as often as it hits — he often seems a bit bland compared to Hoppe. Russell Baker is probably the most gifted writer of the three, but has trouble finding the themes that will carry his richly wry commentary. Hoppe has more ideas, and better ideas, than either of his rivals. It is easy to suspect, too, that Hoppe is much more the political animal than is either Buchwald or Baker. There is an acid quality in much of his whimsy. He observes the foibles of humans (especially those in government), focuses on one of their more dubious enterprises, then imagines in print that it has been carried to an absurd conclusion. It is political commentary of a very high order.

For all their great value, Caen and Hoppe are much more writers, in effect, than they are reporters. But some of the specialty columnists *do* report and are fairly substantive. Ralph Gleason on pop culture, William Hogan on books, Terrence O'Flaherty on television, and Art Rosenbaum on sports — these are often meaty offerings. But Adeline Daley, Merla Zellerbach, Stanton Delaplane, Ron Fimrite, and Charles McCabe (who now has a general column) most often write cleverly about very little. Count Marco writes offensively about women, and manages to offend man as well as women. Some issues of the *Chronicle* suggest that not a columnist left the building the day before; everything was spun off the top of somebody's head, and the reader seems to be mushing over a mountain of whipped cream.

The *Chronicle*'s approach to society and women's page news is so frivolous that one young reporter terms it "a clarion call to revolution." Although Thieriot rarely interferes with the work of the news department, his hand is heavy on the society pages, where his country club friends appear regularly. The space given to the debutante cotillion set is so far out of balance that some of the society writers are "frankly upset." They want more articles on black women and on the sexual and social problems of modern women.

Thieriot's concern with society even extends to sports, where sports editor Art Rosenbaum has been pushed into covering society golf tournaments. The sports department is not given the money to cover the U.S. Open or the PGA. And the *Chronicle* was the only major paper in the Bay Area which did not staff the "basketball game of the century" in Los Angeles: the Lew Alcindor–Elvin Hayes rematch in 1968, which would have cost a thirty-dollar plane ticket. Sportswriter Dave Bush "covered" it by TV in a *Chronicle* conference room.

Chronicle staff members complain about such matters, but the general morale is quite high. They are almost unanimously in love with the ratty-appearing city room, and they sneer at the "straight" papers which surround them. There is pride in a staff which boasts science writer David Perlman, labor writer Dick Meister, and reporters Keith Power, Michael Grieg, Jerry Carroll, and Bill Moore, among others. If *Chronicle* staff members have a major concern, it is probably over who will succeed Newhall. His health is poor, and it has not been improved during the long months the *Chronicle* has been arguing with federal officials over its joint operating agreement and the future of KRON-TV. The company is on shaky ground in both cases. The Tucson decision makes it likely that agreements of the sort that married the *Chronicle* to the *Examiner* are illegal unless Congress legalizes them.

KRON-TV presents even worse problems. Its license renewal was delayed in part because of complaints by a KRON cameraman, Al Kihn, that his station distorted the news to the benefit of the larger company. When General Motors set private detectives on the trail of Ralph Nader, the *Chronicle* editorialized against snooping. But company officials sent detectives after Kihn. Until Brugmann's *Bay Guardian* revealed this snooping and the FCC forced the company to admit that it had occurred, neither the *Chronicle* nor KRON-TV reported it. FCC eyebrows have been raised high over the whole affair.

Whatever the outcome of these cases, Newhall's retirement is not far away. The young *Chronicle* men, who seem to like both news editor German and city editor Mellinkoff, are betting that one of them will become the new executive editor. Managing editor Pates is also a possibility. The basic question is whether Newhall's successor will continue the *Chronicle* philosophy of fact, truth, and fun — with emphasis on fun. The potential successors have given no sign that they are displeased with the paper's design and purposes; that they have aspirations to national influence comparable to that of, say, the Los Angeles *Times*. And yet, since the merger, there have been no more of the wild pseudo-stories. Moreover, during recent months, while Newhall has been jousting with federal officials and has given less attention to the paper, new strains of seriousness have been threaded through the *Chronicle*. The "talking about" series continues, but there are other international reports, and several of the stringers abroad have been giving as much attention to information as to titillation.

It is still a *Chronicle* cursed by parents who would prefer that their sons be left ignorant of the female form, still a *Chronicle* which seems to smile on fads and foibles no matter how bizarre. But if there is not enough world news to please a professor of international relations, there is at least enough for a high school student to clip for his report on "India Today." In short, the *Chronicle* long ago established itself as a successful barker. The people are in the tent. Now the *Chronicle* must decide whether they are to be offered escapism, or something more.

NEWS AS A BYPRODUCT

Ben H. Bagdikian

Anyone who reports out of Washington has to develop a taste for mimeograph paper and its usual cargo of agency English, an aberration of the native tongue combining the styles of the Victorian novel and real estate deeds.

One day this spring the diurnal tonnage of government paper included one innocent-looking specimen of 176 pages, printed single-space on both sides, labeled, "Federal Communications Commission . . . ABC-ITT MERGER PROCEEDINGS." Most of it abandoned the patois of the bureaucracies to raise the issue of corporate conflict-of-interest in journalism.

In fact, this spring saw an extraordinary crop of government actions involving the business operations of the press. The Department of Justice obtained a consent decree against the Lindsay-Schaub newspaper chain, which it had accused of violating antitrust law by cutting ad rates, taking an intentional $3 million loss between 1956 and 1963 in an attempt to swamp a competitor in Champaign-Urbana, Illinois. The department said the chain offset its loss by profits from its other papers, just one of which, an A.M.-P.M. twin in Decatur, Illinois, with less than 65,000 combined circulation, made more than $5 million during the same period.

The Antitrust Division of Justice obtained this decree while waiting for a final judgment in its Tucson case, where it has accused two one-time daily competitors of illegal collusion. During the same cherry-blossom period it began trial on its charge that the Los Angeles *Times*'s acquisition of a $15 million paper in San Bernardino violated the law.

There were continued private murmurs in the Department of Justice asking whether the syndicate business violates antitrust

---

Spring, 1967.

law by selling wide-area exclusive rights in popular features to big papers to the disadvantage of small ones.

During this same period there was dropped into the Senate hopper S.1312, a bill of sweeping exemptions of newspaper mergers and joint operations from all antitrust action if one of the newspaper parties "appears unlikely to remain or become a financially sound publication." It thoughtfully vacates all past convictions. Even the lobbyists who got through last year's Bank Merger Act, the most sweeping exemption in history, look upon S.1312 with respect. The bill is co-sponsored by fifteen prestigious senators of all ideological shades, whose chief bond is that they all come from states with papers in joint operations that could be affected by the Tucson case.

S.1312 was referred to Senator Hart's subcommittee on monopoly, which may or may not hold hearings. This equivocal prediction is based on the remarkable evaporation of past proceedings on this subject. Those of Representative Cellar suddenly stopped in 1963 and have not been heard from since.

The important issue in the organization of journalism is not business monopoly or giantism in themselves, though these are vexing problems, all the more complicated because the press has an obvious right to protect its business interests. The central issue is how monopoly influences the flow of independent news and commentary.

The action this spring took on overtones of geometry and geology. There was talk of mergers that are horizontal — that is, a marriage of direct competitors, as when the New York *Journal-American* joined the *World-Telegram;* and of mergers that are vertical — consolidation of firms involved in different stages of an operation, as when the New York *Times* bought a half-interest in a paper mill in Kapuskasing, Canada. There was also mention of conglomerates ("that which is heaped together in a mass or compacted from various sources"), the common control of largely unrelated businesses. For example, the parent company of the Los Angeles *Times* has twenty wholly owned subsidiaries that do a variety of things like printing local telephone directories, manufacturing goods, operating in real estate, selling Bibles, and publishing the *Times.*

Such talk gained added meaning when the Supreme Court in

the Procter & Gamble–Clorox case made it plain that antitrust action may be applied to conglomerates even when no direct competitors are involved. (A key argument by the court was the advantage giants like P&G have in newspaper discounts to big advertisers, a point reported blandly if at all in most papers.)

All of these actions defied two of the more solemn pieties among publishers.

One piety is that news companies are under constant siege by hostile government agencies using every possible device to bring the press to heel. The fact is that government in all its branches is more hesitant to apply restraints against corporate transgressions of the press than it is against any other segment of the American economy. It would be nice to think that this comes from a delicate regard for the First Amendment. But there is a broad area of antitrust, antimonopoly, postal, and tax law that is applicable without infringement of the First Amendment; yet the press is traditionally permitted to go farther and is reprimanded more gently than are other enterprises. The basic reason is that no one likes to make enemies with the town crier. If the press and the government are in conflict, it is the press that explains it to the public, or decides whether to mention it at all.

The other piety is that the news apparatus is not influenced by its profit-making activities, including advertisers. It is. Romantics continue to insist that the press is somehow corrupt for making a profit at all, which is to misunderstand a source of the strength of the American press. Another stereotype sees the advertiser as a censor of all the news, which, at least in the printed press, is not true. But this does not mean that there are no serious problems in corporate influence in the news. The reaction of dailies, magazines, and broadcasting to news seriously damaging to tobacco, automobile, and pharmaceutical industries, but plainly in the public interest to see, are good examples. In no such case was there an absolute or permanent blackout. But in each case the level of verification and of public concern had to be higher for these profit-sensitive news subjects than it is for other news. David R. Bowers of Texas A&M in the Spring of 1967, *Journalism Quarterly* found in a survey that publishers most often intervene in newsroom decisions "in areas which conceivably might affect the revenue of the newspaper directly or indirectly" and that publishers did this more than they did "in social issues such as politics, race, labor or war. . . ." The incidence of such influence in broadcasting is so epidemic that advertisers regard control or choice of content as a "right."

Conflict of interest in journalism has almost always been concerned with the individual reporter and editor, where the problems are, admittedly, real enough. In a recent issue of the *Bulletin* of the American Society of Newspaper Editors a number of editors debated about reporters who cover politics and also get involved in politics, sometimes for pay. Ed. A. Fitzhugh of the Arizona *Gazette* said: "Moonlighting for politicians is taboo; it smacks too much of clandestine support for cash. No matter how you rationalize it, in both the public eye and in the eye of the employing politician, the newsman *does* represent the paper." It is the only sound approach to reportorial independence and public confidence in that independence; not enough reporters and editors resist moonlighting that compromises it. Employers ought to pay their men enough and then insist they take no pay from possible news sources.

But what about corporate moonlighting? The reporter who trims his stories to favor his nonjournalistic interests corrupts his own stories. The owner of a press organization who does it corrupts an entire institution. If enough institutions are influenced by the same pressures, then the entire body of public knowledge and social values is distorted.

This is what made the 176 pieces of mimeograph paper from the FCC such a pregnant package of the fertile spring. The first twenty-two pages consisted of an order by a majority of the FCC permitting the biggest broadcast merger in history, between International Telephone and Telegraph Corporation and the American Broadcasting Company (or, technically, allowing transfer of ABC's seventeen stations to ITT; the FCC has no jurisdiction over who owns the network but the seventeen wholly owned stations are crucial to the deal).

The remaining pages were devoted to the dissenting opinions of three commissioners, 118 of them from Commissioner Nicholas Johnson.

For a time, this new Johnson was the most noticeable man of that name in Washington. He is a thirty-two-year-old lawyer in the hell-raising tradition. He asks irreligious questions in simple declarative English and his dissent was primarily responsible for reopening the case.

Among Johnson's reasons for rejecting the merger was ITT's deep financial involvement in areas which ABC News would have to report. ITT has commitments in forty countries and its officers have said that they protect these interests by obtaining sympathetic policies in Washington.

Johnson wrote: "Chile, Peru, Brazil, or India might someday wish to nationalize the telephone companies which ITT now owns in whole or in part. It has happened to ITT in the past and could easily happen again. ABC News and public affairs personnel would have to comment on the affair at length. If one admits the possibility that such nationalizations could be put in a favorable light, the potential for conflict with ITT's economic interest is obvious."

What would happen, he asked, if a rebel movement in Brazil got sympathetic treatment in an ABC news documentary that the government of Brazil tried to block? "The added leverage which the government of Brazil could exert because of ITT's Brazilian holdings would be substantial."

ITT gets 40 percent of its domestic revenues from defense and space contracts. What if ABC wanted to criticize the high rate of this spending?

Johnson asks, "Are we to accept . . . that although ITT may continue to exert pressure as an advertiser on the programming of CBS and NBC, it will exert none as an owner on the programming of ABC?"

This last worry was sharpened on April 20 when reporters for the New York *Times*, AP, and UPI were subpoenaed to testify on ITT's alleged "extraordinary" efforts to influence news about the merger hearings. Eileen Shanahan of the *Times* testified that the senior vice-president of ITT for public relations made "accusatory and nasty" remarks about her stories and asked her "if I didn't feel a responsibility to the shareholders who might lose money as a result of what I wrote." ABC drove the point home by having its affiliates ask members of Congress in their districts to support the merger. It is a dull politician who doesn't wonder if his access to constituents through broadcasting isn't at stake.

Aggressive and inept pressure is nothing novel in news coverage but it does raise the interesting question of what can happen when a reporter or editor is pressured not by an outside force but by his own employer. Or by an outside force with financial influence, as when complaints about some UPI wording in its ITT-ABC stories brought out that ABC pays UPI $250,000 a year for various services.

The issues raised by Commissioner Johnson cast light on the ITT-ABC type of conglomeration that already exists with NBC and CBS.

NBC is owned by Radio Corporation of America, which also has substantial foreign investments (one subsidiary alone, NBC Enterprises, operates in ninety-three countries), is the leading international telegraph company, owns RCA Victor records, Random House books, a drug company (Hoffman-LaRoche), and a car rental firm, Hertz. (ITT owns Avis.)

CBS, according to filings at the Securities and Exchange Commission, has thirty-nine major subsidiaries, fifteen of them in foreign countries, owns Columbia Records, and Fender Musical Instruments. It told stockholders in 1965 that it was working to increase its defense and space orders. It owns no car rental service but SEC records show that in 1965 CBS invested $21 million in the credit affiliates of General Motors, Ford, and Chrysler. At its recent annual meeting it reported increased investment in toys, the acquisition of book publisher Holt, Rinehart, and Winston, and denied plans to merge with Curtis Publishing.

Although diversification and conglomeration create sufficient problems of economic power, the central concern here is with the impact on news when it is controlled by corporations with deep financial involvements of a nonjournalistic nature. We are seeing a shift from journalism companies that moonlight in other work to conventional businesses that happen to moonlight in journalism.

It is a problem looked at only spasmodically, as when a Fred Friendly quits his network. Or when competitors complain that RCA color television gets special breaks on NBC. Or when CBS is suspected of firing a sports announcer because he said unkind things about the CBS subsidiary, the New York Yankees.

Specific stories influenced by specific business interest cannot tell the whole story. Each network and most publications can point to individual productions detrimental to their business investments. Most of them reject outright bribery or crass coercion. One of the greatest exposés of all time was the New York *Times*'s destruction of Boss Tweed's gang, accomplished after the publisher, George Jones, in 1871, turned down an offer of $5 million to suppress the stories. This was pretty crude. Today a syndicate of lawyers and brokers could use the money to get control of a corporation to buy an offending news medium, not just knock out one series of articles.

There have always been ingenious ways to buy influence in the news. Just before World War II the Japanese government secretly took over control of a hundred-year-old respected journal, the *Living Age*, in which it planted its stories. It created a newsletter that went to every American editor. It bought silent, secret interests in *Current History, North American Review,* and the *Saturday Review of Literature.*

Rafael Trujillo regularly bought himself into American news during his dictatorship in the Dominican Republic. He spent two thousand dollars a month with International News Service to have INS move Trujillo propaganda, masquerading as news, into American newsrooms. In 1959 a Trujillo agent handed $750,000 to the president of the Mutual Broadcasting System in return for a promise of fourteen minutes a day of pro-Trujillo material on the network.

These were successful transactions but they are not at the heart of the conflict-of-interest problem. It is true of individual reporters and just as true of their employers that the worst corruption is self-imposed; the expedient, profitable, or comforting bias is rationalized as news.

For more than fifteen years after 1911, the elder Hearst used all his communications agencies to provoke a war between Mexico and the United States. His papers ran headlines like MEXICO PREPARES FOR WAR WITH U.S. He owned the International Film Service, which made films about Mexican plots to overthrow the American government. In the 1920s he ran in all Hearst papers a spectacular series based on documents showing Mexico had bribed four United States senators with $1,115,000.

Most Hearst readers had no way of knowing that the Hearst family owned 2,500 square miles of Mexican mines, timber, chicle, and ranches that were threatened with government seizure.

When the bribery of the senators was investigated it turned out to be untrue; the documents Hearst had paid for were primitive fakes. The New York *Herald Tribune* for January 7, 1928, quoted a Treasury Department handwriting expert: "Anybody who would pass a consideration for these documents must have been in a very acceptable mood."

Most of Hearst's biographers, including W. A. Swanberg, think that when he printed them Hearst honestly believed the documents to be genuine. That is the point: he suffered the human tendency to be "in a very acceptable mood" about anything that supported his private interests.

Newspapers and magazines have these moods. They are generous in their coverage of antibillboard activities. They seldom muckrake their leading advertisers, such as department stores or car dealers. Most reporters and editors know that the system is in "a very acceptable mood" about news that favors the system's financial interests.

Only occasionally do the more explicit influences come to the surface. During the 1964 presidential campaign the fiercely pro-Goldwater Manchester (New Hampshire) *Union-Leader* delivered an astonishing rebuke to Goldwater for criticizing Jimmy Hoffa. It turned out that the Teamsters had $2 million in the *Union-Leader*. Joseph Kennedy put $500,000 into the ailing Boston *Post* at about the time the paper switched its support to John Kennedy.

Monopoly in communications decreases the chances that an interested party will notice and call attention to corporate conflicts in the news. The Hederman papers in Jackson, Mississippi, have done incalculable harm to their state by incitement of destruction and malice and they have also been accused of serving the owners' nonjournalistic investments. Their last competition ended five years ago.

The Wilmington, Delaware, papers belong to the Du Ponts and have been used to protect company and family interests. The Houston *Chronicle* and *Post* are also handmaidens of the ruling oligarchy, which controls much of downtown Houston. In both Wilmington and Houston the distortions to favor owners' interests became known only after tough editors quit or were fired.

But competition is hardly a guarantee of mutual monitoring on the corporate level. There is competition for ads, circulation, and even news in Houston, Chicago, Los Angeles, and San Francisco but it stops short of the executive suites.

Owners frequently respond explosively to questions about corporate conflict in the news. This could be because an owner is truly disinterested, or that he twists the news focus but it is so natural it seems to him true reality. Or he could be thinking of the virtuous as typical of the whole trade. There are publishers and there are publishers. One owner of a daily in a Florida city owned substantial real estate in the town and sold it to avoid any possibility of inhibiting his paper's freedom, and those who know this can point to it as proof of incorruptibility. But there was also a publisher in Connecticut who owned real estate in his city, most of it substandard, and fired a new city editor who ordered an investigation of slums. There are relatively few news staffs that cannot — privately — tell variations on this theme.

The crux of the issue is not the specific bias. It lies in the fact that journalism is more important today than any time in the past. The human race is better educated and equipped with more efficient communications. Dynamic interaction — in communities, in the country, throughout the world — is in response to some kind of communication, usually a form of journalism. If this communication does not reflect reality as rigorously as trained and independent professionals can produce, then the consequences can be profound, and already have been. More than ever journalism needs to be not only accurate but has to be looking at the most important issues.

The ultimate question in corporate conflict-of-interest in the news is whether news and commentary as a whole would be different if news corporations had no outside financial interests. And if different, whether it could come closer than it does today to the needed improvement in reporting and relevant commentary. The resolutions of most urgent issues — war and peace, the growing chasm between rich nations and poor, decay of cities, inadequacy of schools, race relations, contamination of environment — depend on allocation of national wealth, which means both social policy and taxes. If the news and its interpretation are increasingly merely a byproduct of huge corporations whose primary concern must be conventional gain then this is not a minor matter in public information or in the development of social and fiscal policies.

Nevertheless, diversification and conglomerates seem destined to grow: they make too much fiscal sense. In the process more news operations will become appendages to conventional businesses. It is not illegal to include news in a conglomerate. One long-term remedy is the development of professionalism and strengthening of the tradition that helps put a wall of separation between front office and newsroom and to seal the present porosity.

Another could be to inform the public of any news organization's outside financial interests, which might restrain corporate interference with news and at least notify the consumer. Something like this is required of all companies traded on the stock market, but relatively few newspapers and broadcasting stations are openly traded. Yet systematic and locally available reports of this kind would be therapeutic. Publisher opposition would be not much more than 99 percent, and since universal press disclosure would require an act of Congress, it may be necessary to wait for an act of God. Yet the questions asked by Commissioner Johnson of ITT can be fairly asked of every conglomerate corporation that owns a journalistic enterprise.

WHAT THE FCC MUST DO

Nicholas Johnson

Virtually every country in the world treats broadcasting as an activity possessed of unique public responsibilities. In many countries — Scandinavia among them — all stations are owned and programmed by an agency of government or a public corporation. Other nations have recently supplemented their public broadcasting facilities with the competition of privately owned, commercial stations — subject to government regulation. Japan is an example. When England supplemented its world-famous BBC with a commercial "independent television service" the new stations continued to be publicly owned. They are merely programmed, during portions of the week, by various programming companies licensed for fixed terms by the Independent Television Authority (ITA). (Unlike the FCC, the ITA has been quite freely encouraging competition by refusing to renew some companies' authority.)

During the debates on the Radio Act of 1927 and the Communications Act of 1934, senators and congressmen repeatedly expressed their awareness of the potential economic and political power of this industry, its great opportunity and responsibility, and the need for a close public check upon it. As early as November, 1927, Secretary of Commerce Herbert Hoover urged at the Fourth National Radio Conference that each applicant for a broadcast license be required to prove "that there is something more than naked commercial selfishness in his purpose. . . . [W]e should not freeze the present users of wave lengths permanently in their favored position, irrespective of their service. In 1927 and 1934

Winter, 1969–70. Nicholas Johnson is a member of the Federal Communications Commission and author of *How to Talk Back to Your Television Set*. This article is based on his testimony to the Senate Subcommittee on Communications concerning S.2004, the "Pastore Bill."

Congress purposefully provided that an FCC license would be only "for the use . . . but not the ownership" of the assigned frequency. A six-month license term was originally specified. Later, as the industry gained political power, this term was extended to one year and then to three years. (Recently the industry has been urging a *five*-year term!)

After the original term the FCC must make *an affirmative finding*, every three years, that a renewal of the license will serve the public interest; it is not, like a license to practice law, something that lasts for life unless revoked. The FCC may refuse to renew, and grant the license to another party. Thus the licensee's relationship to the government is very much like that of a highway contractor — he is free to bid against others for an extension of the profitable relationship, but he is not entitled to an additional term as a right. As Judge Warren Burger said for the U.S. Court of Appeals, "after nearly five decades of operation the broadcast industry does not seem to have grasped the simple fact that a broadcast license is a public trust subject to termination for breach of duty."

For a variety of reasons, the system simply hasn't worked as intended. As in so many other instances of "regulation" of an industry, the FCC has permitted irresponsibility to run rampant — under its imprimatur and protection. Lest there be any doubt about the drubbing the public has taken under its leadership, consider these cases:

— The FCC once decided that a radio station proposing thirty-three minutes of commercials per hour would be serving the public interest. (*Accomack-North Hampton Broadcasting Co.*, 1967.)

— It permitted the wholesale transfer of construction permits from one licensee to another, prompting the Special Investigations Subcommittee of the House Interstate and Foreign Commerce Committee to conclude in 1969: "The Commission apparently confused its role as guardian of the public interest with that of guardian of the private interest."

— The FCC approved a license transfer application for a station that quite candidly conceded it proposed to program no news and no public affairs at all. (*Herman C. Hall*, 1968.)

— When presented with charges that a Southern station was engaged in racist programming, the FCC first refused to let the complainants participate in the case, then found that the station's performance entitled it to a license renewal. (*Lamar Life Broadcasting Co.*, [*WLBT*], *1965; 1968.*) Even technical violations get little attention. Recently the Commission refused to consider revoking the license of a station whose owner, it was charged, had ordered his engineer to make fraudulent entries in the station's logbook, operated with an improperly licensed engineer, and whose three stations had amassed eighty-seven other technical violations over a three-year period.

Violations of the most elementary principles of good business practice don't arouse the Commission to action. Recently the FCC examined the record of a station guilty of bilking advertisers out of six thousand dollars in fraudulent transactions. The local Better Business Bureau had complained. The station was already on a one-year "probationary" license status for similar offenses earlier. The result? The majority had no difficulty finding the station had "minimally met the public interest standard," and it therefore renewed the license. (*Star Stations of Indiana, Inc.* [*WIFE*], 1969.)

Every industry requires *some* minimal standards — in this instance, of programming, advertising, ownership patterns, technical performance, and business practices. The FCC is not providing them. Nor is the industry doing any better with "self-regulation." The New York Code manager of the National Association of Broadcasters Code of Good Practice, Warren Braren, recently resigned rather than continue to work with an organization so little concerned about its own standards. When the Eisenhower Commission on Violence addressed the matter of the industry's "self-regulation" of violence, it concluded: "The television industry has consistently argued that its standards for the portrayal of violence and its machinery for enforcement of these standards are adequate to protect the public interest. We do not agree."

If FCC regulation hasn't worked, and industry self-regulation is even weaker, what alternatives are there?

There are two principles to which we are deeply committed in

America: competition and democracy. Institutions spring up from time to time that deviate from these principles, but we eventually bring them into conformity. And if we cannot create pure "competition" or "democracy" in a situation we try to simulate them; to make the institutions work *as if* competition and popular control were a check upon them. So it has been with broadcasting.

We want the American people to have "the best" — the best cameras, copying machines, television programming. Every businessman takes a risk of losing his position in the market. A multimillion-dollar plant can become worthless overnight. Bankruptcy rates are high. Those are risks the American people, and their government, are willing to take; those are risks the American businessman is willing to exchange for the opportunity to make great profits. When the Polaroid camera came on the market, no one concerned himself about providing protection to conventional camera makers and their "right" to continue in business. No one thought of requiring Xerox first to prove that conventional copying machines were not serving the public interest, before displacing other manufacturers' positions in the market. What we do as a people, in effect, is to subject the products offered for sale to a "comparative hearing"; the one that wins is rewarded with handsome profits, the one that loses may suffer losses in the millions.

This kind of pure competition cannot work in TV programming. There are only a limited number of available frequencies; the demand exceeds the supply. There is no way that the new programming idea can find its way into the marketplace. Our typically American solution has been to try to simulate that market process. Congress has provided that no one has a "right" to have his station license extended beyond its original term, that competing applications can be filed, that they must be considered by the people's representatives (the FCC), that programming proposals will be compared, and that the people will thus be assured "the best" in television programming as in other areas of their lives.

To select "the best" is a pragmatic approach. The best may not be very good. It may be an unexpected deviation from our previous standards. But standards tend, by their nature, to be minimal and conventional. One of the beauties of competition is that it is innovative. You cannot "predict" a Polaroid, a Xerox, or a transistor; but you want a system that makes them available to the people when they come along. It is impossible to define the "perfect note." But it is possible for us to determine which of two notes is the higher. That is what the FCC must do when comparing programming proposals.

Not only does competition lead to innovation from newcomers to an industry; it also offers a spur to improve performance on the part of those already in the business. The broadcasters have complained that unless competing applications are curtailed, those in the business will have to cut back on investment in programming. In fact, the broadcasters' response to competitive challenges has not been to cut back upon programming; they have responded to competition like any other industry. *Variety* reports:

> The recent wave of license challenges . . . has without question raised the level of program aspiration in most major markets, and particularly in those where the jump applications were filed. There is on the whole discernibly more local involvement, more community affairs and educational programming, more news and discussion and more show-casing of minority talent since the license challenges than there were before.

This is healthy; it's American; it benefits everyone.

The argument is made by some broadcasters that they cannot fight "blue sky" promises from a fly-by-night applicant for their license. Of course, this could be a theoretical problem. But the FCC has had more than forty years' experience in evaluating programming proposals — and the financial and professional ability of applicants to deliver on them. Its record is pretty good. It can be expected to continue to be biased in favor of the existing operator, and to take a very realistic look at competing proposals. Moreover, the incumbent operator is in the very best position to reply to impractical proposals. He may have tried some of them, and can explain why they didn't work. The "blue sky" objection to competing applications simply cannot withstand close analysis.

The benefits of competition are not limited to comparative evaluation of programming proposals. Ownership is also a legitimate consideration. In many communities the FCC has permitted the owner of the only AM station to acquire the only FM because there were no competing applications for the FM. The public is better off, the majority has reasoned, with the additional service run by a monopolist than without it at all. If there is only one man in town who wants to run the morning and evening newspaper, TV station, and AM-FM radio stations, there's not much the FCC can do about it short of shutting down some of these facilities. When a potential new operator comes along there is.

Nor is competitive ownership limited to considering the number of commercial operators. Blacks, who now own less than ten of the 7,500 operating stations and none of the nation's TV stations, believe themselves even further excluded from participation in the ownership of the most valuable stations by the "Pastore Bill." It is no solution to argue that minority groups should be satisfied with access to ownership of the most undesirable properties — those which at best promise short-term losses and a minimal possibility for long-run viability. Nor can we expect that blacks will be able in the near future to acquire the most desirable properties by bidding in the virtually free market for broadcast licenses. This bill will cut off the only avenue to responsible minority participation in the ownership and operation of broadcast stations. And "minority groups" change. That's why ownership should remain as flexible ten years from now as today. Mexican-Americans and the American Indians are beginning to get organized. Senior citizens, the young (a major portion of the radio audience), and the new-found "Middle America" are also "minority groups."

There are other alternatives to station ownership by white businessmen. Congress and the FCC have provided a great deal of encouragement to the competition known as "educational broadcasting." Hopefully, we both intend to provide it even more support. But many communities are now without VHF educational TV stations, or AM educational radio stations. Should competing applications for these facilities from public broadcasting stations be forever prohibited in these communities? There are now audience-supported radio stations in the area of New York, Los Angeles, San Francisco, Houston, Seattle, and St. Louis. These stations provide a noncommercial service so valued by the audience that it is willing to sustain the programming with voluntary contributions. This is yet another pattern of alternative ownership and competition.

What if a community group offered to operate a local commercial station on a nonprofit basis, plowing the money from commercials back into programming and other broadcast-related activities? Should the community be denied this service? Should consideration of this "competing application" be refused until the FCC has first found that one of the local stations is not serving the public interest (or, in Chairman Burch's proposed language, that it is not "substantially . . . attuned to meeting the needs and interests of its area")?

The practical advantages of competition aside, there is even some question as to whether the "Pastore Bill" is constitutional. The First Amendment flatly bars Congress from enacting laws abridging the freedoms of speech and the press. If Congress were to state that only one, two, or three persons would be permitted to operate newspapers in any one community, such a law would clearly violate the Constitution. And if Congress were to state that no more than three named persons could use "soapboxes" to speak in a public park at a time, such a law would also violate the Constitution. Free speech is not truly "free" if one is forced to speak in a closet. The First Amendment sanctions, not just "speech," but "effective speech" (*Edwards v. South Carolina*, *1963*; *Saia v. New York*, *1948*); the effectiveness of this speech depends on the existence and nature of an appropriate forum. There is no more appropriate "public forum" today than the radio and television media. It does no good to say that citizens have the rights of free speech and press, and then deny them access to the most important methods of communication to modern man: the broadcast media.

So much for "competition." The other basic principle is "democracy," or as the redundant expression has it, "participatory democracy." Our country is caught up in a wave of citizen and consumer participation. We have suddenly become aware of just how unrepresentative and unresponsive our major institutions are. We are reforming our national party structure and procedures. Citizen panels are being established to review complaints against the police, and to participate in local educational policy. Increasing amounts of education, leisure time, and disposable income are creating an exponential growth in the number of people who want, and know how to get, "a piece of the action."

Broadcasting cannot expect to be immune. During the 1968 presidential campaign each candidate made participatory democracy a part of his program. President Nixon talked of listening posts to hear directly from the people; George Wallace urged the return of more power from Washington to local communities; Robert Kennedy spoke of "participatory democracy"; and Eugene McCarthy, of "the new politics." Hubert Humphrey used similar rhetoric. The challenge is to devise systems that leave the people as much opportunity as possible for participating in the decisions that affect their lives. In a densely populated, highly industrialized nation there will be a need for a great many national decisions.

In broadcasting, we must arrive at some national plan for the allocation of TV channels across the country. But who operates those stations, and what they program, need not be determined nationally. There is a balance between popular control and federal regulation. When we can devise ways meaningfully to involve the public in the regulatory process we thereby reduce the need for government-initiated regulation.

What can we do? FCC Commissioner Kenneth Cox and I have set forth our modest efforts at programming evaluation and standards in opinions dealing with renewals in Oklahoma, New York, and the Washington, D.C., area. These studies — especially the latter two — represent an effort to rank stations by common criteria. It is an effort to stimulate competition, or the comparative hearing process. It provides a means whereby the Commission could, if it so chose, undertake a more thorough review of the performance of those stations that rank in the bottom 25 percent or 10 percent. So far, as Professor Louis L. Jaffe has noted, "the Commission has not seen its way clear even to respond on the merits" to this suggestion.

Congressman John Moss of the House Interstate and Foreign Commerce Committee has urged that public renewal hearings be held in the communities where the stations are located. Local hearings might prove impractical for all communities, but encompassing the top hundred markets would require less than three additional hearings a month for FCC examiners.

There are other ways of telling the public of its rights in the license renewal process. Full-page ads and repeated, intelligible radio and TV announcements could be used — instead of the present small-print legal notices and rare and perfunctory broadcast announcements. The FCC could provide the same kind of information and assistance to public groups interested in the renewal process that it now provides broadcasters when its top staff travels about, speaking, answering questions, and distributing literature and helpful hints to licensees about to fill out renewal forms. Most important, if public participation is to work effectively, Congress and the Commission must recognize the tremendous handicap in financial and professional resources that any public group confronts when competing against a well-established broadcaster. There must be some economic incentive for the protesting group. The possibility of competing applications, with the ultimate reward of obtaining the license, is such an incentive — and another reason why competing applications should not be discouraged.

The law has often recognized the need for such incentives. Treble damages are awarded in some antitrust cases, as an incentive to private policing rather than the alternative of more government action. Statutes provide the award of attorneys' fees in some instances. Other agencies — like the National Labor Relations Board or the Neighborhood Legal Services Project of the Office of Economic Opportunity — provide lawyers directly to complaining parties.

There are 7,500 stations in this country. All the licenses in a given state come up for renewal at the same time. With three-year terms, this means roughly 2,500 a year. Even if the FCC were to take away two or three licenses a year — something it has yet to do during its forty-two-year history — we would still be providing rubber stamp renewals to 99.9 percent of the stations. Professor Jaffe has posed the question "whether a communication industry financed by private capital can be run on a three-year basis." Given an industrywide average 100 percent rate of return annually on depreciated tangible investment, and a 99.9 percent (or better) probability of license renewal, I would agree with Professor Jaffe that "once the question is asked it appears to be almost rhetorical."

The really outstanding broadcaster has little to fear. He knows the people of his community and they know him. He heads off legitimate complaints before they become serious. He seeks out representatives from all segments of his audience, including potential protestors, even before they look for him. He knows such an approach is good, audience-building business — as well as public service. Any group seriously looking for a license to challenge is going to go after the station with the worst record in town, not his station.

Further, there is no reason why the FCC need hold long, useless, harassing hearings. Administrative practice is flexible enough to permit the FCC to draft hearing issues tightly, and to use informal prehearing procedures, to dispose of the frivolous cases quickly. (In fact, the most innovative current development has been the negotiated "settlements" in Texarkana and Rochester between outraged citizens and local broadcasters; renewal hearings were contemplated, then dropped, in exchange for concessions.)

Finally, if anyone in or out of the industry is seriously interested in helping to draft standards for the comparative evaluation of stations' license renewal, their contribution will be most welcome. In our renewal opinions, Commissioner Cox and I have called on the academic community to devote some of its intellectual resources to this problem. So far there has been no response.

It is significant, I believe, that the FCC is officially on record as opposing the "Pastore Bill." Its members feel deeply enough about it to have presented an unusual number of personally prepared statements. Some believe the present procedure — if made to work — is best. Others have attempted to fashion compromise positions that give away less than the bill. None, however, on the old commission, offered the bill their enthusiastic support. Only one commissioner does so now, in a most summary and general statement.

The issue before us ought to be stated starkly. It is, quite simply, who is to retain the potential to rule America. We know, if we are honest with ourselves, which segments of the economic and social structure have the loudest voices in the decision-making process in Washington. But the *potential* for popular check remains. It remains, however, only so long as the people can obtain education and information, only so long as they can communicate with each other, only so long as they can retain potential control over the mass media of this country. So long as we preserve the people's *potential* to rule — their *potential* opportunity to participate in the operation of their mass media — there is some hope, however small, that some future generation — perhaps the next — will use this potential to rebuild America.

PASSING COMMENT

The March on Washington— to Save Commercials

Since 1929, the National Association of Broadcasters has administered codes of good practice for commercial broadcasting. The present radio and television codes forbid certain offenses against taste and limit the time devoted to commercials — to no more than 4 minutes 15 seconds, for example, in a half-hour program.

The benefits to viewers and listeners from these codes are likely to be illusory, for 170 of 580 television stations and 3,116 of 4,946 radio stations do not even adhere to the code. Many who do profess to find the standards inexpedient. Moreover, the codes have little to say about orderliness on the air, about the "clutter" of advertising and promotion.

Two years ago, the Federal Communications Commission began to look into the matter. (To the broadcasters, this appeared to be another example of the FCC's rapacity; to outsiders, the FCC looked like an overworked body that would hardly undertake more duties without public demand.) The FCC sought an easy path — adoption of the broadcasters' own standards into the FCC rules.

Judging from the reaction of much of the broadcasting industry, one would have thought the FCC had proposed the Communist Manifesto. *Broadcasting* magazine said that the industry should forget that it ever had codes. Vehement broadcasters staged a "march on Washington" and were greeted with warmth by friends in Congress, one of whom introduced a bill to keep the

---

Winter, 1963–64.

FCC from touching the question. Some broadcasters even resorted to the dubious argument that because broadcasting had dropped commercials after the assassination of the President, regulation was unnecessary.

Under the pressure, the FCC wilted and on January 15 gave up the idea. The episode offered little hope for either the ability of the FCC to act independently or for the statesmanship of many in the broadcasting industry. An enlightened exception was LeRoy Collins, president of the NAB, who insisted that broadcasters live up to their codes.

The broadcasters' victory has not made the issue go away, but has reshaped it. The absence of a government code makes it all the more incumbent on broadcasters to clean house themselves. One can sympathize with station owners' resistance to annoying regulation — by either the government or their own association. Nonetheless, there is still truth in the words of the first government bureaucrat who regulated broadcasting, Secretary of Commerce Herbert Hoover: "It is inconceivable that we should allow so great a possibility for service, for news, for entertainment, for education and for vital commercial purposes to be drowned in advertising chatter."

Broadcasters can scarcely deny that parts of their programming are being so drowned. It is a measure of their failure to grasp the issue that one of their friends in Congress (Cunningham of Nebraska) said in effect that viewers should put up with the annoyance of commercial interruptions as the price of free enterprise.

What a reversal — to have the public's air looked on as a vehicle for the enrichment of license holders. Shades of Commodore Vanderbilt! Unless the industry abandons this dinosaur kind of thinking, unless it takes hold and develops good practices and good manners that will stay far ahead of codes and government rules, there may eventually be a viewers' "march on Washington" — that is, a redoubled public demand for government intervention. As in the ratings mess of 1963, parts of the broadcasting industry are so far inviting the thing they most hope to avoid.

PASSING COMMENT

Something for the Press

Judging from its title alone, the Newspaper Preservation Act, which became law on July 28, might be thought to be aimed at saving quaint old editorial offices as museums. There is at least a glimmer of truth in this idea, for the act may salvage some quaint old newspapers by shielding them from the normal functioning of antitrust law. This is the first point to remember about the act: by legalizing "joint operating agreements" it grants a kind of antitrust immunity allowed no other unregulated United States industry. It is, as the July 20 *Time* stated, A LICENSE TO FIX PRICES.

The United States Supreme Court, in a legal test of such agreements under prior law, last year ruled the agreements illegal in the Tuscon *Star/Citizen* case. The right of separately owned papers to trim overhead by sharing mechanical plants and business staffs was not disputed. What was in question was the fixing of advertising rates and pooling of profits without relationship to costs. To advocates of the act, approving this seems an acceptable price for "preserving competitive editorial voices" in a community. To critics such as Paul Conrad, former general counsel of the National Newspaper Association (representing seven thousand small daily and weekly newspapers), it seems both morally repugnant and conducive to precisely the opposite effect.

"A joint operation," says Conrad, "is the most formidable barrier that can be erected to discourage newcomers in the same market, because it effectively brings together the combination of two organizations and divides the market between them. . . . We don't think the legislation would serve the newspaper industry as a whole. . . . In the present climate, I think it is unfortunate

---

Fall, 1970.

that anyone in our business feels he has to ask Congress for . . . legislation, particularly antitrust action."

Moreover, as Stephen R. Barnett has pointed out in *CJR* ("Newspaper 'Preservation' — or Monopoly?" Winter, 1969–70), the act's immediate beneficiaries (certain to be joined by others, who must come hat in hand to the Attorney General for approval) scarcely are uniformly destitute. Indeed, "approximately one-quarter are owned by large chains such as Scripps-Howard, Newhouse, Hearst, Knight, and Cox."

Let there be no mistake: the law was not designed to save a few sturdy independents who happened to run into financial trouble. It will help out urban businesses of considerable size — managements the Blackfoot (Idaho) *News* called "barefoot millionaires." Powerful millionaires, it might have added, with enough awesome influence on public careers to assemble heavy majorities in both houses — majorities cutting significantly across party and ideological lines in this, an election year for every United States representative and for one-third of the United States Senate.

Is it possible, as the act's advocates contended, that by any logical reasoning its passage was a victory for press freedom? If so, then one can only wonder why there was so little editorial crowing about its passage — especially in cities alleged to be its beneficiaries. In a sampling of twenty out of forty-four "joint operating agreement" newspapers in the week the act passed the Senate, *CJR* found that only thirteen carried stories mentioning the passage, and of these only five listed the twenty-two cities affected. Of these five, only two — the Nashville *Tennessean* and Salt Lake *City Deseret News* — named themselves as specifically benefited by the act. (The Scripps-Howard chain, for one, later did circulate an editorial in which member papers acknowledged, and defended, their beneficiary roles.)

Shortly after the act was signed — again without fanfare — by President Nixon in San Clemente, a suit testing its constitutionality was filed in San Francisco by the Bay Guardian Company, publisher of an independent investigatory newspaper, and by its editors, Bruce B. and Jean Dibble Brugmann. The defendants named are the publishers of the two San Francisco daily newspapers and their joint agency, the San Francisco Newspaper Printing Company. Among the principal charges: that the Preservation Act allows the defendants to "monopolize and preempt" San Francisco advertising revenues, thus abridging the "freedom of the press guaranteed to the plaintiff"; that the act "bears no rational relationship to the financial condition" of its beneficiaries now or "for the unlimited future"; and that, to enter into such an agreement henceforth, one must satisfy the "unique requirement" of approval by "a high governmental official" — the Attorney General. In setting up the test, the *Bay Guardian* is performing a saving function that more formidable elements of the newspaper business should be doing for themselves.

SEVEN

Blights and Fixations

THE NEWS FROM MOSCOW: A CORRESPONDENT'S VIEWS

Harrison E. Salisbury

The question of American press coverage of the Soviet Union has been subject to periodic analysis since shortly after the establishment of the Bolshevik regime on November 7, 1917. The first, and still in many ways the classic analysis of American press coverage of Soviet events is that done by Walter Lippmann and Charles Merz and published under the title "A Test of the News" as a special supplement to the *New Republic* of August 4, 1920.

In their study Mr. Merz and Mr. Lippmann scanned the columns of the New York *Times* for reports of the fall of the Bolshevik regime, the assassination of the Bolshevik leaders, the annihilating victories of the White Russian armies. Their conclusion was sobering. The most reliable of American newspapers had reported *scores* of times that the Red Regime had been overthrown. Yet it survived and even flourished.

The American press might, perhaps, be forgiven its ineptitude in that early period. Knowledge of Russia was scant. Specialists in the field hardly existed in the United States. Even the names of the Bolshevik leaders seemed difficult to establish. It was in this period that some unknown wire service man, compelled by the exigencies of style to provide a first name for the Bolshevik known as N. Lenin, provided him with the given name Nikolai. To this day in many American reference works the name Nikolai Lenin is studiously listed despite the fact that Vladimir Ilych Ulyanov who did use the pen name "Lenin" or, occasionally "N. Lenin" (N in Russia is the equivalent of our X) never signed himself

Fall, 1963. Harrison E. Salisbury of the New York *Times* was Moscow correspondent from 1949 to 1954.

"Nikolai Lenin." To this day, it is not uncommon to find American press references to "Nikolai Lenin," an error as glaring to a Russian as would be a Soviet reference to "Alexander Lincoln."

The Lenin error is fairly characteristic of American reporting of the Soviet revolution in the early days. There were few correspondents in Petrograd or Moscow. Sensational rumors circulated as fact. Many of the wildest asseverations, still not uncommonly attributed to Soviet life, had their origin in this period — the "communization of women," "free love," the cartoonlike representation of the Bolshevik leaders as bomb-throwing anarchists, state rearing of children, and countless stories of the atrocity type.

Some vivid reporting from "inside" the Revolution did find its way into the United States press. The reports of John Reed, Louise Bryant, Albert Rhys Williams (all of them sympathizers in the Bolshevik cause) appeared in a variety of publications that included *Masses*, the Philadelphia *Public Ledger* and some of the New York dailies. Biased as these accounts were, they did report firsthand impressions of the "Ten Days that Shook the World," as Reed called them. And to this day they represent valuable historical source material.

If we find these accounts inadequate, patchy and partisan, it may be said in their defense that this American reporting was the best of the period (excepting, perhaps, the book journalism of Bruce Lockhart and the late Sir Bernard Pares).

With the stabilization of the Bolshevik regime in the early 1920s American journalism in Russia took firmer root. It was in this period that such men as Walter Duranty of the New York *Times*, William Henry Chamberlain of the *Christian Science Monitor*, and Louis Fischer of the New York *Evening Post* and the *Nation* began their work.

Although reporting conditions were far from normal in Soviet Russia, all three of these men (and a number of others who corresponded from Russia in that period) enjoyed what would now be regarded as extraordinarily close contacts with high Soviet officials. They were often aided and assisted in presenting to the world materials of historic importance. In the earlier part of this period Max Eastman, himself deeply involved in Soviet politics, wrote a number of brilliant dispatches on the emerging conflict between

Stalin and Trotsky and presented in the New York *Times* such historic documents as Lenin's famous testament, long a semisecret document in the Soviet Union.

Once again in writing the history of the 1920s and up to the purge period of the mid-1930s, one turns again and again to the brilliant reporting of these American correspondents. Each had his bias. Duranty has often been criticized in the postwar period as having been too sympathetic to the Stalin regime; Chamberlain made a sharp and clean break with the Russian scene and devoted himself to history; Fischer followed the classic course from sympathizer to critic; Eastman went over to the most energetic kind of anti-Communist reporting.

Alongside these brilliant examples of U.S. coverage of Russia there continued a flow of mediocre and tendentious reports. Much of the agency material, much that appeared in the Hearst press and in other less responsible media continued at the lowest level.

A phenomenon that became more and more frequent as the Soviet regime grew older was that of the reporter who arrived on the scene as a partisan or enthusiast but who lost his enthusiasm in the harsh light of Soviet reality. An archetype of this correspondent was Eugene Lyons, who went to Russia early in the 1930s for the United Press an ardent Communist sympathizer and within a few years became a violent antagonist. His *Assignment to Utopia* summed up his classic experience. It set a pattern for much correspondence in the following decades. Not all of Lyons's correspondence from Moscow was of quality standards. His reporting was marred by inaccurate or exaggerated reports of fighting on the Russo-Japanese frontier (it was for such reports that he was expelled from the Soviet Union). In this same period Duranty's reporting also suffered serious lapses, notably in underestimating the turmoil, violence, and famine resulting from collectivization of the peasantry.

The mid-1930s in American reporting were characterized by the emergence of the "exclusive interview" with Stalin — first scored by Roy Howard, followed by Lyons, Duranty, and others. These were utilized by Stalin to propagate his line of the moment. The period was also characterized by poor and confused reporting of the famous "purge" trials. Many American reports tended to follow the line of United States Ambassador Joseph E. Davies, who became convinced of the essential validity of the charges. None of the American reporters' accounts came close to the keen and accurate analysis of the purges and the significance of the trials revealed in the since-published dispatches of George Kennan to the State Department.

American press reporting of Russia in World War II was little better than mediocre. Because of partisanship at the time of the Soviet-Finnish war, almost all U.S. correspondents had been withdrawn from Moscow. When the Nazi attack came only three American reporters were on duty there. The *Times*, for example, was not represented for many months until C. L. Sulzberger made his way into Russia via Iran.

The gap in reporting was filled in very poorly with propaganda materials supplied by Sovinformburo (the Soviet Information Bureau). These were largely glorifications of the Red Army and atrocity accounts of the Nazis provided by various Soviet war correspondents and authors known in the West, such as Ilya Ehrenburg and Mikhail Sholokhov.

To go with this, American papers published a good deal of "expertise" from pseudo-military experts, largely designed to show that the Soviet would not be able to stand up long under Nazi assault. Until Pearl Harbor American newspapers published substantial quantities of information originating with the Goebbels propaganda ministry.

American reporting of the Soviet scene improved by 1944 and 1945, with the dispatch to Russia of large numbers of able correspondents. However, Soviet censorship and restrictions prevented balanced accounts of many situations.

American reporting of Russia in the postwar period — up to the death of Stalin — was undistinguished. With the advent of cold war and the tightening of press restrictions in Moscow most American media withdrew their correspondents. By 1950 there were only four or five United States reporters in Moscow. The *Times* was the only newspaper represented. Most of the Soviet materials in the United States press originated with agency pickups of Tass broadcasts in London. There was heavy emphasis on "interpretation" and a strong tendency to accentuate the negative and play down the positive. The average reader began to get an almost exclusively black picture of the Soviet scene. So much was published of Soviet deficiencies, defects, inadequacies, failures, and repressions that when the Russians began to overcome the handicaps of war damage and to produce nuclear arms, much of the American public was so conditioned against accepting any achievement of Russia as to doubt the existence of Soviet atom bombs — an attitude of skepticism which persisted even after the first Soviet sputnik.

The greatest failure of the American press in Russia undoubtedly occurred in the period 1945–53 when, instead of reporting the country in depth and with pristine objectivity as would befit intelligent appreciation of a potential enemy, it either ignored or distorted the Soviet reality beyond recognition. Even those correspondents remaining in Moscow were almost continuously criticized for publishing "Soviet propaganda," instead of being hailed for their efforts.

Since the death of Stalin and the advent of a comparatively lighter regime in Moscow, U.S. reporting on Russia has improved substantially. Not only has the press corps in Moscow expanded to a score or more of well-qualified men but the interest of the press, generally, in accurate and factual information has mounted year by year.

The average U.S. correspondent in Moscow today had some background training before going there. A majority of the reporters have language ability. Through the concentrated efforts of the U.S. academic community this country possesses a body of scholarship and a cadre of specialists in the Soviet field second to none. American scholarship in many fields of Soviet affairs is superior to that in the Soviet Union itself. The press increasingly reflects this fact.

Today, U.S. press coverage on the Soviet Union comprises more than the handful of reports from a few lonely correspondents in Moscow. It is made up of a steady flow of expert dispatches from agency men and special correspondents. It is augmented by a constant stream of specialists and reporters for individual newspapers (even small-town papers) who go to Russia and "see for themselves." Their reports may be largely color and may often incorporate error and inexactitude, but the sheer volume of accurate reports tends to offset the minor inaccuracies.

Moreover, the stream of Soviet visitors to the United States forms a subject for interviews, impressionistic stories, and features. The American reader has a background of translated literature from Soviet authors, films from the Soviet studios, and miscellaneous materials of every kind to flesh out his impressions.

As a result it may safely be said that the quality of U.S. reporting on Soviet affairs today is higher than ever before and probably higher than the quality of reporting we are now getting from any other nation. In volume the news report from Moscow has begun to equal or exceed that from such long standard datelines as Paris, Rome, or Tokyo. Sometimes it will exceed even that from London.

All this being said, there still remains room for improvement, particularly in the provincial press. The reader of the New York *Times*, the New York *Herald Tribune*, the Baltimore *Sun* or the Washington *Post* can fairly say that he is accurately and reliably informed on the Soviet Union. The same cannot yet be said for the reader of the provincial press. This is not basically the fault of the agency bureaus in Moscow. Henry Shapiro, United Press International chief, has been there since the early 1930s. His reports are authoritative and reliable. The Associated Press bureau is well staffed and equally to be relied upon.

However, smaller papers cling to the old habit of reporting the sensational rumor — the vagrant report that "Khrushchev is on the way out" or even that "Khrushchev is dead" while the intelligent surveys and analyses are consigned to the wastebasket.

Until this handicap has been overcome, vast areas of the United States will continue to be deprived of news concerning the subject which may be vital to our very existence.

BLIGHTED AREAS OF OUR PRESS

Ferdinand Kuhn

One way to put the American press into sharp focus is to get far away from it. A traveling writer on foreign affairs develops a keen eye for the merits and faults of American newspapers, especially if he has had to depend for a few months on papers abroad.

Whenever I come home from Africa or Asia, it cheers me to rediscover American papers. But this time I am newly conscious of a blight upon them. Commercialism pollutes the back pages and Sunday sections like the smog in our city air, the muck in our lakes and streams.

I remember newspapers' air of superior virtue during the television scandals of six or seven years ago. Radio and television stations had been slipping unlabeled plugs for advertisers into their programs. "Sneaky commercials," the Federal Communications Commission called them. The press was right to squawk, and it did so, loudly.

One who protested in those days was the president of the American Newspaper Publishers Association, D. Tennant Bryan. The sins of television, he said, proved the wisdom of newspapers in keeping news, editorials, and advertisements in "separate, airtight compartments." To the publishers' association in 1960 he repeated an old refrain: no good newspaper lets its advertisers influence its news columns.

Maybe it was true in 1960. Is it true now? In all but a few big-city papers, one has only to look to know that the press adulterates its news with unlabeled advertising. The line between news and salesmanship is hard to find in the pages and sections that deal

---

Summer, 1966. Ferdinand Kuhn, long a newspaper reporter and foreign correspondent, based this article on his Henry F. Pringle memorial lecture at the Columbia Graduate School of Journalism.

with food, fashions, and travel. In real estate pages the line has almost disappeared.

The pollution of real estate news is worth the urgent attention of publishers, editors, reporters, and schools of journalism, for three reasons:

First, the pseudo-news of real estate blurs the line between news and advertising. Second, it shows a failure to use freedom of the press, which, as I know it, means the freedom to dig, to inquire, to challenge. Third, and above all, most real estate news columns amount to week-by-week confessions of a deeper failure. They neither report nor even reflect the crisis in our metropolitan areas.

Real estate news, after all, deals with where and how Americans live and will live. These questions cut to the heart of the problems of our cities and suburbs. Millions of Negroes and the poor of all races live cooped up in city slums and ghettos. They need houses and cannot get them; when they can get houses they cannot afford them.

Millions of others can find houses or apartments, but discover that it is harder every year to ride to work and home again. This is no specialized subject affecting a few readers. Two thirds of all Americans now live in urban areas. They know, as real estate editors apparently don't, that our cities are strangled with traffic and choked with fumes, that our suburbs are starved for adequate schools and other services.

Do you find any word, any hint, in most real estate news about the plight of the cities and suburbs? Have you ever seen stories or pictures in these pages about low-cost housing, public or private? Can you find any serious discussion of the future shape and character of our metropolitan areas? No; I sometimes think that all but a few real estate editors prefer to see nothing, hear nothing, report nothing, know nothing of the actual America around them.

The pattern of real estate news is familiar. A big office building may be about to go up on a whole square block. The architect's sketch, complete with shrubbery, stretches across three or four columns. The news story tells how much the building will cost, who will finance it, who has designed it, what luxuries the tenants will enjoy.

But I want to know more. What used to stand on that square

block before the bulldozers came? If homes used to be there, how many people have been displaced, and what provision, if any, has been made for them? How will the new building fit in, or not, with the design of other buildings nearby? Will it create new traffic and parking problems for the city?

Or, to take another example, a couple of hundred ranch-type houses are about to fill what used to be open country, outside the suburbs. The pseudo-news story quotes the developer; he says his tenants will have easy and swift travel over uncongested highways into the city. How easy? How swift? A reporter could easily have clocked it and checked the developer's story if this were worth mentioning at all.

A reporter could have asked a few more relevant questions that the handout didn't cover. How near is a school? If two hundred families move in, will the school have room for their children? What are the municipal authorities doing or planning to cope with the newcomers?

In real estate copy such questions are seldom asked or answered. Reporters are seldom turned loose on such stories. Real estate copy is not meant to tell; it is meant to sell.

One example of such puffery, a relatively innocent example, I found the other day in the Milwaukee *Journal*. It was a UPI feature headed WHY HIRE A DESIGNER? — the word "designer" being a euphemism for interior decorator. The story argued that everyone furnishing a new home should hire a designer. It attributed the advice to a designer who is a consultant to a firm of fabric makers. "The homeowner pays no more than he would pay at a store," the story said. And "designers are as interested in a $300 room as they are in a $5,000 room." As I was reading, I found my eyebrows rising until they almost hit the roof of my head.

I suppose someone could write a genuine story on interior designing — on the men and women who work in it, their training, their pay, their role in developing American taste and economy.

But the UPI feature was not a story at all. Although it did not mention any brand name, it was a sales talk. I would sum it up with an honorable four-letter term that seems to have gone out of style. The term is "advt."

I have asked editors how they explain or justify this kind of copy. One of them told me it was only "shinplaster to keep the ads from bumping." But shinplaster has two definitions. One is medical; the other (from the unabridged Webster III) is "a piece of poorly secured and depreciated paper currency." That says it. That's what fills page after page of these sections every week.

How many reporters complain that their pieces have been cut or killed for lack of space? How many news editors grumble because they can't find space for the good stories? How many publishers wail about the price of newsprint? Never mind; there has to be shinplaster to keep the ads from bumping.

Another explanation of pseudo-news is that papers must offer not only news but "service" to their readers. The story about interior decorators was, presumably, such a "service." Obviously every good paper provides service of many kinds, as all of us discover during a newspaper strike.

Weather forecasts, television and radio programs, lists of the day's events, reports on what's plentiful in the food markets are all legitimate services. Real estate advertising itself is a service to anyone — any white person, that is — who is looking for a home.

But to be a service at all in the news columns, the information has to be disinterested and honest. When a writer simply tries to persuade his readers to buy, he is no better than a tout.

To sniff the rank fragrance of salesmanship in real estate news, I suggest a look at the usual run of pseudo-news about apartment buildings. I found a rousing sales pitch not long ago in the Philadelphia *Inquirer*, under the byline of its real estate editor. It happened to be a day when the paper bulged with apartment advertising. The lead sentence of the lead story asked: "Is there an apartment in your future?" The editor answered: "Probably." According to him, "there is a tremendous demand for the kind of carefree living that is only possible when the landlord takes on the chores of lawn care, snow removal, and redecoration."

At this point I looked for that four-letter term "advt." and couldn't find it. If the story had been fair reporting instead of hawking, it would also have mentioned a tremendous, insatiable demand for houses — for peace and privacy, for space and quiet, for one shade tree and one little flower.

Real estate editors find no difficulty in switching their love from apartments to houses from one week to the next. If the section features advertising for houses rather than apartments, the editor will be glad to conform in his news columns. Conflicting advice poses no problems. If a city happens to have competing papers, the reader can enjoy contradictory advice on the same weekend, as I often do in my own city of Washington.

On May 13, for example, the *Evening Star* ran an advertising pullout of four pages, one page for gas air conditioners, the next three pages for new houses with gas cooling systems. On the fifth page, by coincidence, I suppose, the main display in the news columns went to a signed article by the residential sales manager of the Washington Gas Light Company. The head stretched across five columns. What was the news under all this display? His company had opened a new showroom in a Maryland suburb, and he wanted the customers to see it.

The next morning, in the competing paper, the Washington *Post*, gas air conditioning was gone. The paper ran a double-page advertisement of the Potomac Electric Power Company. This time the shinplaster of pseudo-news, fore and aft, was as thick as a featherbed. On that single day the paper printed 145 column inches, almost seven columns, not labeled as advertising, about the delights of electrified home life.

It told of the joys of electric heating, cooling, floodlighting, and gadgetry unlimited, including an electrically warmed birdbath. The words "wonderful," "intriguing," and "remarkable" dripped from this copy, and one other adjective especially struck my fancy. When a story dealt with electric heating, the writer was careful to include the adjective "flameless."

It struck me because last winter I used to listen to the morning news on the *Post*'s own radio station, WTOP. A commercial of the same Potomac Electric Power Company, dinned into my ears morning after morning, said of electric heating: "It's flameless!" — and sang the praises of "flameless electric living." Again, I suppose, any resemblance to a paid commercial in these news columns was purely coincidental.

When World II began in 1939, the New York *Times* carried a front-page box to put its readers on their guard: "Dispatches from Europe and the Far East are now subject to censorship." In all decency, should not real estate sections carry a similar box saying: "News in this section is furnished by advertisers"?

On television, the remedy that stopped the practice of concealed advertising — for a time — was exposure. When the evil was brought to light, the stations were at least abashed, if not ashamed. I suggest that most of our big-city papers need such exposure, too. AP and UPI editors might also take a searching look at the shinplaster turned out by their feature services.

I have enough faith in newspapers to believe that responsible publishers will give their real estate editors stiff brushes and strong detergents, and will tell them to scrub their columns clean.

I do not want to leave the impression that we get no independent reporting and no careful coverage of metropolitan sprawl and urban decay. These have become subjects of growing concern. Especially in cities that are proud of their beauty, like San Francisco and Washington, the newspapers print news stories, letters, and editorials about highways and bridges, slums and blight, growth and crowding.

But these stories, as a rule, do not appear in the real estate section, the only part of the paper wholly concerned with metropolitan living. They have to struggle for space in competition with other news and features. By their nature they require pictures and maps, and these call for space that often is not available. There would be more room for serious news and discussion of the metropolitan future if publishers would clear out their real estate junk.

In the meantime, a few papers are setting good examples, trying to break with the shoddy commercialism of the usual real estate sections.

Of the papers I have seen, the outstanding one in this field is the Louisville *Courier-Journal*. Its management proceeds from the assumption that the changes around us are too important to be left to the real estate advertisers and their handout men. The *Courier-Journal* renamed its real estate section, accurately, "City and Countryside," and reshaped it. It put the section, not in charge of a salesman who is called an editor, but under an urban affairs editor, Grady Clay, and a building editor, Simpson Lawson.

Mr. Clay has now taken a new post at the school of journalism at Northwestern University, where he will train and recruit writers on urban design. He has said that city planning in the European sense, including architecture, is "one of the most significant stories of our generation." He and his paper have proved that it is possible to banish the trash and make room for the story.

If downtown Louisville has developed a clutter of light poles, signs, and other ugly street furniture, the *Courier-Journal* editors don't hide it from their readers. They put it into a feature, with pictures, on the front page of their City and Countryside section. If commercial zoning is gobbling too much residential space, they dip into this subject too. Their choice of stories is as wide as the field of urban design. They dig up examples, contrasts, ideas applicable to their city, from other cities and other countries.

Louisville, of course, is a one-ownership town. Its papers run no risk of losing real estate advertising to a shoddy-minded competitor. But even in a competitive city, decent newspapering will not necessarily drive out revenue. A disgruntled real estate advertiser cannot switch to television. Obviously, a home hunter cannot take a television program with him while he searches; he uses printed advertising as his guide. This is why 80 percent of all real estate advertising money is still spent in newspapers. In real estate more than in food, fashion, or travel copy, the odds favor a newspaper.

A few pioneering papers are showing the power of example in another way. Each has assigned a talented writer to roam freely over the subject of the urban and suburban environment — which includes the planning of buildings, parklands, transportation, and housing. Lewis Mumford has been the trailblazer in this field of American journalism, but he has written primarily in a magazine, the *New Yorker*. I happen to know of only five who have followed the same trail in daily newspapers.

One is Grady Clay of Louisville, whom I have mentioned already. The others are Ada Louise Huxtable of the New York *Times*, George McCue of the St. Louis *Post-Dispatch*, Allan Temko in the San Francisco *Chronicle*, and, my favorite of the lot because of the inexhaustible range of his interest, Wolf von Eckardt, of the Washington *Post*. They differ in their style and in the scope of their work. But all of them, I think, belong on the same roll of honor. They are pioneers and public defenders, and their papers deserve honor for having hired them.

Why can't every metropolitan paper give its readers a service of this kind? One answer is that qualified writers are difficult to find. To fill the gap, other schools of journalism might well copy the experiment now begun at Northwestern. What is needed, in my opinion, is not an architect, but rather a reporter with specialized knowledge and generalized interest. The field of the metropolitan environment is too huge, too varied, for anyone but an informed generalist.

Architecture is the most public of the arts. Everyone can see it every day. Urban planning affects everyone in the community. Public interest may be more sophisticated than the salesmen-editors imagine. Last year, for example, nontechnical magazines printed more than three times as many pieces on city planning, four times as many on water pollution, as they did in a year in the early 1950s.

I would guess that newspaper coverage has grown just as fast. It would grow still faster if so much news space were not wasted on real estate handouts and commercialized rubbish.

In the next five years, I believe, every big-city paper will feel the need of someone to cover this field. And if a publisher has any pride in his craft, he will want to clean his slums in the news columns, his blighted areas in the real estate sections, and substitute news and comment that matter.

THE FANTASY WORLD OF TRAVEL SECTIONS

Stanford N. Sesser

With the initiation of the Boeing 747 jumbo jet, the doubling in the sixties of the number of Americans spending vacations overseas, and myriad problems associated with a travel boom, it seems particularly urgent that attention be given one of the most woefully inadequate areas of American journalism — the newspaper travel section. It is almost axiomatic that a person choosing a vacation spot relies for advice on friends and travel agents, not on the various pieces of puffery sandwiched in most Sunday papers between ads for Florida hotels and three-week-Puerto-Rican-vacations-for-two-from-$87. This could be attributed to a natural defense mechanism that sets in after the thousand-and-first description of smiling natives, swaying palm trees, and sumptuous Hilton hotels that always "exemplify the unique culture" of each foreign land. But now with travel such big business and with millions of Americans visiting distant points, it becomes relevant to ask why travel can't be reported in a considerably more professional and probing fashion than it is.

While most other parts of a newspaper make at least some attempt to come to grips with reality, most travel sections determinedly seek to avoid it. Words like "dictatorship," "racism," and "poverty" don't exist; they are avoided almost as assiduously as "bad weather," "expensive," and "grotesque." Publicity releases are passed off as news, and reporters or syndicated columnists write glowing descriptions of airlines, hotels, and vacation spots while somehow failing to mention that the subjects of their articles

---

Spring, 1970. Stanford N. Sesser, a *Wall Street Journal* reporter, investigated the travel beat on assignment for his newspaper.

have paid all the bills for their trip. Moreover, the style of travel writing too often resembles that of the publicity man, where nothing is allowed to be beautiful and optimistic unless couched in the clichés of hack writing.

In some cases it might almost be suspected that newspapers lay down an edict that travel articles be so dull as not to distract from the ads. Take one Sunday's travel articles in the Newark *News:* of a total of nine, six were releases from airlines, travel agencies, or state tourist departments. They included AMERICAN EXPRESS WILL SHOW MOVIE ON EUROPE, PAN AM INAUGURATES 747 SERVICE TO PUERTO RICO, and ALASKA TRAVEL DIVISION OFFERING HIGHWAY MAP. The seventh was a short unattributed puff about the island of Curaçao, describing "the crystal clear water, blue skies, and powdery white sand, along with an occasional seagull to break the solitude." (We will hear more about Curaçao later; when a hot, arid island dotted with oil storage tanks is struck by rioting, as Curaçao was last summer, that is a sure sign travel writers will be flocking in, usually on free junkets, to assure everyone it ain't necessarily so.) The eighth Newark *News* article, carrying the by-line of a staff reporter, urged vacationers to visit Sarasota, Florida, which, he wrote, is "on the verge of rediscovery, this time by modern tourists." Finally, there was a column by the *News* travel editor on Expo '70 — consisting solely of an interview with the director of the Japan National Tourist Organization's New York Office.

Only a few voices in the newspaper industry have reacted against such pap. One is Norman E. Isaacs, outspoken editor of the Louisville *Courier-Journal* and a man who takes the concept of "ethics" and "standards" seriously. About two years ago Isaac's paper dropped a syndicated travel columnist when Isaacs discovered that the writer was taking free junkets to the faraway spots he described in his columns; and recently the paper reduced its travel section to a couple of pages of ads and assigned its travel writer to other duties. "The big question in my mind is why travel can't be handled like all other news," Isaacs declares. "I never see anything that comes close to being criticism. It's all, 'Oh, gee whiz.' I'd never read one of those damn things to tell me where to travel."

Dropping a travel section is scarcely the ideal solution, but it does indicate the depth of the problem. Even the handful of newspapers that pay all expenses of their travel editors — they include the Los Angeles *Times*, the Washington *Post*, and the New York *Times* — still don't attempt to enforce on their travel sections the high standards that exist for the rest of the paper. For example, Los Angeles *Times* travel editor Jerry Hulse is widely considered to be the best in the country; his stories are frequently critical, and the paper spends twenty thousand dollars a year to finance his travels. Yet the Los Angeles *Times* travel section still contains scattered publicity releases disguised as articles. One such article begins: "For a swinging vacation with a 'Latin' flavor, Henry Miele Travel Service recommends Matson's *SS Monterey* cruises to the Mexican Riviera this spring." And the paper also uses syndicated columnist Richard Joseph, who often mentions airlines without noting that he flew on them free.

Not every travel writer is happy with the junketeering. "I'd love to pick up and go anyplace, but my paper just wouldn't agree to it," says Bill Hughes of the Cleveland *Press*, a highly profitable link in the Scripps-Howard chain. Bruce Hamby of the Denver *Post*, who has persuaded his paper to finance most of his travel, declares, "I fight like hell; I don't want to take any free trips at all." When Hamby does accept something free he mentions that fact in a box accompanying the article.

Not very many travel editors, however, are making this fight. Virtually all are over forty years old and veterans of years or decades of city-room reporting, and few are eager to risk an enjoyable job by requesting a twenty-thousand-dollar expense account. If there is to be an initiative for better travel reporting, it will have to come from a realization by newspaper management that today's travel sections alienate both readers, who skip over them because of the puffery, and advertisers, who thereby get a lower readership response.

The New York *Times*, whose Sunday travel section has a staff of twelve and can encompass forty or fifty pages, also offers an illustration of some deficiencies in travel writing. While the *Times* travel section has done excellent articles such as reports on the complexity of airline fares and chaotic customs procedures at Kennedy Airport, most of the section still seems to picture the world as a sort of giant museum that exists for the benefit of American tourists. The articles on foreign countries not only ignore political and sociological factors generally but also tend to gloss over anything negative. When something unfavorable happens in the travel field that can't be overlooked, such as this year's disastrous New Orleans Mardi Gras or the dropoff this past winter in Florida tourism, the event is recorded in the general news columns rather than the travel section.

Last fall, for example, four months after serious riots in Curaçao, Hyman Maidenberg, a *Times* Latin American reporter, visited the island for a travel article. It is now safe for tourists to return, Maidenberg stated, and he recalled: "This reporter remembers tourists telling him at the time how Negroes escorted frightened foreigners back to their hotels that Friday afternoon. Some tourists, who thought they were being abused verbally on the streets, realized later in calmer moments that they were being advised to go to their hotels in *papiamento,* the local patois."

All this may have been true, but the travel article omitted mention that on Monday, June 2, four days after the rioting began, the same Maidenberg had reported in the *Times*'s news columns that "hundreds of tourists — many of them Americans — have been trapped in hotel lobbies since Thursday night waiting for outbound transportation." Also, that "some 70 percent of the resort's businesses have been destroyed or damaged." While a visitor would be pleased to know he is safe in Curaçao, he might also wonder about the attention given to underlying grievances which had led to the rioting — unless he wanted to gamble on spending four days of his vacation sleeping in a hotel lobby. In addition, he could legitimately ask how badly shopping and night life had been hurt by the riots; certainly they had been affected to some extent. Similarly, a *Times* travel article on Haiti spoke of "an optimistic spirit" among the Haitian people, who "give the impression that even though they lack the material abundance of some parts of the world, they share the pride that comes with independence." Not only is this description directly contradicted by articles on Haiti in the *Times*'s regular news columns, but the travel story also fails to point out that dollars spent by visitors to Haiti go into the pocket of dictator François Duvalier, who desperately needs hard currency to prop up his repressive regime.

To the *Times*'s credit, however, one of the worst abuses in its travel section has been eliminated. Until this year the paper consistently ran at least one puff on Florida right next to the Florida hotel ads. The Florida articles were moved to the back of the section after Robert Stock, formerly a deskman for the *Times* Magazine, became travel editor January 1, replacing Paul J. C. Friedlander, who now writes a weekly column. At this writing, it is too early to tell whether there will be further improvements, and Stock is reluctant to discuss specific plans, but there is one hopeful sign: the *Times* travel section of March 1 led with a significant and well-reported story on discrimination by foreign countries against young, long-haired American tourists.

The way newspapers handle travel writing assignments provides part of the explanation for what finally appears in print. In some newsrooms editors accept for themselves the most appealing free trips and distribute the rest of the invitations among favored reporters. Other papers use the position of travel editor as a reward to a staff member who in addition takes on less glamorous duties. The travel editor of one Philadelphia paper, for example, is also in charge of comics, maps, puzzles, stamps, gardens, schools, and the bridge column.

Most newspapers insist that their travel writers work out as many free deals as possible, and a surprising number won't reimburse them for extra expenses. John McLeod, travel editor of the Washington *Daily News*, wrote in the Scripps-Howard house organ:

> The main problem of a travel writer is staying solvent. Any trip away from home costs money. You may be the guest of an airline; hotels may compliment some of your bill; your sightseeing may be provided; you'll be exposed to a lot of banquets and booze. Still it costs money. There are tips and taxis and airport taxes. There are a lot of dull, lonely evenings when you have to provide your own entertainment.
>
> How do we do it? One travel editor buys stamps as he travels for a hometown dealer. Another writes a confidential hotel report for travel agents. Another collects antiques. Another scouts for novelties for a mail order firm. Still others write books and magazine articles or have a radio or television show on the side.

Airlines, hotels, and foreign governments anxious for favorable publicity arrange for lavish excursions. Of course, they carefully read what appears in print, and blacklisting of an overly critical writer is not unknown. "We want travel writers to be honest," the publicity agent for a Caribbean island puts it. "But we hope that 80 percent of what they write is affirmative." One way airlines sometimes have arranged for a free trip is illegal, in the opinion of the Civil Aeronautics Board: under a letter of agreement the travel writer buys his plane ticket and the airline agrees to pay him for "reprint rights" to his articles. The two sums are often suspiciously similar: a CAB proceeding against Trans World Airlines charges that Richard Joseph, who writes *Esquire* magazine features as well as a widely syndicated newspaper column, was paid $675 for reprint rights in connection with a $676.60 plane trip; and that Wade B. Franklin of the Chicago *Sun-Times* received $1,500 in connection with a trip worth $1,577.10. Franklin says TWA flew him and his wife from Bombay to Chicago, with part of the trip first class.

Richard Joseph denies vigorously that he plugs the airlines in return for a free trip; he says that he even pays for some of his excursions himself. Nevertheless his columns show that he is favorably impressed with a number of the world's airlines. On a trip to Venezuela, he noted, "Pan Am put together a really perfect flight"; on a flight to South Africa, Alitalia provided "some of the most attentive service I've ever enjoyed aboard an airplane"; Kenya "is still very much BOAC country." Joseph also appreciates his hotels: in a column from Nairobi, he wrote that "I've heard good things about the Inter-Continental, and I can say only good things about the Hilton." Joseph started his African trip this year in South Africa, and large excerpts from his column datelined Johannesburg were reprinted by the South African government in a news release. "If this is darkest Africa," Mr. Joseph wrote, "then somebody must have put on the lights." Naturally, the column never mentioned apartheid.

The travel writers also supplement their free newspaper trips with bargain excursions sponsored by their organization, the Society of American Travel Writers. Three of every four SATW annual meetings are held outside the United States, with charter jet air fare virtually the only cost to members for a week's trip to, say, Turkey (1967) or Vienna (1968). This year the society will hold its convention in Finland; a one-week trip, including plane, meals, hotel, and sightseeing, will cost a member just $250 for what an SATW officer describes as "very exceptional VIP treatment." Sometimes not even a token amount is paid; the society's Middle Atlantic chapter this year accepted an all-expenses-paid invitation from the government of Costa Rica to visit that country.

It is, then, hardly surprising that the most consistently probing travel articles come from a writer whose paper pays every cent of his expenses — Jerry Hulse of the Los Angeles *Times.* Hulse once described Atlantic City, New Jersey, as "the Skid Row Riviera." He added: "The nicest thing about visiting Atlantic City is the drive out of town. Visiting Atlantic City is like taking your vacation in military boot camp."

In another instance Hulse, after paying his own way to Hawaii for the dedication of a new Hilton hotel, devoted his column to a tongue-in-cheek commentary on the four-day party Conrad Hilton sponsored for reporters and for "200 elite from Bel Air and Beverly Hills." His only comment on the hotel, in fact, was contained in a single paragraph: "There is a certain sameness to all Hilton openings, of course. Good plumbing and dry martinis."

Not only does paying his own way give a travel writer liberty to criticize, but it also frees him from the confinements imposed by his hosts. Generally when travel writers take junkets to foreign countries the local tourist organization plans every minute of their time to make sure they see only the "approved" sights. Georgia Hesse of the San Francisco *Examiner* — who is unusual among travel writers for her fluency in several languages and for her interest in the customs and culture of countries she visits — describes what happened when she went to India as a guest of the Indian government: "I spent a month in India and it was three weeks before I was able to walk down the street myself. They do have some really serious problems, so they suspect travel writers wouldn't be happy visiting the areas where people live."

"How can you criticize an airline or a hotel if you've just had a $2,500 free airplane ride and free room and meals?" asks Hulse. "It's time the travel writing profession grew up a little bit. We deserve the same right to criticize that a stage or movie critic has. You don't read many travel stories that are critical — most of the time the sky is blue, the sand white, and the palm trees green."

PASSING COMMENT

"All the News"

There it was, among stories in the August 31, 1969, Cleveland *Plain Dealer* such as NAVY TOLD TO RELEASE PACIFIST, COMMON PLEAS FASTER IN RIOTS, and CELEBRATIONS BY VETS CLIMAXED BY PARADE. The headline, with a two-column photo, said 17 CHEVROLET SALESMEN WIN TRIPS TO EUROPE. A story listed all seventeen, with dealership affiliations. In a city the size of Cleveland, in a large chain-owned (Newhouse) newspaper, what editorial criteria made this "news"? What, indeed, makes similar puffs "news" on real estate, business, sports, and feature pages? The answer is a few typewritten lines — if they carry the right signatures, such as (below) those of (1) an advertising agency president, and (2) an executive editor.

Summer, 1970.

The Letters:

August 25, 1969

Mr. Edward O'Connor
General Advertising Manager
The Cleveland Plain Dealer
1801 Superior Ave.
Cleveland, Ohio

Dear Ed:

Here's the BIG NEWS EVENT of the year for the CLEVELAND CHEVROLET DEALERS which we want you to cover with a photographer and a reporter *without fail!*
The 17-winners of the Chevro-Laddies salesmen contest which ran to 3 months have been announced (winner's list attached) as the European group tour winners.
Saturday — August 30th — 3:30 P.M. the Chevro-Laddies and their wives will meet at the Air Canada check-in counter at Cleveland Hopkins Airport to prepare for their 4:50 P.M. flight departure . . . starting a two week vacation trip to Scotland, England and Paris, France. (Trip itinerary also attached).
Once again may I stress the importance of your news coverage on this event at the request of all the Cleveland Chevrolet Dealers!

Thank you,

Leroy F. Lustig
President

ENC: (2)

Memo

To: Ted Princiotto

From: William Ware

Dear Ted:

This is a photo coverage that I fear we are obligated to handle. These are the winners of a contest conducted by the Chevrolet Dealers Association. The advertising which went along with the contest has been running in The Plain Dealer. I would think perhaps a photo and underlines would do the job with perhaps an agate listing of these 17 names. I would think the photo might be stashed away some place in either the Sunday or the holiday papers.

William M. Ware

WMW/*mjl*
Attch.

A *DIGEST* CASE: A WARNING FROM THE MAILMAN

Arthur E. Rowse

Timothy J. May does not often write letters to editors. That may be fortunate for the editors. For when he writes, he means business.

May's recent letter to the editor of the *Reader's Digest* may never be printed — the *Digest* does not print letters from readers — but it may leave an imprint on the policies of the *Digest* as well as many other magazines and newspapers.

May is the general counsel of the United States Post Office Department. He was writing to Hobart Lewis, president and executive editor of the *Digest*, to say that an advertisement in the November, 1967, *Digest* "was inconsistent with the spirit and intent" of laws governing publications with second-class mailing privileges.

The ad that bothered May was an eight-page "pull-out" containing several articles in the traditional type and format of *Digest* articles. The articles touted the research, brand names, and pricing policies of the prescription drug industry. The ad, the first of four in a $1 million series planned by the Pharmaceutical Manufacturers Association, was introduced by a half-page teaser notice advising *Digest* readers to:

Winter, 1967–68. Arthur E. Rowse is a Washington writer who specializes in consumer matters.

Detach and keep this "magazine within a magazine"

On top of the first page of the detachable section was the phrase: "Special Advertising Section." (These three words were missing from one million reprints distributed to doctors' waiting rooms, hospital reading rooms, and members of the general public who wrote in.)

The only indication to readers of the *Digest* that the section was a paid advertisement was the three-word notice on the first page and the following phrase in small print at the bottom of the last page:

First in a Series Published as a Public Service by the
Pharmaceutical Manufacturers Association
Washington, D.C. 20005

Charges of deception were voiced by several senators at a hearing of the antitrust and monopoly subcommittee of the Select Senate Committee on Small Business. The subcommittee had been investigating drug industry prices and prescription practices.

The subcommittee chairman, Gaylord Nelson, Wisconsin Democrat, called the ad "calculated deception . . . designed to avoid disclosing that it is in fact an advertisement." He accused the drug organization of trying to appear as a "non-industry philanthropic group." Senator Mark Hatfield, Oregon Republican, read another article type of ad in the same issue for a hemorrhoid drug and called for an investigation of the *Digest*'s "entire advertising policy."

Nelson cited a report from the Food and Drug Administration saying that the articles themselves were misleading and that one of them "totally disregarded historical fact."

But this was not what bothered the Post Office Department's general counsel when asked for a ruling by Senator Nelson. May told Nelson that he had informed the *Digest* that "the manner of marking the advertising of the Pharmaceutical Manufacturers Association in your November, 1967, issue was inconsistent with the spirit and intention of the above cited statutes and regulations. Accordingly, the practice as exemplified in this particular advertisement should be discontinued."

The letter cited Section 4367 of Title 39 and Section 1734 of Title 18 of the U.S. Code entitled "Marking of Paid Reading Matter."

The latter section says: "Whoever, being an editor or publisher, prints in a publication entered as second-class mail editorial or other reading matter for which he has been paid or promised a valuable consideration, without plainly marking the same *advertisement*, shall be fined not more than $500" (italics in original).

Why was the *Digest* not prosecuted? May said it was because the law did not specifically require the word "advertisement" on each page. He said that the department had drawn up a regulation specifying this practice but that it had never been published officially in the *Federal Register*. He felt that this put the department in a weak position to prosecute. He said the regulation would be published soon.

Asked about special advertising sections in newspapers containing paid editorial copy along with the ads, May replied that his office had recently advised the Washington *Post*, in response to an inquiry from that paper, that each page of such supplements must be marked "advertisement."

May acknowledged that newspapers and magazines "often" run advertisements in the form of articles and that they do not always comply with the law by marking them "advertisement." But he said his office did not have the personnel to do monitoring and would not be doing any in the future.

He said that his office relied on the Postal Inspection Service and on complaints from the general public. But he conceded that few people seem to be aware of the law and that complaints have been few.

Of the *Digest,* he said, "I have no doubt that the *Reader's Digest* knew precisely what the law was. They have people who spend full time just on mailing operations."

A few days before the Postal Office letter to the *Digest,* the Federal Trade Commission issued a statement advising that the word "advertisement" should appear on each page of an advertisement resembling a news or feature article. But it added that in some cases this was not enough to avoid deception.

"In some instances," it said, "the format of the advertisement may so exactly duplicate a news or feature article as to render the caption 'advertisement' meaningless and incapable of curing the deception. The commission believes that it is in the public interest that publishers and advertisers avoid any possible deception by not placing advertisements whose format simulates that of a news or feature article. Inclusion in such an advertisement of a byline, particularly when accompanied by the writer's title (such as 'feature writer' or 'editor') may also mislead readers as to its nature. Accordingly, the Commission cautions advertisers to avoid use of such devices in their advertisements when they may tend to mislead readers."

The FTC statement applies to all publications, whether or not they are mailed with second-class privileges, but it is the Post Office Department that may cause the greatest concern to newspapers and magazines, for most of them have second-class privileges, and many have not been complying with the letter of the law.

The *Digest*'s own performance in 1967 was spotty. Last April, the magazine ran a twenty-page section for Celanese clothes with some pages appearing to be articles. Each page had the words, "Special Advertising Section," at the top.

Yet in May a twelve-page section appearing as a pictorial travel guide to Expo '67 had the words, "Special Advertising Section," only on the first page.

In July, a one-page ad for Anacin Tablets appeared as an article, with the trade name only in the body type. There was no other indication that it was an ad.

In October, the *Digest* ran a one-page ad for Geritol in the format of an article and with the word "advertisement" at the top.

The *Digest* frequently uses the editorial technique to sell itself. In September, it ran a full-page article entitled "One of Our Best Opportunities," by Emile Kief, for the purpose of selling the *Digest* to schools. The December issue carried a subscription promotion appearing as an article by Joan Crawford and entitled, "A Very Special Gift."

In addition, there are numerous other layouts where it may not be easy for a reader to tell whether he is reading an advertisement or article, especially when illustrations are involved.

Although federal agencies cannot police all publications for such practices, they can draw lines beyond which publishers should not go. The day apparently has arrived when ads can no longer with impunity be dressed up as news or features without plainly marking them for what they are.

PASSING COMMENT

Drug News and Non-News

The public should be able to assume that American journalism is at its most cautious and scrupulous in matters affecting the lives and health of its audience. That such has not invariably been the case is demonstrated in the new book by Morton Mintz, *The Therapeutic Nightmare*. (The author, it will be recalled, is the Washington *Post* reporter who uncovered the thalidomide botch.) His study, drawing in great part on congressional investigations of the drug industry, is only secondarily a critique of the press. But he does show that newspapers, magazines, and broadcasting have been victimized in the past by pushers of nostrums, and that news media have been less assiduous in reporting adverse news about therapeutic drugs than they have in reporting new triumphs. As Mintz puts it: "Drug Success = News; Drug Failure = Non-News." He notes, too, the continual complaint by doctors about patients who read of a new remedy in the lay press and demand that their physicians use it on them. Moreover, he finds a connection between such reports on new drugs and speculation in drug-manufacturing stocks.

Although Mintz's examples are drawn from the recent to not-so-recent past, the instances he cites are recognizable enough. For example:

The case of the Sunday supplement, *This Week*, which carried in 1964 a column bearing the seal of the American Medical Association that still failed to report adequately the side effects of an oral contraceptive.

The offer — rejected, of course — to Alton Blakeslee of the Associated Press to write a planted article mentioning a new drug, for a sizable under-the-counter payment.

Winter, 1965–66.

The time, ten years ago, when a company gave news of a new drug to reporters at a cocktail party, then piously lamented to doctors how word had leaked out. The National Association of Science Writers demanded and received an apology, but the damage had been done.

More recent examples come to hand easily enough. The kind of article that puts pressure on doctors still abounds. On the cover of the July, 1965, *Cosmopolitan* is a line that reads: "The new pill that promises to make women more responsive." A warning that the "pill," estrogen, can "lead to unpleasant and dangerous consequences" if taken without supervision is buried on the fourth page of the article inside. *Look* for January 11, 1966, has a more cautious treatment, by one of the physicians who developed estrogen. It carries a separate warning against self-medication. Still, the general tone of the article will obviously put doctors under pressure to use a radical procedure that is still far from universally accepted.

The road to better protection for readers is simply the path already being taken, as Mintz makes clear, by the more alert segments of journalism: first, the development and hiring of the kind of specialists who will not be victimized by premature medical miracles; second, more systematic coverage of the agencies charged with safeguarding the public against therapeutic disaster; and, even without the money to take these steps, at least the circumspection to avoid hasty publication of sensational drug stories. In this matter, journalism does not carry the entire responsibility; it shares the load with government, the drug industry, and the medical profession. But journalists can at least keep themselves from being the channels of speculation, in drug stocks or in health.

PASSING COMMENT

The Karafin Case

Harry J. Karafin operated in real life the kind of racket that — fortunately for the newspaper business — has usually cropped up only in B movies. He used his powers as an investigative reporter for the Philadelphia *Inquirer* to collect from those who might be exposed by his stories. His ingenious variations on this gambit led to an income from "public relations" fees that multiplied many times his modest *Inquirer* pay. He lived in a style to which Philadelphia reporters have been unaccustomed.

Or he did so until March 2, 1967, when his paper discharged him. The immediate cause was Karafin's effort, via lawsuit, to stop publication of an article about him in a local magazine called *Philadelphia*. The *Inquirer* gave him his severance pay and *Editor & Publisher* carried a routine personal item to the effect that Karafin was entering the public relations field.

Judging from the time that lapsed before anything further happened, the *Inquirer* would gladly have let the matter drop at that point. But *Philadelphia* came out on April 4 with its article, a highly detailed exposé of Karafin's complicated involvement with a variety of rackets. A day or so later, *Time* magazine started digging into the story, as did *Newsweek*. But the two uninvolved Philadelphia papers (one under the same management as the *Inquirer*) and wire services did not.

Not until April 10, when it became clear that the story would get national publicity, did the *Inquirer* put its own reporter on the story. Once the step was taken, the *Inquirer* was committed to a unique self-exposure — public confession that its top investigative

---

Spring, 1967.

reporter had abused his paper and his profession. It did the job with a vengeance — a long story that was "a brutal, public interment," as *Philadelphia* magazine called it. It borrowed freely from *Philadelphia*'s story, but did not credit the magazine by name. The *Bulletin* and the *Daily News* remained silent.

Before the Karafin case is forgotten, newspapermen in Philadelphia and elsewhere might ask themselves what it meant. Why did a theoretically competitive paper not touch the story? Is news about newspapers still a special category? What does it say of a paper's standards that manipulation on Karafin's scale can be carried on through its news columns? How free are other papers of such enterprises? If the newspaper business is fortunate, these questions may be more annoying than substantial. But they should be asked.

DEPARTMENT OF CORRECTION

Edward W. Barrett

Have you been misquoted or otherwise misinterpreted lately? If so, did you get it corrected — and how? The process is becoming increasingly difficult in many print media and remains all but impossible in broadcasting. If you are clearly libeled, the correction is easy. Short of that, it is not.

Our own one-man, nonscientific continuing survey of press critics indicates that this is one factor behind the widespread grousing about the media, particularly among those opinion leaders to whom gradations of meaning are important.

The Review has dealt, in the past and in the most recent issue, with the odd reluctance of the *Reader's Digest* to print corrections or dissents of any sort. It is not clear whether this springs from a profound fear of admitting fallibility or from the simple mechanics of having no convenient place for such items in its tidy makeup. In any event, we submit, it is a failing in what we like to regard as a press committed to free expression.

The *Digest* is not strictly alone. In broadcasting, one who has been personally attacked or who represents an organization opposing a broadcast editorial may demand time for reply and, if he is bold enough, woodenly face a camera or microphone and read his rebuttal. If he is simply misquoted or otherwise misrepresented, the average station won't give him the time of day. When did you last hear a broadcast correction?

Some newspapers, too, are falling into the pattern. Indeed, it is easier today to get a fact or a nuance corrected in the most widely deplored newsmagazine than it is in many a newspaper. The New York *Times* has become a case in point.

Spring, 1968. Edward W. Barrett is chairman of the Board of Advisory Editors of the *Review*. This article is one of a series he wrote under the heading "Editorial Notebook."

The *Times* long had a letters column open to those who felt that their utterances had been misrepresented, their identity confused, or simply that a vital fact had been garbled in a news story. This is no longer the case. In an effort to make the letters column more vital and interesting, the editorial page editors have converted it to a department for discussion of issues. Meanwhile, the news department editors fight to avoid those embarrassing little squibs entitled "A Correction," and there are subeditors who appear to spend most of their time writing letters that express regret but decline to correct.

A small illustration among many: Last year the warmly regarded head of the New York Community Trust unveiled a small plaque in the Waldorf noting that General MacArthur had long lived there. The *Times* covered the event with a picture and a light story indicating that the plaque was "not quite accurate" in identifying the General. Stung by the implication that he had erred in bronze, the gentleman wrote a rather gay and charming letter to the editor arguing that the *Times*, not the plaque, was in error. It was good reading, but it never saw print. There was no place for it. The gentleman is still offended.

Today the *Times*'s letters column is filled with support for, or dissent from, the paper's editorials or with criticisms of foreign policy and parking meter placement. If the news columns contain an error short of libel, however, the chances of correction are slim. An examination of thirty issues turned up only five printed corrections.

Some years ago a *Times* editorial writer and I appeared on a panel together. The *Times*'s two-paragraph report misconstrued his remarks, and he paid me the compliment of calling to ask advice on how to get the matter corrected in his own paper. I suggested a letter to the editor, which was duly published. He could not achieve that today. The reason is that he has become editorial page editor and has changed the character of the letters column.

You *Review* readers who are print or broadcast editors might well think of what you would do if your speech were misinterpreted by some unfortunate staffer. It might provide one clue to the seemingly growing complaints about the media. It might even suggest some small but important policy change.

EIGHT

Folkways

ON LOOKING INTO CHAPMAN'S *NEWS*

A. J. Liebling

When a man writes a book about a newspaper where he is still employed, there are likely to be serious omissions. In the case of *Tell It to Sweeney: the Informal History of the New York Daily News*, (Doubleday, 1961) by John Chapman, who is the *News*'s esteemed drama critic, the omissions have greater potential interest than the inclusions. The words present form a typographical parenthesis around those that aren't.

Chapman, for example, furnishes a considerable body of uniformly respectful reminiscence about Captain Joseph Medill Patterson, who founded the *News* in 1919 and died in 1946. This is territory more than amply covered by previous biographers. He says nothing of the characteristics or proclivities of the men who have shaped its policies since then — a stretch of fifteen years. He notes, indeed, that by Patterson's will F. M. Flynn and Richard W. Clarke, now president and vice-president, respectively, of the *News*, "as trustees but not legatees were to head the management team which now was to direct the destinies of the *News*." But he says nothing at all about what kind of fellows they are, whether either ever had an idea, or if so, what.

Nor does he describe the authority wielded over the *News*, or say that it is not wielded, by the officers of the Tribune Company, of Chicago, although he furnishes a simplified diagram of "the basic corporate structure of the New York *Daily News*" that shows that the Tribune Company holds control. He does not name the

---

Fall, 1961. A. J. Liebling, who wrote "The Wayward Press" column for the *New Yorker*, was the author of *The Wayward Pressman, The Press*, and other books.

owners or officers of this paramount organism at all, much less discuss their notions, although he does furnish some deadpan notes on Colonel Robert Rutherford McCormick, Captain Patterson's cousin and survivor, who ran the Tribune Company until his death in 1955. When did informal history end, in 1946 or 1955? Upstairs in Chicago, downstairs in New York, what are the new brains like? The essential information about a newspaper is the character of its owners.

Newspapers are not waifs. They reflect their source, and Chapman leaves us without a clue. This is the more annoying because he himself sets up the question he never answers:

"When Patterson died in 1946 the road ahead for the *Daily News* was chancy," he says. "Should the paper be preserved as a monument to its creator, following as best it could the dictates and odd whims of its founder? Had it really been a one-man show, and should it henceforth be operated by a ghost?"

Has it been? When Patterson died he was in an acute phase of illiberal chauvinism that had lasted since his bitter quarrel with Franklin D. Roosevelt in late 1941. He had, as Chapman relates, been a warm and potent supporter of the President from the beginning of his first candidacy, in 1932, until their open split over the Lend-Lease Bill. The *News* had supported all of Roosevelt's social legislation, and had been a prime advocate of United States recognition of the U.S.S.R. The break came not over any issue of left versus right but of Patterson's ingrained isolationism against Roosevelt's belief in the need to intervene. His paper had followed his swing as fast as a sports car follows the wheel, but it is conceivable that that man of "odd whims" might have swung in some other direction had he lived. Roosevelt was dead, war against Germany no longer an issue. He was, after all, an old socialist, although he had been a rich one.

"It will be interesting to see what changes, if any, his death will bring," the *Times*, quoted by Chapman, had editorially noted.

There have been none in the *News*'s editorial orientation. It has continued on, as if guided by an Iron Mike, until it now refers to itself on its editorial page as a "nationalist" newspaper, implying that all others, except the Chicago *Tribune*, are "internationalist," which = Socialist, which = Uknowhat.

Reuben Maury, who wrote the pro-Roosevelt, pro-Social Security, pro-TVA editorials for the Captain — Maury went there in 1926 — and who wrote the anti-Roosevelt editorials after the Captain changed his mind, is now writing pieces about how McCarthy was right, and others under heads such as SOCIALISM IN THE SICKROOM (medical care for the aged) and FASCISM ON THE FARM (Administration agricultural program). Both these ran on the same day, June 5.

C. D. Batchelor, the equally suggestible editorial cartoonist, furnishes gems like that of June 8 showing Uncle Sam, with a skull in his left hand — the skull labeled PEACE HOPES — in a cemetery filled with headstones marked LEAGUE OF NATIONS, R. I. P., NUCLEAR TEST BAN, and TO LET. The *News*'s isolationist chauvinism of 1940 has changed to an extremely bellicose brand. Batchelor, who used to draw "War" as a lady with a skull for a face, may begin any day to make her look pretty.

Maury's notion of proving that McCarthy was right — the Captain, incidentally, died before McCarthy appeared, and might not have liked him — is to lift to the editorial page a news item about a State Department announcement that it had dropped sixteen employees as homosexuals. McCarthy's most famous charge was that the State Department contained 205 card-carrying Communists, not one of whom he produced. The incidence of homosexuals is probably about the same in the State Department as in newspaper offices.

On none of these points does Mr. Chapman, who is a nice fellow, say anything. Is he afraid of the ghost?

With the *News*'s swerve to the right, in 1942, its circulation leveled off. The period of growth had ended. Between 1932 and 1942 circulation rose from 1,400,000 to very nearly two million. It was still that in 1959, the last year noted on the graph of comparative New York newspaper circulations that serves as endpaper to *Tell It To Sweeney*. In the same period of seventeen years the population of New York City had risen by a million, of what the census calls the New York Metropolitan Area by a great deal more.

Whether this contrast between a gain of 43 percent in ten years and a flat standstill in the next seventeen was a coincidence or had any significant correlation with the paper's switch is a great "not proven." The author, while he concedes that "in the first happy days of the New Deal" the *News* had stated that its support of Roosevelt had "stood well in the top row of reasons for its growth," concludes dutifully that the change "had no measurable effect on the paper." It has, however, suffered arrested growth in a growing market, where there were four morning papers, including the *News*, in 1959 as in 1942.

The *Times*, which does not compete with the *News*, in the same years increased its circulation by 50 percent, according to the same obliging graph.

Patterson himself, as a young man, once wrote that a new newspaper proprietor comes to town full of zeal for the underdog and avid for circulation, fights for the first, gets the second, and joins the fat cats when the money rolls in. Then, he went on, growth ceases and deterioration begins.

The *News* has reached its plateau, but has not yet fallen over the edge, a position the curious reader expects even an informal historian to comment on. I am tempted to try for myself, but that is not a reader's function. Between ourselves, I hold with the early Patterson.

HOW I TRIED TO WRITE A LETTER TO THE *TIMES* AND FOUND MYSELF CUT TO THE QUICK

Robert Yoakum

This informal study of the tightwad policy of the New York *Times* on preelection comment from readers was inspired by my own failure to crack the letters column of that paper before two elections, leaving me vulnerable to the charge of being, simply, a sorehead. But the history of man's expanding knowledge is filled with examples of irritating personal experiences that led to great discoveries, so I'll proceed in the hope that this is one more such.

A week and a half before the bizarre presidential election of 1964, I fired off a letter to the *Times*, in which I pointed out that the man they had endorsed in our district for the United States House of Representatives was, unlike many Republicans in the East, a supporter of Senator Goldwater. It was a one-page letter, devoted entirely to a recital of key issues on which the Republican candidate agreed with Goldwater and on which the Democratic candidate agreed with the *Times*. The Republican was Thomas Meskill, mayor of New Britain from 1962 to 1964. His Democratic opponent was Bernard Grabowski, an incumbent congressman by virtue of having won the representative-at-large seat in 1962. The two were contesting in the new Sixth District of northwest Connecticut.

I was certain the letter would be printed. It even seemed possible that the *Times* would change its endorsement. Admittedly, I

Winter, 1966–67. Robert Yoakum, former city editor of the European Edition of the New York *Herald Tribune*, writes from London and Connecticut.

had never heard of such a thing, but that only made my Mitty-like speculations more exciting. Would the apologetic editorial point to my letter as the reason for the switch? Would this be a journalistic "first"? Even in retrospect, my reasons for being certain back in 1964 seemed good:

1. I knew of no other instance in which the *Times* was supporting a Goldwater man.

2. I knew of no other instance in which the *Times* was advocating the dumping of an incumbent congressman who agreed with them.

3. Readers who did not know points 1 and 2 would be seriously misled if no letter or comment appeared at all.

The only letter that appeared, however, was not in print and it was to me, not from me. It was written by John B. Oakes, editor of the editorial page. I quote it in full:

> We were glad to have your expression of opinion on the relative merits of the candidates in the Sixth Congressional District in Connecticut, even though it differed from our own.
>
> We made our judgment on the basis of reports from *Times* correspondents in Connecticut and Washington that Representative Grabowski was not a very effective member of Congress, despite a superficially attractive voting record, and on the fact that Mr. Meskill's record as Mayor of New Britain indicated that he was a man of considerable ability and moderate views.
>
> May I call your attention to the fact that this morning's *Times* carried a story, a clipping of which I enclose, listing Mr. Meskill as one of seventy-five Republican nominees regarded by the Ripon Society as potentially the best the party has to offer. This is a leading anti-Goldwater group.

Mr. Oakes's letter arrived only four days before the election, giving me too little time to proselytize the Ripon Society *and* the editorial board of the *Times*. Grabowski won handily without the support of the *Times* or my letter.

This time, in 1966, things were different. Representative Grabowski had to run without the help of Barry Goldwater, the greatest vote getter for the Democrats in these parts since Grover Cleveland. For this and a number of other reasons (including the presence of a "peace candidate" on the ballot), it was clear that the vote would be close. I was dismayed, therefore, when the *Times* again endorsed Mr. Meskill. Again, I sent off an issue-by-issue letter to the editor, contrasting Grabowski's voting record and the *Times* editorial record with positions advocated by Meskill in 1964 and 1966, and enclosing several press releases to show that the Meskill quotations I had used were in context. Later, when I learned that Meskill (the only Republican congressional candidate in Connecticut endorsed by the *Times*) was the only candidate in Connecticut to be endorsed by the ultraconservative Americans for Constitutional Action, I relayed that fact to Mr. Oakes by telegram.

For five days nothing happened. Then, on November 1, I received a call from a Miss Liebowitz, who told me that my letter would be run but that it had to be cut. Instructions to run a shortened letter, she said, had come down to her from Mr. Oakes by way of her superior, Miss Huger, who was in charge of the letters department. I agreed that the letter was too long and called back a little later with a shorter version.

Miss Liebowitz called back later to say that it was still too long. It would have to be cut quickly to three hundred words, she said, and again explained, as she had on the first call, that the pre-election pressure on the *Times* letters section was enormous. "You can understand, I'm sure," she said. "We aren't even able to give that much space to people writing about campaigns right here in New York." I expressed sympathy, but pointed out that nowhere else, to my knowledge, had the *Times* put its prestige behind a man who sounded like Ronald Reagan. "After all," I added, "the winner will be one of the 435 men who will vote on taxes, wars, and such. They will have no small influence on the fate of mankind."

"Well, I only work here," she replied.

My next version was ready a half hour later. It was still forty words over the three hundred limit, according to Miss Liebowitz in yet another call, but it would be set in type anyway, and Mr. Oakes could look it over. I went to bed that night thinking that the *Times* editorial page was still faithful to Section VI, Part 2, of the Canons of Journalism, which says: "It is the privilege, as it is the duty, of a newspaper to make prompt and complete correction of its own serious mistakes of fact or opinion, whatever their origin."

Miss Huger herself called the next day. She said that the letter was still too long. As a matter of fact, she said, Mr. Oakes now wanted it reduced to "one or two paragraphs." Poor Miss Huger! Poor Miss Liebowitz! Caught between Mr. Oakes's deescalation and an increasingly irate reader from Connecticut! Their position was unenviable, and I did not and do not wish them ill. I wanted only to get into their paper a point-by-point challenge of the *Times*'s mysterious choice. I explained that a one- or two-paragraph lump generalization from a Mr. Yoakum in Lakeville would have no meaning. "That's too bad," said Miss Huger. "We won't be able to use anything, then. You probably don't realize how much election material we have to run from other areas." On that familiar note our strained exchanges ended.

I had noticed that for a couple of days prior to Miss Liebowitz's call no letters dealing with the election had appeared at all. Afterward, I watched for the deluge of election comment that I had been told was still to be run. The deluge never came. There was one heavy day, Saturday, November 5, when 47 inches of letters were used, all dealing with the campaign. But the next day — two days before the polls were to open — there was one 2¾-inch letter about the campaign and 60 inches of correspondence that had nothing to do with the imminent vote.

After the election, which Meskill won by 81,973 to Grabowski's 79,458, I wondered whether any of the decisive 1,258 citizens had taken the advice of Forty-third Street and switched to what a loyal *Times* reader would assume — with no evidence to the contrary available in that paper — was a liberal Republican. Propelled by this concern, and by ordinary curiosity, I decided to find out just how much preelection comment or contrary opinion had been admitted.

Some of the eight newspapers that enter my home daily were letting their campaign letters spill over to a second editorial page — which the weekday *Times* conspicuously lacks — and they evidenced a free and formidable flow of protest and even occasional humor. Even I, however, was surprised at the results of my survey of the *Times*. In the two weeks preceding the election, *nonelec-*

tion letters in the Times *outmeasured those dealing with the campaign by more than two to one.* On four days the *Times* let in no outside comment at all on election issues, which had occupied, over the preceding months, yards of space in the columns produced by their own editorial writers. The total from October 25 through November 7 was 172 column inches of election-related letters — about twelve inches a day.

My letter, set in type, ran to nine or ten inches. More than forty inches was printed in three Sunday editions (October 23, 30, and November 6) on the subject of unrest in Nigeria. I am ordinarily interested in Nigeria, but during a congressional showdown I should think this kind of illumination, lifted from a letter two days before the election, could be postponed: "While roundly and ethnocentrically condemning the Ibo's cultural heritage, Mr. Muffett does not mention that the Hausa-Fulani hierarchy of bureaucratic emirs was well suited to the imposition of British colonial rule as directed by Frederick Lugard in 1900, and that the easterns' communal village life could not be well integrated into the colonial system. . . ."

I know the *Times* must bear the torch for the long trip, and I am aware that the *Times* can't exhibit the same proportion of generosity to its letter-writing readers as the Berkshire *Eagle*, for example. (The *Eagle*, with 30,000 circulation, ran 435 inches of political letters from October 22 through November 5 — more than double the *Times* space). Just the same, Big Daddy should make room for a steady and large stream of debate during those weeks when Americans, including *Times* readers, are making up their minds about how they will vote. In that same November 6 paper, quoted above, where readers' views on the campaign were given 2¾ inches, 10 inches were given to "Canyon Dams Opposed," 11 inches were given to "U.S. as Debtor in 'Brain Drain,'" and one foot went to "For World Law."

It should be admitted, though, that they are even-tempered up there on Mount Olympus. The reply from Mr. Oakes this time, as in 1964, was friendly, even though my cover note had included some testy jabbing. He was also, as in 1964, silent about why the letter hadn't been run.

His letter ended my dialogue with the editorial department of the *Times*. I now feel even greater sympathy for that worker for *Time* magazine (no relation), who, according to the *New Yorker*, felt so oppressed by the air of omniscience around him that he had an occasional strong impulse to rush into the corridor and shout, "*Time* is not omniscient!" He feared, however, that this might bring the building down around him. So, out of caution and respect, I won't say that the *Times* editorial board is not omniscient. I do think, though, that the building wouldn't tumble if they made room for a little more dissent, particularly around election time.

FROM MY QUIP BOARD

Alan L. Otten

To quip, the dictionary tells us is to make "a clever, usually taunting, remark; a witty or funny observation or response, usually on the spur of the moment."

For obscure reasons, however, reporters insist on using the word to describe the dullest, most leaden of comments. The remarks are rarely advanced as humor by the people who make them; it's the reporters who decide to elevate the remarks into gems of purest wit serene. Comments described almost daily in the public press as "quips" have about as much laugh-appeal as Hamlet's soliloquy.

During the recent presidential campaign, for instance, the Washington *Evening Star* reported that a group of students in San Francisco had walked out on Democratic vice-presidential candidate Edmund Muskie. The *Star* then described the senator's reaction: "This reminds me of my campaign 14 years ago," quipped Muskie.

Now isn't that a grabber?

Jet magazine chalked up another: "Apprised of his nomination as chairman of the President's Equal Employment Opportunity Commission, Clifford Alexander Jr. quipped: "It's another challenge in my life."

Another gasser came from UPI some time back, when Sargent Shriver was still head of the federal antipoverty program. Mr. Shriver appeared at a White House news conference with President Johnson, and Mr. Johnson warned that he planned to drop over soon to visit the antipoverty office:

Winter, 1968–69. Alan L. Otten heads the Washington bureau of the *Wall Street Journal*.

Then Johnson quipped that he "went over to see Humphrey yesterday, and he wasn't on the job."
"I was there," Vice-President Humphrey laughingly exclaimed.

Laugh? Mr. Humphrey was practically overcome.

The quip syndrome isn't confined to political reporting. To quote a New York *Times* profile of a young labor negotiator who had just had an all-night session: " 'It seems that youth has a place in marathon negotiations,' quipped the thirty-five-year-old lawyer."

During the 1967 Ford strike, the *Times* reported a speech by economist Walter Heller, a witty man who occasionally does let fly with a quite legitimate quip. This time, however the *Times* had Mr. Heller "quipping" the following: "If the strike ends by Thanksgiving, we will have something to be thankful about."

There are several possible explanations for this journalistic compulsion to hail as humor the most humdrum remark. The reporter may want to build up the man he's covering by assigning to him a number of warm, attractive qualities — including wit. Or perhaps the reporter isn't equipped with a sense of humor, and doesn't know a quip from a clinker.

Probably the most reasonable explanation, though, is that early in his career, the reporter had drilled into him, by some city editor or journalism professor, the need to avoid repetition of the word "said" in reporting what someone was saying. He has consequently accumulated a stable of substitutes that he uses indiscriminately and often improperly.

His subjects "assert" remarks actually advanced extremely tentatively, "suggest" ideas that are really stoutly maintained, "opine" when they are asking questions, "charge" when they are merely indicating, and "quip" when they are only trying, often rather uncomfortably and unsuccessfully, to come up with some kind of answer to the reporter's stupid questions.

This theory is supported by the quiplike synonyms that are employed from time to time. A number of reporters, for instance, like to have their subjects "chuckling" away rather idiotically, even though these men and women are only offering some obvious platitudes to keep up their end of a tedious conversation. Former Treasury Secretary Henry Fowler was a well-known Washington chuckler, and the *Star* last summer related this one: "Joe Fowler revealed a new side last evening. Long before he sank to his present job, he observed with a chuckle, he wrote sonnets in Latin."

The *Star* also related an encounter between Tijuana Brassman Herb Alpert and former White House aid Walt Rostow and Mrs. Rostow: "Both Rostows were chuckling later at the message Alpert sent their daughter, Ann, for whom Mrs. Rostow had asked Alpert's autograph. Hearing that the eleven-year-old Ann plays both piano and clarinet and wants to play the trumpet and snare drums, Alpert, in addition to greetings, sent along this injunction: 'Practice!' "

Not too hard to get a chuckle out of those Rostows, is it?

The *Times* recounted a press conference to announce plans for a new Columbia University library. After brief remarks by two speakers, the late *Times* board chairman Arthur Hays Sulzberger, was called on and contributed this bit of hilarity to the occasion — or, to quote the *Times* more accurately, he "added with a chuckle": "I think this is the first time a presentation has been made when there wasn't a long speech."

That must have sent them rolling on the floor.

"Shot back" is another journalese signal that the reader ought to be doubling over with laughter.

Not too long ago, there was a New York City movie premiere at which everyone was supposed to arrive in a vintage car. Senator Javits drove up in a "sleek blue Cadillac," however, and the *Times* reported the ensuing exchange:

> "We've got thirty-six vintage cars lined up on Park Avenue, and you come up in this?" asked Henry Fonda, the actor.
>
> "I guess we didn't have time to make all the arrangements," the senator shot back jokingly.

During the National Governors' Conference in Cincinnati last summer, the *Enquirer* managed a rare double coup, with both a "quip" and a "shot back" in the same story. It reported a project to take a plaster cast of the handprint of each governor, for preservation in a local hotel lobby as a memento of the Conference. A large batch of plaster was whipped up for the occasion, and as Governor Rhodes of Ohio approached, this exchange took place:

"I want you to roll your face in it, Rhodes," quipped Gov. Norbert T. Tiemann, (R. Nebr.)
"I think you ought to sit in it," shot back Rhodes.

With wit like that, who needs statesmanship?

TO COUNT A CROWD

Herbert A. Jacobs

Crowd estimates may be the last area of fantasy in the newspaper business. The city editor insists on direct quotations that reflect what the speakers actually said. He wants correct addresses and accurate spelling of names. But it is a different story when it comes to estimating the size of the crowd. The editor may grumble but he will let an "official" do the guessing for him. Reporters, aware of this foible, tend to get together at rallies, and jointly agree on a "reasonable" figure.

The trouble with all these guesses is that they are themselves based on guesses. Old-time political reporters cover many meetings and observe crowds of various sizes. They soon adopt a scale of values, having seen police officials and their own colleagues estimate crowd sizes. But nobody, including the police, actually stops to count. It is a symposium of guesses, usually erring on the side of generosity.

Only a few newspapers — the Louisville *Courier-Journal* is one — make their reporters count heads and report the figure as part of the story.

"Crowds are part of politics," Theodore H. White wrote in *The Making of the President 1960*, and the business of "crowdmanship," or bragging about who attracted the biggest crowds, was part of their success picture that both major candidates tried to create in 1960.

The size of the crowd is a factor in state and local politics as well, because it tells something about the popularity of a candidate, and about the intensity with which issues are affecting the people. Should not this figure, then, be given as careful attention as that

---

Spring, 1967. Herbert A. Jacobs, who worked as a newspaperman in Wisconsin for thirty years, is a lecturer in the department of journalism, University of California, Berkeley.

accorded to quotations and statements of policy? (The problem arises largely at outdoor gatherings. Halls have known seating capacities, and it is easy to estimate the size of the crowd by noting whether most seats are filled, and whether there are standees.)

Samuel G. Blackman, general news editor of the Associated Press, conceded in a letter to me that the wire service had "no foolproof system for estimating the size of a crowd, and will be in the market for an IBM crowd-estimator any time they invent one."

Earl J. Johnson, retired vice-president of the United Press International, wrote: "Our Washington reporters who travel with national political candidates are pretty savvy about crowd sizes. If Merriman Smith [head of UPI's Washington bureau] reports that 5,000 came to the railroad station at Coshocton to hear Goldwater, we accept his estimate, although we may report that local Republican leaders said the crowd numbered 7,000."

The New York *Times* has used a three-ply estimate at political rallies, giving the police judgment (at the same time noting the political allegiance of the local administrator), the politician's own estimate, and also that of the covering reporter. The reporter's is usually the consensus of the press corps covering the candidate. Turner Catledge, executive editor of the *Times*, supplied to me a "memorandum from the city editor":

> For years the police in New York City were *the* source for crowd estimates. It was usually the highest-ranking police officer in charge of patrolling the parade route or rally who made the guess and always erred on the side of generosity. As the years went by, the estimates seemed to become more and more unrealistic.
>
> In the post-mortems which followed the Truman victory over Dewey in 1948, it became apparent that if more attention had been paid to the size and the behavior of the crowds, Truman's strength might have been seen. Thus, the accurate estimation of political crowds assumed a new importance.

Just how accurate are the police and other estimates on which reporters generally rely? A sampling around the country indicates that they are often double or triple and sometimes as much as twenty times the actual number.

When Vice-President Nixon stopped at the Milwaukee airport during the 1960 campaign, a Republican party official estimated the welcoming crowd at twelve thousand. The police put it at eight thousand. A reporter said there were five thousand. The Milwaukee *Journal* enlarged a crowd picture and counted heads; the number turned out to be near 2,300. Even counting those along the fringes, or possibly obscured by other heads, "the crowd could not have been more than 3,000," the *Journal* said.

Democratic leaders estimated Nixon's 1960 crowds in the New York campaign at 600,000, White points out in his book, but Governor Nelson A. Rockefeller said they numbered two million. Democrats put John F. Kennedy's parade crowds in New York at 1,250,000. This was a remarkably modest claim, in view of some of the whoppers perpetrated in the name of civic pride.

For instance, when General Eisenhower returned in triumph from Europe at the end of World War II, a police official "counted" six million welcoming him, but the commissioner cautiously cut this to four million. A few weeks later, Major General Jonathan M. Wainwright, hero of Corregidor, drew crowds looking only half as big. But the loyal police still said four million.

A high tide of estimating came in the parade for General Douglas MacArthur in 1951, when a police commissioner put the crowd at eight million. John Hohenberg, in *The Professional Journalist,* points out that this guess was emblazoned across eight columns of at least one New York paper, although it totaled as many people as there were in the city.

In 1960 the New York *Times* used official city maps, measured sidewalk widths, and calculated that the traditional ticker-tape parade route from Battery Park to City Hall could hold no more than 141,436 spectators. Even allowing generously for those hanging out of office windows and watching from side streets, the total could not be more than 500,000, the *Times* concluded.

Hohenberg also writes that measurements show that Times Square, where New Year's Eve crowds were formerly reported at 500,000 to a million, can actually hold no more than 250,000.

Ben Reeves, managing editor of the Louisville *Courier-Journal,* has pointed out how far astray estimates of even small crowds can wander:

I recall once traveling on the campaign trail with our U.S. Senator John Sherman Cooper. In the little town of Manchester, Kentucky, a veritable hotbed of Republicanism, I asked a constable his estimate of the crowd that heard Cooper speak. He looked around over the crowd and allowed it numbered "about 3,000." That looked a little inflated to me, so I moved on and put the question to the little town's chief of police. He thought there were 1,500 to 2,000 present. Cooper's P.R. man guessed it at 3,000 to 4,000. Later, en route to the next campaign appearance, I asked Cooper himself. He said he'd spent the time during a long-winded introduction in counting heads, and had arrived at a figure of just over 600. That was about right.

In another instance, I counted 375 heads at a rally down in western Kentucky. When the speaking was over, I asked the rally chairman, a Baptist preacher of some local reputation, how many people he estimated were there. He looked out over the audience and whispered, "Oh, there's probably more than 5,000."

I wondered whether a tentative beginning might be made in developing an estimating formula that even a novice reporter could use. The Berkeley campus of the University of California furnished an excellent site for this kind of research, for the following reasons:

1. I was able to obtain blueprints of the Sproul Plaza rally area, giving exact measurements, so that one could determine what square footage a crowd occupied.

2. Much of the plaza is divided by stone pavement lines into squares of twenty-two feet each, and some of the squares are crossed by brick diagonals, and thus quartered.

3. The campus community is activist, speech-prone, and rally-prone, giving abundant opportunity for measurements.

The architect and city planner Victor Gruen, in his book *The Heart of Our Cities* says that "a thin man in a subway" takes up two square feet. A fat man, Gruen says, takes up five square feet. The California Health and Environmental Safety code requires a minimum of seven square feet to a person for dance floors and other places of public assembly — and be it remembered that the seven-foot formula was made when dancing was still a body-contact sport. Thus it is probable, considering Gruen's thin and fat men and the building code, that an average standing person is believed to occupy three or four square feet. My researches indicate, however, that he — or she — actually occupies about six or eight square feet, at least in Berkeley's Sproul Plaza.

By counting people standing in a square, one could figure out how many square feet each spectator would cover. It was also possible to take pictures of the entire crowd from an upper floor of Sproul Hall, rather than merely obtain a ground-level view. Thus a mathematical determination of density could be verified by head count.

During December, 1966, and January and February, 1967, there were many rallies. Shouldering aside FBI men and police chiefs of various cities who were looking for Communists, and also brushing away Communists looking for recruits, I infiltrated the crowds. I counted representative squares, and quarters of squares, noting the time and the speaker. And then I would dash to the upper floors of Sproul and take a picture of the same crowd. The crowds tended to be slightly denser close to the microphone.

With the squares measuring 22 feet each way, for a total of 484 square feet, if I counted 85 people standing within a square, a calculation indicated that each person averaged 5.7 square feet of space. The photograph with its head count gave a check on the mathematical computation. I am happy to report that they pretty well agreed.

The density of the crowds varied. On some occasions, apparently when the topic did not interest any students at all, the person at the microphone would be speaking to an indifferent parade. Nobody stopped to listen. On other occasions the plaza would be full of spectators. Yet even when it seemed full, there was always some movement within the crowd.

I was even able to obtain a sit-in density formula. At a Students for a Democratic Society rally, the speaker urged the audience to move forward and sit down, so as to open up a lane for foot traffic. The group did move forward — should one say that it was as Moses parted the Red Sea? — and the steps were covered. A photograph count gave a density figure of 6.7 square feet for each seated person. It was a mixed group. Perhaps the square footage would be greater with a predominantly female crowd.

Only once did the density, according to my calculations, reach four square feet to a person. The usual density on other occasions was between 6.5 and 8.5 square feet to a person. On February 10, a chance count showed 9.5 square feet to a person when the activist leader, Mario Savio, was addressing the plaza for the first time since the dismissal of President Clark Kerr.

I wondered whether a formula might not be developed by which a reporter could quickly calculate the approximate size of a crowd. I determined from comparing photographs, density counts, and the blueprints of the plaza, that this could be done. If the reporter paced the length and width of the crowd, and multiplied these two footages together, he could divide by a number — say, seven — that could approximate the density of the crowd, and get a figure that would probably be within 20 to 25 percent of what an actual nose count would show.

Another, simpler method, but suitable only for medium-sized crowds of around five hundred to five thousand in size and approximately square in shape, is to add length and width, and multiply by a density factor. If the crowd seems fairly loosely composed, that is, if people can be seen moving into and out of the middle, multiply the sum of length and width by seven. If the crowd seems more compact and few persons can be seen moving within it, multiply by ten. Since there are few remaining mountain peaks available for naming, I will call this the Jacobs Crowd Formula.

When Berkeley students voted on December 1, 1966, to approve a strike, after an incident the night before involving the presence of policemen on campus, Bay Area papers estimated the crowd at eight to ten thousand. Some papers published photos. I obtained an 11-by-14-inch enlargement of one photo taken at the height of the rally. I ruled it off in one-inch squares, and with a magnifying glass counted heads. They totaled 2,804. Even allowing 20 percent more for those on the fringes just outside the picture, the crowd could not have been more than 3,400.

On February 7, 1967, Stokely Carmichael spoke to a Sproul Plaza gathering, estimated by the San Francisco *Chronicle* at "between 6,000 and 7,000 students." I took photographs and again counted noses. The long count. Such a count takes about four hours; it totaled 2,366.

I have labeled this study tentative. There are cross-cultural implications crying for attention. Do Eskimos stand more compactly because of the cold climate? There are already weighty studies indicating that the volatile citizens of Rome or Naples stand farther apart than do Americans, because they need room to wave their arms. Finally, one could also ask whether constant reading of Mao Tse-tung's thoughts causes Chinese crowds to be more or less dense.

FLAPDOODLE WRIT LARGE: ASTROLOGY IN MAGAZINES

Mervin Block

Astrology has been denounced, discredited, and declared dead by scientists for centuries. But a casual reader of magazines and newspapers might never realize it, judging by the recent flurry of articles reporting a resurgence of public interest in astrology. Although the alleged resurgence may be only illusory, there has been a demonstrable resurgence among editors, with each new article generating even more interest — by other editors. No matter what their intentions, many editors thus lend respectability to the laughable, reinforce the credulity of the gullible, and earn the gratitude of the culpable.

The first general magazine to concentrate on astrology in the current wave was *Harper's Bazaar*, in October, 1968. The cover promoted several stories about astrology, including "The Cult of the Zodiac" and "Astrology & Wall Street." All the stories treated as established fact the notion that stars and planets influence people's lives. In addition, there was a horoscope, which also is a monthly feature in two other Hearst magazines, *Town and Country* and *Cosmopolitan*.

Ironically, another Hearst magazine, *Good Housekeeping*, was once praised by *Scientific American* for an investigation of astrology it published in November, 1940. The author, a Pulitzer Prize winning reporter, Henry Pringle, quoted a Princeton professor as saying, "The fallaciousness of astrology ceased to be debatable three hundred years ago." Pringle also quoted a Boston researcher as saying, "Astrology is always, in every way, a delusion and a

---

Summer, 1969. Mervin Block is a TV newsman and editorial writer in New York.

fraud." Dr. Morris Fishbein, then editor of the *Journal* of the American Medical Association, said, "Astrology is the bunk." Pringle concluded: "Astrology . . . is nonsense."

Science, also in 1940, reported that a learned society (the Boston and Cambridge Branch of the American Association of Scientific Workers) had condemned astrology as lacking every conceivable scientific foundation as well as being psychologically harmful and contrary to the public interest. The chairman of the group, Harvard astronomer Bart Bok, said: "Astrology should not be tolerated as a cheap aid to salesmanship and advertising, and newspapers of good repute should not print daily columns of mushy astrological advice."

Back to 1968: About the time of *Harper's Bazaar's* excursion into the bizarre, *Time* (October 25) printed an astrological forecast for the candidates in the approaching presidential election. The story began: "Richard Nixon is lucky. He is a Capricorn, which is the sign of government, and men born under its goat symbol make the best executives. Moreover, the planet of good fortune, Jupiter, has come to his aid, and in early November the planets will be in a favorable aspect for him. But he must be careful. Pluto, the planet of change, conjuncts with Mars on October 30, portending potential violence, and the fact that both Uranus, the planet of the unexpected, and Jupiter, are moving toward Humphrey's sun is favorable for him."

On October 27, *This Week* ran a two-page piece, "Astrology Picks the President." Jess Stearn, who who has written several books about the occult, wrote: "Have the planets something to say about the coming Presidential election? They have, indeed." Stearn quoted a former president of the Astrologers Guild of America as saying that "the planets have clearly expressed their preference for Richard Nixon — a Capricorn — over Gemini Hubert Humphrey." (On February 23, 1969, *This Week* published another Stearn story about astrology, this one about an architect who suggests that people live in homes designed to conform with the life style dictated by their stars.)

Next came the New York *Times* magazine, which devoted its cover December 15 to a psychedelic illustration of the zodiac that proclaimed: "the stars are right for astrology." The index said the artist is among the "increasing number of moderns high on the ancient art of astrology." The article, "The Signs Are Right For Astrology," mentioned the galaxy of newspapers (some 1,200) that print daily horoscopes and the specialized magazines that print only horoscopes. The *Times* article contained several cautiously worded disclaimers, including one disclaimer qualified by another disclaimer: "While no serious scientist appears to regard the casting of horoscopes and prediction of the future as more than arcane flapdoodle, there are at least a couple who think that the electromagnetic fields of the sun and moon and the planets closest to the earth may influence life here in many still unrecognizable ways." The article and accompanying photographs seemed to convey the general impression that astrology is fun.

Three weeks later, on January 6, 1969, *New York* magazine gave astrology six pages. Featured were the predictions of five astrologers. One of them went so far as to venture that "the key word for [New York City] this year is . . . 'change.'" There was only one disparaging remark about astrologers. It was attributed to psychiatrists, who in the next breath, were disparaged in turn.

On January 13, *Newsweek* weighed in with a story labeled in the index "Astrology's New Zenith." The story said psychoanalyst Carl Jung took astrology seriously and added that Marshall McLuhan considers astrology "one of the message-senders of the media age." *Newsweek* asserted: "There is no doubt that astrology is gathering followers in every quarter."

On February 9, *Parade* joined the procession with a lighthearted account of a reporter's uncritical flirtation with astrology. A picture of Frank Sinatra and his former wife, Mia, bore a quotation in the cutline: "It's not the astrologer's fault if things don't turn out."

On March 2, the Washington *Post*'s Sunday magazine, *Potomac*, burbled that astrology had "arrived" in Washington. The enthusiastic story ended by saying, ". . . the importance of astrology today evokes the cliché 'Astrology tells it like it is.'"

On March 20, the *Wall Street Journal* printed a column and a half about the pervasive influence of fortunetelling in South Vietnam. The page 1 story carried this head: SOOTHSAYERS' FORECASTS/ ARE A SERIOUS MATTER/FOR VIETNAM OFFICIALS. Over the head was an italicized line, "Writ in the Stars." (On April 3, *Newsweek*'s Feature Service distributed to its clients a story headed ASTROLOGY IN VIETNAM: IT'S ALL WRITTEN IN THE STARS.)

On its March 21 cover, *Time* portrayed a famous astrologer. In the fourth paragraph of its six-page story, *Time* asked: "Isn't astrology just a fad, and a rather absurd one at that? Certainly. But it is also something more." *Time* then went on to say the fad had become a phenomenon. The article reported Jung's use of astrology and quoted McLuhan as saying, "Mysticism is just tomorrow's science dreamed today." *Time* did mention that one element of what it characterized as the "astrology boom" is the "crass exploitation of people's credulity," yet *Time* constructed an elaborate, full-page horoscope for President Nixon, replete with jargon that Sir William S. Gilbert might well have dismissed as "merely corroborative detail, intended to give artistic verisimilitude to a bald and unconvincing narrative." The article also quoted two psychology professors as reporting, in the November issue of the social science monthly *Transaction,* that they found the mail-order marriage counseling of eighteen sample astrologers "generally valid and useful." Two weeks later, *Time* printed a letter quoting Edmund in King Lear: ". . . when we are sick in fortune, often the surfeit of our own behavior, we make guilty of our disasters the sun, the moon and stars. . . ."

Why did *Time* do a cover story on astrology? The managing editor, Henry Anatole Grunwald, replied: "I just thought it was an interesting, off-beat subject that had an unusual revival, especially among the young." Does Grunwald think *Time*'s coverage might have bolstered the belief of the susceptible? "I don't think so, because we're fairly careful to demolish the pretensions of these people. I think our story made absolutely clear that we didn't believe a word of it [astrology]."

Grunwald described the newstand sales of that issue, with an astrologer on the cover, as "moderately successful." A *Time* circulation executive told me the issue enjoyed sales about 10 percent higher than average.

On its April cover, *Ebony* plugged a six-page spread: BLACK ASTROLOGERS/PREDICT THE FUTURE. The index said the Age of Aquarius was the age of ascendancy for blacks. Among the predictions: "Dick Gregory will be offered a position in the President's cabinet" and "The Messiah will return as a black man."

In May, the *Reader's Digest* cover carried a sticker announcing the title of a story: "The Signs Are Right for Astrology." The title also was publicized on cards placed in magazine racks. So widespread was this campaign that an unsophisticated or superstitious passerby who didn't even buy a copy might be impressed by what he considered an endorsement of astrology. The *Digest* story, a condensation of the New York *Times* Magazine article of December, 1968, was preceded by the signs of the zodiac and this head: BE IT ARCANE FLAPDOODLE OR PRESCIENT SCIENCE, THE ANCIENT ART OF/THE STARGAZERS IS ENJOYING AN EXTRAORDINARY COMEBACK.

On its May 13 cover, *Look* said: "ASTROLOGY/Fun, fraud or keyhole to the future?" *Look*'s answer inside was not "fraud." The four-page spread prompted this letter, published in *Look* of June 24: "When a professional astrologer reads an article [*Look*'s] which attempts to be objective and fair, it behooves her to express gratitude. Your piece and its author . . . deserve my appreciation and that of others who attempt to serve clients in a meaningful, scientific manner. . . ." (*Look*'s index page had called attention to the story with advice: "This month you will experience an elevation of interest in the influence of the stars. A good period to find a private astrologer for a personalized reading.")

Why did *Look* print a story about astrology? The editor, William B. Arthur, said: "Simply because there has been a great deal of interest in astrology, and we decided to look into it." Is he concerned lest *Look*'s coverage encourage acceptance of astrology? "No, I don't think it necessarily does that, at all."

The July *Ladies' Home Journal* ("The Magazine Women Believe In") spotlighted an astrology story on its cover. The story—and a full-page diagram—provided "a completely original way for you to discover your secret self, and the influence of stars on your life." In addition, the *Journal* carried its regular monthly horoscope by Sybil Leek, who described herself as a "white" witch—one who does not practice black magic. The *Journal*'s masthead lists her as a contributing editor.

The Washingtonian also hitched its wagon to the stars in July. The local magazine began its cover story: "Astrology is in. Television shows are scrambling for astrological features, staid suburban clubs invite astrologers in to speak, and department stores promote glassware and lingerie emblazoned with signs of the zodiac." The author later asserted that astrology "has never been disproved."

What is the cumulative effect on the populace of all these stories about astrology? "It's pernicious for reason and rationality," said the director of the department of psychiatry at Manhattan's Mount Sinai Hospital, Dr. M. Ralph Kaufman. He said the stories "tend to bring those who are on the fence to believe [in astrology] and confirm those who already believe." Dr. Kaufman said one reason he is especially concerned is, "faith in astrology keeps its adherents from coming to grips with reality."

The May *Natural History*, published by the American Museum of Natural History, carried an article that said flatly: "Ancient astrology is derided to this day by all scientists." Others are equally firm. Daniel Cohen, in his book *Myths of the Space Age*. (Dodd, Mead, 1967), wrote: "Clearly it is not any scientific discovery that has brought about the rebirth of astrological interest. On the contrary, every discovery makes astrology more untenable." And Patrick Moore, in *Suns, Myths and Men* (W. W. Norton, 1968), said of astrology: "I can only echo the famous remark made by the Duke of Wellington in a different context: 'Sir — if you will believe *that*, you will believe anything.' "

On May 29, *Newsweek*'s Feature Service sent out an astrology story that — in contrast to almost every other article examined in this study — knocked down astrology in the first sentence and minced no words demonstrating that it is unadulterated buncombe. Jacquin Sanders's story began bluntly:

> The astrology fad marches on — over its own dead errors.
>
> Though it doesn't seem to hurt business, some of the most prominent astrologers have been coming out with some of the most misguided predictions since Chicken Little passed the word that the sky was falling.

Next, Sanders attributed a prediction to the prominent astrologer, Carroll Righter, whom *Time* had presented on its cover March 21. This prediction, Sanders wrote, had been made early this year (but was not quoted by *Time*): "The race problem will be with us through May 1. Then people will start to work things out on a constructive basis."

In addition, the summer issue of *Horizon* carries a two-page article, "The Astrologers," by J. H. Plumb, of Cambridge. He pooh-poohs astrology and brands newspaper horoscopes "silly," "foolish," and "pathetic."

Incidentally, on March 25, Washington's *Editorial Research Reports* — published by the Congressional Quarterly Service — distributed a one-page article about astrology to newsrooms across the country. But no exposé, this. The article began with a reference to the story that appeared in *New York* January 6:

"The stock market, says New York astrologer David Williams, is due for trouble April 4. On that date, Jupiter and Uranus will be in exact conjunction in the heavens."

But if Williams — or *New York*, or *Editorial Research Reports* — had consulted a calendar instead of the heavens, he would have observed that April 4 could not be a bad day for the market or any kind of day except a holiday, Good Friday.

THE ROVING LISTENER

Melvin Mencher

Now I know how the fellow felt who was stuck in a Chinese fortune cookie factory. For three months this last summer I was trapped in my automobile and in remote cabins with only a radio for information about the world outside.

Help.

Driving through the Sioux country one night, I tuned the radio to a nearby station to get the news. There was a fanfare and the announcement: "News in Depth." I settled back to catch up on Vietnam or the President's political fortunes. The announcer credited the program to something called the American Security Council, and the tape began to spin. A Rhodesian press official in Washington was interviewed about democracy back home. When he remarked that the "indigenous peoples" were delighted with their government and that only a few radicals opposed it, I tuned elsewhere in the search for news.

A station in the town thirty miles ahead came in, and for the fifth time that day I heard the same state news that had been ripped from the wires most of the day. The first item was the number of traffic fatalities in the state for the year, with a description of the latest death; next, an endless rundown on bids on state highway construction; then the weather — temperature, wind velocity, barometric readings, the highs, the lows, and the anticipated readings for every section of the state.

It was like this from Canada through the Midwest into the Southwest. Local stations sounded alike. Traffic accidents, arrests, judicial actions, deaths — courtesy of the local mortuary — statements by the mayor, the governor, a senator. All of it from the record, as dry and as concealing as dust on the highway.

Fall, 1966. Melvin Mencher is a member of Columbia's journalism faculty.

Much of the energy of the local news staffs seemed to go into the gathering of news for the bulletin board type of program. Kiwanis Club members were told when they would meet next. The Order of DeMolay had a new leader. The American Association of University Women would meet next Wednesday to discuss a scholarship program. The transient listener could learn a little about the community from these programs. As we moved west, the meetings of parent associations and bridge clubs were joined by announcements of the district rodeo association and the Future Farmers and 4-H clubs. On the swap-shop programs, baby cribs and the sixty-dollar '55 Pontiac that "runs pretty good" were joined by a "gentle saddle horse" and a Cessna airplane "just right for the family."

But the kind of local happenings and flavor that make the United States so diverse, that make Joplin different from Pueblo and Austin unlike Tucumcari, were not being broadcast when I was listening.

The homogenization of local news is not limited to the United States. While on an island in the French River in Ontario, Canada, for almost three weeks, I had to rely for news on a radio station in Sudbury, the nickel capital of the world. Squeezed between endless replays of a nonmusical record hit, "They're Coming to Take Me Away," were local newscasts of traffic accidents and police reports.

One day I heard something about a dispute over a miner's lunch pail that led to a strike. What seemed a frivolous matter apparently was serious, for the station continued to refer to a shutdown in the mines. The issues and the extent of the strike were never made clear, and I had no understanding of the strike until I was able to buy a newspaper weeks later. I wrote to the manager of the station expressing my distress at being unable to learn about the strike, or any meaningful local news, for that matter.

He replied that he thought the station was meeting its listeners' needs because it had more listeners than its competitors.

"We must be doing something right," he wrote, incisively putting me in my place.

Radio news was not all bad. In Canada, the Canadian Broadcasting Corporation's slow-paced newscasts were a pleasure to hear.

Occasionally in the United States a local station showed a spark of imagination. A station in Nebraska, for example, gave in full detail a bird count made at a wildlife refuge. There was not an English sparrow or a pigeon in the count.

Every now and then a station had the makings of a good story, but the newsmen, whether local or at the wire service state news desk, refused to find answers to the most interesting questions. A Denver University student was arrested and charged with growing marijuana in his window box, local police reported. The mind wandered. Who spotted it? A nervous landlady? A neighboring floriculturist? Does Denver have a police patrol that surveys window ledges and empty lots?

A prisoner in the South Dakota State Penitentiary filed a writ of habeas corpus in the state supreme court. End item. Again, the mind wandered. Did he draw it up himself after reading some of the recent court decisions? Is there a self-trained lawyer in the penitentiary who has been turning out writs for fellow cons? A call to the penitentiary would have added the human dimension missing from so many stories.

AP and UPI wire news was read slavishly. Announcers were as bored as their listeners. In western Missouri, on a warm afternoon, a disc jockey read about the United States and Russia "singling a duet." An event took place on "Denmark's northeastern coast . . . [pause] . . . make that northwestern coast."

It really didn't matter. In the lush countryside of the Ozarks, Denmark was another planet. What were the people doing in the Ozarks that day? According to the newscasts, they were killing each other on the highways, shooting one another, planning a seven-story building somewhere.

Once I was swept up in the excitement of life around me. A severe windstorm struck an area near Winner, South Dakota, and a local station tracked its whereabouts for listeners.

Mrs. Stanley Goudy called in from her farm to report that the wind had ripped a concrete cover from a cistern. Another housewife, ten miles from Mrs. Goudy, said the wind had lost some of its violence when it reached her place. As the station faded out, we were assured that the wind was spent.

In the incessant search for a new top in newscasts, the trivial is bloated. Old events newly discovered are read with an intensity that baffles the attentive listener. On the largest station in New Mexico, a congressman was described as having introduced a bill to give farmers greater disaster relief benefits. At the end of the item, the listener learned in a final sentence that the bill was old; it had cleared a committee and was on its way to the other chamber.

As the mountains of New Mexico passed into the distance and the hills of western Texas hove into sight, I turned on the radio again. An Amarillo station gave a two- or three-sentence account of a farm workers' march on Austin. Not until hours later, on the Morgan Beatty NBC newscast did I learn the reason for the march. Moreover, NBC added an essential dimension to the event with some background about the differences between Governor John B. Connally and Senator Ralph W. Yarborough.

The Amarillo station's handling of a big state story reminded me of the Sudbury station's lack of interest in its major local story. It indicated that the news of the march was either distasteful to the station, or the news staff was amateurish.

During the summer, I was introduced to a program called *Lifeline*. Immersed, I should say. H. L. Hunt followed me throughout the Midwest and Southwest. I had heard about H. L. Hunt in New Mexico years ago when I was covering the state capital. Mr. Hunt, a Texas billionaire, so they said, had picked up every oil and gas lease in the state. Apparently, he was now in the market for softer goods.

Lifeline is a favorite public service program of the small stations. After a while, it became a late-evening favorite of mine. I enjoyed the relentless pursuit of the deep-voiced announcer, ever on the trail of those who would subvert the sovereignty of the Republic.

My favorite *Lifeline* show, introduced by the local announcer on a Michigan station as "background to the news," concerned the pitiable condition of some of America's youth. The *Lifeline* announcer contrasted the fresh-faced Young Americans for Freedom with the bearded, radical, pimpled young leftist. Until that moment of truth, I had never known that acne had a political coloration.

MY INTERVIEW

Philip Sheehan

If the American newspapers have trouble getting and keeping good men, my brief case history may help explain why. The point is not that one paper missed a good man in me, but that the reasons for excluding me no doubt exclude many good men from many papers.

My appointment was with the man in charge of hiring editorial personnel for several papers. He was imposing, but not forbidding. Lightly tanned, dignified lines in a square face, gray eyes, steel-gray hair brushed straight back. He would have looked powerful if he had had prominent eyebrows.

"Good morning," I said. "My name is Philip Sheehan, and I'm here to see about a job on one of your newspapers."

"Have a seat," he said, "and we'll talk it over." His voice was quiet, but not weak; like the eyebrows, it was a minor disappointment.

I had done television and magazine work for about eight years, and explained to him why I thought I could do newspaper work.

"Have you ever done any newspaper work?"

"No. I thought I made it clear that I was not a newspaperman, but would like to be one."

"I mean at all," he explained. "Didn't you work on a paper in high school or college?"

"Well, yes, I did, but I didn't count that. I worked on the high school paper, and for a while on the college paper."

"But you didn't stay with it?"

"My college career was interrupted by the army, a wife, and

Fall, 1967. Philip Sheehan is a New York writer who has worked in educational TV.

several children. The last two years I didn't have much time for extracurricular activities."

"You're still saying you didn't stay with it."

"No, I suppose I didn't."

"Let me tell you something: when I graduated from college, I had already worked on newspapers for seven years. I started out in newspaper work, and loved it, and stayed with it. You tried it, and obviously didn't love it."

I didn't think that was a reasonable comparison, and tried to tell him why without being insulting.

"If you really wanted to work on a paper," he said, "you would have been working on one before now. I don't think you have the commitment you would need for a newspaper job."

"Possibly I don't have a commitment to newspapers. I do have a commitment to journalism — to the truth of what happens and to the clear expression of that truth. That's enough for many jobs."

"Well, it isn't the same thing. If you don't love newspapers, you wouldn't be much of a newspaperman."

The rest of the interview was boring, except for a few words on the subject of money.

"For us to give you as much money as you'd expect, we'd have to pay you more than some of the people who have been with us for years. That wouldn't be fair to them."

"It wouldn't be unfair if I'm better than they are."

"Well, I don't think you are. We had another fellow in here from television before, and he wasn't much good at all."

"Maybe he wasn't much good in television either."

"That may be, but we're suspicious of people from radio and television. They don't worry about spelling and punctuation, and we don't think they know much about it."

I had long before decided the interview was pointless, and now decided to end it. "What you mean is that you don't have any job that you would offer me."

"That's not true. We do have a few openings, but one of them was just filled. We had a young fellow in here, just finished graduate journalism school, and I bet he can write better now than you can."

I hadn't been asked to write anything, and no one had looked at my samples or called my references. I suggested that such a judgment, therefore, was a bit hasty.

"Possibly you can write," he allowed, "but I'd have to bet against it. And as I said, the salary is not in your range at all. This other lad now, he has his master's degree, and some years of experience, and we're giving him $105 a week. And he's glad to get it."

I resisted the urge to tell him he had obviously hired a nitwit. I took the application form he offered, and said I would send it back with some samples when I got a chance.

I'm keeping it as a souvenir.

NINE

Shapes of the Future

WHY WE LACK A NATIONAL PRESS COUNCIL

Norman E. Isaacs

For me, it all began with the stress on "good news" in the worrisome, penny-pinching days of the Great Depression. As a young, still untutored reporter in Indianapolis I found it hard to understand why stories about job layoffs should be relegated to short spaces inside the newspaper and why any prediction by any business spokesman about better things to come was almost certain to appear on page 1. As I learned more about newspaper shortcomings and oversights, I swiftly became aware that concerns about newspaper performance were being expressed in many places. It was infuriatingly common to hear the line, "You can't believe what you read in the newspapers."

I also learned a bit about publishers. Young newsmen of that era were impressed and fretful about the surging growth of radio and of *Time* magazine, which had been launched in 1923 by two twenty-four-year-old newspapermen, Briton Hadden and Henry Luce. But the publishers and editors were scornful of these intruders. We young reporters felt humiliated in 1935 when the American Newspaper Publishers Association bitterly opposed the proposed Child Labor Amendment. The publishers wanted laissez-faire for themselves in the use of youngsters to deliver newspapers and they had not the slightest hesitancy about falling back on the First Amendment. There was also what we considered disgraceful opposition to the Wages-Hours Act in its applications to news-

---

Fall, 1970. Norman E. Isaacs, longtime Louisville *Courier-Journal* and *Times* editor and a past president of the American Society of Newspaper Editors, is Editor in Residence at the Columbia Graduate School of Journalism.

papers; there was long and tendentious argument before a compromise was reached, fixing newspaper executive salaries at thirty-six dollars.

Hence it was little wonder that we perked up in early 1943 when it was announced that Henry Luce had given $200,000 and *Encyclopaedia Britannica* $15,000 for a study into the state of the press and the prospects for its continued freedom. We were buoyed also by the fact the study would be run by Robert M. Hutchins, the lively chancellor of the University of Chicago. We turned resentful later when it was disclosed that Dr. Hutchins had named to the Commission on Freedom of the Press only scholars and had failed to choose even one journalist.

We should have had enough sense, of course, to recognize the capacities of men like Zechariah Chaffee of Harvard; John M. Clark of Columbia; Harold Lasswell of Yale; Archibald MacLeish, who was not only a poet of distinction but had served as an Assistant Secretary of State; Reinhold Niebuhr of the Union Theological Seminary; Beardsley Ruml, then chairman of the Federal Reserve Bank in New York; and the senior Arthur Schlesinger of Harvard. Whatever suspicions I had nurtured vanished the moment I read "A Free and Responsible Press," the Hutchins report, in 1947. I was tremendously impressed and moved.

My publisher, Elzey Roberts, was outraged by the report. Even though his St. Louis *Star-Times* was one of the few liberal newspapers in the country, Roberts's visceral reaction was like that of at least 95 percent of his fellow publishers. Up to then, Hutchins had been one of the most influential and effective of citizens; within a year his public standing had been shredded by the distortions of editorial vilification.

What was the heinous crime of which the Commission was guilty? In essence, all it had pleaded for was a press both responsible and accountable. It felt that freedom of the press, while not in immediate peril, was endangered in the long run by the growing crisis in society. The Commission appealed for a moral approach to journalism, saying, "There is a point beyond which failure to realize the moral right will entail encroachment by the state on the existing legal right." While it cast aspersions on the economic structure of communications, the Commission's great sin was in recommending the establishment "of a new and independent agency to appraise and report annually upon the performance of the press." It was a sweeping concept.

Even now — twenty-three years later — people like me who applauded the report feel that the Commission went too far in the task it envisioned for the new agency, which was to be independent of both press and government. It was fine in stipulating that the new body "help the press define workable standards of performance," it was farsighted in wanting "inquiries in areas where minority groups are excluded from reasonable access to the channels of communication," it proposed to serve journalism better in conducting "a continuous appraisal of governmental action affecting communications," it was in proper but risky territory in advocating the investigating of instances of "press lying, with particular reference to persistent misrepresentation of the data required for judging public issues." But the Commission clearly strayed afield when it looked ahead to seeking ways of "supplying service where it is lacking or to provide alternative service where the drift toward monopoly seems dangerous." Unfortunately, because of the fury of the publishers, the nobly worded constructive portions of the report were foredoomed to join the frivolous segments on shelves reserved for small, unobtrusive reference books. (See "The Hutchins Report: A Twenty-Year View," Summer, 1967.)

But the need remained for some kind of agency to appraise press performance, or at least to consider grievances against it. For a yawning credibility gap was widening year by year. Less than twelve months after the Hutchins report, for example, there was widespread disillusionment about coverage of the Truman-Dewey campaign. The denouement of that race, of course, was the photograph of the beaming Harry Truman holding aloft an early edition of the Chicago *Tribune* reporting Thomas Dewey's "victory." To its vast embarrassment, the great preponderance of the country's press simply had refused to believe — and report — what its reporters were seeing and hearing: that the "silent majority" of that day were following Truman's campaign and turning out for him. (During the campaign, when a top Kansas City political reporter incredulously told St. Louis colleagues that the "Boot Heel" part of Missouri was Truman country and he was urged to write it, he replied, "My God, no. I'd be laughed out of the state.")

Retrospective unhappiness over 1948, however, turned to professional anger in the 1952 campaign. Adlai Stevenson made his bitter comment about a "one-party press." There were evidences of gross slanting in news columns. The anger surfaced at the 1953 national convention of Sigma Delta Chi. There Irving Dilliard, editor of the editorial page of the St. Louis *Post-Dispatch,* who had been making challenging speeches around the country about one-sidedness, showed as one of his most telling exhibits a copy of the Indianapolis *News*'s page 1, made up as a billboard for an appearance by General Eisenhower in that city. The society voted for an investigation of the press's conduct. I was not at the convention, nor did I take part in the public debates. But I was chosen to head the SDX Ethics Committee charged with conducting the examination.

The assignment was not unwelcome. Since 1947, mainly through the Associated Press Managing Editors Association and to a lesser degree within the American Society of Newspaper Editors, I had been increasingly involved in the movement for self-examination by newsmen, and principally for higher ethical standards and practices.

(The issue of internal criticism had been one of the chief motivations for the reorganization of APME in 1948. Though the group had been largely a docile appendage of AP, some "young Turks" were pushing for more far-reaching activity. Among the leaders were Kenneth MacDonald of the Des Moines *Register & Tribune,* Lee Hills of the Knight Newspapers, and William P. Steven of the Minneapolis *Star & Tribune.* I had shared their ardor for "action," and quickly joined the movement. After the 1947 meeting, Kent Cooper — for a quarter of a century AP's famed general manager and executive director, who now was facing retirement against his will — advanced the idea of an independent APME. He had incorporation papers drawn up specifically barring publishers from membership, and some twenty of us were among the incorporators of APME, Inc. Out of this came a glowing decade for the "Continuing Studies," the first mass self-examination project in American journalism. They were of varying quality and importance, but they provided individual editors with the opportunity to challenge both specific story coverage and also raise questions of news policy and emphasis.)

The SDX election-coverage study turned out to be both fascinating education and a harrowing experience. What was clearly needed was some kind of intelligent method of assessing performance. It called for study by research experts. "Seed money" for this phase came from the Fund for the Republic, then associated with the Ford Foundation. Raymond B. Nixon of the University of Minnesota and Chilton R. Bush of Stanford collaborated in bringing together virtually every top academic research specialist. Out of this consultation came a moderate, though far-reaching, proposal. It was agreed that it was impossible to pass judgment on election coverage after the fact. The proposal, therefore, was for a widespread on-the-scene study of the 1956 presidential campaign.

Safeguards were scattered all through the projected study. Editorial pages, columns, and cartoons were to be disregarded. The exploration was to involve merely basic fairness of news coverage. The difficulties of gathering information were to be weighed. Edition schedules were to be taken into account. No judgment was to be passed without direct consultation with the editors involved. The cost was estimated at $700,000.

Repeated consultation with foundation executives made it clear there was no hope of a grant unless at least a majority of the nation's publishers saw merit in the proposal. This meant selecting a list to be polled. It should come as no surprise that one can question fewer than seventy individuals and cover all the major newspaper properties in the United States, as well as many middle-size and smaller ones. After all, when one questions a chain owner, he ticks off a good many big-city dailies in one call. But there is no need to dwell on detail. Only seventeen publishers in the country voted "yes" to having their newspapers studied for fairness during the 1956 campaign. The remainder voted "no" — a number of them vehemently.

It was clear that most of those who owned American newspapers were determined to resist self-examination. I had to conclude that they would not take the slightest step without the greatest of pressures being exerted upon them.

By 1960, however, it turned out that the Sigma Delta Chi experience had not been entirely an exercise in futility. The New England Society of Newspaper Editors voted to have that fall's presidential campaign coverage studied, and I became chairman of the special committee. Because there were almost no expense funds, it had to be a limited study. Sevellon Brown, then editor of the Providence *Journal* and *Bulletin* and NESNE president, helped as he could. My colleagues were the late Carl Lindstrom of the Hartford *Times* and Ted Rowse of the Washington *Post,* who had written the book *Slanted News.* After considerable thought, we decided to focus on the handling of two stories.

One story was about official Roman Catholic church opposition in Puerto Rico to the election bid of Governor Luiz Muñoz-Marín because of his statements on birth control. The other had to do with a reported loan to Richard Nixon's brother by Howard Hughes. Our reasoning was that if there was going to be any bias in news presentation, including overplays or underplays, it was most likely to show up in these two stories. We thought the first story more likely to capture attention because of the heavy Roman Catholic population in New England and the past attention to birth control, plus the fact Senator Kennedy was a Catholic. The other story stemmed from a Drew Pearson column implying possible future favoritism for Hughes, who was involved in several cases with the government. AP and UPI had picked up the story, and we felt its handling might disclose bias.

The result startled us. The election coverage in New England newspapers — with only two exceptions — was casual, erratic, and at times incomprehensible. Our report concluded that the general performance had been "so slapdash as to give an impression of bias," even though we could pinpoint none. It was an indictment of newspapering simply on the issue of inadequate news coverage.

Newspaper attainment of accuracy depends on deskmen as well as on reporters. One story told over and over is that of teachers at a Newspaper in the Classroom session in Louisville. Questions and answers flowed smoothly until one woman arose to say, "I have great respect for the *Courier-Journal* and the *Times.* But something bothers me. I really haven't had a great deal of experience with it — perhaps five or six times. But each time I've known anything about an event, there's been something wrong with the stories."

"Such as what?" came the quick challenge.

"Well," she said, "such as the paper reporting the meeting being in the wrong place . . . or the time being wrong . . . or the names of the people being wrong, or misspelled. Little things, I know. But all wrong, and it makes me wonder how much more accurate all the other stories are about what goes on around the world."

There was a long silence while I looked out the window at the University of Louisville, and then came the most telling remark about my calling that I have ever had to make: "You know, I have to agree. It has been true of almost every story I have ever been involved in personally. The fellows at the office know how much I hate to have my speeches covered. We try so hard to be right. It's the one goal all of us have. And we fail so often. We've got to do more about it than we have done."

Barry Bingham was trying to do something more when he appeared before Sigma Delta Chi in Norfolk in 1963 and proposed the creation of local press councils. He had thought it out carefully and listed the ingredients he thought a council should contain. These included a representative group of a community's citizens, but specifically excluded government officials or political spokesmen of any party. In its purest sense, he was urging local grievance committees which could accept public complaint against the newspapers, study them, ask the editors questions if they so desired, and issue reports on press performance when and if they wished. We tried everything we could at the time to induce Louisville citizens to move on the suggestion. None was so inclined, and we were unwilling to sponsor one on our own, believing that this would properly be considered window dressing.

The seed did not fall entirely on barren ground. Ben Bagdikian had become president of the Mellett Fund. This consisted of stock left to the American Newspaper Guild by Lowell Mellett of the Washington *Daily News* to "stimulate responsibility in the press while maintaining freedom." It seemed to Bagdikian that local press councils offered just such an opportunity. In 1967 the Mellett Fund offered financing through university sources for press councils in four smaller cities: Bend, Oregon; Redwood City, California; and Sparta and Cairo, Illinois. (See "Local Press Councils: An Informal Accounting," Spring, 1969).

The Cairo experiment was the only outright failure. "The trouble there," says Bagdikian, who now is national editor of the Washington *Post*, "was that the community's whites wouldn't even sit down to talk with the blacks." The other three turned out to be less than press councils, but nevertheless highly successful. They opened communication between the editors and the citizens on a regular face-to-face basis. Redwood City's effort ran smoothly, but has now been discontinued. Bend, where the *Bulletin* is a daily, and Sparta, which has a weekly newspaper, continue because the publishers in those cities like the idea of informal monthly meetings for frank discussions.

Based on the success in the three smaller cities, the Mellett Fund stretched the move to two major centers, Seattle and St. Louis. Both of these called for a university professor to serve as chairman, to seek systematic examination of facets of news coverage, and to reach out into community problems. The St. Louis experiment is moribund. Only one newspaper was sufficiently interested to take part, and the project itself, Bagdikian reports, was "too unstructured." The Fund learned a lot from the experience, he says.

Seattle is a different story. Henry McLeod, managing editor of the Seattle *Times*, calls it "immensely useful." The Seattle council has been a movement tapping the Negro community. After a few bristling sessions about the newspapers and TV and radio stations in Seattle, the meetings have become educationally beneficial for both sides. There has been examination of the handling of trials in Seattle, and some regular testing of community attitudes. "I do believe," says Bagdikian, "that the existence of the Seattle council has avoided serious trouble for that city." Reports of the editors and the electronic journalists seem to bear this out.

For some months, Philip Geyelin, editorial page editor of the Washington *Post*, has published informative editorial comment on misplays within the communication field, heading these FYI. Now the *Post* has moved further with the appointment of an assistant managing editor in charge of oversight, and some of the early results are encouraging. A yearlong feud between the Honolulu *Star-Bulletin* and the city administration came to an end early this year when a Honolulu media council came into being, under the chairmanship of Dr. Harland Cleveland, president of the University of Hawaii. And in Milwaukee, there has been the unusual development of a TV station (WITI-TV) carrying an editorial calling for an end to the long battle between the Milwaukee *Journal* and Mayor Henry Maier. It was unusual because of news organizations' reluctance over many years to offer public criticism about one another, even when desperately needed.

"It takes two to tango," commented the TV station. "The *Journal* Company has every right to editorialize against the Mayor, but it is also perpetuating this feuding. . . . If the Mayor and the *Journal* want to fight, let them do it in the backroom. Other media want no part of this time-wasting. Neither does the public."

Publishers and editors around the United States, however, paid scant attention to these experiments or to the Louisville newspapers' appointing an ombudsman to receive complaints on news coverage. It has been business-as-usual for the press, even though it has been increasingly obvious that the tinder pile has been growing more rapidly. Joseph McCarthy and Governor George Wallace tried putting the match to it, but it didn't burst into flames. There is now some reason to believe they left it smoldering, ready for Vice-President Agnew to ignite it.

If the polls are correct — and I do not challenge them — journalism cannot continue to sweep the idea under the rug. One fairly recent Gallup Poll reported that only 37 percent of the public feels newspapers deal fairly on political and social issues. Some 45 percent think newspapers unfair. Listed as not sure were 18 percent. It is significant that the more highly educated the person questioned, the stronger the feeling that newspapers are unfair.

Vice-President Agnew has capitalized on serious weaknesses in journalism. (And it is notable that much of Agnew's editorial backing comes from newspapers whose owners and editors are bitterly opposed to any thought of self-examination.) I considered and still consider the Agnew attacks a form of intimidation of the press. Though his more recent approaches stress "sensible authority," it is not inconceivable that a drive for "sensible authority" could be stretched to the creation of an overview agency by government ostensibly to preserve and protect the First Amendment freedoms. Far better, I hold, for the press to create its own protections.

Our troubles in 1968 began well before the Democratic Convention. Pierre Salinger had screamed "foul" to ASNE over the Indianapolis *Star*'s carving on a New York *Times* editorial to serve its anti-Kennedy purpose. (See "The Indiana Primary and the Indianapolis Newspapers," Summer, 1968.) Salinger sent a wire on a Sunday demanding instant investigation and a public report before Tuesday's primary. Vincent S. Jones, ASNE president, rejected Salinger's thrust as a political ploy. But Jones thought it bad journalism and made clear to associates he would have put the matter to the Board if Salinger had invoked the ASNE Code of Ethics. In mid-May Salinger sent Jones a more thoughtful letter, saying: "[If] ASNE is unwilling to look into the practices of its own members, then who will? Certainly, you would be among the first to admit that the government cannot do this, and that it has to be done by the industry itself."

Chicago was in the offing. That story needs no replaying here. What does bear repeating is the response of the public to what it saw on its TV screens and read in its newspapers — the flood of protests all adding up to the fact people did not believe what they were seeing and hearing.

I believe it fair to question whether we of journalism hadn't been inviting this kind of public response. Each time wise, thoughtful men had asked us as a profession to look into our standards and our practices we had taken refuge in the First Amendment. At various times some of us had challenged publishers' concepts of that Amendment. We had held that it had been written to protect the free expression of opinion, that under it the patriots of early America had created their own underground press. There was nothing in the First Amendment, we had said, that gave a man with a printing press the right to exert a stranglehold on a community's lifeline of information. The press had ignored university poll reports of years ago that showed teen-agers believing that newspapers ought to be under firmer control. We needed to be rebuilding faith in the American press; the shrugging off of inaccuracy and slanting in news columns was the most dangerous course we could follow. An ethics or grievance committee — or, if you will, a press council — seemed to be an effective way to deal with the situation.

What might a grievance committee or press council, under proper auspices, be constituted to do, and how might it do it? Those of us who have been studying the issue believe it should be set up to consider and pass upon serious complaints charging deliberate distortions, unfairness, or grossly inadequate or misleading coverage of news. Clearly, a first requirement ought to be that a complainant must have sought redress and failed to get it from the newspaper. The system of a complainant's waiving the right to use Council findings in a libel suit has been so successfully used by the British Press Council that this concept ought to be adapted to our own uses. There might be panels of editors set up around the country to assess complaints in their regions. All of the discussions have emphasized that there should not be any enforcement powers; that all that is necessary is the expression of approval or disapproval. At the outset, such an agency could well expect a flood of complaints of little or no substance. These can be promptly disallowed or screened out, as has been the case in Britain. William Dickinson of the Philadelphia *Bulletin* has predicted that within a short time there would be only a handful of cases serious enough for investigation and action.

Most of those who oppose press councils on a rational rather than emotional basis customarily raise two warnings. One is the potential impairment of an editor's freedom of action through community pressure as brought through a council. The other is that councils open the door to the licensing of journalists. Erwin Canham of the *Christian Science Monitor* has long held a dour view of licensing. He has argued that a majority given the right to pass on the credentials for a professional might easily be led to deny the right of expression to one with whom they disagreed strongly.

Earlier this year the issue was raised anew by Dr. W. Walter Menninger in a National Press Club speech. Dr. Menninger's comments arose out of his service on the Commission on Violence. Later, in a talk in his hometown, Topeka, Kansas, he clarified his remarks. Concerning licensing, he said:

The phenomenon of the eye of the beholder was dramatically demonstrated in the reactions of some members of the media to the National Press Club address, which included a suggestion of standards for journalists in the form of certification or licensure. While a number of journalists responded thoughtfully and nondefensively, many responded with defensive protestation and emphatic rejection. . . .

What were the provocative comments? "A time-honored question in a free society is, Who shall guard the guards? Freedom of the press is the only guarantee of the Bill of Rights which cannot be exercised by each individual citizen. Practically speaking, this privilege can be exercised only by those in the journalistic profession. . . . In other professions with a public trust — medicine, law, education — laws for licensure and certification assure the public that the practitioner has fulfilled minimum standards, met certain requirements for training and demonstrated competence in the profession. The public is entitled to similar safeguards in the quality of the practitioners of this most important cornerstone in our democratic society, the news media."

Obviously, the thought of "licensing" springs from my medical background. Thus I may have chosen the wrong word to emphasize a concern about professional standards in journalism. It is clear that certification or licensure doesn't guarantee competent performance of professionals. It does no more than assure the public that practitioners have met minimum standards. And there are undoubtedly many legal, constitutional, and procedural problems that would make certification or licensure of journalists by law well nigh impossible. Ideally the question of standards is a matter for the professional journalists to address, but the public has a right to be deeply concerned about these standards.

Dr. Menninger quite justifiably could not resist the temptation to remark about the statement by Sigma Delta Chi's professional development committee in 1966 that "the time has arrived — it is long overdue, in fact — for the profession of journalism to establish its minimum standards, announce them to the public, and begin enforcing them." Dr. Menninger noted that the proposal had been rejected by the SDX convention and then delivered a tap on our professional Achilles' heel: "It is fascinating to note that none of the discussion of this rejection was reported in the media, despite the presence of the media and their reporting of other convention activities."

As to pressures which might be brought on editors through press councils, the opponents of such proposals often quote the eloquent J. Russell Wiggins, former executive editor of the Washington *Post*, who has said:

> The committee might become in many cities the channels through which the very worst special-interest groups would bring pressures to suppress or withhold news. They might make the collective opinion of the community irresistible at the very moment when that opinion was the most misguided and most in need of contradiction and restraint. . . . The real danger of such committees, of course, is that they might make the press even more subservient to the mores of the community and more than ever the prisoner of the Establishment.

At the risk of sounding cynical, most newsmen can swiftly point out that most middle-sized and smaller newspapers are already, to some degree, prisoners of "the establishment." Although there was a substantive degree of compassionate judgment involved, Wiggins was himself victim at one point of his newspaper's vulnerability to "establishment" pleas. One must also include as parallel victim the Washington *Star*.

This instance concerned the arrest of Walter Jenkins, President Johnson's assistant. The request for "consideration" was made to the editors of Washington's newspapers by former Supreme Court Justice Abe Fortas. The story had been confirmed by reporters in the morning. That day's editions of the *Star* contained no mention of the arrest. The *Post* published nothing of its own, nor had it moved to do so, until UPI carried a story on its wires. None of us in American journalism can claim to have been without guilt, at some point or another, of accommodating ourselves to our communities at some moment of particular stress — or, perhaps, to some individual case, poor or rich, as the episode might have been. I raise the awkward matter of the Jenkins case with full sympathy for all the editors involved simply as an honest offset for Wiggins's fears of what dangers a council might bring in the way of exerting pressures on editors.

By April, 1969, when the wheels of time had ground me into the presidency of ASNE, one of my main goals was to establish a grievance committee. Vincent Jones, vice-president and executive editor of the Gannett chain and my predecessor as head of ASNE, became chairman of the small, select committee to try to work out the grievance idea. Committee members were Barry Bingham; John S. Knight, chief of the Knight properties; Otis Chandler of the Los Angeles *Times;* the youngest of the ASNE members, James Hoge, Jr., of the Chicago *Sun-Times;* and the present-day sage of Great Plains journalism, William Allen White's protégé Whitley Austin of the Salina *Journal.* Robert U. Brown of *Editor & Publisher* had helped counsel in the selection of the small group, and *E & P* carried a careful supporting editorial about the effort.

At no point in the ASNE's consideration of grievance machinery has the subject of licensing of journalists been given the slightest consideration. Nor has the possibility of prepublication pressure entered the picture because this was never the intent. All the effort has been the other way: to establish a means by which a citizen or organization with a complaint of substance against a newspaper could appeal for hearing. From the outset it has been made clear that there is not the slightest interest in the trivia of what we might call civic-club pressures, or in the small omissions which occur daily as a result of space pressures in daily journalism. The thrust was summed up well in the statement by Jones when he first assumed the chairmanship in April, 1969: "Our assignment is to ask whether the Society needs a new definition of purpose; whether, in keeping with the noble sentiments of the preamble of our constitution and the widely admired Code of Ethics, the Society should be able to speak firmly and clearly for the best in American journalism, to set standards of behavior and performance, and to function as the top leadership of our profession."

In the labors to find the key to unlock the door to approval by the ASNE Board, Jones's committee went through a series of changes. The first group (named earlier) served until a meeting in London last fall. Knight and Chandler asked then to be relieved because of the press of business and they were replaced by William Dickinson of the *Bulletin* and Warren Phillips of the *Wall Street Journal.*

The London meeting was the regular fall board meeting. It was called in England to give the members opportunity to examine the workings of the British Press Council. Many arrangements were made by H. Philip Levy, counsel for the International Publishing Corporation (the Mirror newspapers) and author of the definitive book *The Press Council.* A small group of us drove far into the lovely English countryside to have a luncheon meeting with Lord Devlin, who as chairman of the Press Council was credited with a great deal of its success. One thing we learned at this session was of Lord Devlin's introduction of the waiver procedure, under which the Council declined to accept any serious complaint against a newspaper unless the complainant signed a waiver stipulating that none of the Council's investigative findings could be used in legal action against the newspaper. A quid pro quo was that the editor of the newspaper concerned signed a note agreeing to publish the Council's findings.

Lord Devlin was proud of what had been accomplished under the waiver, and we were to find the leading English publishers and editors agreeing thoroughly. Indeed, the statement was made several times by editors that the waiver had undoubtedly reduced the number of libel actions against newspapers. There was not the slightest doubt that the majority of British journalists were in favor of the Council's work. Indeed, in June, 1969, the *UK Press Gazette* had published a survey showing that 86 percent of newspapermen questioned thought that the spreading of the Press Council movement throughout the world desirable.

At this point, some of us were misled into a euphoric state. What we had seen, what we had been told, and our board discussions all seemed to point to an early, favorable decision by the Board to approve a grievance committee. I agreed to call a special meeting in Chicago to receive a new, specific report from the Jones committee. All of this was said publicly and was reported. Stanford Smith, general manager of ANPA, told me in New York that he hoped ASNE would go ahead and added, "When you've got a firm plan, come to us first. This is what the ANPA Foundation is for." It was to be one of the few bits of good news to come in the next months. For the politics of American journalism had come into full play.

Describing here what happened at the Chicago and the subsequent San Francisco Board meetings is difficult as a matter of personal ethics. Some things, however, are self-evident. Obviously, the Board is badly split or a decision would have come long ago. What can only be described as a muzzle was placed on Board members on the question of what has transpired. A few Board members protested, saying the membership should be told what had happened. I can testify that the worst position to be in during a conflict is as presiding officer; one is stripped of the advantages of attack; he is judge, seeking to conduct a fair trial.

The only recent information the membership of ASNE has is a letter published in the ASNE *Bulletin,* sent to the new Committee on Ethics which was named in San Francisco to replace the Jones group. That letter was written by the new ASNE president, Newbold Noyes of the Washington *Star,* to Erwin Canham, the new Ethics chairman. There is no confidentiality that I know concerning the naming of the new committee.

Noyes, with whom I differ philosophically but with whom I enjoy a warm friendship, originally wanted me to serve in his term as Ethics chairman, but my plans to enter academic life made that impossible. We then agreed that an Ethics Committee made up of leading past presidents made sense. I suggested Canham as an ideal "alter ego" for me. Noyes agreed. My other choice was Jones, Noyes's two nominees were Vermont Royster of the *Wall Street Journal* and Michael J. Ogden of the Providence *Journal.* Canham and Jones were looked on as proponents of the idea of self-examination; Royster and Ogden as opposed. Later, Noyes and I agreed on Kenneth MacDonald of the Des Moines *Register & Tribune* as the fifth member. MacDonald describes himself as attracted to the idea, but concerned about some of the "practical" aspects.

In retrospect, I confess to a major error as chairman at San Francisco. Certainly I should have insisted on a direct vote in the Board about the confidentiality of the proceedings. As it stands, I am palpably guilty of participating in the same hypocrisy I have always condemned in others: denouncing public groups such as university regents for conducting executive sessions, then drawing a cloak over one's own functioning as a trustee of a newspaper organization. That no member of the Society rose in open session to inquire about the grievance matter suggests a question that might be asked about American editors; that no reporter covering the meetings — and there were many — queried any officer is also something to think about.

The ASNE Board met again in early October in Sorrento,

Maine. The Ethics Committee had been specially invited. Unfortunately Canham, as chairman, had been occupied as a member of the National Commission on Student Unrest and there had been no committee sessions. Sorrento, therefore, was the group's first canvass of the situation, and it seems fair to say that there is a good distance to go before any definitive statement will be made. There the matter stands.

Clearly, at some point a proposal is going to have to be put before American journalism. ASNE seems to me the most logical sponsor (though it could come through an organization such as the Association for Education in Journalism, which voted approval of the idea of an oversight agency). The question is, what will move ASNE? Under ASNE's constitution, the Board has full authority to conduct the Society's business. But some, strongly opposed to the grievance proposal, have threatened to take the issue to the convention floor, where they are convinced they can win easily. They may be right. Like all professional organizations, ASNE is the victim of its history. Under the membership requirements, every member is the representative of his publisher.

Therefore, while many editors might look upon a grievance proposal favorably, it is conjecture as to how many would feel free to commit themselves in a public vote. Publishers have been known to bring personal pressure on other publishers, even if to no avail. Eugene Pulliam, for instance, was not averse to calling the publisher of one ASNE Board member to protest comments made by the editor. The thought will occur to many that one way of conducting a vote in which editors can express themselves freely is simply by a closed ballot not requiring signatures. ASNE members can smile wryly as they contemplate the long floor wrangling before this could occur. Nonetheless, it has to be conceded this is a sane way of obtaining a democratic expression of true opinion.

In the final analysis, what is called for are enough editors willing to put their jobs on the line for what it is they believe in. I know it is asking a lot. But I have done it myself on occasion and so have some others, because we happen to think that's what being an editor ought to mean.

RIGHT OF ACCESS: A MODEST PROPOSAL

Ben H. Bagdikian

The 150 members of the Agua Caliente Band of Mission Indians in Southern California own 32,000 acres in and around the valuable desert resort of Palm Springs under the guardianship of the Riverside County Superior Court.

A couple of years ago enough Indians had grumbled about the court's handling of their property to cause the Riverside *Press-Enterprise* to assign a reporter, George Ringwald, to poke around. There followed more than a hundred stories and editorials that described, among other things, how one judge encouraged local lawyers to have their Indian clients name the judge as executor of their wills, how another judge received $250,000 for his services to the Indians, and how one Indian estate had 88 percent of its income paid to officers of the court.

The U.S. Department of the Interior said the court protection had been "a failure . . . encumbered with some venality." The *Press-Enterprise* won a Pulitzer Prize.

But Judge Merrill Brown, presiding justice of the superior court in that district, told the *Press-Enterprise* publisher, Tim Hays, that he wanted an explanation for the stories. Hays didn't explain. The judge issued an order for Hays's arrest. Fortunately for the quality of Hays's sleeping accommodations but unfortunately for clarification of the law, the county clerk declined to serve a warrant for the publisher's arrest.

This is hardly typical of court-newspaper relations, but neither is it unique. Gene Wirges in Arkansas, Hazel Brannon Smith in

---

Spring, 1969.

Mississippi, and J. R. Freeman in Colorado have all felt the tender mercies of local authorities enraged at the idea of someone espousing minority causes or unorthodox views.

Among other things, this tells us that judges make bad newspaper editors.

Professor Jerome A. Barron of George Washington University Law School tells us something else: a lot of newspaper editors make bad newspaper editors.

"Bad" in this case means unresponsive to a wide range of voices in their communities, unfair in treatment of people and issues, and unwilling to give aggrieved subjects of news and commentary the right of reply. In a large, urbanized society, individual free speech does not guarantee access to the marketplace of ideas. After all, even in Hitlerian Germany or Stalinist Russia, a man was always free to go into his own soundproofed closet and deliver an attack against the regime. In a democracy, political existence requires access to an audience and today newspapers and broadcasting stations are that access.

Professor Barron has been suggesting for two years a fundamental change in the interpretation of the First Amendment. It now protects freedom of the press. Professor Barron would have it expanded to include the right of the individual to have a fair chance at access to the press, with the courts or legislatures deciding what is fair.

He first suggested this in the June, 1967, *Harvard Law Review* and more recently in the March, 1969, *George Washington Law Review* ("An Emerging First Amendment Right of Access to the Media?").

Barron is not likely to receive testimonials from publishers and broadcasters, but he deserves gratitude for raising the issue in a rational and clear way (and I say that not just because I disagree with him).

He accentuates an important principle: each person in a free society should have a fair chance of being heard and today that inevitably means access to the mass media.

But there is a parallel principle: the right of the speaker — including the one who happens to own a printing press or broadcasting transmitter — to say what he wants no matter what his enemies think about it.

News organizations have acted as though these principles were contradictory, but they are not. Both lie beneath the growing problem of *inequity* in access to the public. *Equality* of access is an impossibility except under special conditions. But the inequity today lies in the bias, sometimes unconscious and sometimes deliberate, in favor of those who have bureaucratic, financial, or political power, and those with skill in dealing with large organizations. Lone individuals or unskilled groups aren't heard and get attention by meeting the convention of news that calls for melodrama. They carry placards, or burn their draft cards, or their neighborhoods, or themselves.

One result has been that until very recently most American journalism didn't recognize social change until there was social explosion. If this deficiency is not remedied on a large scale each new generation will have to turn to violence to get attention and produce change. Today's rebels will become tomorrow's stuffed shirts and will require exposure to unwelcome danger signals that the smug always heed. Letting a maximum number of voices be heard regularly is not just a nice philosophical notion. It is the best way any society has yet discovered to detect maladjustments quickly, to correct injustices, and to discover new ways to meet the continuing stream of novel problems that rise in a changing environment.

Even with unresponsive broadcasting stations, required by law to be fair, there has been no practical remedy for the individual. The FCC has just lifted its first television license in over twenty years of mass television.

For the individual stuck with an unresponsive local paper there is absolutely no remedy. The idea of unhappy readers rushing to court to force a publisher to print an item is anathema to traditional free journalism. But after the suggestion has been anathematized, let the denouncers then answer the question: what else can the reader do?

Insensitivity among mass media operators exists, on a large scale, usually by omission. Some simply do not see themselves as having responsibility for maintaining the local marketplace of ideas. Others accept the role but don't understand how much the world has changed; they think they're covering the marketplace when all they're doing is polishing their friends' pushcarts. Some make honest mistakes but react with the prevailing convention that you admit error publicly only under threat of a viable libel action.

There are still a fair number of operators who see their function as obliterating the marketplace rather than encouraging it. Every political campaign has its quota of cases where some publisher or station owner blacks out the candidate he dislikes. When that happens there is a standard scenario:

— The campaigner makes a public complaint of unfair treatment by a local publisher;

— The visible evidence is that the publisher has been unfair;

— The publishing hierarchs issue their standard proclamation of outrage that anyone should imply that any newspaper could possibly be wrong;

— Most editors and working professionals know that these proclamations are flapdoodle and that their spokesmen are journalistic delinquents but they remain silent; and

— The general public comes to believe that "the press" is a monolithic, arrogant corporation telling every complainer to go to hell.

Now Professor Barron is telling the complainers to go someplace else — to court or to their legislatures. And there is evidence, as he points out in the *George Washington Law Review*, that the courts are creeping up to the idea that access to an audience has standing in the law.

Barron cites a number of cases, perhaps the most interesting being *Food Employees Local 590 v. Logan Valley Plaza, Inc.* A shopping center in Altoona, Pennsylvania, obtained a local court injunction against union members' picketing of a store on the shopping plaza, which was private property. The local court said the pickets had an alternative off the private property, on pathways leading to the center. The Supreme Court overthrew the injunction, saying that since the pickets' audience was the shoppers in the store and since the shoppers couldn't read the strikers' placards if they were carried on the adjacent pathways, the alternative suggested was meaningless.

Furthermore, the Supreme Court said, while the shopping center was private property, its "dedication to public use" diminished its private prerogatives, and it took on special obligations as an important communications center.

Barron notes: "The Court reasoned that in the automobile-centered suburb, the shopping center is a focal point for the community, so that access to its parking lot may be indispensable to secure access to that community.

If the courts take the same attitude toward news organizations ("dedication to public use" and special obligations as an important communications center) there will be, Professor Barron acknowledges, tough problems deciding who has access to what.

His answer is that the courts have handled similarly thorny questions in deciding standards of obscenity.

The history of obscenity decisions may not be a good parallel. It is one thing to enjoin the authorities from interfering with the publishing of James Joyce's *Ulysses* and another to order a particular publisher to print *Ulysses* whether he wants to or not. More important, there is a simple drift to obscenity decisions from "less freedom" to "more freedom" as world communications and historical insights improve, and it becomes clear that whatever the difference between exposed female kneecaps in 1890 and 1920, and between bare-breasted Polynesian maidens and the ladies at Schrafft's, these differences are not those of criminality. Almost inevitably, local legal restraints on such matters will diminish.

But courts, in deciding who will have access to the press, would be passing judgment on political and social values in which there is no simple scale or historical standard as in obscenity. "More freedom" and "less freedom" have little meaning in deciding which voices deserve more attention in the matter of foreign policy, theories of learning and structures of schooling, work-residence patterns, and economic policy. The courts or legislatures deciding who shall be permitted to place his mouth to the megaphone will have the same problems as the most conscientious editors — and less time to think about it.

It would be easy to find absurd — though interesting — applications of the doctrine of forced access to established media of communications. *Editor & Publisher*, the Old Testament of newspaper printing, might be ordered by a court to feature the latest release from the National Association of Broadcasters claiming television to be a superior medium of advertising. *Broadcasting,* the weekly encyclical of electronic movie-attendance, would be forced to give equal space to FCC Commissioner Nicholas Johnson. It would take ten full issues of the magazine to let Johnson catch up, by which time the Tobacco Institute would have sued *Broadcasting* for letting this period go by without quoting in full a speech by Senator Ervin on how much the tobacco industry has done for the economy of North Carolina. The Tobacco Institute would have to buy prime time to show colored slides of malignant lung tissues and John F. Banzhaf III would have to make a commercial for L&Ms without coughing. Station breaks on NBC would urge viewers to switch to CBS and ABC would promote the New York Yankees. Meanwhile, back at *E&P,* Robert U. Brown would be composing a poem in praise of the International Typographical Union while the *Guild Reporter* would run a front page piece saying that George Hearst, Jr., was justified in trying to break the unions in Los Angeles. Hearst would do a column in his Los Angeles *Herald-Examiner* telling readers that Otis Chandler's *Times* was really a better newspaper, while Los Angeles Mayor Sam Yorty would sue Chandler (again) demanding that *Times* cartoonist Paul Conrad draw a picture of Yorty looking intelligent. Conrad would petition Heaven for injunctive relief.

The more likely extension of Professor Barron's idea is that news organizations would tend to become common carriers of other people's views with no control over content, like telephone and telegraph companies.

This is already true for most advertising. The courts have made plain that they will not permit arbitrary denial of advertising space in a monopoly or near-monopoly medium.

Is this a reasonable doctrine for news? It is not. One function of news is the professional judgment of what is more and what is less important at any given hour. There can be only one lead, one second lead, one third lead. Despite all the flaws in these decisions, someone has to do it, and judges and legislators are not able to do it better.

Then what does one do about unfair treatment of individuals and groups in the news, about restrictive policies on letting community groups speak, about silence or narrowness on issues?

The Barron proposal is thoughtful and dramatic. But there are more modest possibilities whose weakness is that they depend on widespread adoption throughout the press on the initiative of the press itself. So far the press as a whole has resisted changes on a scale sufficient to win back public confidence and to meet urgent social needs. Some of these more modest ideas are:

— Start a new journalistic form: the occasional full page with a skilled journalist writing clearly and fairly six or seven ideas of the most thoughtful experts on solutions of specific public problems. The editorial would still survive as the paper's own opinion. But the reader would be exposed to others, presented in clear language in a standard, attractive format offering a series of possible answers. Instead of bits and pieces of harangues on the welfare problem, for example, let the serious reader see a display of all the more interesting alternatives: negative income tax, guaranteed income, keeping things the way they are, forced labor camps (let people face the implications of what many feel), guaranteed public jobs, total abolition of any aid. It would help end the sense of frustration that comes because the news is such an efficient carrier of problems and such an inefficient carrier of solutions. And it would provide a local outlet for ideas that are now sequestered in universities, research organizations, special journals, and newsmagazines.

— Devote a full page a day to letters to the editor, some days for random letters and others on a particular issue. This would send ax-grinders, psychopaths, and common scolds rushing for the stationery, but that is manageable: that's what they said about popular voting. There aren't enough letters to fill that much space in most papers but in communities of any size that tells more about the papers than it does about letter writers. Once the practice was accepted as a genuine open forum that did not require a doctorate in English literature, once readers came to believe that what they had to say would be accepted, they would write. It would be a relationship with the community that papers ought to encourage. Most papers of any size have at least eight columns of junk — "anytime" early page-makeup material — they could replace with the letters page. If they don't have the space it would be worth killing some ads to get reader reaction. Besides, the contents would be free.

— Appoint a full-time ombudsman on the paper or broadcasting station to track down complaints about the organization's judgment and performance. The Louisville *Courier-Journal* does it and has discovered things about itself that exist in most papers undiscovered. Then print corrections of errors. If papers think that not printing corrections improves reader credibility, they have not been reading the opinion polls. Let readers in on a secret: newspapers are human institutions and when human beings compose 250,000 words in a few hours they make mistakes.

— Organize a local press council of community representatives to sit down every month with the publisher. The community people will learn something about newspapers and the publisher will learn something about his community.

There are other ways of keeping the press a relevant institution close to the lives of its constituents. These include a national press council that would, among other things, investigate and make public findings on claims of gross malpractice, public accounting consistently denounced by the hierarchs but which they have never been willing to do themselves. Whatever does evolve as a way to keep the institutions responsive it will not be the prevailing official ritual of endless self-congratulation for having successfully negotiated the nineteenth century.

THE "NEW JOURNALISM" WE NEED

Gerald Grant

Several months after Benjamin Bradlee left *Newsweek* to become managing editor of the Washington *Post*, a series of staff shakeups began. After the first wave one of the editors invited a dozen young city staff reporters to lunch. As he sipped his Dubonnet on the rocks we nervously wondered about our fate. Most of what he said now escapes me. But I have a vivid recollection of his curiosity about the social circles we traveled in. Whom did we see? What parties did we go to? Whom did we know? His point was that a good deal of what went on in Washington could be learned at dinner parties — or at least that those who were able to establish a social relationship with sources after working hours were most likely to be privileged to the inside story on the job. Some of the best journalists in Washington had grown in reputation as their sources had grown in responsibility; in some cases they had been lucky enough to be classmates.

At the time his message struck me as mildly offensive. Not that it was pointless; his own prominent social connections had not hurt his career. As I look back, however, his inquiry no longer strikes me as saying so much about upward mobility of journalists as about patterns of thought in journalism. His comments underscored the idea that talent in journalism is often a skill for finding out what somebody *else* thinks or knows about something. It may be an oversimplification, yet it is true that lively concern for whom a journalist knows reflects weak appreciation for how he thinks.

Spring, 1970. Gerald Grant is a Nieman Fellow and former Washington *Post* reporter.

What separates most journalists from the few great ones is that the latter are not content with knowing what their sources think. They exhibit an independent intelligence that seeks to wrest meaning from the torrent of events rather than acting as mere transmission belts. They ask better questions because they have a better concept of what the "story" is.

There are some journalists who think, as Richard Hofstadter has said, in terms of configuration and style, thus delineating patterns as well as describing events. One recalls the work of Philip Meyer of the Knight Newspapers, who has effectively used social science skills to analyze current issues; of the perceptive reporting of Joseph Lelyveld and Anthony Lukas of the New York *Times*; of the probing exemplified by the work of Laurence Stern's and Richard Harwood's Insight Teams on the Washington *Post*. There has been a gratifying tendency on a number of papers such as *Newsday* and the Los Angeles *Times* to give reporters the time and freedom to do serious, thoughtful journalism. But as Daniel P. Moynihan said in his brilliant eulogy for Paul Niven: "[Journalism is] that most underdeveloped, least realized of professions. Not a profession at all, really. Rather a craft seeking to become such out of the need to impose form on an activity so vastly expanded in volume and significance as desperately to need the stabilizing influence of procedure and precedent and regularity."

Max Ways, in a *Fortune* article last October entitled "What's Wrong with News: It Isn't New Enough," attributes journalism's shortcomings to its failure to adopt new forms and new definitions of "the story." As a result of applying old yardsticks to events, he says, journalism continues to focus on what can be easily measured and told, to the neglect of more complex and important events unfolding in the society. But were the yardsticks ever any good? My guess is that journalism in 1870 failed in much the same ways it does today. The underlying explanation, then as now, is the kind of mental habits and attitudes most journalists bring to bear on events.

Journalists work by a code that makes many of them moral eunuchs. The professional, in print at least, generally pretends to be without opinions or convictions. His objectivity differs from that of the scientist who demands freedom to develop a fresh hypothesis but then remains objective in the sense that he will look in an unprejudiced way at the results of his experimentation.

Reportorial objectivity has been under vigorous attack by the "New Journalists." Citing Norman Mailer and others, they rightly sense that newsroom objectivity may result in untruth. It masks feelings and stifles imagination. More importantly, it can produce a trained incapacity for thought in the young journalist. Unconsciously he comes to believe that what he thinks doesn't matter. He regards himself as a conduit. The reporter calls an expert for a quote as an unfortunate shortcut to thinking the problem through himself. He asks not what do I think, but what do they think? That can be a habit difficult to break. He seldom has a sense of personal responsibility for what he writes.

This is why Michael Arlen, writing in *Living Room War*, is right when he characterizes much current journalism as propaganda. Not that experts shouldn't be interviewed, or that reporters must be philosopher-kings; but they should be something more than tape recorders. Most journalists are caught in a netherworld. They are neither men of action, forced to confront a problem by struggling with it in an operational sense, nor men of true imagination or contemplation.

Yet uncritical enthusiasm for the New Journalism of passion and advocacy may cost more in the loss of the valuable skepticism of the traditional newspaperman than can be gained through the new involvement. The trouble with advocacy may be that it leads writers who haven't thought or felt much to portray cardboard emotions. Most readers would rather hear the experts. The challenge is to make sense out of the experts and of events. We don't need a whole new breed of novelists in action, we need more cogent journalism that tells us about problems rather than sketching conflict, that gives us the arguments rather than two sets of opposing conclusions. We do not need more passion but more intellect, more understanding.

While there are heartening signs of change, it remains depressingly true that the rewards in journalism tend not to go to the writer who painstakingly thinks a problem through and expresses the subtleties, but to the author of jazzy personality pieces, scoops, and exposés. Exposés are nominated for prizes (often rightly so, of course) while a complicated piece of analysis wins the epithet "thumbsucker." These attitudes are related to the city-room environment where keen — often counterproductive — competition encourages reporters to jealously guard their scoops and current projects even from their co-workers. There is no incentive for the kind of intellectual sharing and discussion of first drafts that is common in an academic community or in any profession where the contributions and criticisms of one's colleagues are considered essential.

Work tends to be defined as scurrying about and asking questions. It is the rare reporter who has the fortitude to sit at his desk and read a book on a subject he intends to write about. Not infrequently one reads a long newspaper series — in which hundreds of man hours of reporting and travel time have been invested — and it is glaringly obvious that some of the most basic books written in that field have not been glanced at by the writers. I once asked Nicholas von Hoffman of the Washington *Post* how he avoided the usual pitfalls of newspaper writing. His exaggerated reply: "I never read newspapers."

Interestingly, von Hoffman was in his thirties when he turned to journalism, having been a community-action organizer with Saul Alinsky. Perhaps that thought-provoking apprenticeship also protected him from learning the bad intellectual habits that are bred into many young reporters. There may be something of a pattern in his experience, although it could just as well be explained by genetic endowment. The careers of a number of exceptional journalists reveal some catalytic intellectual experience outside the newsroom: Walter Lippmann's association with Santayana and his diplomatic experience; David Broder's opportunity to break out of the usual journalistic formulas on the *Congressional Quarterly;* Nick Kotz's background of Phi Beta Kappa and study at the London School of Economics before his present assignment with the Des Moines *Register* and *Tribune;* Willie Morris's residence at Oxford before tackling the Texas *Observer,* and now the editorship of *Harper's;* Anthony Lewis's immersing himself in the Harvard Law School as a Nieman Fellow before doing his exceptional reporting on the United States Supreme Court; Alan Barth's sojourn with the Schlesingers while he was a Nieman; Joseph Lelyveld's Fulbright year in Southeast Asia before joining the *Times*.

Journalists pride themselves on being generalist-specialists. Ridicule of academic specialties ranks high as newsroom sport. Yet the methods by which journalists are trained tend to be extremely narrow, even though most are probably college graduates. On most large papers today reporters specialize early in fields in which few have any general background: transportation, politics, education, or perhaps even elementary education. But the academic, whose specialty or current research may be narrowly focused, usually has had a broad intellectual base that emphasizes the interrelationships of knowledge and common methods of inquiry. The journalist learns his lore on the job. He is steeped in the concrete and specific phenomena pertaining to his beat, learning in the syncretic, associative way. Thus, he often lacks a broad conceptual framework of his subject, or a method of analysis. Hence he is usually very good in predicting what will happen tomorrow, but seldom about the shape of things five years from now. Similarly, he often remains unaware of historical parallels of current events, or of cross-cultural comparisons.

The aims of journalism differ crucially from those of scholarship. The academic investigating police behavior, for instance, wants to tell it all once, thoroughly, exhaustively. His intellectual aim is to formulate a theory or model that will explain the seemingly variable surface events, and perhaps predict the shape of things to come. The newspaper has a vested interest in the concrete and specific, in telling the same story again and again in a way that makes it sound new and different. Thirteen petty robberies must be written in a way to make them sound as different and interesting as possible.

Both approaches have their strength, however. If the journalist often obscures the general truth in mountains of fact, the scholar frequently remains blinded to the specific truth of a particular situation because of his faith in his abstractions, and occasionally, his ideology. Noam Chomsky has shown in *American Power and the New Mandarins* how frequently the latter is true. He convincingly pairs Neil Sheehan's description in the New York *Times* of fetid slums in Saigon with some scholarly accounts of the supposed benefits of American-sponsored "urbanization" in Vietnam. He writes:

> Many have remarked on the striking difference between the way the press and the visiting scholar describe what they see in Vietnam. It should occasion no surprise. Each is pursuing his own craft. The reporter's job is to describe what he sees before his eyes; many have done so with courage and even brilliance. The scholarly adviser and colonial administrator, on the other hand, is concerned to justify what he has done and what he hopes to do, and — if an expert as well — to construct an appropriate ideological cover, to show that we are just and righteous in what we do, and to put nagging doubts to rest.

Paradoxically, the limited generalization characteristic of most journalism is often a great strength. It doesn't care what the general theory is, but what is true in this particular instance. Ignorance of what is supposed to be true may have the productive result of puncturing myth or forcing scholars to reevaluate old evidence.

Much more could be said of the sins of academe — of its petty jealousies, blindnesses, and irrelevancies. My aim, however, has been to probe the roots of what Norman Isaacs of the Louisville *Courier-Journal* once called the "mental prearrangement" that passes for thought among many journalists. More weight could be given to exceptions to some of the norms cited. But the point is precisely that there are such norms, though they are increasingly being violated.

The more general question that obtrudes is how can the norms be changed? To begin with, journalism schools could profitably follow the developments of law, education, and business schools whose faculties are no longer top-heavy with former practitioners, although they have an important place. Faculty are needed from the academic disciplines who are interested in applying their knowledge to the problems of mass media and who will teach students more thoughtful modes of analysis in a realistic setting. Such new faculty could also play a vital role in strengthening journalism schools' much-neglected role of critically assessing the performance of the press.

Newspapers should also recruit from law schools and graduate schools of sociology and political science. A great many more skilled young academics in the social sciences could be attracted to new careers in the mass media if given responsibility to tackle significant issues. Newspapers need not become miniature graduate schools, but neither should they produce the kind of shabby analysis that they do of city budgets and school reading scores. Personnel practices must change. Salaries must rise. Sabbaticals should become standard. Research assistants will be needed. Change might be so drastic as to free the average reporter from drudgery and scut work in the way that the average elementary school teacher has been liberated in New York City. The costs of carrying out these suggestions might prove a considerable financial drain on many smaller papers — at least until their benefits could be established. For that reason, such programs ought to be worthy of foundation support.

But these are long-term changes. What about now? Newspapers have only begun to take advantage of outside expertise. Academic skepticism of "newspaper writing" can be overcome with the right kind of assurances from sensitive editors that copy will be responsibly handled (not to mention massage of professorial egos with promises of the right kind of display). This puts a premium on editors who are aware of the outside expert's area of competence and interest and who can frame issues in an intellectually stimulating way. Outsiders should also be involved in seminar-like lunches, planning sessions and critiques of coverage. This use of experts as "consultants" has become fairly common among magazines but is employed less frequently by newspapers.

A bolder necessary step is to go beyond hiring the free-lance talents of academics to hiring the academics themselves. But the twist here is to employ them for their skill as teachers, as catalysts who would develop new concepts and methods of reporting. Distinguished teachers and thinkers could be brought to newspapers for short periods to head special projects and reporting teams. Some might come on sabbatical; others for only a semester or a few months or weeks. They might come from think tanks, foundations, publishing houses, and universities as well as from the ranks of free-lances and other diverse social critics. Why not ask Ralph Nader, Saul Alinsky, or James Baldwin as well as sociologist Nathan Glazer, psychologist Robert Coles, economist Robert Lekachman?

There are scores of candidates, though perhaps not all as well known, in every large city.

Under such a system, a small team of reporters might be assigned to work for a month preparing a series on the police, or an assessment of educational programs in the slums, or a survey of changing racial attitudes. They might work with a political scientist, a sociologist, a social psychologist. They would read and jointly discuss several books and perhaps a half-dozen relevant articles, attempting to define issues, identify historical trends, decide where reportorial energies should be directed.

Instead of rushing out to interview sources, reporters might spend time digging into census documents, examining attitudinal research, and drawing some conclusions of their own. There would be some debate about what the story is — with one result that the series would not be, like so many others, merely an elaboration of the obvious. Interviews would not be sought until there was some evaluation of what had been written, what the questions were, and the kinds of sources that could best answer them. In the case of the racial attitude series, reporters would have a chance to learn about constructing a survey, how data is fed into a computer, and some elementary notions about principles of statistical inference.

David Riesman, commenting on a draft of this article, noted that more reflective social scientists are under attack today by some of their radical activist colleagues. Although generally enthusiastic about the suggestions here, he added, "I could imagine the ironies of academicians in the newsroom being more journalistic than the journalists."

One should not overlook the benefits that would accrue to academics as a result of immersion in the newsroom. They would come away with a more realistic sense of the possible, of how complicated things really are in the concrete. It might broaden the outlook of many scholars about what their fields of inquiry ought to include. It could prove an interesting testing ground for many kinds of hypotheses and have benefits in research terms, including research about the mass media. New and better academic publications might be another byproduct. The hostility of many journalists toward academics — perhaps a result of their unconscious resentment at their dependence on the experts — might be reduced. There might be a similar gain in understanding on the part of the academics, who are frequently jealous of the journalists' power (and angry at what they regard as its misuse), and who sometimes resent journalists who "cream off" the fruits of their research.

The whole notion of a newspaper as an educational institution — internally as well as externally — is central to this concept. The possibilities of encouraging greater cross-fertilization within the newsroom are limitless. Outsiders would be astonished at how little information or expertise is exchanged or developed among newspaper staffs, which have an exceptional range of talent and great opportunities for such development. A consulting firm like Arthur D. Little would close tomorrow if internal staff growth processes were as moribund as those on even our largest newspapers. Newspapermen, though they would vigorously deny it, jealously guard their imagined status and small prerogatives within the newsroom, and nothing in the way the place operates is likely to encourage them to do otherwise. One way is to bring in a catalyst from whom all learn as they teach each other. The multiplier effects of such a process could be surprising. Journalism could expand your mind.

THE MIRACLE *LE MONDE* WROUGHT

Jean Schwoebel

For most of a century, technology has been changing the physical profile of journalism. Now, almost unnoticed, a companion revolution has begun. Still embryonic but clearly irreversible, it has to do with who within a journalistic institution can raise basic questions about it and receive meaningful answers; the extent to which journalists shall be free to exercise professional skills within corporate structures they do not own; and ultimately, the question of whether distinguished, sophisticated journalism can thrive in an organization in which fundamental editorial arrangements are determined by fiat.

In the interview below, Jean Schwoebel, diplomatic editor of *Le Monde* and architect of its pioneering staff-controlled management structure, describes his historic experience in Europe.

The Society of Journalists is the vehicle through which staff control of Le Monde *is exercised. How did it begin, and why?*

Two factors produced the Society of Journalists. We had the historic Revolution in France; we have this tradition. Then there was the liberation of France in World War II. The Occupation was very hard. Many papers had accepted the law imposed by Occupation forces. So at the end of the war there was a general idea that the press was not valuable because it had collaborated with the Germans. So there was a law after the Liberation to expropriate — confiscate — properties of editors of the old press, and

---

Summer, 1970.

their estates were put in charge of national societies. The idea was that we were to create a new press.

At the end of the war we had big illusions and big hopes, and we thought we could keep the press free of economic control. We could see that freedom of the press must not only be freedom from oppression by the State; the State in a way is an expression of the democratic majority. To a certain degree the press was in control of political parties, with a degree of protection against central power. But we also could see that economic progress depends more and more on very large investments, and freedom of expression is given only to people who can assemble formidable capital. So in a modern society freedom of the press is not only a question of structures which give freedom to journalists in relation to political powers, but also to economic powers. In the Resistance that idea was commonly accepted. That was a very revolutionary period.

Of course, we live in a capitalist country, so these ideas were progressively abandoned. More and more the "new" owners have changed their minds, and they are exactly like their predecessors. Except for one — *Le Monde*.

Le Monde was directed by Hubert Beuve-Méry, who had been asked to found a newspaper with the property of the old *Le Temps*. He had a very high conception of the press. When he was obliged for many reasons to submit his resignation in 1951 there was a rebellion on the editorial board. The editorial staff was a very strong force because *Le Monde* practiced a very high level of journalism, and its quality depended very much on us. Influential elements in France — the universities and the elite — were waiting for a declaration from us. The thought that *Le Monde* would have any other direction was a kind of scandal. So we were in a good position with the owners, and in 1951 we obtained the first agreement — it was not the last — entering into ownership.

Why did the editorial staff insist on sharing ownership?

If you want to exert influence in a capitalist country there is only one way, and that is to have part of the ownership; the rest is without value. It was a good time to ask for part of the ownership.

The capital of the country was very low. The Liberation could take over such estates. It was something of a special situation.

In Europe the status of journalists is very low because we work in a commercial framework. And what is the law of commerce? It is to make maximum profit. And what is the way to maximum profit? It is to have a maximum of receipts and a minimum of expenses. If there is any reduction it is in expenses. So in general the papers of France have very low-paid journalists. Because they don't pay them, of course, the journalists are not of the quality required in view of their profession. We say that is a stupidity and a danger to the future.

We have the conviction that in modern societies progress depends on the high quality of citizens. To have a high quality of citizens you must have a high quality of education. It is a very common thing now to learn to read. Every country knows we must free the people of illiteracy. We must move to a higher level now. We must have citizens able to choose representative people in any field of activity. And they can do so only if the citizens know the real facts — the factors of every situation. If you don't have that it is a caricature of democracy. That is why we say that only a society which has highly qualified journalists can progress.

We contend that present structures do not offer to citizens the guarantee of a high quality of journalism. And so this is an idea which is more and more being adopted by journalists in France.

What are the prospects for shared management on other French newspapers?

Thirty-two societies have been created, within all the big papers of France. They have been created in the hope of having the same arrangement we have at *Le Monde*. They have been opposed systematically by the managers. So they have federated, and I am president of this federation, to try to act in the political field, to act on the deputies, the senators, the government. We were on the point last year of winning the battle to pass a law. We had many friends. De Gaulle was playing his cards politically. As with Algeria he tried to make compromises. He was not prepared to go as far as we were.

Was a bill introduced?

One of the main reasons why de Gaulle fell was this question. All the conservatives were fanatically opposed to any kind of participation, because in France there is a very old tradition of management authority. In a way I think the United States is much more advanced on the question of cooperation and work in teams. That tradition does not exist in France, and that in my view is a paramount question. If we don't change on the question of the authority of middle age, we cannot change much else. We have a very strong concentration of that kind.

So a commission was created by the government to study our ideas, but with the departure of de Gaulle and the reaction of the managers and owners the issue has been tabled.

If de Gaulle had not fallen would you have had a realistic chance?

It would have been difficult, but we were on our way. But we will have our day. Already there is a tendency to come back to our conception because it is necessary for the future, and because it has had an impact on countries around us. I have been to Germany, to Italy, to England, to Belgium, and to Spain, and I see everywhere the same state of humiliation, of dissatisfaction among journalists over feudalistic power.

In fact, at *Le Monde* we have succeeded not only in quality of information but in quality of administration. And that is very important. We did not surprise the industry on the first point, but on the second. We have a profitable enterprise, and the discipline is exceptional because we are conscious of the important questions of what is best for the structure, for the organization, for its ethics. But the daily administration we do not determine at all.

How successful is Le Monde *as a business?*

Le Monde has high profits. It has a modern mechanical plant. Its circulation is high. These are the reasons why our example has been followed in Germany. We were able to give them all the materials and concepts. We already had twenty years of experience — and not abstract experience. It was experience in the responsibilities of a major enterprise. We know the realities of an enterprise. That gives us real force. That is why in Italy last year I was invited to speak to Catholic journalists, and two months later, to all the journalists of Italy.

You have named newspapers and a magazine. Could this apply to television also?

Television is another problem. The Society of Journalists was contacted two years ago about TV, but the Department of Television has been in chaos. So there is no more a Society of Television. The TV situation is very difficult, because it is in a sense directed by the State.

How does the Society of Journalists function?

We are not like the American Newspaper Guild. We decided first to be a "commercial" society. Now we are a civil society. We do not want to operate like capitalists. We do not want part of the profits. We want part of the ownership not for the profits — that is for the investors — but only for the juridical rights the property gives. As soon as we leave the paper we have no more rights.

The Society of Journalists has an assembly and a council of administration. We try to unite the journalists in a common conception. To unite journalists is very difficult. You succeed only if you pick very solid, very reasonable arguments. And in my view we have united on very sensible, responsible problems.

There has been an epidemic of criticism of the news media in the United States. If your success were duplicated there, might there be fewer such criticisms?

We have had no relations with American journalists on this question. But in my view we are all, of whatever country, journalists, with common responsibilities. I think that in the future the journalism profession will be most important. It is not a question of nationalism — of nations. We must have a solidarity among journalists to improve their status.

Political men may be very authentic men, but they are dependent in large degree on the man who elects them, and it is on journalists' courage and quality that we depend to raise the quality of citizens. Our profession must push the legislative man to courage, because he is so dependent. So in a way we have to sustain him.

Since Le Monde *is an elite newspaper, should we assume by analogy that the most likely place for your idea to take root in the United States would be on an elite or quality newspaper?*

Very possibly it could happen someday at the New York *Times*, *Christian Science Monitor*, and maybe the Washington *Post*. But I know perfectly well that conditions are different in America. You in the States are advanced in something which is necessary — efficiency, energy, and so on. But maybe you are slow to realize that the real cause of chaos in the future will involve a dimension beyond efficiency.

Your journalists are much dependent on a society which still believes much in profitability — which is necessary. I think the view of profits, of commerce, in American society in a certain measure represents progress; in another way, not. I believe sincerely that it is much more difficult for American journalists than for us because in such a society as yours it is not regarded as a scandal that economic processes control the press. In European societies it is looked on as a scandal that economic processes control the press. In my view, control of the press by economic processes is completely anti-American.

In ten years I am sure this philosophy will have taken root in America. I say that not only journalists have a right, but clerks or workers have a right to press for their rights. But journalists are different. We are the defenders of truth. Now progress is a question of dialogue. We are at the end of a certain kind of journalism — of magisterial journalism — and of a certain kind of journalist: the magisterial journalist. And we must accept the dialogue.

"REPORTER POWER" TAKES ROOT

Edwin Diamond

One of the most significant and underreported social experiments of 1969 took place in the small northern California community of Willits. There, forty-three-year-old George Davis, a football coach who describes himself as "a small man with nothing to lose," fielded a football team each Saturday using the principle of participatory democracy; the players themselves voted on who should be in the starting lineup. The team lost its first four games of the season but rallied and ended in a tie for the league championship. This record, of course, might have been as much due to talent as to democracy. Still, the implications of the Davis experiment are clear: in an era marked by the pervasive and passionate questioning of all authority, even the football coach — that traditionally rigid hierarchical figure — is trying to bend with the times.

In American news media most communications caliphates are more like Vince Lombardi than George Davis — they are big men with a lot to lose, so to speak — and so the principle of electing editors or announcers has not yet been established. But a sampling of attitudes in a number of city rooms, magazine offices, and broadcast studios indicates that day may not be far off. In various cities journalists have banded together to impress their professional beliefs and occupational misgivings upon management.

At the Gannett papers in Rochester, New York, editorial staff members have begun sitting in with the papers' editorial board on a rotating basis. In Denver, a new Newspaper Guild contract signed in mid-March establishes an ethics committee and a hu-

---

Summer, 1970. Edwin Diamond, a former *Newsweek* editor, is a senior fellow in political science at MIT and a media critic for WTOP-TV in Washington.

man rights committee that will meet regularly with management. The human rights committee plans to take up the question of minority employment (women as well as blacks) at the *Post;* the three-member ethics committee, which will meet with three representatives of management, wants to discuss such hoary *Post* practices as trade-outs — editorial puffs written about an advertiser to fill out a special section. And in Providence, Rhode Island, a Journalists Committee has held several meetings with management about specific staffing and policy changes on the *Journal* and *Bulletin.* The Committee acted after surveying a sizable portion of the editorial staff, then compiling the survey and mimeographing it for distribution.

Guild contract negotiations are still grimly contested in the news media, as are labor contracts in most business enterprises. But the new benefits that journalists have begun to seek go far beyond the usual guild bargaining points of wages and hours. The new grievances involve, first of all, moral — almost theological — concerns. When the Association of *Tribune* Journalists was formed by reporters at the Minneapolis *Tribune* last February, for example, it carefully stated that the group was not a collective bargaining unit but an agent for bringing "our best thoughts into a dialogue with management." There had been the usual grumbling at the *Trib* about shortages of staff and space, but there was a new element in the talk. As an association member later explained, "There was a feeling on our part of loss of respect. We were being treated like army privates and the editors were officers; we were to do what we were told and like it and no one gave a damn if we thought our orders were sane or insane."

On May 25 the *Tribune*'s enlisted men and women moved decisively to assert "rights of participation" in the choice of their junior officers: when two *Trib* assistant city editors announced that they planned to leave the paper, the local Guild unit adopted a resolution stating that "reporters, photographers, and copydesk editors should advise and consent to management's nominations." The next day management met with the Guild and said that while it was not giving up its prerogatives it was willing to take the staff's nominations into account. It is a small step for the *Trib*, but a giant leap for American journalism — which more and more is moving toward the model of *Le Monde* and other European publications.

Similarly, the men and women who produce programs for public television have formed an association concerned not with residuals but with, among other subjects, the social content of programs and the racial hiring practices of their industry. And reporters in several cities have founded journalism reviews.

The concerns that have stimulated these various activities are immediately recognizable as the concerns that have dominated much of the news covered by media men and women in recent years. Journalists who have followed the fight of parents to decentralize schools, the demands of students to have a say in the investment policies of the universities, and the blacks' and radical whites' challenge to the established institutions of society, have now begun to think about applying to their own lives principles of community control, participatory democracy, and collective action.

The development of this new consciousness is fairly recent. Ten or fifteen years ago, unions battled to win wage increases and to protest mergers, but the way a publication or station was run — from the color scheme of the newsroom walls to the overall editorial policies — remained the prerogative of the owner. The journalist's attitude was, typically, acquiescent; after all, was it not management's bat and ball — and ball park (although in broadcasting, the air *does* belong to the public and the station owner has only the loan of it)?

With affluence, the new temper of times, and the seller's market for young talent, this attitude has changed. Media executives now know (and graduate school studies show) that the brightest young people, on the whole, are not going into journalism, and that even those who are graduated from journalism schools often choose public relations work over reporting jobs. Even more alarming to an editor or news director with proper regard for talent is the attrition rate of good young newsmen and women after two or three years in the business. Money and bylines alone are no longer sufficient inducements; if executives want to attract and keep good young people, they must be attentive to or at least aware of their opinions. As often as not, a good university-trained reporter who is now in his or her late twenties picketed for civil rights while in high school, spent a freshman summer in Mississippi or Appalachia, and sat in at the dean's office during senior year — or covered these events for the school paper. Now they are turning reformist toward their own profession.

Recent unrest at the *Wall Street Journal* is a case in point. The *Journal* reached its present eminence in part by hiring good young people right out of college, training them, and giving them the time and the space to develop long, informative reports and trend stories. Now, says an older hand at the paper, "these younger people are much more activist-minded and more willing to needle management." During the Vietnam Moratorium Day last October, several younger reporters wanted to march on Broad Street, a block from Wall, with at least one sign saying WALL STREET JOURNALIST FOR THE MORATORIUM. Management's position was that it didn't mind the marching but didn't think the wording of that one sign was proper because it might "raise questions about the *Journal*'s objectivity in the reader's mind."

A confrontation on Moratorium Day was avoided — according to one witness, the sign was carried but not held up. But the young activists then dispatched a petition to management asking for a clarification of the *Journal*'s "position" on what they could do with their private lives. In response, executives Warren Phillips and Ed Cony issued a memorandum noting that "we must be concerned not only with avoiding bias in our news columns but also with avoiding the appearance of bias." They concluded: "It is the individual's obligation to exercise sufficient judgment to avoid such embarrassment." The younger reporters also have expressed their concern about what the *Journal* does on the editorial page; when the *Journal* ran an editorial that seemed to blame New York City's telephone troubles on allegedly slow-witted welfare mothers hired to operate switchboards, a newsroom caucus told management that reporters didn't want to be associated with a paper that had such mossback views.

The *Journal*'s radical "cell" remains largely an *ad hoc* group springing to life when an issue presents itself. At the Minneapolis *Tribune*, however, the new consciousness of younger journalists has manifested itself in a formal organization. Last fall, by all accounts, the *Tribune* had a morale problem compounded by a high turnover and some admitted paranoia on the part of the staff. A group of reporters began meeting on Sunday mornings — for a while they were known as the Underground Church — to see if anything besides complaining could be done. The Underground Church members repeated the usual litany of city-room complaints — the need for more phones, better files, more out-of-town exchanges — but they also were concerned with such traditional domains of management as the size of the travel allowance, the company's fiscal and budgetary procedures, and the circulation breakdown by area. More important, the Underground Church challenged the *Tribune*'s news judgment, most particularly on those issues that have polarized so much of the country. One young reporter drew up the following indictment:

> The Trib's sins tend to be those of omission, rather than commission. We sent no one to the Chicago Conspiracy trial despite repeated requests from staffers who wanted to go. We sent no one to Washington last November with the thousands of Minnesotans who participated in the Vietnam Moratorium. We do have a D.C. bureau which handled Moratorium coverage but we did not, like our rival paper, the *Star*, see fit to send anyone on the buses of demonstrators from our state. . . . The November Moratorium was our right-hand, front-page lead story, with a front-page picture of masses of marchers going along peaceably. The story by Chuck Bailey of our D.C. bureau devoted the first five paragraphs to general comments on the demonstration. The next six paragraphs were on the violence that occurred there. Then followed twelve paragraphs on the speeches, color, etc. We used only the official 250,000 figure for the number of participants and did not mention any higher estimates.
>
> On the second front page only one of the five pictures showed a peaceful scene (Coretta King marching). One was rioters getting teargassed, another a draft-card burning, another an American flag being carried upside down, and the fourth a flag-burning which turned out, on close inspection, to be counter-demonstrators burning a Vietcong flag. According to our own figures, one-250th of the people at that demonstration got at least three-fifths of the pictures on the second front page and about one-fourth of the main story. . . .
>
> We do, of course, often do a good job breaking a story. Give us a cyclone or a postal strike or the Governor saying he won't run again,

and we're all over it. We get the sidebars and the reactions and the whole thing. But in trying to explain what the hell is happening in this society in any larger way — perspective, context, whatever you want to call it — the *Trib* just ain't there."

The Underground Church soon realized it could go in two possible directions: the reporters could start a publication modeled after the *Chicago Journalism Review* which would regularly monitor the local press's performance on stories like the November Moratorium, or they could try to work within the organization by establishing a "dialogue" with management. The Church chose the former course, and plans for a *Twin Cities Journalism Review* were put on the back burner. Early this year, John Cowles, Jr., president of the Minneapolis Star and Tribune Company (and also the majority owner of *Harper's* magazine), and Bower Hawthorne, vice-president and editor of the *Tribune*, were invited to meet with some of the staff and discuss the paper's direction. Hawthorne, meanwhile, had invited all staff members to his own meeting to discuss the paper — the two invitations apparently crossed in the interoffice mail. The meetings took place — "by this time we were communicating like hell," one reporter recalls wryly — and the dissidents formally organized into the Association of *Tribune* Journalists.

The managing editor, Wallace Allen, drew up an extensive questionnaire which was distributed to some hundred staff members; forty-seven returned their forms. Allen's own summary of the responses reflects the low opinion the workers had for the paper and the management. Five of the nineteen "impressions and conclusions" he drew from the replies are especially noteworthy:

— You want a great deal more information about company direction, through direct and personal communication with management up to the highest level.

— Some of you feel strongly that staff members should play a part in policymaking and decisionmaking. You do not wish to run the newspaper but you would like to be consulted on what is done and informed in advance of both major and minor decisions.

— You feel that news policy and direction are not being handed down fully or clearly. You have only a vague idea — or no idea — of what we are trying to do and where we are trying to go.

— You feel that our approaches to covering the news and the ways we present it are not up to date. You want to see change and progress in an orderly, responsible but exciting way.

— Many of you feel that the *Tribune* was a progressive and exciting newspaper until about six months or so ago. You indicate that the letdown may have come from confusion in management's mind about news direction when it discovered the silent majority. You feel management switched direction in an attempt to respond to changing social conditions but switched in ways that revealed ignorance of basic issues.

Allen's efforts at communications apparently had a calming effect on the staff, which by and large adopted a "wait and see" attitude. As of late spring the Association continued to meet every other week or so and was reviving plans for the *Twin Cities Journalism Review*.

The Association of Public Television Producers, another group of journalists who went "above ground" out of a deep concern about their professional lives, has also become engaged in management matters. Men and women on every level in public television are worried about the continued unfettered operation of noncommercial TV in the United States, especially because the new Corporation for Public Broadcasting has to go to Congress each year for funds. The Association came forward during congressional hearings last year to discuss alternative plans for financing public TV; its spokesman, Alvin Perlmutter, a National Educational Television producer, told the Pastore Committee that he personally favored financing PTV by a tax on the profits of the commercial networks rather than the present arrangement in which public TV is dependent on the goodwill of 535 congressmen. Perlmutter was rewarded with a lecture from Senator Pastore, advising him not to bite the hand that is feeding him. More recently, the Association publicly protested the decision of some local public TV stations not to show the NET documentary. *Who Invited US?*, a highly critical study of U.S. foreign policy. Like the reporters at the Minneapolis *Tribune*, the public TV producers want to see certain stories run — and they are prepared to challenge past assumptions about whether the people who have the bat and ball can make all the rules of the game.

The women's movement at *Newsweek* also has been willing to try its case in public. The conditions that the *Newsweek* women found objectionable — segregation of women into the scut work of research, the lack of writing opportunities (fifty male writers to one woman), and the general atmosphere of exclusion — had for years existed unopposed except by one or two editors. In the last year or two, however, many of the young women had been covering the black revolution and student unrest. As reporters they had listened to the rhetoric of "power to the people"; they had been "used" by militants who staged news conferences and other media events to get across their messages. When the *Newsweek* women decided to press their collective claims they arranged a media event: they timed the release of their complaint to the Equal Employment Opportunity Commission in Washington to coincide with the Monday morning newsstand appearance of the *Newsweek* cover story "Women in Revolt." They called a news conference and phoned contacts at other news organizations to insure full coverage. Then they appeared in force, well groomed and intelligent, flanking their lawyer, a young, attractive black woman named Eleanor Holmes Norton. Their widely covered action had the desired effect, galvanizing the top echelon of *Newsweek* into a long series of meetings with the women and winning from management pledges to open the entire editorial hierarchy to women.

The editor may justifiably grumble that the women should have come to his office first, but the women believe it was the public nature of their action that produced results. Their experience replicates that of a Minneapolis *Tribune* reporter who now believes the "only power that we staff members really have in these matters is the power to embarrass management." This power also was demonstrated last March when a group called Media Women flooded into the office of the *Ladies' Home Journal*'s editor and publisher, John Mack Carter, to stage the first "liberation" of a mass magazine. The resulting publicity may not have immediately hurt the *Journal*'s advertising revenues or circulation, but it certainly affected that evanescent quality known as aura — and it made many readers who heretofore had not paid much attention to the feminist cause conscious of the magazine's assumptions.

For the time being at least, the tactics of "liberation" have been the exception rather than the rule. If there is a pattern in developments around the country, it is the tactic of internally rather than publicly making the case for a larger staff role in policymaking. Thus, some sixty New York *Post* activists (over as well as under thirty) have been meeting with the *Post*'s publisher, Mrs. Dorothy Schiff, to force a break from the penurious policies and lackluster journalism of the past. The reporters have asked for more specialist beats, a larger travel budget, more black and Puerto Rican staff, and more coverage of minority groups. At the New York *Times* a loose confederation of reporters and editors have also met to discuss a long list of grievances, some of them water-cooler complaints but others centering on the *Times*'s coverage of politics, race, the Chicago Conspiracy trial, and the Black Panthers. Some of the *Times* reporters are chafing under what they consider the harsh yoke of Managing Editor A. M. Rosenthal and his bullpen editors, and one step being considered calls for the selection or election — in the *Le Monde* and Minneapolis models — of a top editor.

And in Philadelphia, the senior editors of the *Bulletin* have been conducting regular Monday afternoon "seminars" with some fifteen of the younger — and more activist-minded — staff reporters. The weekly seminars began last March after managing editor George Packard had heard complaints from staff members that story suggestions and opinions about news coverage were not "trickling upward." A typical meeting allows equal time for a senior editor to explain his particular operation (newsdesk, photo assignments, etc.) and for reporters to ask questions or otherwise respond. The trickle — some say, torrent — of underclass feelings loosed by the seminars has already resulted in some changes in the way the *Bulletin* handles racial identifications in stories. *Bulletin* editors are also opening up channels so that younger reporters can get story ideas into the paper's new "Enterprise" page, and no one seems more satisfied with these developments than Packard himself.

A number of issues could transform these informal internal discussions into overt action groups. Working reporters have been made visibly nervous by recent efforts to subpoena reporters' notes, raw files, and unused film. The *Wall Street Journal* "cell" and the Association of *Tribune* Journalists, among others, have formally protested to their managements about cooperating in such government fishing expeditions. More significantly, two groups of journalists, cutting across corporate and media lines, have banded together on the subpoena issue. One group consists of some seventy black men and women journalists who placed an ad to announce their intention to oppose the government's efforts (the government's first target in efforts to obtain reporters' notes was a black journalist for the New York *Times*, Earl Caldwell.)

The second group, called the Reporter's Committee on Freedom of the Press, consists of both black and white newsmen, and J. Anthony Lukas of the New York *Times* has been one of its early organizers. The Reporter's Committee met early in March at the Georgetown University Law Center in Washington. The discussions — attended by men from the Washington *Star*, the Washington *Post*, *Time*, *Newsweek*, the Los Angeles *Times*, NBC, and CBS — reflected some of the feelings of staff men that interests of management and employees may not always be congruent in the matter of subpoenas. Rather than rely on lawyers of their individual companies and corporations — who by and large have been uncertain trumpets in recent months — the Georgetown group wants to explore the legal thickets of the subpoena issue directly with law schools and scholars. Already, the group is cooperating with the Georgetown Law Center on an information center and clearinghouse, and with Stanford University on a legal study of the whole area of confidential material.

Two other issues could also serve to "radicalize" the working press. One issue is race. Black reporters in the San Francisco area and in New York City have organized their own associations, partly to get together to talk about matters of common interest and occasionally to speak out with a collective voice. The other radicalizing issue is the war in Indochina. Shortly after Mr. Nixon ordered American troops into Cambodia, more than 150 *Newsweek* employees met to debate whether they should bring pressure on their magazine to come out against the war; one form of action considered was an antiwar advertisement in *Newsweek*. At the New York *Daily News* more than one hundred editorial employees attempted to place just such an ad in their paper, but were refused space by the paper even though they had collected $1,100 to pay for it. The *Daily News*men promptly took their ad to the New York *Times*, where it was accepted — double embarrassment for the *News* management.

As of mid-1970 then, media activists had a great deal in their favor, including management's fear of a talent drain and its abhorrence of adverse publicity. Ultimately, too, they can count on the *amour propre* of the ownership: the proprietors have a selfish interest in listening. John Cowles, Jr., for example, told his *Tribune* reporters that it wasn't at all pleasant to hear, in his words, that he was "the captain of the *Titanic*." Perhaps a "dialogue" can achieve a new arrangement of authority that recognizes the best qualities of passion, spontaneity, and social concerns of the younger journalists while preserving the established professional virtues of fair play and balance.

NOTES ON THE CO-EDITORS

James Boylan edited the *Columbia Journalism Review* from its founding in 1961 until 1969. He is a graduate of Cornell College, Iowa, and the Columbia University Graduate School of Journalism; he also holds a doctorate in history from Columbia. Before coming to Columbia in 1957 as assistant to the Dean of Journalism, he worked for the New York *Herald Tribune* edition of *This Week* magazine.

Alfred Balk became visiting editor of *Columbia Journalism Review* in 1969, when James Boylan went on leave for doctoral study. He is a graduate of the Medill School of Journalism (B.S., M.S. with honors) at Northwestern University; has been a newswriter-producer for WBBM-TV (CBS) in Chicago; a reporter for the Chicago *Sun-Times*; a magazine writer for the J. Walter Thompson Company; a freelance author for national magazines; special writer under contract to the *Saturday Evening Post;* and feature editor and editor-at-large of *Saturday Review.* He is the author of *The Religion Business* (1968) and *The Free List: Property Without Taxes* (1971), and was executive producer of the film "*That the People Shall Know*": *The Challenge of Journalism,* narrated by Walter Cronkite.